*Divided Visual
Field Studies of
Cerebral Organisation*

# Divided Visual Field Studies of Cerebral Organisation

Edited by

*J. Graham Beaumont*
Department of Psychology,
University of Leicester,
England.

1982

ACADEMIC PRESS
*A Subsidiary of Harcourt Brace Jovanovich, Publishers*
LONDON   NEW YORK
PARIS   SAN DIEGO   SAN FRANCISCO   SÃO PAULO
SIDNEY   TOKYO   TORONTO

ACADEMIC PRESS INC. (LONDON) LTD
24–28 Oval Road,
London NW1

*U.S. Edition published by*
ACADEMIC PRESS INC.
111 Fifth Avenue,
New York, New York 10003

*British Library Cataloguing in Publication Data*

Divided visual field studies of cerebral organisation.
1. Visual perception – Addresses, essays, lectures
2. Neurophysiology – Addresses, essays, lectures
I. Beaumont, J. Graham
612.8'4      QP471

ISBN 0–12–084080–4

LCCCN 81–67898

Phototypesetting by Oxford Publishing Services, Oxford
Printed by St. Edmundsbury Press, Bury St. Edmunds

# CONTRIBUTORS

M. ANNETT, *Department of Applied Social Studies, Coventry (Lanchester) Polytechnic, Priory Street, Coventry CV1 5FB*

J. G. BEAUMONT, *Department of Psychology, The University, Leicester LE1 7RH*

G. COHEN, *Department of Experimental Psychology, University of Oxford, South Parks Road, Oxford OX1 3UD*

C. J. COLBOURN, *Department of Psychology, University of Southampton, Southampton SO9 5NH*

J. DAVIDOFF, *Neuropsychology Unit, Neuroscience Group, The Radcliffe Infirmary, Woodstock Road, Oxford OX2 6HE*

H. FAIRWEATHER, *Department of Social Science, Middlesex Polytechnic, Enfield, Middlesex EN3 4SF*

M. D. RUGG, *Psychological Laboratory, University of St Andrews, St Andrews, Fife KY16 9JU*

A. W. YOUNG, *Department of Psychology, Fylde College, University of Lancaster, Bailrigg, Lancaster LA1 4YF*

# PREFACE

THE ABSENCE of any coherent treatments of divided visual field studies and my increasing difficulty with the literature as I pursued my own research interests, as well as the lack of any publication to recommend to my students, gave me the idea for this book. The published literature on studies of cerebral organisation using the divided visual field technique has grown to a very considerable size over the past decade, and it is a literature which has more than its share of contradictions and inconsistencies. I have often had the sensation, in trying to grasp its form and meaning, of tramping through a particularly wet and sticky bog. The aim of this book is to plant some guideposts in the bog, to make travelling easier for those who follow.

The purpose of the book is therefore simple: to provide a comprehensive and critical review of what we may learn about human cerebral organisation from studies of human performance which have employed a particular experimental paradigm, that of divided visual field presentation. I hoped the book would both cover the main studies in the field and provide critical commentary on them. I also hoped that out of the review may arise a clearer view of the findings of this area of research, and the more general implications for neuropsychology. This clearer view may result in the development of our theoretical understanding of how human abilities are organised in the brain, and certainly a more precise concentration of research effort on the current key issues in the field.

The book is intended for advanced undergraduate students, postgraduate students and research workers in neuropsychology and related fields. I also hoped that it may be used by undergraduates as a concise guide to an area of research which is of increasing importance in experimental and clinical psychology, as well as neuropsychology. Its interest and utility should be clear to postgraduate students and researchers in the field, but it is also designed to be of value to postgraduate students in clinical psychology and in allied medical disciplines. The summaries at the end of each chapter are intended to aid those who wish to take information selectively from the book.

Following a brief introduction, there is a consideration of the methodological parameters and theoretical bases which underlie the divided visual field technique. This is in turn followed by the two central chapters which review the studies with normal human subjects in some detail, treating the studies with non-verbal and verbal stimuli respectively. This division is somewhat arbitrary, but seems the most sensible for historical, if for no better, reasons. These reviews are then reflected by a discussion of the theoretical interpretations which have been proposed for the results of the studies. The next four chapters deal with variables associated with divided visual field asymmetries and with individual differences, by reviewing the findings relating to developmental parameters, electrophysiological variables, sex and handedness. Studies with two abnormal groups, the 'split-brain' and psychiatric patients, are reviewed before the final concluding chapter.

There are merits and demerits to any book which incorporates a number of diverse contributions. I felt that the merit of having a comprehensive and authoritative review of the area (as well as some slight variety of perspective) justified inviting other workers to contribute to the book, while taking great care to ensure a reasonable uniformity of style and approach. I am sure that I am not the person best placed to judge whether it has been possible to create a fully integrated volume, but I am delighted with the result, and I think that the worst demerits of a contributed volume have been avoided. I should like to record my thanks to the contributors, not only for what I believe to be the high quality of their contributions, but also their co-operation in the effort to produce a coherent and well-integrated volume.

Lastly I should like to record my thanks to Rita Benford, a patient, long-suffering and accurate typist, for her contribution to the book, and to my family, students and friends for their tolerance and help.

J. GRAHAM BEAUMONT
*Leicester, March 1981*

# CONTENTS

# 3. Studies with Non-verbal Stimuli
*Jules Davidoff*

# 4. Studies with Verbal Stimuli
*J. Graham Beaumont*

### 5. Theoretical Interpretations of Lateral Asymmetries
*Gillian Cohen*

### 6. Developmental Aspects
*J. Graham Beaumont*

# 1

# INTRODUCTION

*J. Graham Beaumont*

THE LOGIC of divided visual field (DVF) studies is essentially very simple. The cortex of the human brain is divided laterally into two similar hemispheres which are interconnected by the corpus callosum and other smaller commissures. Visual stimuli received at the retina of the eye are transmitted along the visual pathways directly to the hemisphere which is contralateral to the side of space in which the stimuli originated. That is, visual stimuli to the left of the current point of fixation are transmitted, via both eyes, to the visual cortex of the right hemisphere (RH). Those to the right of fixation, in the right visual field (RVF), go to the left hemisphere (LH). So, by arranging for stimuli to be presented in the left or right visual field, we can be certain that these stimuli will be initially transmitted to only one of the cerebral hemispheres, and subsequent response, in terms of the accuracy or speed with which some task related to the stimuli can be performed, can be referred to the hemisphere which received the stimuli.

While the logic may be simple, the problems which attach to putting it into effect, and to interpreting the data obtained, are not so simple, as the discussions which follow in this book will show. There are many methodological difficulties attached to arranging for the presentation of stimuli at a specific locus in one of the visual fields. Given that this can be achieved, and differences in performance contingent upon the visual field of presentation are found, what can be validly inferred from such findings? There are a variety of models of what happens after receipt of the information by the visual cortex as there are differing views as to how the processes which underlie the task being executed are undertaken. These naturally lead to different interpretations of differences in performance "between the hemispheres". Nevertheless, it is valuable that the inherent logic is so simple, and the simplicity of the logic, as

1

well as the techniques generally employed to effect it, has been a significant factor in the popularity of this field of investigation over the past decade.

## The Background

The origins of contemporary DVF studies can be traced in at least three areas: in clinical neuropsychology, in the "split-brain" studies, and in general experimental psychology.

### *Clinical Neuropsychology*

While there is evidence that the Ancient Egyptians knew about the contralateral organisation of the sensory and motor systems as early as 3000 B.C. (Gibson, 1962), as did Hippocratic writers in Classical Greece, the relation between the cortex and contralateral receptors and effectors was not understood until the second half of the nineteenth century.

Galen had described the corpus callosum in the second century A.D. and Vicq d'Azyr had described its possible role in interhemispheric communication in the eighteenth century. Willis in 1664 had introduced the term "hemispheres", but it was not until the role of the cortex in mental processes was appreciated, and the localisation of visual function was accurately described, that real advances were to be made in understanding cerebral organisation for psychological functions. Although Dax had described the lateralisation of cortical speech functions in 1836 (subsequently published in 1865), it was in the 1860s that the factors all came together to produce the germ of modern neurology and neuropsychology. Broca presented his patient "Tan" in 1861, and from this time current interest in cerebral localisation and cerebral organisation can be said to date. (Excellent introductions to the history of neurology and neuropsychology are to be found in Benton, 1978; Clarke and O'Malley, 1968; Joynt, 1974; Meyer, 1971. Walsh's excellent introductory textbook to clinical neuropsychology (1978) also contains a good summary of the historical background.)

A rather grimmer set of circumstances was responsible for the opening of the modern era of neuropsychology, for the origins of contemporary theories and practices are to be found in the study of brain-injured casualties of the Second World War. In the study of such patients, Paterson and Zangwill (1944) in Britain, Teuber and his associates in the U.S.A. (Teuber, 1962), and Luria in the Soviet Union (Luria, 1966) were to observe that deficits in cognitive abilities were more commonly associated with lesions of either the right or the left cerebral hemisphere. Over a long period this was a matter of the collection of data from which inferences about specific abilities could be made, and there was little integration between the findings related to specific tasks. However, attempts were eventually made to suggest principles upon which these diverse specialisations might be based, of which the seminal paper by Semmes (1968) was an important contribution.

Nevertheless, the state of clinical neuropsychology, certainly until the last few years, was for there to be a mass of observations which related specific functions to the anterior or posterior regions of the left or right hemisphere, and with which specific tests were associated which might be utilised to demonstrate a deficit of the particular function. The principle of relative localisation was, however, well established, with the concept of lateralisation to the cerebral hemispheres well demonstrated in clinical material. The role of individual differences, particularly handedness, as an important correlate of differences in cerebral organisation, had also been established.

## The Split-brain Studies

The second stimulus to DVF investigations came from the study of "split-brain" or, more properly, cerebral commissurotomy patients. The origins, and a description, of these studies follow in a later chapter, but briefly the operation in which the corpus callosum and other cerebral commissures are sectioned for the relief of intractible epilepsy, so disconnecting the two cerebral hemispheres from direct intercommunication with each other, provided a new stimulus to the study of cerebral organisation.

Although originally introduced by Van Wagenen and Akelaitis in about 1940, it was the re-introduction of the operation by Vogel and Bogen, and its subsequent study by Sperry and Gazzaniga from 1960, which is the significant event. Sperry had previously been working on the split-brain preparation in animals (Sperry, 1961), and the fortuitous availability of patients with a similar surgical lesion enabled the work to be extended to human subjects.

As a human surgical procedure which seemed closely parallel to the animal preparation had become available, it seemed that the opportunity was suddenly present for the scientific and controlled study of each cerebral hemisphere acting alone and in isolation from its partner. The opportunity was actively exploited by Sperry with others, and the ingenious and creative experiments designed by Michael Gazzaniga ensured that much important research, of a high quality, was conducted on these patients through the 1960s (Gazzaniga, 1970). It was Gazzaniga who, it seems, should be credited with the introduction of tachistoscopic DVF presentation for the study of these patients.

In retrospect, as will be made clear in Chapter 10, the methodological problems of studying these patients were initially underrated, and quite excessive extrapolations were made from the data which were obtained. Considerable reappraisal of the findings with commissurotomy patients has been necessary in recent years. What, however, is important in an historical context is the stimulus given to experimental neuropsychology by the writings of Sperry and his coworkers. Not only was the interest of neurobiologists and psychologists fired by the split-brain experiments, but a great deal of popular interest was shown in this work. Specifically, in considering the DVF technique, the commissurotomy studies showed that laboratory investigations of cerebral organisation in normal intact subjects might be possible, and suggested that one of the techniques which might be used to pursue such investigations was that of DVF presentation.

## Experimental Psychology

The investigation of human performance contingent upon lateralised tachistoscopic visual presentation had been pursued for a considerable period before its significance for neuropsychological research was fully realised. It was one of those situations, which fascinate the historian of science, in which the techniques were largely available, and all the components of the theoretical ideas were openly discussed and yet a considerable period passed before stimulation from other areas sparked off the kind of investigation which has been prevalent in the last decade.

Poffenberger, as early as 1912, had hit upon the idea of using direct and indirect stimulus-to-response pathways in reaction-time studies (a good discussion of the historical setting of this work appears in Swanson *et al.*, 1978). Trials on which the same hemisphere received the visual signal and initiated the motor response were contrasted with trials on which transfer across the callosum was required between the hemisphere receiving the stimulus and the hemisphere which was to perform the response. This was hypothesised to introduce an additional synaptic transmission of the information.

A series of sporadic studies followed, including the papers of Wagner (1918), Glanville and Dallenbach (1929), Crosland (1931, 1939), Anderson and Crosland (1933) and LaGrone (1942). It was in the early 1950s, with the papers of Mishkin and Forgays (1952) and Orbach (1952), the seminal paper of Heron (1957), and the papers of Harcum from 1957 (Harcum, 1978), that a particular interest was shown in DVF presentation. However, although the experimental technique was employed, it was not within the theoretical context of the investigation of cerebral organisation. Writers in this period were interpreting their data in terms of reading habits, and the concept of post-exposural scanning which was related to these. Data, particularly from alphabetical material, began to be collected in some volume, but there was little interest in cerebral lateralisation, or "cerebral dominance" (the contemporary term) as an explanatory hypothesis.

The consideration of cerebral lateralisation as relevant to the DVF studies does not seem to have a clearly identified origin. However, from the mid 1960s it came to have an increasingly important place alongside the other hypotheses discussed, as shown in the reviews of White (1969a, 1972) and of Harcum (1978). This was partly as a result of the emergence of papers on the split-brain patients, and partly as a result of the development of dichotic listening, through the work of Doreen Kimura, as a parallel technique for the investigation of cerebral organisation in normal subjects.

From about 1970, and with publication of the books by Dimond (1972), Dimond and Beaumont (1974a) and Kinsbourne and Smith (1974), DVF presentation has become a major field of investigation in experimental psychology, in which neuropsychological concepts have been employed in the interpretation of the data. This area of experimental psychology, now an important area of "cognitive psychology" has become merged with experimental human neuropsychology, and in the past decade there has been a considerable number of investigations which have employed the technique of DVF presentation.

## The Contemporary Field

The contemporary field of DVF investigation has to be seen within the context of a number of other methods of investigation which also contribute to the study of cerebral organisation. The investigation of patients with clinical lesions continues within the practice of clinical neuropsychology, and data obtained from such patients are no less relevant to the study of normal intact subjects. The data are largely supportive of the models derived from DVF studies with normals, but it is intriguing that a number of differences between the two sets of data continue to go unresolved.

With normal subjects there are also parallel techniques which are of relevance. The dichotic listening technique (Berlin, 1977; Krashen, 1976), although now more commonly directed to investigations of psycholinguistic and neurolinguistic questions, is perhaps the closest of these parallel techniques. The logic of dichotic listening is to undertake in the auditory modality what has been attempted in the visual modality in DVF studies.

Another parallel line has been the investigation of tactual presentation. Again the simple logic of lateralised presentation can be employed, and despite a paucity of early studies there is now an increasing interest in this technique of presentation (Gardner and Ward, 1979). The study of lateral eye movements, or the lateral deviation of the direction of gaze shown by subjects when engaged upon some cognitive task (Ehrlichman and Weinberger, 1978), has also been conducted within the conceptual framework of cerebral lateralisation, and may have important implications for theories of cerebral organisation.

Perhaps the most exciting development has been the introduction of electrophysiological recording into studies of hemisphere lateralisation (see Chapter 7). The recording of such variables, as an adjunct to one of the other experimental techniques, or with subjects freely engaged upon some cognitive task, permits for the first time the opportunity to observe physiological events and psychological cognitive events occurring together in real time. Although the techniques are difficult to implement, and the methodological problems are considerable, this field holds considerable promise for the future development of neuropsychology.

Three more specialised techniques should also be mentioned. Although confined to small numbers of clinical patients, the use of intracarotid sodium amytal, the "Wada technique", to temporarily suppress the activity of one of the hemispheres continues to yield relevant information (Rasmussen and Milner, 1975). Also, the study of the cerebral blood flow, "rCBF" studies, contingent upon cognitive activity (see *Brain and Language*, 1980, Vol. 9, Part 1) is pertinent to the DVF studies. Studies of asymmetries in cerebral anatomy (LeMay, 1976) have also produced data which, a little more distantly, must have a place in any account based upon the lateralised organisation of the cerebral cortex.

One problem common to all these methods, and it applies no less to DVF studies, has been the failure to consider some of the basic conceptual problems which underlie experimental neuropsychology. Perhaps it is more proper to say that progress has only been made by ignoring such problems. Nevertheless, perhaps part of the conceptual and theoretical difficulties which beset the field at the present, and which are amply demonstrated in this volume, spring from this failure to resolve a number of basic issues.

Undoubtedly the clearest, and most intransigent, of the problems is the failure to resolve the whole issue of the mind–body problem. The lack of any secure philosophical position from which to discuss the interrelationship between mental events and physiological events makes for particular difficulties in constructing models in this field. This is too great an issue to be discussed satisfactorily here, but it is promising that there is increasing interest in, and awareness of, the problem by neuroscientists. A number of recent works have also made valuable contributions to the debate, particularly the proceedings of the CIBA symposium "Brain and Mind" (CIBA, 1979), and the recent book by Bunge (1980). There still remains the difficulty of knowing what we mean when we refer to a "function", of understanding what is implied when it is "localised" to some region of the brain, and of creating valid models of the relationship between brain events and psychological events. This is not an esoteric problem, for it may simply not be sensible to attempt to describe mental processes in terms of cerebral topography. Whether this is so or not, and happily there are arguments to suggest that it is not (Bunge, 1980), experimental neuropsychologists should be aware of the foundations of their models, and should be prepared explicitly to support them by conceptual analysis. It seems unlikely that significant progress will be made in neuropsychology until issues of this kind are more satisfactorily treated.

A quite separate difficulty has been the degree of enthusiasm with which some of the more restricted scientific ideas in this area have been taken up and extrapolated well beyond reasonable generalisation. Some scientists within the field have not been without blame in this respect. Goleman (1977) presents a critical survey of some of the wilder ideas under the heading "Split-brain Psychology: Fad of the Year", and Gardner (1978) has been critical of what he terms the "academic hucksters".

The findings from DVF studies, together with the related techniques of investigation, apply in a very restricted context to some aspects of cognitive function, and from which some rather extended inferences may be made to certain aspects of cerebral organisation. Even to accept this cautious approach would be to ignore many considerable methodological and theoretical difficulties. Nevertheless, it has been proposed that aspects of cerebral specialisation account for a whole range of individual differences including occupational and educational adjustment, (Bracken et al., 1979), and for differences in the development and philosophical foundations of different cultures (Ornstein, 1977). Even more alarming is the suggestion that educational systems might be modified to account for the different processes attributed to the right and left cerebral hemispheres in order to develop the full potential of the "styles of thought" which characterise each (Bogen, 1977; Galin, 1976). A method to develop the potential of the right hemisphere based upon Shakespeare's Hamlet has even been published (Shuman, 1978), as well as more general methods for modifying "hemisphericity" (Reynolds and Torrance, 1978), although a more cautious note is sounded by Hellige (1980b). Hemisphere-related models of processing style have been proposed in vision therapy for the treatment of esophoria and exophoria (Birnbaum, 1978). We have seen the appearance of neurolinguistic sociology and anthropology (Dawson, 1977; Kaplan and Tenhouten, 1975; Tenhouten et al., 1976) which seek to attribute the foundations of social systems to the relative operation of the two cerebral hemispheres. Questionnaires have appeared to assess the balance between the hemispheres in an individual's cognitive strategies (Torrance and Reynolds, 1980; Zenhausern, 1978), and Julian Jaynes' (1978) work on the development of consciousness, attributing the "voice of the gods" to the right hemisphere, is well known.

It may well be that I do an injustice to some of these writers, and it may well be that some of these hypotheses will be supported by evidence in the future, although it is difficult to see how some could be supported by scientific investigation. What is important is to make clear, as the contents of this volume will demonstrate, that such hypotheses go well beyond the evidence which is at present available and should not claim a sound scientific basis for their support. Echoing the views of Oliver Zangwill in his Presidential Address to the British Psychological Society (1976, p. 309) we should "be wary of an updated phrenology that seeks to provide a scientific justification for some . . . irrational and disturbing trends in modern thought".

Despite this cautious and critical approach, it should not be forgotten that DVF studies do have a wider and practical relevance beyond the bounds of purely scientific enquiry. The most obvious of the areas of relevance is the contribution which experimental neuropsychology makes to clinical neuro-psychology. Acting not only as a stimulus to new approaches in clinical neuropsychology, but by also generating fundamental data, developing models of brain-behaviour relations, and allowing the testing of clinical issues within an experimental context, DVF studies have played a part in recent advances in the understanding of the effects of injuries to the brain. With increasing interest not only in the assessment of such patients, but also in behavioural methods for the rehabilitation of the brain injured, we should anticipate a growing practical relevance of the findings of DVF investigation.

Another exciting development has been the interest in the neuropsychology of psychiatric disorders (Gruzelier and Flor-Henry, 1979). Models of psychiatric disorder which involve central nervous system components have suddenly become received with enthusiasm, rather than the contempt they might have encountered a decade ago. (It is of some interest, and a sign of the degree to which this area has captured the popular imagination, that as early as 1969 in *A Pelican at Blandings*, P. G. Wodehouse has Galahad Threepwood say, "that something had gone wrong with the two hemispheres of her brain and the broad band of transversely running fibres known as the corpus callosum and that she was, in your crisp phrase, potty".) The techniques of experimental neuropsychology, and particularly DVF presentation, are playing a major role in the expansion of this field. While a highly critical appraisal of this area at the present time might conclude that there are few really secure findings, the field holds considerable promise, and at least one new direction for the development of psychiatry.

Lastly, models of neuropsychological function are intimately related to cognitive models in psychology. DVF studies have therefore a place in the general theoretical development of psychology. They provide an opportunity to test the validity of cognitive models in terms of the cerebral "hardware", and to suggest directions for the evolution and improvement of such models. There has always been a valuable cross-fertilisation between general experimental psychology and neuropsychology and there is every reason to expect that this will continue into the future.

These then, rather sketchily presented, are the origins of DVF studies, some of the general difficulties which they encounter, and some of the areas of relevance which they possess. It seems however, after a decade of active investigation, that DVF investigation has reached a critical point in its scientific development. There have been a very large number of published studies over the past 10 years, neuropsychology has been and to some extent still is fashionable, and the dissertations and theses of undergraduate and postgraduate students have added to the bulk of data amassed. During this period there has been little in the way of significant methodological development, and while there have been important theoretical contributions, we are little nearer to a valid and well-established model of lateralised hemisphere function.

The purpose of the chapters which follow is therefore to provide a statement of the current state of our knowledge, and of the theoretical issues at stake. While it may be over-optimistic to hope that significant solutions will be presented, it is hoped at least to illuminate the way forward. The following chapters will provide a critical guide to the recent literature, a clear summary of the conceptual and theoretical issues currently under discussion, as well as original contributions to these issues where these can be formulated. As a result we hope that new directions may emerge, and that a better understanding can be attained of performance asymmetries contingent upon lateralised visual presentation, and what can be inferred from these about the organisation of the human brain.

# 2

# METHODOLOGICAL AND THEORETICAL BASES OF VISUAL HEMIFIELD STUDIES

*Andrew W. Young*

## Introduction

MANY INTERESTING FINDINGS have emerged from studies involving the presentation of stimuli in the left and right visual hemifields (which will be referred to as divided visual field, or DVF studies), but it is known that the outcome of DVF studies can be influenced by a wide range of procedural factors which complicate the comparison of results from studies that used different methods.

This chapter will examine the principles on which DVF studies are based, and the advantages and limitations arising from the different methodological choices available to investigators. The intention is not to establish the supremacy of any particular method over all others, but simply to state the pros and cons of each. Attention will, however, be drawn to common methodological deficiencies and sources of invalid inference, insofar as these are known. Because it is often the simplest points of methodology that are most easily overlooked no attempt will be made to refrain from stating the obvious or banal.

The body of the chapter is divided into three general sections dealing with basic methodological principles, the choice of subjects, stimuli, tasks, responses and measures, and the difficulties involved in making between-group or between-subject comparisons. Each general section is subdivided as necessary. A final section provides a summary and conclusions.

11

## Basic Methodological Principles

All divided visual field (DVF) studies of cerebral organisation depend upon the fact that, for the primary visual system, information concerning stimuli falling to the left of the point at which a person is looking (in the left visual hemifield, or LVF) is initially projected to the right cerebral hemisphere, whereas information concerning stimuli falling to the right of the point at which a person is looking (in the right visual hemifield, or RVF) is initially projected to the left cerebral hemisphere. Of course, the presentation of a stimulus outside central vision usually results in the person moving his eyes in order to bring the stimulus into central vision. For this reason it is customary to use brief exposures that present the stimuli used in DVF experiments for less than the reaction time needed for such an eye movement.

From this simple description of the essential principles of DVF research it is clear that further consideration must be given to the arrangement and functions of the optic pathways and the commissural connections between the cerebral hemispheres, to the range of stimulus presentation times that can be regarded as acceptable, to the ways in which it can be ensured that subjects fixate as instructed, to the range of eccentricities at which stimuli may be presented, and to the relative merits of unilateral stimulus presentations (in which stimuli are only presented in one visual hemifield on any particular experimental trial) and bilateral stimulus presentations (in which different stimuli are simultaneously presented in each of the visual hemifields). These points will be examined in turn. The section will conclude by mentioning some of the methods that can obviate the need for brief stimulus presentations by providing continuous lateralised input.

### *Optic Pathways and Commissural Connections*

For the purposes of this chapter, only the primary visual system, whose optic nerves project to the cerebral cortex, will be considered in detail. The known functions of the optic nerves projecting to the superior colliculus (Schneider, 1969; Trevarthen, 1974a) are such that they are unlikely to contribute to the findings of most DVF studies.

The optic nerves of the primary visual system are arranged so that nerve fibres from each of the nasal hemiretinae project to the visual cortex of the ipsilateral cerebral hemisphere, whereas the projections from the temporal hemiretinae are to the contralateral cerebral hemisphere. Thus, although each eye has projections to both cerebral hemispheres, information concerning LVF stimuli is projected to the visual cortex of the right cerebral hemisphere and information concerning RVF stimuli is projected to the left cerebral hemisphere. The cerebral hemispheres are themselves linked by a number of nerve tracts, or commissures, of which the corpus callosum and anterior commissure are the most notable.

Two questions concerning this general arrangement of the primary visual system immediately arise. First, how complete is the separation of ipsilateral and contralateral optic projections at the midline of the retina of each eye? In other words, is there any degree of overlap? Secondly, how is information from the two visual hemifields integrated by means of the cerebral commissures? Unfortunately, the answers to these questions are not definitely established at present, and the available evidence must be viewed cautiously.

Most of the physiological evidence comes from studies of the cat. For present purposes, however, this will be set aside, and attention will be concentrated on the findings of studies of the monkey and of man.

Stone et al. (1973) identified a vertically oriented strip in the centre of the monkey's retina which gave rise to both ipsilateral and contralateral optic projections. This strip was about 1° wide, and passed through the centre of the fovea. Similar findings were reported by Bunt et al. (1977) who also noted, however, that the bilaterally projecting vertical strip widened to pass around the fovea, which is itself 2° wide, giving a total of some 3° of overlap at this point.

Such direct evidence is not available for humans, but it is hard to believe that a similar arrangement would not be found. The "sparing" of foveal vision often noted in the presence of visual-field defects following unilateral injuries (Huber, 1962; Koerner and Teuber, 1973; Williams and Gassel, 1962) has sometimes been taken as evidence that bilateral projections exist in the central retina of man, but the interpretation of such observations is complicated by difficulties of controlling fixation and attention, and by the finding that some patients exhibit "splitting" of the fovea instead of sparing (Koerner and Teuber, 1973; Williams and Gassel, 1962).

Most of the commissural connections between the visual cortex of the left cerebral hemisphere and the visual cortex of the right hemisphere pass through the splenium of the corpus callosum. These callosal connections are again largely restricted to a strip some 2–3° wide bordering the vertical meridian of the visual field (Berlucchi, 1972; Karol and Pandya, 1971; Selnes, 1974). It would thus seem that the vertical strip that is bilaterally represented by means of the splenium of the corpus callosum is for the most part somewhat wider than the strip with direct bilateral projections (Berlucchi, 1972). The functions of these callosal connections, and the significance of the bilateral representation of the visual midline by means of both direct and commissural connections, are not understood. It may be the case though, as Berlucchi (1972) points out, that the needs of stereopsis are involved.

It is tempting to conclude that the bilateral representation of retinal cells adjacent to the visual midline should be taken to imply that DVF studies should avoid presenting stimuli in this region. However, this need not necessarily follow. If the bilateral connections were to subserve central stereoscopic vision, for instance, they might have negligible effect on the results of DVF studies that present stimuli on a flat surface. In fact both Harvey (1978) and Haun (1978) have demonstrated visual hemifield asymmetries for foveal stimuli similar to those found for non-foveal stimuli. These findings suggest either that the bilateral representation of the visual midline has little functional significance or that its functional significance relates to conditions not normally encountered in DVF experiments.

In addition to the connection of visual cortical cells adjoining the midline of the visual field, there are a number of other levels of commissural integration of visual information (Berlucchi, 1972; Gazzaniga and Le Doux, 1978). It is unfortunate for DVF studies that these are again poorly understood. Gazzaniga *et al.* (1975), Gordon *et al.* (1971), and Risse *et al.* (1978) have reported what would appear to be interhemispheric integration of information about quite complex visual stimuli in partial split-brain patients with intact splenium or anterior commissure. It is not at present clear, however, how directly such findings can be related to the normal functioning of the cerebral commissures, and the possibility of complex cross-cueing and guessing strategies mentioned by Gazzaniga (1970) is always difficult to rule out entirely. Moreover, none of these studies paid much attention to analysing the level or levels of information processing at which interhemispheric coordination and integration might have taken place.

Given the lack of understanding of the functions of the cerebral commissures, then, investigators using DVF methods are at present limited to knowing only to which of the cerebral hemispheres stimuli were initially projected, and the interpretation of obtained laterality effects is correspondingly difficult.

## Stimulus Presentation Times

The most obvious factor affecting the acceptability of stimulus presentation times is the latency of the saccadic eye movement needed to bring a laterally presented stimulus into foveal vision. Although saccadic movements are to some extent voluntary, it is difficult for people to resist the temptation to fixate a newly presented visual stimulus. For this reason it is usually held that the latency of the saccadic eye movement involved should be used as a limit to the upper range of stimulus presentation times.

Saccadic eye movements have been extensively studied, and reviews include those of Alpern (1962a, 1971), Carpenter (1977) and Miles (1936). Although the mean saccadic latencies observed are often in the range 180–200 milliseconds mentioned by Cohen (1977), there are a number of factors that can affect latencies. These include the number of alternative positions a target stimulus can occupy (Heywood and Churcher, 1980), target intensity (Cohen and Ross, 1977), type of stimulus (Pirozzolo and Rayner, 1980), the subject's level of practice and ability to anticipate the positioning and timing of stimulus onset (Alpern, 1971; Carpenter, 1977; Hackman, 1940), and the distance of the necessary movement, with longer times for very short (less than 0·5°) and also for long (greater than 10°) movements (Bartz, 1962; Wyman and Steinman, 1973).

Since the value of the saccadic latency is not fixed, it is advisable to make use of values taken from the studies that most closely approximate to the conditions obtaining in the majority of DVF experiments. These will be taken to be the use of relatively complex stimuli (rather than the target lights used in many studies of saccadic latencies) presented some 2–6° left or right of the subject's point of fixation, occuring at intervals and in positions not entirely predictable to subjects.

None of the existing studies exactly meets these specifications, but those of Rayner (1978a) and Pirozzolo and Rayner (1980) are quite close, as are some of the data of Bartz (1962). Bartz (1962) gives mean latencies of about 200 ms for digits presented 5° left or right of fixation. Rayner (1978a) found mean response latencies of about 180 ms for words 1–5° left of fixation and 170 ms for words 1–5° right of fixation. Pirozzolo and Rayner (1980) found mean response latencies of about 195 ms for words and symbols presented 2–5° left of fixation to right-handed subjects, and about 180 ms for words and symbols 2–5° right of fixation. In view of these findings of shorter latencies for words and symbols presented to the right of fixation the data from earlier studies that had collapsed across left and right positions (reviewed by Miles, 1936) has been set aside.

Of course, it is the nature of mean latencies that many people will be able to initiate an eye movement in less than the mean time taken by whole groups of subjects. The standard deviations of the mean latencies that have been considered are mostly of the order 20–25 milliseconds. Hence the use of exposure durations up to a maximum of 150 ms should, for most subjects, preclude the possibility of eye movements to bring stimuli into foveal vision, and this would seem to be a suitable upper limit for studies employing a number of subjects. For studies involving only a few subjects, however, and also when comparisons of individual subjects are proposed, it would be better to use a maximum time of 120 ms, which is close to or below even the fastest latencies for individual subjects under any of the conditions reported in the literature.

These recommended maximum times are shorter than those often used in DVF studies. However, they are based on the times needed for subjects to initiate eye movements and, as Fudin and Masterson (1976a) point out, the time needed to actually bring a lateral stimulus into foveal vision will be longer. Saccadic movements themselves take some 20–30 ms to execute (Carpenter,

1977; Rayner, 1978a), and there may also have to be small changes in convergence and accommodation. Moreover, there is evidence to suggest that perceptual sensitivity is substantially reduced both during an eye movement and for some 40–50 ms before and after the movement begins (Latour, 1962; Volkmann, 1962; Volkmann et al., 1968). For these reasons the use of presentation times of up to 200 ms, as advocated by Fudin and Masterson (1976a), need not be seen as particularly worrying, though it cannot be recommended in view of the fact that perceptual sensitivity is not entirely eliminated by the factors discussed.

A minority of researchers have made use of presentation times considerably in excess of even 200 ms and have still found laterality effects. Although Moscovitch et al. (1976) offer reasons to justify this practice, it is inadvisable in the absence of continuous and accurate monitoring of subjects' fixation, since it can otherwise confound effects arising from LVF and RVF stimulus processing with those arising from asymmetries in left and right eye movement latencies.

Having discussed the upper limit of acceptable stimulus presentation times, consideration needs to be given to whether it is advisable to use relatively long or short presentations within the acceptable range. The answer appears to depend on the type of stimulus used. For words, most studies have provided little reason to suppose that presentation time is of much importance within the range 20–150 ms (see Chapter 4). For faces, however, Leehey et al. (1978) have maintained that as long a presentation as possible should be used in order to permit encoding of the stimulus as a face.

These comments on the use of different presentation times within the acceptable range are at best vague, and more systematic studies would be helpful. The problem is that it is difficult to disentangle effects attributable to presentation time from effects due to such other variables as task difficulty and stimulus clarity.

Finally, it is necessary to draw attention to the fact that some studies use fixed presentation times for groups of subjects whilst others use individual times determined for each subject, or even for each condition of an experiment. The potential advantage of the latter method is that it can avoid variations in overall performance between subjects or across conditions, but this is difficult to achieve in practice as the fluctuations in the performance levels of individual subjects can be as marked as the original differences between subjects or across conditions.

## Fixation Control

In order that stimuli are presented to subjects in the required retinal positions it is essential that they fixate carefully as and when instructed. Most DVF studies employ a central fixation position, but there is not a commonly agreed method for ensuring that subjects carry out the instruction to fixate. Some investigators are willing to trust adults to do this, and make use of no other fixation control. This is unwise, since the consequence is often that results from studies without fixation control that conform to the pattern established by studies that did employ fixation control are accepted, whilst those that do not conform, and which may be highly important, are disputed on the grounds of the lack of fixation control.

The available methods of fixation control can be divided into two types. Indirect methods make use of the quantitative and qualitative differences between foveal and non-foveal vision, whereas direct methods involve adaptions of the various methods of monitoring and recording eye movements reviewed by Carpenter (1977) and by Young and Sheena (1975).

The most well known of the indirect methods is that made popular by McKeever and Huling (1971b). Instead of a fixation spot, they used a small fixation "space", surrounded by a pattern of radiating lines. On each experimental trial this space was filled by a digit presented simultaneously with the lateral experimental stimuli. Subjects were required to report this digit before carrying out the experimental task of reporting the lateral stimuli. The greater acuity of foveal than non-foveal vision allows the digit to be arranged so as to be sufficiently small to be only clearly visible if central fixation is occurring. Trials on which the digit was not reported correctly were regarded by McKeever and Huling (1971b) as those on which central fixation might not have occurred.

This method illustrates well the advantages and disadvantages of indirect fixation control. It is simple to use, and does not require complex equipment. It is not, however, well suited to reaction time studies, and it cannot be used to ensure central fixation before stimulus presentation. The accuracy of the method, in terms of its ability to detect trials on which central fixation did not occur, is limited by the probability of subjects' guessing the central stimuli correctly and the extent to which these stimuli can be identified from non-foveal vision. For these reasons, high accuracies are seldom attainable in practice. None the less, the mere presence of a reasonably effective check will discourage most subjects from adopting strategies based on not fixating centrally.

A possible problem with McKeever and Huling's (1971b) method of fixation control is that the additional task of reporting central stimuli may interfere with or modify the processing of the laterally presented stimuli. Hines (1972a) was one of the first to voice this fear, but his arguments were largely refuted by

McKeever *et al.* (1972). Some studies have compared laterality effects when using central digits to control fixation to those obtained without any fixation control. These inevitably confound absence of the task of reporting the central digit with absence of fixation control, and will not be discussed. Kershner *et al.* (1977) and Carter and Kinsbourne (1979) both maintained that the nature of the fixation control stimuli could affect asymmetries obtained with children as subjects and laterally presented digit stimuli, but Hines (1978) did not find this result with adult subjects and word or random-shape stimuli. The stimuli and subjects used in Hines' (1978) study are more typical of the majority of DVF experiments in which this method of fixation control has been used, and Carter and Kinsbourne (1979) do not report what presentation times they used. It thus remains to be established that the central stimuli of McKeever and Huling's (1971b) method actually do interfere in any important way with the processing of the laterally presented stimuli.

Modifications of McKeever and Huling's (1971b) method have been made by Kershner (1977) and by Schmuller and Goodman (1979). In both cases these have involved replacing the central digit with a simpler stimulus drawn from a smaller number of alternatives. This considerably reduces the accuracy of the method.

A somewhat different indirect method was introduced by Young and Ellis (1976), who brought trials with central as well as with LVF and RVF stimuli into their study, reasoning that subjects who were fixating centrally should show better performance with central than with either LVF or RVF stimuli. This method suffers from the disadvantages that it requires additional experimental trials and that it can only attain modest accuracy. Its principal advantage is that it can be used in cases, such as studies of children, where McKeever and Huling's (1971b) method would probably be unsuitable.

A further indirect method used by Gibson *et al.* (1972) has involved the Haidinger's Brush phenomenon, which only occurs with foveal vision. As this phenomenon is perceptible only to the subject, however, the method does little to control fixation beyond providing him with feedback as to whether he is fixating or not.

The simplest direct method of controlling fixation is to watch subjects' eyes. Maddess *et al.* (1973) have shown that this can be remarkably accurate. An added advantage is that stimulus presentations need not be triggered unless central fixation is occurring. As described by Maddess *et al.*, however, the method requires the presence of two experimenters. This can be avoided by using a video camera to effect the monitoring in the manner described by Geffen *et al.* (1972) or by Young *et al.* (1980). These methods do not require excessive technical competence to set up, and can tolerate some head movement on the subject's part.

Other direct methods that have been used include electrooculography

(Dimond and Beaumont, 1972b) and a sensor system utilising the differential reflectivities of the iris and sclera of the eye (Dimond and Beaumont, 1971b). These methods can also be used to turn off the stimulus if an eye movement occurs, thus allowing continuous lateralised input whilst the subject fixates centrally. The method utilising the differential reflectivities of parts of the eye can be arranged in order to achieve very high levels of accuracy, but for the purposes of conventional DVF experiments the video method is sufficiently accurate when properly set up, and the extra technical investment involved in more sophisticated methods is not repaid.

## *Stimulus Eccentricity*

Even when a person thinks that he is fixating a point, his eyes are subject to the very small movements known as "tremor", "drift" and "microsaccades" (Carpenter, 1977). The largest of these, however, seldom exceed 5′ of arc, so that they are not very important in determining acceptable stimulus eccentricities for DVF studies. In addition, despite the bilateral projections of the central retina, it has been noted that the studies of Harvey (1978) and Haun (1978) found laterality effects for stimuli presented within the range of foveal vision.

It would thus seem that there is no known physiological reason to preclude the use of small eccentricities for stimuli in DVF experiments. It would be prudent, however, to avoid the bilaterally projecting areas whenever possible until their functions are more clearly established. Moreover, it assists the accuracy of methods of fixation control if stimulus offsets of more than 1 or 2° are utilised.

Acuity along the horizontal meridian of the visual field falls quite markedly with increasing distance from fixation (Alpern, 1962b). The extent to which stimuli may be laterally displaced from fixation thus depends on the extent to which they can remain sufficiently clear to subjects. Most investigators have kept within an outer limit for stimulus presentation of 5–6° from fixation, but there is no evidence to indicate any change in the nature of laterality effects obtained with stimuli offset by more than 6° (see Chapter 4). Some studies have also tried to establish whether the magnitude of visual hemifield asymmetries is affected by the extent to which stimuli are offset from the central fixation position. This is difficult to ascertain, as stimulus eccentricity tends to be confounded with changes in visual acuity and task difficulty. However, in most cases eccentricity has not been found to affect visual hemifield asymmetries (see Chapter 4).

In summary, then, whilst it is generally convenient to present stimuli 2–6° from fixation, studies which present stimuli outside this range will often prove to be perfectly acceptable.

## Unilateral or Bilateral Presentation

Unilateral presentation involves the use of a single laterally presented stimulus on each experimental trial. Usually the order of trials with LVF and RVF stimuli is random, so that subjects do not know where the next stimulus will appear. Blocked trials with LVF or RVF presentations should only be used when accurate fixation control is available.

Some investigators have, however, preferred to use bilateral rather than unilateral stimulus presentations. For bilateral presentation different stimuli are presented simultaneously, with one in the LVF and one in the RVF. A number of advantages have been claimed for this procedure. Dimond (1972) maintained that the use of a simultaneous input to each of the cerebral hemispheres might cause them to function to some extent as independent channels, and thus give a more accurate assessment of the capacities of each. The presence of LVF and RVF stimuli on each trial prevents the possibility that subjects will adopt a strategy of guessing where the next stimulus is to appear, and fixating that position (if there is no fixation control). Twice as much data can be gathered from a given number of experimental trials, as compared to unilateral presentation.

There are, however, two difficulties encountered with bilateral presentation, though neither is insuperable. The first is that it is best suited to studies in which accuracy is used as the dependent variable. For reaction time studies one of the stimuli on each trial would have to be treated as a dummy, losing some of the potential advantages of the method.

The second difficulty is that when both LVF and RVF stimuli are to be reported the first reports will often be more accurate than the second reports, and may implicate rather different cognitive processes. Consequently, obtained lateral asymmetries can be influenced by subjects' tendencies to report in a left-to-right or in a right-to-left direction. The importance of report order may be greater for picture and letter string stimuli than for pronounceable non-words and certain types of word (Coltheart and Arthur, 1971; MacKavey *et al.*, 1975; McKeever, 1971; Smith and Ramunas, 1971; Young *et al.*, 1980). Simple methods for counterbalancing order of report are described by Schmuller and Goodman (1979) and Young *et al.* (1980), and this should be done whenever more than one report from each experimental trial is possible.

Studies have been carried out in order to compare the magnitudes of visual hemifield asymmetries obtained under unilateral and bilateral presentation conditions. In some cases no differences obtained (e.g. Hines, 1976), but when differences have been found they have always been such that bilateral presentation produced the larger asymmetries (e.g. McKeever, 1971), provided that fixation was properly controlled. Such results should be viewed cautiously in view of the general lack of control for order of report in the bilateral conditions.

Two further variations on bilateral presentation should also be mentioned. When letter strings are used as stimuli they are often presented bilaterally in the form of one continuous string across the fixation point. Hirata and Bryden (1976) have shown that the introduction of a gap at fixation (making the letter strings into separate LVF and RVF strings) can increase RVF superiority. Kershner (1977) presented pairs of bilateral words arranged in such a way that only one was correctly reported. This procedure avoids order of report difficulties, and is analogous to the idea of using a "dummy" stimulus mentioned earlier.

At present, then, there are no compelling reasons to favour unilateral or bilateral presentation, and the choice can still be made according to the preferences of investigators and the requirements of particular studies. When bilateral presentation is used and both stimuli are to be reported, however, order of report should be controlled.

## Methods That Can Give Continuous Lateralised Input

These will be dealt with briefly, as they are not in common use.

Two general approaches have been used. The first is to monitor eye movements and arrange that the stimulus is only illuminated when the eyes are in a specified position (e.g. Butler and Norrsell, 1968; Dimond and Beaumont, 1971b). Although this allows stimuli to remain present for as long as fixation can be maintained, it does not permit the scanning of stimuli by means of eye movements.

The second approach is to restrict the extent of the visual field by means of special contact lenses (Dimond et al., 1975; Zaidel, 1975). This allows eye movements to be made, but care must be taken to ensure that the contact lenses do not slip and change position.

# Choice of Subjects, Stimuli, Tasks, Responses and Measures

These will be examined under four headings: specification of subject groups; choice of stimuli and tasks; choice of responses and measures; and effects of practice and set size.

## Specification of Subject Groups

Special or unusual subject groups are considered elsewhere. Here, the only concern is with the specification of typical subject groups used in DVF studies.

The most common requirement is that subjects should be right-handed, in order to ensure a high probability that they will have left-cerebral dominance for speech and some degree of right-hemisphere superiority for visuospatial skills.

Handedness can be defined in terms of preference for the use of one hand or the other, or in terms of the relative skill of the left and right hands. Most DVF studies rely on measures of hand preference, usually assessed by such simple tests as writing a word, by self-report, or by questionnaires (Crovitz and Zener, 1962; Oldfield, 1971). Richardson (1978) has demonstrated that the various items used for self-report and questionnaires load on a single factor. Although measures of relative skill are for some purposes preferable to reports of preferences (Young, 1977) they are cumbersome to use. Since preference and relative skill are closely related for difficult tasks (Annett, 1976; Brown, 1962) the needs of most DVF studies can be met by using reports of hand preferences for tasks such as writing, and reasonable sample sizes.

A small proportion of right-handed people, however, may have right-cerebral dominance for, or bilateral organisation of, speech functions (Branch *et al.*, 1964). It has been thought that these unusual patterns of cerebral organisation may be associated both with familial sinistrality and with the use of an inverted writing posture, though the available evidence is far from conclusive (Bradshaw, 1980; Levy and Reid, 1978). For these reasons the added precautions of using right-handed subjects who write with an upright hand position and who do not have parents or close relatives who are left-handed are sometimes taken. More precise criteria for determining familial sinistrality remain to be agreed.

Although it was at one time customary to try to determine the eye dominance of subjects in DVF studies it is now accepted that there is no reason to suppose that this is a useful indicator of cerebral organisation (Porac and Coren, 1976).

## Choice of Stimuli and Tasks

The choice and construction of the experimental stimuli and tasks used in DVF studies involves a number of important methodological decisions. However, as such choices are often constrained by the aims of particular studies, and as their consequences are discussed throughout the rest of this book, they will not be discussed in detail here. It should be noted, however, that a potentially important feature of DVF tasks which is seldom discussed in this context is the use of stimulus-masking techniques. The presence or absence of masking stimuli, and the type of masking employed, can have profound effects on the processing of briefly presented stimuli (see Coltheart, 1980a, for a review of this topic).

## Choice of Responses and Measures

It is customary for DVF studies to use a manual or vocal response, and accuracy or reaction time as a measure. In most cases studies in which the principal measure is accuracy have involved vocal responses, whereas reaction time studies have involved manual responses. There are also, however, some studies of vocal reaction time.

Accuracy is the simplest measure to use, and is relatively free from theoretical problems, though difficulties can arise in deciding how to compare hemifield asymmetries for stimuli that led to different levels of overall accuracy (Coltheart, 1980b). The main drawback of accuracy is that it is unlikely to be a very sensitive measure, especially in conjunction with matching tasks, for which the probability of answering correctly by guessing is usually substantial.

Reaction time is potentially a more sensitive and direct measure than accuracy, but it needs to be used and interpreted carefully. The use of manual reaction times will here be given more extensive consideration than vocal reaction times, though many points are common to both methods.

Most of the methods used in DVF studies of manual reaction times involve subjects in deciding between two alternative possibilities (same or different, member or non-member of memory set, word or non-word, and so on). The times taken to make each type of responses need to be measured separately, unless a "go/no-go" task, in which the subject only responds to one of the two possibilities, is employed. The two types of response should preferably be made using a centrally positioned apparatus. In this way unwanted stimulus-response compatability effects, in which the fastest responses are made to the side on which the stimulus is presented (Craft and Simon, 1970; Simon, 1968; Wallace, 1971), can be avoided. The type of movement required to initiate a response is also important, since there is evidence that fine motor movements, including movements of individual fingers, may involve a relatively high degree of contralateral cerebral control as compared to gross movements of the whole arm (Brinkman and Kuypers, 1972, 1973; Trevarthen, 1974b). Whether or not a relatively high degree of contralateral control of the motor response is required depends on the aims of particular studies. It is also often necessary to counterbalance the hands used to make each type of response.

In reaction time studies it is essential that the variance of the reaction times is kept as low as possible (Schmuller, 1980). For this reason, many reaction time studies make use of subjects performing at high levels of practice. In addition, however, it is usual to discard or repeat trials on which errors were made, and those resulting in very short and very long reaction times, or to transform the data in various possible ways in order to reduce the otherwise disproportionate influence of long times. Such decisions require careful scrutiny, since there is as yet no agreed general procedure.

The ideal of reaction time studies is to have subjects responding as quickly as possible whilst making few errors, and instructions should emphasise this. Error-free performance levels should be avoided, as they may fail to reveal visual hemifield differences in reaction time. Substantial error rates are even worse, since they are often associated with complex subject strategies involving tradeoffs of speed and accuracy. This possibility is particularly worrying when the processing of stimuli presented in one of the visual hemifields is found to be faster but less accurate than the processing of stimuli presented in the other visual hemifield. In such cases one cerebral hemisphere can appear to be both superior (faster) and inferior (less accurate) in performance, and no satisfactory interpretation can be made. It is thus necessary to ensure either that error rate in reaction time studies do not vary between visual hemifields or that one visual hemifield is associated with both faster reaction times and greater accuracy (less errors).

These requirements of reaction time studies are not difficult to achieve when normal adults are used as subjects, though they need very careful attention when such subject groups as children, poor readers, or clinical patients are involved. There are two further problems, however, that are at present less tractable. The first is that the assumption that faster performance results from more efficient or effective stimulus-processing need not always be valid. The second is the difficulty of deciding how to combine the interpretation of two different sets of data deriving from the two responses usually involved in reaction time experiments. The use of a "go/no-go" task does not solve this problem, it only avoids it by arbitrarily eliminating one half of the available data. Both of these problems reflect the lack of satisfactory theoretical models of the cognitive processes involved in the matching tasks usually used with manual reaction time measures.

A minor problem with the use of manual reaction times is that they are unsuitable for certain tasks, and particularly for naming tasks. Recent studies have, however, demonstrated the feasibility of using vocal reaction times (e.g. McKeever and Jackson, 1979). It is now evident, despite the fact that vocal responses will nearly always be initiated by the left hemisphere, right-hemisphere processing superiorities can none the less be demonstrated for certain tasks (Berlucchi *et al.*, 1979).

## Practice and Set Size

The importance of these factors is not at present properly understood, and they are also discussed in other chapters in this book. Whilst set size has been shown to be an important factor in DVF studies (Miller and Butler, 1980; Young and Bion, 1980a) it is clear that it cannot account for all visual hemifield asymmetries (Schmuller, 1980). Effects of practice reported in the literature are complex and inconsistent, and studies have not been successful in disentangling effects attributable to practice at given tasks from those that may have arisen from increased familiarity of stimuli and from covert and overt changes in subject strategies. Control of the latter factor would at present seem more important to DVF studies than control of level of practice *per se*.

## The Difficulties Involved in Making Between-group or Between-subject Comparisons

In a number of DVF studies the focus of interest has been the possibility of differences in cerebral organisation of function between different groups of subjects (adults v. children, normal v. poor readers, clinical patients v. normal controls, left- v. right-handers, and so on) or the possibility of differences in the performance of various tasks between individual subjects who seem to be more or less "lateralised" in terms of the sizes of obtained visual hemifield asymmetries. The execution and interpretation of these studies presents special difficulties, which will be summarised and discussed in terms of differences in DVF asymmetries between subjects or groups that are not due to differences in cerebral organisation of function, and in terms of lack of reliability or lack of understanding of the measures used.

### Differences Not Due to Differences in Cerebral Organisation

This problem is discussed with reference to specific types of between-group comparison by Naylor (1980), Young (1981), and Young and Ellis (1981). As these reviews demonstrate, there are a number of possible sources of between-group differences in DVF asymmetries which, for the purposes of studies of cerebral organisation, should be regarded as artefactual and which investigators should take care to eliminate by careful design of studies and choice of control groups. These include between-group differences in fixation, in the stimuli recognised, and in the strategies or processes used to solve experimental tasks. In addition, between-group differences in performance level are also problematic, as the tasks used may then have different sensitivities (Chapman and Chapman, 1973).

Clearly, then, studies of between-group differences in DVF asymmetries need to ensure that subjects in the groups studied are dealing with the tasks used in the same way. The same point applies to between-subject as well as group comparisons, but the use of DVF methods with individual subjects also involves additional difficulties discussed under the next heading.

## Lack of Reliability or Lack of Understanding of the Measures Used

For between-subject comparisons using DVF task it is necessary that the chosen procedures are reliable. Whether satisfactory reliabilities can be attained is a question that has received little attention. Fennell *et al.* (1977a, 1977b) found that reliable performance, in terms of significant correlation of LVF and RVF scores across testing sessions, only occurred after the second of their four sessions with a DVF task. The initial instability may, however, have resulted from subjects changing their strategies, as this factor was not controlled.

Although promising reliabilities were obtained by Fennell *et al.*, they were far from perfect, and would not be of much use in predicting an individual subject's cerebral organisation. As Satz (1977) explains, when there is a strong *a priori* probability that a certain type of organisation exists (as would be the case for, say, left-cerebral control of speech in right-handed people), a test must be highly reliable before it can improve on the null hypothesis that a tested individual conformed to the typical pattern.

Although the points made by Satz (1977) are of great importance to those interested in dichotic and DVF asymmetries, it must not be forgotten that lack of understanding of the nature of these asymmetries is also a basic problem for between-subject comparisons, since it is not clear what is actually being measured. In particular, it should be noted that DVF tasks involve asymmetries for stimulus-processing, and it is not known to what extent these should be expected to be stable across different stimuli, task conditions, levels of practice and subject strategies, and to what extent they should be expected to map on to asymmetries for speech production or even speech perception (see Bryden, 1965; Zurif and Bryden, 1969; Fennell *et al.*, 1977a, 1977b).

This lack of understanding of the measures that can be used for between-subject (and between-group) comparisons has formed the basis of an important critique of the practice of measuring "laterality" by Colbourn (1978). The statistical properties of the possible measures deriving from DVF asymmetries also present difficulties, and have been discussed by Birkett (1977), Marshall *et al.* (1975), Richardson (1976), and Stone (1980).


## Summary and Conclusions

Three general problems hinder the interpretation of DVF studies. These are lack of understanding of the functions of the cerebral commissures, lack of understanding of the cognitive processes involved in solving the tasks used, and the lack of an adequate theory with which to account for the lateral differences that have been found.

In the monkey, and most likely also in man, a vertical strip down the centre of the retina of each eye is bilaterally represented in the visual cortex by means of direct and commissural nerve connections. There is reason to believe that these bilateral projections of the visual midline do not subserve functions of importance to the majority of DVF studies, and it is prudent to avoid them whenever possible. The other major determinants of acceptable eccentricities for laterally presented stimuli are the acuity of vision at different eccentricities and the accuracy of any chosen method of fixation control. Fixation control is always advisable, and indispensable when comparisons between individual subjects or between groups of subjects are involved. McKeever and Huling's (1971) method of fixation control is satisfactory if properly set up, but it is not appropriate to all DVF studies, and direct methods are preferable.

A conservative estimate of the upper limit to acceptable stimulus presentation times would be 150 ms for studies with moderate or large numbers of subjects and 120 ms for studies with small numbers of subjects and those involving comparisons of individual subjects, but the use of presentation times as long as 200 ms is not particularly worrying. Longer presentation times should not be used unless methods that permit continuous and accurate monitoring of subjects' fixation are available. Within the range 20–150 ms the factors affecting the choice of suitable presentation times for particular studies are not well understood. Both unilateral and bilateral stimulus presentations are acceptable, but order of report should normally be controlled when bilateral presentation is used and subjects can achieve more than one report from each trial.

Although reaction time measures are potentially more sensitive and more direct than accuracy measures, they need to be carefully arranged. The policies adopted with regard to excessively short and long reaction times, data transformations, errors, and the like, should be determined before subjects are run.

In all DVF studies investigators should pay careful attention to the strategies available to their subjects, and should normally aim to achieve a high degree of uniformity in the strategies actually used. They should be cautious in the inferences they draw from studies of asymmetries for processing visually presented stimuli, and beware of prematurely concluding that they constitute an index of some form of general "lateralisation".

# 3

# STUDIES WITH NON-VERBAL STIMULI

*Jules Davidoff*

THE CLASSIFICATION of stimuli as non-verbal would appear to be a clear definition by exclusion but in practice there is a continuum of verbalness. Without doubt there are slight differences between stimuli of colour or shape which are very difficult or at least cumbersome to put into words, yet some verbal description is usually possible. The reverse is also true and Chapter 4 discusses the relationship between the imageability of words and hemisphere-processing. However, the aspects of verbal stimuli which are hard to verbalise do not seem to be important and are certainly not consistent in changing visual field advantage (VFA). Non-verbal stimuli are less reliable than verbal in giving VFAs: is this because we *are* likely to verbalise them? Without some *a priori* notion of the ease with which a stimulus can be labelled, we must be careful in interpreting findings which do not produce a left VFA (LVFA) (and hence associated with the right hemisphere: RH) as deviating because of verbalisation. While some rough-and-ready evidence is available that ease of labelling can change the VFA (Umilta *et al.*, 1974; Marzi and Berlucchi, 1977) some intuitively easy-to-label stimuli such as the times on a clock face still give an LVFA (Hatta, 1978). Naming has also not been shown to be an important variable in changing the LVFA for faces (Umilta *et al.*, 1978b) nor association value in altering the LVFA for shapes (Fontenot, 1973). Therefore, rather than considering the VFA with respect to verbalness or non-verbalness it may, in the end, be more fruitful to ask under what circumstances reliable LVFAs occur. To effect this aim, the present survey of what has become an increasingly expanding literature arranges studies under stimulus characteristics.

Every stimulus has both location and extension, which if equated for the two visual fields, leaves only very simple aspects of the stimulus as candidates for producing asymmetries. Such stimulus properties as intensity, colour, depth, and motion are all known to involve the striate cortex and each of these perceptual abilities is clearly not the sole prerogative of one hemisphere. The contralateral half of visual space is mapped on to the visual cortex of each hemisphere, which if destroyed, means the loss of all perception (but note the work on blindsight, e.g. Perenin and Jeannerod, 1978) for the corresponding half-visual field. For simple perceptual abilities one must dismiss the notion of complete dominance of the RH—the striate cortex of the left hemisphere (LH) cannot be just a relay station. However, it is by no means impossible that the RH is in some way more sensitive to stimuli than the LH is and the evidence for this hypothesis will be considered.

After considering what could be called "non-spatial stimuli" in that their extent in space is not what distinguishes one stimulus from another, we shall turn to stimulus attributes which do involve space, such as localisation, direction and shape.

## Detection

Given the undoubted bilateral involvement for early stages of visual analysis, it is surprising how compelling is the clinical evidence showing that the RH is preferentially involved for stimulus detection. An increased latency to a light flash for RH compared to LH damage has often been noted (Arrigoni and De Renzi, 1964; De Renzi and Faglioni, 1965; Colonno and Faglioni, 1966; De Renzi and Spinnler, 1966a, b; Russo and Vignolo, 1967; Faglioni *et al.*, 1969). The most obvious confounding factor, that RH lesions are larger, has been found not relevant (Benson and Barton, 1970). It is therefore reasonable to ask whether LVF stimuli are better detected in normals.

The pioneering deduction of callosal crossing time for a manual RT to a light flash (Poffenberger, 1912) as 4 ms (which still holds in recent research, see Berlucchi *et al.*, 1977) hides a quite markedly quicker RT to LVF compared to RVF light flashes for the two subjects. This was not commented on by Poffenberger and it was not till 1970 (Bradshaw and Perriment, 1970; Jeeves and Dixon, 1970) that significant advantages for the LVF were noted and the RH implicated. This was replicated for ten-year-old males (Jeeves, 1972). Umilta *et al.* (1979) found this LVFA for latency applied to finding a solid dot among empty dots. They also report a left-hand advantage. When the display was presented across the midline (1·3° either side), the left-hand advantage persisted despite the disappearance of the LVFA. Umilta *et al.* (1979) suggest that the left-hand advantage might be due to the direct neural connections to the RH.

Mandelbaum and Sloan (1947) noted, in passing, that most subjects show greater acuity when the fixation point is to the right of a target but presented no data analysis. Specific tests using accuracy, rather than latency, measures have confirmed this superiority for the LVF by a simple yes/no procedure (Davidoff, 1977) or by more sophisticated signal-detection analysis (Wickelgren, 1967; Gardner and Branski, 1976; Allard and Bryden, 1979; Boles, 1979). Differences between the VFs are less likely to be observed from conventional threshold measurements which suffer from response biases. Non-significant hemifield threshold differences may then not be meaningful either because of continued presentations to one visual field without blank trials (Kimura, 1969) or if letter thresholds are found at the same time (Warrington and James, 1967a; Warrington and Rabin, 1970).

## Provisos

There are provisos to any blanket statement that detection is always better for the LVF. Berlucchi et al. (1977), for example, only found this for stimuli near the midline. The main aim of their study was to investigate compatability effects of side-of-light flash to responding hand. In reaction-time (RT) studies, Berlucchi et al., take the view that anatomical connections should be considered as well as compatability of response. Connections between visual and motor areas of the same hemisphere, it is argued, always make for shorter latencies irrespective of whether the hands are crossed or uncrossed. Harvey (1978) for a choice RT replicates this advantage for intrahemispheric connections with the four subjects showing particularly long latencies for left-hand responses to RVF flashes.

Compatability is nevertheless important and provides considerable alteration to the latency of response (Wallace, 1971; Brebner, 1973) and could easily mask any VF difference. The fact that VFAs can sometimes survive compatability effects is therefore worthy of note. Studies which only use the preferred hand to measure RT (Kobrick, 1965; Filbey and Gazzaniga, 1969; Haines and Gilliland, 1973) cannot be expected to verify VF differences for detection. According to Cotton et al. (1980), compatability can even determine which hemisphere deals with the stimulus. For an RT decision of top v. bottom, compatible hand-VF responses are allocated to "top" decisions because, they argue, such responses are more salient. Incompatible hand-VF responses are allocated to "bottom" decisions. Such a division of labour is sure to nullify any VF superiority.

The generality of the LVFA for detection for all subject groups has also been questioned. Davidoff (1977) found the effect only for male subjects. Bryden (1976), who at first reported no significant VFA for detection, subsequently (Allard and Bryden, 1979) found the LVFA to be more pronounced for females. An investigation of sinistrals (McKeever and Hoff, 1979) showed the LVFA only for those who wrote in the inverted fashion. This group of subjects were suggested to have the normal contralateral motor control combined with a dissociation of the LH visual area from the LH motor area. Smith and Moscovitch (1979), however, obtained results compatible with Levy and Reid (1976) with inverted writing sinistrals having ipsilateral motor control. It is difficult to comment on the question of VFA from the study of Smith and Moscovitch (1979) as hand-usage was varied between, and not within, experiments. Certainly in all studies which produce significant LVFAs for detection, there is always a substantial minority of subjects who do not follow this pattern. Schaller and Dziadosz (1975) have suggested a bimodal distribution for dextrals with two-thirds showing an LVFA. Such a distribution would explain non-significant trends towards an LVFA (Knehr, 1941) with the use of relatively few subjects.

There are other non-significant VF differences available in the literature (Filbey and Gazzaniga, 1969; Dimond, 1970; McKeever *et al.*, 1975; McKeever and Van Deventer, 1975; Chastain and Lawson, 1979) with somewhat of a trend to an RVFA for a vocal RT (Filbey and Gazzaniga, 1969; McKeever *et al.*, 1975). These could represent the tip of an unpublished iceberg of non-significant differences in detection between the left and right visual fields. However, non-significant findings are easy to obtain, especially when detection differences between the visual fields are not the aim of the study. It is more important that the tally of significant findings is quite large and always in the direction of an LVFA. However, even when obtainable the LVFA for detection is also without doubt small and easily distorted. It is just this smallness of effect which should make it more likely to be found using accuracy measures with difficult-to-detect targets (Davidoff, 1977; Boles, 1979). Any differential hemisphere-processing time for a readily seen target must be small compared to the variance of RT and unlikely to be found especially from those studies which seem content to use relatively few trials.

## Attention

As there are so many provisos attached to the studies which do produce significant LVFAs for detection, there must be some consideration to the view that VF superiorities are, in general and for detection in particular, caused by fluctuations of attention. Uncertainty of side of stimulus presentation has disrupted the LVFA for detection found when stimulus location is known (Anzola *et al.*, 1977; Berlucchi *et al.*, 1977), but most other studies use random presentations to the LVF or RVF as a matter of course and this has not prevented the finding of an LVFA (e.g. Bradshaw and Perriment, 1970; Jeeves and Dixon, 1970). Even though fixation is constantly monitored (Anzola *et al.*,

1977; Berlucchi *et al.*, 1977), random presentations to the VFs would seem a better way of ensuring fixation. However, Posner (1980) has shown that attention may be allocated to points away from fixation and one could therefore maintain an attentional explanation of VFAs for detection if one were to believe that it is easier to allocate attention to the LVF.

A more detailed account of the operation of an attentional mechanism views hemispheric involvement with a task as depressing (Kinsbourne and Cook, 1971) or as enhancing (Kinsbourne, 1973) concurrent activity for another task. Confirming the former view, Rizzolatti *et al.* (1979) found that no VFA to light flashes occurs unless the other hemisphere is occupied. Confirming the latter view, quite substantial (though non-significant) LVFAs for gap detection (Kinsbourne, 1970; 1973) change to RVFAs with verbal activity. This priming effect has not been replicated (Gardner and Branski, 1976; Boles, 1979) in studies which do find an LVFA without the supposed priming activity. Random presentations of verbal and non-verbal stimuli should make each hemisphere equally activated. Berlucchi *et al.* (1974) using this experimental design found VF superiorities for faces and letters (hence contradicting Kinsbourne, 1973) but little evidence of an LVFA for light flashes. The design of the experiment, however, mitigated against any such finding as different subjects were used for left and right stimuli.

Differential hemisphere-priming continues to be reported (Heilman and Abell, 1979) and still merits further investigation. Attentional effects have been considered for other tasks besides detection (see Chapter 5) but attentional theories of VFA, if one is not careful, may be used to confirm every finding and predict none.

Sustained attention is also seen as being distinguished on a hemisphere basis (Dimond, 1979a); the RH being responsible. If this is the case, then LVFAs should be associated with the later parts of a divided visual field (DVF) experiment. Time spent in the experiment will also be related to familiarisation with the stimuli and this could be a confounding factor if stimulus familiarisation is essential in establishing perceptual asymmetries (Hardyck *et al.*, 1978). Familiarisation, however, may not be a problem as Schmuller (1980) casts doubt on Hardyck's proposal since his changing VFA was accompanied by shortening latencies and decreasing variances. In any case, one would have thought that familiarisation for a light flash and its location would be easily accomplished, so effects of VFA over time may repay further investigation.

## Masking and Visual Persistence

Superiority for detection in the RH might be expected to be associated with a greater resistance to masking for that hemisphere. Contrary to this prediction, Oscar-Berman *et al.* (1973) found superior resistance to masking for both letters and nonsense shapes in the RVF. Their procedure of continuing presentations (increasing the interval between stimulus and mask until recognition) to one hemisphere is open to response biases associated with classical threshold measurement. Mixing the nonsense shapes with letters is unacceptable in this circumstance. McKeever and Suberi (1974) also found an RVF superiority for resistance to masking for letters but not for intervals between stimulus and mask of up to 20 ms. Hellige and Webster (1979) have shown an LVF superiority for these short intervals. The resistance to masking of letters will depend not only on the detectability of the stimulus but also on the rate at which the stimulus is encoded. The LH superiority for verbal encoding seems not sufficient to compensate for an RH advantage for reduced stimulus input. The time of 20 ms fits well with the RH advantage for visual persistence as measured by Cohen (1976). Marzi *et al.* (1979) dispute Cohen's result as she did not obtain the essential partial-report superiority of the Sperling (1960) paradigm. Marzi *et al.* (1979) did obtain partial-report superiority and also found no difference in decay rates between the hemifields even though visual field superiorities existed for recognition of the stimuli. However, the cues to report in Marzi *et al.* (1979) were not given till at least 300 ms after stimulus offset which they admit may not provide a fine enough measure for an advantage in persistence of only 20 ms.

A stimulus kept on the retinal site irrespective of eye movements (i.e. stabilised) will fragment. Presentation of stabilised retinal images in the VF by McKinney (1966, 1967) led to reports of greater resistance to fragmentation for the RVF. This effect interacted with the hemiretina receiving the stimulus and needs replication.

## Hemiretinal Differences

There are psychophysical studies (Aulhorn and Harms, 1972) which have investigated detection across the visual field and might be expected to provide information for a comparison between visual fields, but almost all such studies use just one eye for the task. The investigation of VF differences with respect to an RH involvement for non-verbal stimuli must take account of all possible optical pathways. The RH is accessed via the left eye by contralateral fibres from the nasal half of the retina and via the right eye by ipsilateral fibres from the temporal hemiretina. In the cat, contralateral afferent projections activate more cortical units than do ipsilateral projections (Hubel and Wiesel, 1959). Kimura (1966) has proposed that there is at least a functional dominance of the contralateral pathways over the ipsilateral pathways in humans. Kershner and Jeng (1972) make use of this dominance hypothesis to explain their finding that, even in binocular vision, there is a greater LVFA for left-eye dominant subjects in discriminating between geometric forms. Attempts to show a superiority of contralateral fibres in humans have rarely been linked to the study of VFAs, but any study which uses monocular viewing conditions should be aware of possible artefacts if optical pathways are not considered.

Poffenberger (1912) reported a nasal retinal advantage for an RT to a light flash at 10°, 30° or 45° but not at 3° eccentricity. Poffenberger controlled for both hand of response and eye stimulated. Both of these factors are important. If there is hemisphere specialisation for a task, then use of only one eye is not acceptable given differential activation by contralateral and ipsilateral pathways. As Berlucchi *et al.* (1977) have shown that quicker responses are achieved if the response is activated from the same hemisphere which receives stimulation, it is also important to control for hand or foot of response. Hemispheric advantages cannot be properly commented on from studies using monocular viewing which do not use all combinations of hand/foot and eyes (e.g. Rains, 1963; Frisen and Glansholm, 1975; Gilliland and Haines, 1975; Maddess, 1975; Osaka, 1978).

Leaving aside the issue of hemisphere superiorities, the nasal retinal advantage (which is said also to apply to verbal stimuli and not considered here) is repeated by Maddess (1975) but not by Harvey (1978) even after exhaustive testing. The use of accuracy rather than latency measures seems to make the report of nasal retinal superiorities less likely. They are nevertheless reported for depth estimation (Wyke and Chorover, 1965) and a motion after-effect (Beaton, 1979) but only for some conditions of the studies and by Oostenbrug *et al.* (1978) for one subject's temporal discrimination. Such equivocation does not apply to the compelling effect reported by Crovitz and Lipscomb (1963). Simultaneous presentation of colours to the nasal and temporal hemiretinae produced reports of only the colours given to the nasal fibres. Using accuracy measures, significant temporal rather than nasal retinal superiorities have been reported (McKinney, 1967; Markovitz and Weitzman, 1969) and there are rather unclear reports (Travis and Martin, 1934; Luria, 1974) in which both nasal and temporal hemiretinal superiorities emerge. Reports of temporal retinal advantages for latencies (Dimond and Beaumont, 1971b; 1973; Jeeves, 1972; Jeeves and Dixon, 1970) probably result because eccentricities for the two hemiretinae have not been equated. Marzi (1980) has offered some reconciliation of these conflicting findings by noting that the density of ganglion cells differ in the nasal and temporal hemiretinae according to the eccentricity of the stimulus.

A hemisphere superiority for a non-verbal task found using the dominant optical pathway may not be strong enough to be exhibited using the non-dominant pathway. This may explain VFAs which depend upon eye of entry McKinney, 1967; Beaton, 1979). On the other hand, there is some evidence that the particular optical pathway used is irrelevant to the production of

VFA. Studies producing both no VFA for non-verbal stimuli (Lordahl *et al.*, 1965; Adams, 1971) and significant VFAs (Carter, 1953; Rizzolatti *et al.*, 1971) have given no interaction of VF with eye of entry. It would seem better to avoid using monocular viewing in any investigation of VFAs unless an analysis of the contribution of the optical pathways is at issue.

## Brightness

In the early part of the twentieth century, the perception laboratory of Cornell University conducted a large number of experiments to determine which aspects of stimuli compelled attention. Curtis and Foster (1915), for example, contrasted size with intensity using two well-known vision experts (E. G. Boring and F. L. Dimmick) as subjects along with one of the authors. Two stimuli were presented tachistoscopically with one either side of fixation. Both the eminent perception scientists saw the stimulus on the left as brighter and for Boring it needed a four-fold increase in the area of the other stimulus to compensate. Bowman (1920) in a similar study, which included Karl Dallenbach as a subject, repeated this finding, concluding that spatial position was "a major disturbing influence" in the experiment.

Dallenbach was clearly inspired to investigate the phenomena and replications, albeit with a limited subject population, followed (Dallenbach, 1923; Dewey and Dallenbach, 1924; Friedline and Dallenbach, 1929) with an opposite visual field advantage for sinistrals (Burke and Dallenbach, 1924; White and Dallenbach, 1932). Indeed, Dallenbach (1923) gave functional hemisphere asymmetry as the causal factor for the asymmetries in brightness in the visual fields. He suggested that because both his subjects were dextrals, stimuli arriving at the RH would be free of interference compared to those arriving at the LH which was also controlling the right hand. In fact, as manual responses were not used, it would have been better to have argued that the LH was busy controlling speech. Dallenbach reasoned that "when man became man's greatest danger it was the weapon held in the antagonist's right hand and therefore appearing at the left which demanded attention".

More recent experimentation (Davidoff, 1975a) has verified these early results and has been found also to apply to the brightness of coloured stimuli. However, nothing more than a small trend towards a RH advantage was observed by Basso *et al.* (1977) for the effect of background contrast on a grey rectangle. This could be due to the rectangle being placed across the midline since part of the VF may be represented in both hemispheres. A VFA for brightness does not fit well with the view that brightness constancy has a retinal origin (Pöppel, 1977). It may be interesting to compare tachistoscopic with non-tachistoscopic brightness estimation to see if the LVFA is still maintained. It is a general weakness of the DVF methodology that it stresses temporal factors for any task.

## Colour

Clinical evidence suggests that RH damage causes greater impairment of some colour vision tasks than does LH damage (De Renzi and Spinnler, 1967) though Meadows (1974a) insists that the lesions have to be bilateral for complete loss. For colour naming, the clinical literature clearly implicates the LH (Kinsbourne and Warrington, 1964). An RH centre for colour vision has been deduced by Pennal (1977) from latency data with normals through a comparison of all combinations of visual field and hand of response. However, hemianopic colour vision loss has been reported for just the LH–RVF combination (Albert et al., 1975) and it would seem more likely that any asymmetry would be relative rather than absolute.

It is obviously important to avoid labelling if the colour vision task is to be considered non-verbal. Any coloured stimulus held in memory is likely to be labelled, as are coloured stimuli in any experiment if they are few in number and/or cover a wide spectral range. The McCollough after-effect uses just this type of stimulus and is still stronger in the RH (Meyer, 1976), but the McCollough effect cannot depend on verbal coding. Studies which involve difficult colour discriminations have given an LVFA (Davidoff, 1976; Hannay, 1979). Easy discriminations with a delay between stimulus and forced-choice response produce RVFAs (Malone and Hannay, 1978). Hard colour discriminations are very difficult with a delay and while producing no VFAs are also performed very close to chance level (Hannay, 1979). Delay between stimulus and response is likely to change the task to colour-naming which either gives no VFA (Dimond and Beaumont, 1972d; Dyer, 1973) or an RVFA (McKeever and Jackson, 1979) for latency measures. Grant (1980, 1981) obtained an LVFA for accuracy of colour-naming with children but just because accuracy measures were being used the exposures had to be short and therefore perceptual rather than naming processes were emphasised.

An LVFA for a simple colour discrimination (Pirot et al., 1977) must arouse some suspicion. These authors maintain that the accompanying left-hand advantage reinforces the view that there is an RH locus for colour perception but it may, by compatability, have caused the VFA. A simple discrimination task for the colouring of letters does not produce an LVFA unless it causes Stroop interference (Schmit and Davis, 1974) and also involves memory (Warren and Marsh, 1978).

## Line Length

The estimation of the strength or quantity of a univariate variable poses problems. Subjective intensity is related to the physical intensity of stimulation by functions investigated by various psychological methods (Stevens, 1975). There have been no attempts for colour or brightness to see if these functions differ between the hemispheres. However, Greenwood *et al.* (1980) have looked for hemisphere asymmetry in line length by both magnitude estimation and cross-modal matching in both normal and split-brain patients. The former methodology asks the subject to assign a number to represent the sensation, the latter asks the subject to press a button for a duration thought to correspond to stimulus sensation. For magnitude estimation of line length there was no difference between the hemispheres for the functions relating subjective and physical intensity. Split-brain patients were unable to do the task with the RH and so any conclusion that there is equal hemispheric involvement in normals must be tentative. The cross-modal matching task was performed similarly by both hemispheres in both normals and splits. Greenwood *et al.* conclude that any supposed RH superiority for perceptual tasks must be held suspect. Hemisphere equivalence for simple perceptual tasks is a parsimonious explanation but it cannot be held proven from the cross-modal results. If one hemisphere sees a line as longer it may also feel that a button push is longer. In which case, the same length of button push for the two hemispheres does not necessarily mean that line lengths are also perceived equally.

Distortions of line length by other lines, as in the case of the Muller-Lyer illusion, has been found by Clem and Pollack (1975) to give differential illusion for the two hemispheres. Simultaneous presentation of line and distorting fins gave more illusion in the LVF but presenting line and fins sequentially gave more illusion for the RVF.

## Depth

The number of studies which have related depth perception to visual field asymmetries is not large. Richards (1970) provides data which, though not analysed statistically, show an LH advantage for disparity detection of line stimuli. As the study was not performed in order to find visual field asymmetries a bias is not likely but the result is even harder to countenance, especially for those who find it hard to believe in hemisphere asymmetry for simple perceptual tasks, than the RH advantage shown by Durnford and Kimura (1971). The latter study found the LVFA only for binocular vision unlike Dimond *et al.* (1975) who found the RH advantage monocularly. Slippage of the contact lens in the Dimond *et al.* (1975) study cannot be ruled out.

Using random dot stereograms, which have the advantage that the subject cannot predict the response required but the disadvantage that form perception is also involved, Durnford and Kimura (1971) again found an RH advantage. Julesz *et al.* (1976) could not repeat this result despite obtaining a top v. bottom field difference. Pitblado (1979a) says that a VF difference was not obtained by Julesz *et al.* because the dot size they used was too large and that for fine detail the RH disparity detectors are superior.

## Motion

The DVF technique has been applied to motion perception in only a restricted number of studies as might be expected because of the difficulties in maintaining fixation. Studies of perceptual simultaneity are discussed below with duration studies and it is noted that the VFAs obtained have differed between studies. This disagreement may be reflecting a combination of opposed-hemisphere activities. The LH has been implicated in the clinical literature for dealing with sequences of simple visual stimuli (Goldman *et al.*, 1968; Carmon and Nachshon, 1971) though not if spatial tasks are involved (Kim *et al.*, 1980). The LH dominance for sequential behaviour which Kimura and Vanderwolf (1970) assign to all motor activity (not just language) has some support from early DVF research on motion detection. Jasper (1932) found the phi-phenomenon to be more pronounced in the LH. This was not the case for sinistrals who had an RH superiority, nor for stutterers who showed no dominance. Jasper and Raney (1937) replicated the result for normal children, and Carter (1953) showed that the RVFA was not related to ocular dominance. It is hard to reconcile this RVFA for the phi-phenomenon with the LVFA for velocity discrimination reported by Bertolini *et al.* (1978). An RH which is more accurate for judgments concerning motion is also suggested by Beaton (1979). This interpretation is offered after finding that an illusory motion after-effect lasts longer in the LH, but one could just as well argue for an LH superiority for sensitivity to motion from this result.

## Duration

An LH which is controlling sequences of movements might suggest cerebral asymmetry for duration estimation. For brief light-flashes there seems no indication of any difference in accuracy between the hemispheres (Bertolini *et al.*, 1978). If the stimuli became visually complex then the RH was found to be more systematically affected (Polzella *et al.*, 1977; Koch *et al.*, 1980). Polzella *et al.* (1977) consider that hemisphere-processing for time estimation might reflect Thomas and Weaver's (1975) two-process model for time perception. Polzella *et al.* suggest that the LH perceives duration from the output of a timer and the RH from the output of a visual information processor.

Duration estimation for brief stimuli depends on the numerosity, chromaticity and size of stimuli, but these main effects are found for either visual field. Any differential effects between the hemispheres for duration estimation are found only as a result of complex interactions and must remain tentative. For the estimation of the duration of an extended series of flashes to one hemisphere, Vroon *et al.* (1977) could again find no evidence of any cerebral asymmetry though they did for auditory presentations.

Efron (1963b) has proposed that the LH contains a centre for the judgment of the simultaneity of visual stimuli. Efron found (for dextrals) that the LVF stimulus had to come on before the right for them to be processed as simultaneous. An earlier report (Hirsch and Sherrick, 1961) that simultaneity judgments were not differentially affected by the LVF or RVF stimulus coming first was deduced only from graphical inspection which, while clearly not being a stringent procedure, does make the point that VF effects are small. A corollary from the existence of a simultaneity centre is that there should be transitivity in the judgment of simultaneity and this was given support by Corwin and Boynton (1968). They found that one could predict the temporal interval needed for simultaneity between two stimuli A and C by knowledge of the interval needed between A and B and between B and C. As Corwin and Boynton (1968) was not a DVF study, LH instrument cannot be held certain. A little better supporting evidence comes from a study of the temporal discrimination of light flashes (Oostenbrug *et al.*, 1978). The use of only one subject and a slight imbalance of experimental design for the use of left and right eyes is somewhat ameliorated by the careful optical procedures and the use of thousands of trials. The LH superiority was not tested for significance and was clearly much smaller than the nasal over temporal retinal advantage.

Contrary evidence against an LH centre for simultaneity judgments has been found: results more in keeping with the RH advantage for visual persistence have been seen in some masking studies. Kappauf and Yeatman (1970) asked subjects to fixate between two lights which went on and off in recurring two-second cycles. For dextrals, the LVF stimulus had to go on after (contrary to Efron's finding) and go off before the RVF stimulus for them to appear simultaneous, resulting in a greater RH persistence for the cycle which was estimated at 10 ms.

Kappauf and Yeatman argue that Efron was, in fact, measuring off-latencies with the brief (1 ms) flashes he used. Newman and Albino (1979) think the discrepancy to be more likely due to Efron discarding 11/20 subjects because of high variances (more than 7 ms). Newman and Albino (1979), who allowed

their subjects to initiate stimulus onset, repeated the RH advantage of
Kappauf and Yeatman and with very much the same magnitude. There was a
slight increase in this RH advantage with left-eye viewing which was considered due to the superiority of the nasal retinal fibres.

A possible explanation of the LVFA is a left/right scanning bias. With
central fixation, the left/right scanning bias associated with reading should
mitigate against finding an LVFA. However an LVFA could arise from a scan
of the whole visual field in iconic storage. Annett and Annett (1979) say such a
bias must be responsible for the consistent advantage found for light flashes on
the left of a display. In support of a scanning bias they note that Sekuler *et al.*
(1973) found that the leftmost of two stimuli was seen first irrespective of visual
field. Newman and Albino (1979) were unable to replicate this with light
flashes instead of the letters or crosses used by Sekuler *et al.* (1973). They
found no VFA when the two flashes were placed in the same hemiretina of one
eye: any small difference that did emerge was in the direction of faster
transmission for fibres nearer the fovea.

## Localisation

The RH is often described as specialised for visuospatial functions rather than
simply for visual or perceptual functions. It must be presumed that the spatial
aspects of the stimulus are deemed important for engaging the RH. If the
cumulative results of the studies prescribed above for detection etc. are considered to show RH superiority, this is not necessarily the case. The clinical
evidence for the simple spatial task of localisation is, in fact, both negative
(Ratcliff and Davies-Jones, 1972) and positive (Hannay *et al.*, 1976b) on the
issue of RH superiority. The same is true for evidence from studies using
normal subjects.

Localisation of a small dot using the DVF technique has been shown better
in the LVF by Kimura (1969). Robertshaw and Sheldon (1976) report an
LVFA for position of letters and Dick (1972), without details, notes a trend in
the same direction. Levy and Reid (1976) clearly considered dot location to be
a reliable RH task since to test their theory of contralateral v. ipsilateral motor
control in writers with normal and inverted hand positions they chose this task
when any RH task would have done. LVFAs were found for dextrals with
normal hand position for writing and for inverted positioned sinistrals but an
RVFA for normal positioned sinistrals. Smith and Moscovitch (1979) found an
LVFA for all these groups though somewhat reduced for normal positioned
sinistrals.

Turning to reports which do not give an RH superiority for localisation, we
found them to be as numerous as the positive findings (Pohl *et al.*, 1972;

Bryden, 1973, 1976; Birkett, 1977; Allard and Bryden, 1979). Dot localisation has even been reported to show an RVFA (Bryden, 1973). Far from making the task more fitted for the RH by allowing a relational judgment for a spatial arrangement, placing the dot inside a frame also gives an RVFA (Pohl *et al.*, 1972). It is certainly possible to verbally code the position of a stimulus, especially if a frame is supplied, but the necessary conditions for this and other factors to nullify or change the LVFA are not clear.

## Enumeration

It is fairly hard to view the RH superiority for dot localisation as proven but, if granted, it should follow that there would be an RH advantage for enumeration as there will be fewer errors in counting the stimuli if one is sure of their positions. The use of very simple and easily labelled stimuli (White, 1971a) or fairly peripheral stimuli viewed monocularly (Adams, 1971) does not, nor would be expected to, produce an LVFA for enumeration. More demanding tasks (Kimura, 1966; McGlone and Davidson, 1973) do find an LVFA but Cohen (1975b) says this only occurs if the subject expects a non-verbal display.

## Direction

In DVF studies using putatively non-verbal stimuli there must be the likelihood of labelling; which, for direction estimation, will increase if the number of alternatives is few and the stimuli are aligned along the major axes. Such stimuli give no VFA (Dimond, 1970) or an RVFA (White, 1971b). A reasonable case for the VFA found for orientation depending upon codability is given by Umilta *et al.* (1974). They found an RVFA for the commonly labelled meridians but an LVFA for less obviously labelled axes. The position of a line is more codable if surrounded by a square frame and, indeed Pitblado (1979b) finds no VFA for accuracy in orienting a line to the vertical if surrounded by a frame, but an LVFA without the frame (the speed–accuracy tradeoff present must, however, caution against the certainty of the finding).

It would seem to follow from Umilta *et al.*'s (1974) study that LVFAs should only be seen for orientations which are not easily verbalised, but this is not the case. An LVFA is found for telling the time from a clock face (Hatta, 1978; Berlucchi *et al.*, 1979) and for a discrimination between the horizontal and vertical (Schaller and Dziadosz, 1975). This last study and others that have produced LVFAs for direction used short exposure times (Fontenot and Benton, 1972; Phippard, 1977; Hatta, 1978; Sasanuma and Kobayashi, 1978) or multiple stimuli (Atkinson and Egeth, 1973; Longden *et al.*, 1976; Marzi *et al.*, 1979), suggesting that to obtain an LVFA considerable information should be in the display or little time allowed in the processing. The LVFA for orientation discrimination seems fairly robust (the non-VFA study of Adams (1971) leaves much to be desired) if these conditions are met.

## Form Perception

### Recognition Accuracy

Reviewing asymmetries found by the DVF methodology, White (1972) could find no evidence for any asymmetry for form perception in normal subjects. Of all non-verbal tasks, form recognition has been the most investigated, yet despite indications from the clinical literature (Milner, 1971), there appeared to be a genuine ambilaterality for normals. Since the review by White (1972), there has been a considerable increase in the number of studies but any VF asymmetry still remains uncertain.

Some of the early studies giving no VFA (Heron, 1957; Terrace, 1959; Bryden, 1960, 1964, 1973; Bryden and Rainey, 1963; Hirata and Osaka, 1967) either give insufficient details of the stimuli or clearly used simple geometric forms. Is this the reason for the lack of VFAs? Without a convincing metric for visual complexity, there must be a certain arbitrariness in allocating stimuli as simple or complex but, using the number of points (angles) of the Vanderplas and Garvin (1959) figures, Fontenot (1973) found an LVFA for 12-point (replicated by Dee and Hannay, 1976; Hellige and Cox, 1976) but not for 4-point figures. Hatta (1975) reports an LVFA for 8-point figures and Dee and Fontenot (1973) an LVFA for 12-point figures but only if there is a delay introduced between stimulus and response.

There would seem, therefore, to be some indication that VFA depends on visual complexity but further increase in the complexity of the Vanderplas and Garvin figures does not make it more likely that an LVFA will be obtained. Hines (1978) found no VFA for a mixture of 8-, 16- and 20-point figures and while Hellige (1978) gives an LVFA for 12-point figures he gives no VFA for 16-point figures. Twenty-four-point figures have given no VFA (Lordahl et al., 1965; Oscar-Berman et al., 1973) or even an RVFA for resistance to masking (Oscar-Berman et al., 1973). Using other complex shapes, Hatta and Dimond (1980) only found an LVFA for Western subjects and not for Japanese. Inkblots which would intuitively also seem to be fairly complex have been found to give no VFA (Kimura, 1966) or to produce an RVFA (Hines, 1975). On the other hand, fairly simple shapes have given an LVFA for both deaf and hearing subjects (Virostek and Cutting, 1979).

A corollary of making a stimulus visually complex is that it will not be easy to code verbally. Indeed Fontenot (1973) found that the LVFA was not related to the association value of the shapes. However, if a recognition task for visually complex stimuli has to be performed in memory, then the subject (unless possessing eidetic imagery) has no alternative but to try a verbal recoding of the stimulus. No VFAs in memory for complex shapes (Hannay, 1976 (females); Birkett, 1978) or RVFAs (Hannay (1976, males); Hannay *et al.* (1976a); Birkett, (1980, females)) are therefore not surprising. Belivacqua *et al.* (1979) report an RVFA for shape recognition after a 15 s delay but the reversal to an LVFA after a 60 s delay defies easy interpretation.

Finding an RVFA would suggest verbal intervention and those studies reporting an RVFA have simultaneously performed or could be very easily construed as performing verbal tasks. Hellige (1978) directly tests for this effect and finds a shift away from an LVFA for Vanderplas and Garvin figures with a simultaneous verbal memory load. Goldberg *et al.* (1978) also provide some tentative evidence of shapes having an RVFA if codable. The extent of the malleability of the VFA under verbal memory load is considered elsewhere (Chapter 5), but one would certainly feel more confident of a general LVFA for form recognition if it were a little more stable. Nevertheless, Moscovitch and Klein (1980) do provide indirect evidence that the RH is involved in processing the 12-point Vanderplas and Garvin figures. They found that when these figures were at fixation they interfered with the known RH advantage for faces suggesting a common processing mechanism.

## Form Reproduction

A methodology used in certain studies is to ask the subject to reproduce what has been shown in the VF. This clearly leads to problems of scoring, but VFAs with this procedure have been noted. McKeever and Huling (1970a) found an LVFA for the reproduction of dot figures but not for solid figures. White and Barr-Brown (1972) could not get a VFA for either but did not use the same figures. The complexity of the figure to be reproduced may be important since overlapping figures were reproduced better if placed in the LVF (Kershner and Jeng, 1972; Kershner, 1974).

## Latencies

The difficulty in finding an LVFA for form perception has been somewhat overcome by the use of latency rather than accuracy as the response measure. Gross (1972), Beaumont and Dimond (1975), Hellige (1975), White and White (1975), Endo *et al.* (1978), Polich (1978) and, ignoring the issue of memory load, Hellige *et al.* (1979) all found LVFAs using latency responses. These studies are also marked by using complex or multiple stimuli, only Poizner and Lane (1979) do not provide a significant VFA for reasonably complex shapes.

Umilta *et al.* (1978a) have investigated the relationship between visual complexity and VFA. Pairs of polygons were considered complex stimuli if they were the same and had more than 8 sides or were different but only differed by one or two sides. Complex stimuli gave an LVFA and simple stimuli an RVFA. A more recent study (Simion *et al.*, 1980) found an LVFA for judgments of pairs of shapes independently of whether a physical, analogue (size-change ) or nominal identity was called for in the task. The stimuli to be judged were what the Umilta *et al.* (1978a) study would, however, have classed as simple and the argument that a more detailed spatial analysis was required in all the tasks of Simion *et al.* (1980) is not convincing.

Latencies when used with simple forms give no VFA (Dimond and Beaumont, 1972e), an LVFA only for some conditions (Egeth, 1971; Cohen, 1973; Bradshaw *et al.*, 1976b; Haun, 1978) or even an RVFA for some conditions (Paivio and Ernest, 1971; Cohen, 1973; Umilta *et al.*, 1978a). The cause of these RVFAs has been ascribed to strategy changes (Paivio and Ernest), an RH "same" processing mechanism (Cohen) or as we have seen above by Umilta *et al.* (1978a) to stimulus characteristics promoting different coding.

## Signs

The argument that the LH is the locus for all coded visual stimuli, not just words but also shapes (Goldberg *et al.*, 1978) and musical notes (Segalowitz *et al.*, 1979) would imply that one would expect an RVFA for all visual symbols including the hand positions used by the deaf as language.

Adults who cannot read the signs used by the deaf exhibit an LVFA (Poizner and Lane, 1979) or no VFA (Virostek and Cutting, 1979), as might be expected if they are perceived as just shapes. In fact, for nonsense shapes, the latter study showed an LVFA and the former no VFA. It comes as little surprise that for hearing subjects who can read the signs, besides the expected RVFA (Ross *et al.*, 1979; Virostek and Cutting, 1979) there is also an LVFA reported (McKeever *et al.*, 1976). This LVFA is not too unpredictable as the stimuli are unlikely to be as word-like for hearing signers as they are for deaf signers. But deaf subjects do not generally produce RVFAs, only Virostek and Cutting (1979) produce this result consistent with LH coding and then only for the signed alphabet, not for signed numbers. Most often, studies using signs with the deaf give LVFAs (Neville and Bellugi, 1978; Poizner and Lane, 1979; Scholes and Fischler, 1979 (skilled signers only), Poizner *et al.*, 1979) or no VFA (McKeever *et al.*, 1976; Phippard, 1977). A preference for dealing with the signs in the RH arose for both deaf and hearing subjects during the course of the study of Manning *et al.* (1977) which may reflect the subject learning to extract information from a brief flash. On the other hand, it could be arranged that deaf subjects have the visual aspects of language established in the RH but this seems unlikely as either no VFA (McKeever *et al.*, 1976; Scholes and Fischler, 1979; Ross *et al.*, 1979) or an RVFA (Manning *et al.*, 1979) was reported for normal letters. Consistent with this finding, keeping the LH as the cerebral basis of language for the deaf, is the report of Poizner *et al.* (1979) that for moving signs, the LVFA for static signs disappears, though as always one must be aware that the added factor (viz. movement) may have lateralised components (Jasper and Raney, 1937) in its own right.

As we are told that a picture is a thousand words, tachistoscopic presentations should not encourage verbal coding for complex pictures. An RVFA for pictures of nameable objects can be predicted and this does seem to be the case. There is the occasional report of LVFA (Schmuller and Goodman, 1980) and no VFA (Katzky, 1972) but RVFAs are the norm (Wyke and Ettlinger, 1961; Bryden and Rainey, 1963; Klatzky and Atkinson, 1971; Paivio and Ernest, 1971; Juola, 1973; McKeever and Jackson, 1979; Young and Bion, 1981b; Young *et al.*, 1980). Juola notes that the RVFA does not occur for unfamiliar pictures. This is just the type of stimulus that would defy labelling and hence encourage a perceptual analysis.

## Face Recognition

In the survey by White (1972) of unilaterally presented tachistoscopic non-verbal stimuli there is a notable absence of work on face recognition. It is not noteworthy that the data are lacking, as there were only a couple of then recently performed studies which could have been included, but it is remarkable that since that time there have been so many reports of significant VFAs. It is, indeed, hard to find studies which, at least for some subjects under some conditions, do not produce a significant VFA and almost always an LVFA for face perception.

### Procedures Giving LVFAs

The clinical syndrome of prosopagnosia (a specific inability to recognise faces) has been associated with the RH (De Renzi and Spinnler, 1966a). An RH occipital-temporal lesion is also argued by Meadows (1974b) for the disability but only if accompanied by an LH, though not necessarily so posterior, lesion. The LVFA for normals predictable from the clinical data was first confirmed by Rizzolatti *et al.* (1971). They assigned a few faces as targets and compared latencies between VFs for targets and non-targets. Subsequent experiments have replicated the LVFA using this technique (Berlucchi *et al.*, 1974; Rizzolatti and Buchtel, 1977 (males only); Gilbert, 1977 (males, females, dextrals and sinistrals except perhaps familial sinistrals); Suberi and

McKeever, 1977; Reynolds and Jeeves, 1978b (for 14- and 19-year-olds but not for 8-year-olds); Zoccolotti and Oltman, 1978; Rapaczynski and, Ehrlichman, 1979). The last two studies found the LVFA only for field-independent subjects.

Geffen *et al.* (1971) employed a target RT procedure using identikit faces (not too dissimilar from real faces) and obtained an LVFA for a manual but not for vocal RT. They suggest that the vocal response produced LH activation but it could also be that the RTs being slower with vocal responses, the VF difference was not allowed to show itself. The target set size has been greatly increased and, using a signal detection analysis, an LVFA has even been found for recognising half the face (Finlay and French, 1978) or the whole face two days later (Jones, 1979).

It is not necessary for a set of targets to be remembered for an LVFA to be found. Two faces presented in sequence give an LVFA for a same–different judgment (Hilliard, 1973; Ellis and Shepherd, 1975 (signal detection analysis); Moscovitch *et al.*, 1976 (latencies); Hannay and Rogers, 1979). A variation on this procedure again giving an LVFA (Hansch and Pirozzolo, 1980) found latencies for a same–different judgment of a face to a verbal label. The most common variation, though, is to allow a forced choice from alternative faces presented after the lateralised face. LVFAs have been obtained in this way by Klein *et al.* (1976), Phippard (1977, not for deaf subjects); Pirozzolo and Rayner (1977); Leehey *et al.* (1978, males and females); Leehey and Cahn (1979); Ley and Bryden (1979); and Piazza (1980, only for dextrals without familiar sinistrality). Bilateral presentations with the same methodology have given no VFA (Hines, 1975) but usually give an LVFA (Klein *et al.*, 1976; Pirozzolo and Rayner, 1977; Moscovitch and Klein, 1980) with enhanced performance if, when paired with a word, the face is in the LVF and the word in the RVF.

A composite figure, called a "chimera", constructed by joining two different half-figures along the vertical midline was found to give a subjective experience of completion of just one of the half-figures when presented to split-brain subjects (Levy *et al.*, 1972). The half-figure that was completed depended on the task being performed. Labelled figures, including faces, produced completion of the RVF half-figure, whereas a pointing response gave completion of the LVF half-figure. Milner and Dunne (1977) found that if the middle 5° of a chimeric figure was blocked out, normals also experienced the completion effect. Recognition of faces, as indicated by a forced choice, gave an LVFA irrespective of whether or not the central portion was blanked out, but only for left-hand pointing. Schwartz and Smith (1980) repeated the LVFA for chimeric faces which were found independent of either verbal or musical priming. Schwartz and Smith made their subjects point bimanually with hands clasped so that the interaction with hand of response was avoided.

An LVFA for faces which depended on hand of response would be a worrying artefact but this fear is allayed somewhat by latency studies (Rizzolatti *et al.*, 1971; Rizzolatti and Buchtel, 1977; Reynolds and Jeeves, 1978b) which gave an LFVA irrespective of hand used. Suberi and McKeever (1977) found an LVFA for both hands but the advantage was significantly greater for the left hand. The latency difference between the hands was of a small order of magnitude compatible with callosal crossing time. The much larger difference between the VFs was said to indicate a face-processing time difference between the hemispheres. As these two effects were both present, Suberi and McKeever (1977) suggested that the RH must have been in control in their face task irrespective of initial hemisphere registration.

Moscovitch *et al.* (1976) found that the LVFA can also be obtained if the two faces are presented simultaneously or in sequence (Bertelson *et al.*, 1977) to the same hemisphere for same–different discrimination. This was the case only if the "same" judgments were for different views of the same person (Bertelson *et al.*, 1977) or involved a comparison between a cartoon and a photograph (Moscovitch *et al.*, 1976). Strauss and Moscovitch (1981) do show an LVFA for two identical faces but claim that accompanying higher-order face judgments produced this result.

## Schematic Faces

It is worth mentioning that schematic faces do not reliably produce LVFAs. Bradshaw *et al.* (1973) found no VFA for same–different latencies to sequentially presented outline profiles. Cartoons of faces did not give LVFAs (Moscovitch *et al.*, 1976) unless compared to real photographs. Using two sequential schematic faces, Patterson and Bradshaw (1975) report an LVFA only for same judgments when all portions of the second face differed but an RVFA for both same and different judgments when just one feature was altered. Matches from long-term memory gave LVFAs for both types of judgment. Buffery (1974) found that it was the second stimulus of a sequence rather than the first that produced the superior recognition for the LVF.

## Emotion

There are two opposing views concerning asymmetry for the representation of emotion in the cerebral hemispheres. One proposal puts the RH in charge of both positive and negative affect (Gardner, 1975). Alternatively, the LH is deemed crucial for positive affect and the RH for negative (Goldstein, 1939). The VFAs found for facial expressions of different emotions should be pertinent in deciding between these alternative views on localisation. Suberi and McKeever (1977) found a greater LVFA if the target face expressed emotion, but without a significant difference between the different emotions. An LVFA was also found for a simultaneous match of a profile to a stylised drawing of an emotion (Landis *et al.*, 1979) but there was no breakdown between the happy, angry and astonished faces used. Ley and Bryden (1979), using caricature faces, found an LVFA for extreme emotion irrespective of whether it depicted positive or negative affect. Similarly, Buchtel *et al.* (1980) found an LVFA for both happy and sad faces and Lavadas *et al.* (1980) an LVFA for all the 6 basic emotions given by Ekman and Oster (1979). Strauss and Moscovitch (1981), also using the Ekman faces, generally support the RH locus for emotion, though surprise gave a clearer LVFA than either happy or sad faces. Natale and Gur (1980), on the other hand, do report that dextrals rate faces as happier in the RVF but overall the evidence does seem to favour an LVFA for the recognition of all emotions in a face.

An RH basis for emotion is consistent with the finding that the left side of one's face expresses more emotion than the right side (Sackeim *et al.*, 1978). They found that a composite of two left halves of the face was judged to show more emotion than a composite of the two right halves. Similarly the left half of a tachistoscopic chimeric stimulus was also judged happier (Campbell, 1978), an effect which was enhanced if it were the true left side of the face. Contrary evidence comes from Finlay and French (1978) who found superior LVF to RVF recognition for either half-face.

## Hemisphere Mechanisms for Face Perception

Different RH mechanisms for facial expression and identity have been argued (Ley and Bryden, 1979; Strauss and Moscovitch, 1981). However, a covariance analysis (Ley and Bryden, 1979) showed that the identity judgment depended on the expression judgment. Strauss and Moscovitch do show different latencies for the two judgments but the asymmetry with regard to hemisphere function depended on interactions with sex of subject (see Chapter 8 for fuller discussion of sex effects). It is known that expression and identity do represent separate aspects of face perception (Ekman and Oster, 1979) but differential hemisphere bases cannot be said as yet to have been proven with normal subjects.

Recognition of faces can be achieved by stored information of either the physical and/or personality characteristics of the face (Patterson and Baddeley, 1977). Galper and Costa (1980) further argue that encoding of faces by physical or social (personality) aspects has a differential hemisphere locus. They do not find a uniquely RH specialisation for either code but suggest that subjects allocate one hemisphere to faces learned by physical cues and the other to faces learned by social cues. Galper and Costa (1980) is one of the few experiments that does not report an overall LVFA for faces. Other such reports (Jones,

1979, 1980) are for accuracy in judging the sex of a face. The RVFA reported by Jones for this task was less evident for females. Jones (1980) considers that a task involving categorisation will involve the LH even if face stimuli are used. This finding is certainly at variance with the conclusion below concerning the general reliability of the LVFA for faces. As accuracy (signal-detection procedures) was measured and perceptual processes emphasised, this is a further disagreement. Though categorisation of face by sex seems not to have been investigated elsewhere in the DVF literature, face identity and emotion are all judgments requiring categorisation and, as seen above, generally favour the LVF (RH).

Identification of familiar faces relies on different mechanisms to identification of unfamiliar faces (Ellis *et al.*, 1979). Different lesion sites, though both in the RH, have been associated with failure for the two types of face material (Warrington and James, 1967b). The LVFA for unfamiliar faces is documented above. The Warrington and James study would imply that there would also be an LVFA for famous faces. Moscovitch *et al.* (1976) do find this for a cartoon-to-photograph match but Marzi and Berlucchi (1977) found an RVFA for the latency of naming famous faces.

Famous faces are both nameable and familiar. Umilta *et al.* (1978b) tried not to confound these factors in their design which used the lateralised faces of the Rizzolatti *et al.* (1971) study. Each task was performed by different subjects with the same faces and a large number of trials. Naming improved RT but was not related to VFA and therefore naming was implicated at response selection rather than at the stimulus-processing. Familiar faces gave an RVFA and unfamiliar faces an LVFA. In direct contradiction to this result, Leehey and Cahn (1979) found an LVFA irrespective of whether a face was familiar or unfamiliar and Young and Bion (1981a) irrespective of whether the face was familiar or famous. The LVFA for familiar faces was present whether pointing or naming was used as the response measure (Leehey and Cahn, 1979) and unlike Umilta *et al.* (1978b) the faces could hardly be more familiar as the photographed people were known to the subjects. A reconciliation of these seemingly opposed results may be possible because familiarity is not a unitary concept. Some subjects familiarise themselves with dot patterns by isolating features (Hock, 1973), some do not. It is much more likely that a feature-isolating approach would be taken for faces in the deliberate attempt of familiarisation as in Umilta *et al.* (1978b) than for the already familiar faces (Leehey and Cahn, 1979; Young and Bion, 1981a).

Finding an LVFA for familiar and unfamiliar faces or for all types of emotion has the weakness—if one is suggesting an RH basis for these aspects of facial stimuli—that one cannot be sure the VFA was caused by the "faceness" of the stimuli. Indeed, it might be more parsimonious to consider that a VFA for all types of stimuli reflected a general RH superiority for visual discriminations. Yin (1970), however, argues that faces do constitute a special class of stimuli in that they are differentially affected by inversion. An RH-damaged group was only impaired in the recognition of upright and not inverted faces. This was not the case for pictures of houses. Rapaczynski and Ehrlichman (1979) have also found a difference between upright and inverted faces with respect to hemispheric involvement. An upright probe for a set of learned faces gave an LVFA, but an inverted probe gave no VFA. It would nevertheless be unwise to believe that inversion does not disturb the perception of other familiar objects besides faces. Graphic examples are given in Davidoff (1975b, p.160) and Kanisza (1979, p.45). For faces it is the internal features which if inverted disturb perception, as is shown in the striking demonstration of Thompson (1980). Work with prosopagnosics (Benton and Van Allen, 1968) also points to the importance of the internal features of the face for face recognition, as seen by the patients' difficulty in dealing with them.

Using the DVF technique, Ellis and Shepherd (1975) were unable to verify a special RH process for upright faces. Leehey et al. (1978) refute this result, claiming that Ellis and Shepherd only obtained the LVFA for inverted faces because the exposure times used were too short to act on the specialised RH face mechanism. As there was no overall performance advantage for upright faces, this is a reasonable argument. Leehey et al. using longer exposures obtained an LVFA only for upright faces. But the obvious and unanswered question arises as to why the factors contributing to the LVFA for inverted faces in the Ellis and Shepherd experiment have disappeared for Leehey et al. The attempt by Leehey et al. to equate performance levels by decreasing the exposure time for upright faces was unsuccessful. Performance was, nevertheless, said to be above chance, though this is difficult to assess as easy items may raise the chance level. However, if performance had been equated, and equal VFAs obtained for upright and inverted faces, Leehey et al. could, and probably would, argue that the faster exposure times had changed the strategy used for upright faces.

If it takes an exposure of around 40 ms to ensure face identification for central vision (Leehey et al., 1978) then quite clearly laterality studies giving LVFAs for exposures much less than that speed (Ellis and Shepherd, 1975; Finlay and French, 1978) must be achieving the VFA prior to face identification. This may also apply to studies using longer exposures, as Suberi and McKeever (1977) note that subjects were unable to identify the non-target faces when they were shown to them after the experiment. Some part of the LVFA for faces may rely on the use of short exposure times. It is interesting to note that short exposure times can produce LVFAs even for a lexical decision (Pring, 1981a), so some proportion of the LVFA for faces could therefore rely on a general superiority for extraction of visual information, which according to Rizzolatti and Buchtel (1977) males are more likely to show. Decreasing the exposure time from 100 to 20 ms increased the LVFA found for male subjects. There are, nevertheless, plenty of studies (covering a wide range of exposure times) giving LVFAs for female subjects (Hilliard, 1973; Suberi and McKeever, 1977). Lavadas *et al.* (1980) even find an LVFA for females and not for males. Visual complexity, however, may not be an important factor for Lavadas *et al.* (1980) as this would not be pertinent for detecting the higher-order variable of the same emotion as represented in many different faces.

Reynolds and Jeeves (1978b) note that the easiest (shortest latencies) of their four face targets was consistent in producing an RVFA while the other faces gave an LVFA. This again suggests that a certain degree of visual complexity is required to achieve an LVFA. However, this decreased latency was also associated with ease of labelling so we cannot be sure to what extent it was reduced visual complexity or increased verbalisation which destroyed the LVFA. An account of the importance of visual complexity to the establishment of a VFA for face perception would be welcome. Comparison across known studies is unfortunately very difficult on the issue of the relationship between VFA and the rate of information extraction as this will depend not only on the exposure time but on the brightness of the pre-, post- and test-exposure fields—details which are rarely given.

## Predicting Performance From the Visual Field Advantage

If performance on non-lateralised tasks were predictable from scores obtained from DVF studies, then the methodology would have clinical and educational applications. Several authors have attempted to relate performance on non-verbal tasks to VFA. Hannay (1976) and Birkett (1980) both used delayed recognition of Vanderplas and Garvin (1959) figures as their lateralised task. Hannay (1976) found RVFAs only for males, with only the female scores correlated to scores on the Block Design subtest of the Wechsler adult intelligence scale. The lower the Block Design score the more likely females were to show an RVFA. It was female and not male scores on a spatial task which Birkett (1980) also found predictable. Again, low scores went along with an RVFA. In fact, the prediction was possible only for one out of three spatial tasks but this was the only task for which males were superior. Unlike Hannay (1976), Birkett (1980) found that it was the females and not the males who showed an RVFA. A sex-related prediction is also seen in Hannay and Rogers (1979) where only males with good brightness discrimination showed an LVFA for faces.

Hannay and Rogers (1979) were unable to find a relationship between Block Design scores and an LVFA for faces, so the VFA is certainly not always predictive of performance on non-verbal skills. It is also not certain that any correlation that is found is due to a continuous distribution of VFAs; rather it could be caused by a bimodal split into LVFA and RVFA subjects. If the extent of the VFA were related to scores on spatial tasks, then it should be seen for all groups of subjects, not just for subgroups of subjects likely to code the stimulus verbally. The task used by Hannay (1976) and Birkett (1980) is one that encourages verbalisation. Hannay (1979) has, in fact, clearly shown that it is subjects with poor vocabulary who are more likely to obtain an LVFA in a colour task. Using a dichotomy of LVFA v. RVFA for dot enumeration rather than a continuum of VFA, McGlone and Davidson (1973) found the LVFA group to have higher than average scores on a test of spatial relationships. Field-independent subjects as determined by non-lateralised tasks have also produced an LVFA for faces whereas field dependent ones gave no VFA (Zoccolotti and Oltman, 1978; Rapaczynski and Ehrlichman, 1979).

Decrements in non-lateralised task performance have been suggested to arise from a hemisphere overlap for verbal and non-verbal skills. As the main tests of such hypotheses rely on differences between groups of different sex and/or handedness this issue is dealt with elsewhere. However, when considering the contribution of the DVF methodology to this issue, it should be remembered that if all that is predicted from the VFA is the propensity to verbalise for certain subjects, then this is a far cry from being able to measure non-verbal skills by looking at the VFA. If such a strong claim were upheld it would be more important than strategy or coding differences found from VFAs. The latter are not trivial and do find a certain support. The evidence for the former must be regarded, at the moment, as slim.

## Conclusions

Non-verbal tasks have been found to be better performed in the LVF for a variety of what could be called "lower-level", and certainly not categorical, judgments. Such tasks include detection, brightness estimation, colour, motion and depth perception, localisation, orientation and form discrimination. Of these only a few could be said to give reliable VFAs but if a VFA is obtained it is usually for the left. Attentional and subject variables seem to disrupt the VFA too often to be anything but cautious in accepting an RH superiority for most of these tasks. On a role-call of significant findings it would appear that difficult colour and orientation judgments were reasonably consistent in giving LVFAs. Both these stimulus variables have nevertheless been associated with RVFAs. The verbal aspects of the stimuli seem to be important in changing the VFA but without doubt clarification is needed of the supposed verbal mechanism, be it labelling or some familiarisation process. Stimulus characteristics such as visual complexity and exposure duration which make for difficult discriminations are more reliably involved when LVFAs are found. There is a need for systematic study of these stimulus parameters in promoting an LVFA.

Categorical judgments of non-verbal stimuli have been less often studied. While RVFAs are obtainable for easily named line drawings, categorical judgments of shapes and faces do give consistent LVFAs. Face judgments seem particularly well represented among the significant LVFAs for non-verbal stimuli. While judgments of face identity or expression should not rely on non-categorical factors, this is not easy to avoid and we cannot be sure to what extent it is particular lines or areas of brightness contrast that are being matched. LVFAs found at exposure durations below that necessary for face identification in foveal perception suggest that rather simple matching strategies have been used in some studies. This lack of clarity as to the mechanism which produces the LVFA is highlighted by the not inconsiderable number of studies which do not find LVFAs for certain groups of even dextral subjects. Evidence for a specific face (as opposed to an object-recognition) mechanism in the RH remains to be made certain. Once again the need is for large-scale parametric investigation of stimulus and categorical variables and not a multiplication of small-scale studies with few trials and insufficient subjects.

The division of non-verbal stimuli into lower-level and categorical would seem to find support from the clinical distinction between disorders of apperception and disorders of association (Lissauer, 1889). Apperception is disrupted when the patient cannot state whether two visual patterns are alike or different. Disorders of association result in loss of meaning for a visual representation of the object. While these disorders are rare and have been controversial with respect to loss of sensory functions (see Levine, 1978) they do form a rather nice parallel to a distinction between categorical and non-categorical functions. It would seem a more useful distinction than between serial and parallel processing or same v. different judgments which do not provide a sufficient hemispheric basis for either verbal or non-verbal stimuli. Non-verbal stimuli are found to be associated with LVFAs and sometimes RVFAs for all such processing modes.

Non-verbal tasks which could be considered as either categorical or non-categorical have been investigated with respect to VFA. It would be most unreasonable to expect, and there is no good evidence to suggest, that non-categorical judgments are carried out solely by the RH. This could still mean that the RH is superior and the substantial number of LVFA studies for non-categorical judgments would support this view. It is not necessary that there should be any relationship to VFA even for categorical perception and, indeed, some clinical opinion is reluctant to ascribe any unilateral hemisphere basis for non-verbal stimuli, even faces. Nevertheless, categorical judgments could have a sole RH site and this might explain why they give more reliable LVFAs (Moscovitch, 1979).

While non-verbal stimuli are said to be unreliable for obtaining VFAs there are two reasons for being optimistic that this will change. Firstly, VFAs should become more predictable once the effect of stimulus parameters is better known, and secondly, the mechanisms for producing VFAs should become clearer if distinctions are made between categorical and non-categorical perception. Clinical evidence tells us that the RH performs different functions from the LH with respect to visual stimuli; it is also worthwhile being optimistic that LVFAs will help clarify at least some of these RH functions.

## Acknowledgment

The author acknowledges the help of SSRC grant HR 5880 in the preparation of this chapter.

# 4

## STUDIES WITH VERBAL STIMULI

*J. Graham Beaumont*

ALTHOUGH tachistoscopic studies of lateralised verbal stimuli have a relatively long history in psychology, the last decade has seen a change in emphasis in the kinds of model employed to interpret the effects observed. As an important aspect of the growth of experimental neuropsychology, these studies have been considered to illustrate principles of cerebral cortical organisation, and to provide a tool for their experimental manipulation.

Until about 1970, "cerebral dominance" was employed as an explanatory concept in the discussion of divided visual field (DVF) studies, but as one of a number of factors which influence DVF performance. The excellent reviews of White (1969a, 1972) and of Harcum (1978; although only reviewing the literature to 1970) illustrate this clearly. Since 1970 there has been both a growth in the number of published studies, and a growth of confidence in attributing the effects of cerebral specialisation. Possibly because of the number of published studies, and the rather confused nature of the reported findings, there has been no major comprehensive review since White's review in 1972. Neville (1976) indeed admits that "a review of even a majority of the studies designed to explore perceptual asymmetries of the normal adult human brain would be a formidable task". With at least 200 studies of DVF performance with verbal stimuli and normal subjects having been published in the last decade, this has become increasingly true.

There have of course been many briefer reviews and discussions. Among these are useful accounts by Bryden (1978); G. Cohen (1977); Dimond and Beaumont (1974b); Moscovitch (1973, 1979); Neville (1976); Pirozzolo (1977); Springer (1977) and Swanson *et al.* (1978); and a bibliography (Fudin

57

and Masterson, 1975). With the exception of the essays by Bryden (1978) and Moscovitch (1979), which treat certain aspects of the literature critically and in depth, these discussions, while valuable, have summarised rather than reviewed the research literature.

The present chapter aims to provide a digest of the research in the past decade, relatively independent of the discussion of methodological issues which have been treated in Chapter 2, and of the theoretical models to be evaluated in the next chapter. In view of the scale of the literature, and of the space available here, this also cannot constitute a full review, but I hope that it will enable evaluation of the nature and range of the experimental observations which are to be explained and clarify some of the confusion over the effects which are to be reliably observed in DVF performance.

For the purposes of this review, I shall assume that with unilateral presentation of English words at between 2° to 5° of visual angle for less than 180 ms, a right visual field (RVF) advantage is to be observed in accuracy and reaction time for identification or matching. How variations affect the observed asymmetry (and, later, how reasonable this assumption is) will be examined.

## Stimuli

### Words

Examples of the "classic" RVF superiority for words are easy to find in the literature (although some failures will be noted below), and can be exemplified by the study of Gross (1972) who required subjects to match 3-letter words and found an RVF advantage with a manual or verbal response, responding with either hand, and for "same" or "different" matches. For recognition, Cohen (1975b) found the RVF superiority for words, which persisted when they were cued by alternatives or by class. When mixed in a series of trials with single letters, however, the RVF advantage for words was only apparent if the type of stimulus was cued. When target words were mixed with words with visually confusable features, words with similar outlines and acoustically similar foils in a forced choice response paradigm, Pirozzolo and Rayner (1977) found RVF presentation to be associated with greater overall accuracy as well as fewer errors in selecting words with visually confusable features. The same effect was found by Bradshaw *et al.* (1977b), although the effect did not appear to extend to the matching of personal names, at least for "same" responses. Similar effects in both recognition and report have been shown by Hellige (1978), Hellige and Cox (1976) and Hellige *et al.* (1979). With bilateral presentation, Gill and McKeever (1974) found RVF superiority for the recognition of 2- to 5-letter words, and Klein *et al.* (1976) for the report or recognition of common nouns. Even when the letters of 4-letter words are presented successively, the

RVF advantage has been observed (Dimond, 1971). These, with other incidental results from experiments employing a broader range of conditions, suggest that the RVF superiority for words is the most stable effect to be observed with DVF presentation.

## Linguistic Characteristics

Ellis and Shepherd (1974) reported a greater RVF advantage for abstract than concrete nouns, and this result has been essentially supported by Hines (1976, 1977) and by Day (1977). No modulation of the RVF advantage was found, however, by Orenstein and Meighan (1976) or by Bradshaw and Gates (1978); and no lateral effects at all by Shanon (1979). There is similar uncertainty with respect to imageability with evidence both for (Day, 1979; Marcel and Patterson, 1978) and against (Schmuller and Goodman, 1979) an interaction with lateral asymmetry. Lambert and Beaumont (1981a) manipulated concreteness and imageability orthogonally but could find no effects of either not attributable to report order.

Word-frequency effects have also been elusive. The effects of concreteness were found to interact with familiarity in the Hines (1976) study, reflecting effects reported by Marshall and Holmes in 1974, and supported by Bradshaw and Gates (1978, Exp.I). The third experiment of this last study did not, however, also show effects of word frequency, like the reports of Leiber (1976) and Orenstein and Meighan (1976).

There has been little investigation of other linguistic parameters. Marshall and Holmes (1974) reported an RVF effect for nouns against verbs, suggesting a left-hemisphere (LH) noun-facilitation effect, but a related paper (Caplan *et al.*, 1974) reported no difference in the RVF effect for different classes of noun. Shanon (1979) found no difference between nouns and verbs, and Young and Bion (1980a) no effect of age of acquisition. The recognition of words as belonging to various concrete categories does not seem to be associated with an RVF advantage (Day, 1977; M. Martin, 1978). In general, the findings related to linguistic parameters are unclear and can only be evaluated in the light of methodological consideration of particular experiments.

## Letter Strings

Letter strings and nonsense words appear to elicit much the same RVF advantage as real words (Bradshaw *et al.* 1977b; Fudin and Kenny, 1972; Young *et al.*, 1979, 1980). The RVF superiority for the second stimulus in the study of Nice and Harcum (1976), which demands a rather complex interpretation in terms of mutual masking, would also point to this conclusion. There appear to be no effects of approximation to English (Bryden, 1970), and no effects of the pronounceability of non-words (Leiber, 1976). Axelrod *et al.* (1977) reported an RVF advantage for high (pronounceable) approximations to English, but not for low and unpronounceable approximations, but the very low levels of accuracy associated with their low approximations must cast doubt on this result. An estimation of visual persistence by Erwin and Nebes (1976) showed an LVF superiority for random strings and first-order approximations, but not for third-order approximations. The interpretation of the significance of this result is difficult, but the finding may indicate the operation of a lexical factor which would yield an RVF advantage in interaction with right-hemisphere-based perceptual systems.

The significance of the diverging results obtained when letter strings are exposed across fixation (Hirata and Bryden, 1976; Schwantes, 1978; Wolford and Hollingsworth, 1974) are more appropriately discussed with the general issue of bilateral presentation (below).

A curious but intriguing result was reported by Bradshaw *et al.* (1979) who showed that lexical decisions could be made about words below the recognition threshold, and that this was associated with an LVF advantage shifting to an RVF advantage with longer presentation.

Letter strings appear to be associated with an RVF advantage, relatively independently of the experimental task employed.

## Single Letters

As with letter strings, the recognition of single letters, or the matching of pairs of letters, is associated with an RVF superiority in accuracy or response speed (Haun, 1978; Higenbottam, 1973; Schmuller, 1979; White, 1971b). This result has also been reported with "subliminal" presentation (Charman, 1979), and is substantially supported by the studies of Egeth and Epstein (1972), in which the RVF superiority was for "same" but not "different" matches, and of Cohen (1975b) in which the absence of a VF asymmetry with uncued letters was converted to an RVF advantage by the addition of cueing by alternatives.

Moscovitch (1976) asked subjects to match lateralised letters to previously presented binaural letters and found an LVF advantage with the left hand, but no asymmetry with the right. When the two stimuli were simultaneous, however, no asymmetry was associated with matches, but for "different" pairs, when the stimuli were pictorially similar, there was an LVF advantage, and when acoustically similar an RVF advantage.

The addition of masking stimuli to examine short-term perceptual and cognitive processes has, as expected, produced different asymmetries. An LVF advantage has been reported with a mask around the letter with a stimulus onset asynchrony up to 60 ms before or after the letter (Hellige and Webster, 1979), although using critical stimulus onset asynchrony of a pattern mask as the index of performance produced an RVF advantage in the first testing sessions which was not present in later sessions (Ward and Ross, 1977). McKeever and Gill (1972b) presented bilateral letter pairs with an interval of 0·1 ms or 100 ms between pairs, and found a significant RVF advantage on the initial pair when the ISI was 100 ms, but only on the second pair when the ISI was 0·1 ms. Polich (1978) reported an LVF advantage with a lateral mask and no asymmetry without it using four letters mapped to four digit responses, although using four letters in a go/no-go paradigm had been previously shown to yield an RVF advantage (Rizzolatti et al., 1971).

Matrices have been employed to study identification of letters as against their position as a parallel non-verbal task, and found to show the expected RVF superiority in sensitivity (Robertshaw and Sheldon, 1976) and on partial report (Marzi et al., 1979). Scully (1978) presented a matrix across fixation and showed superior identification in the RVF for females, but in the LVF for males.

Single letters have also been presented in pairs for nominal and physical matching. An RVF superiority was reported for nominal matches by Cohen (1972), Geffen et al. (1972) and by Ledlow et al. (1978b), when the location of the stimuli was unknown, and by Segalowitz and Stewart (1979) when one of the pair was presented in central vision. A more complex pattern of results was reported by Hellige (1976): that "same" nominal matches had an initial LVF advantage which then shifted to an RVF advantage.

Unless the experimental conditions encourage direct physical matching, or interfere with ongoing verbal processes, single letters also seem to produce a secure RVF advantage in DVF performance.

## Numbers

Largely on the basis of evidence from clinical populations, digits have always been regarded as primarily verbal stimuli. The DVF research has largely supported this conclusion. The RVF advantage has been demonstrated for vocal reaction time (Geffen et al., 1971), although not when a vocal response which did not require recognition was required; for accuracy (Dimond and Beaumont, 1971a); for matching serially presented digits (Hatta, 1976a); and when presented bilaterally if accompanied by a central digit to be reported first (Hines and Satz, 1971, 1974; Hines et al., 1969). As with letters, digits presented in a matrix were associated with greater RVF sensitivity (Robertshaw and Sheldon, 1976) and superior recognition (Kail and Siegel, 1978; although only for males). Even when perceptually degraded, arabic numbers yield an RVF advantage, and binary dots the same asymmetry following an initial LVF superiority (Gordon and Carmon, 1976). Decisions of numerical magnitude are better performed when presented in the RVF (Besner et al., 1979). That the effects are due to recognition of the numbers and not to any vocal response output requirement was established by Geffen *et al.* (1973) who employed digits in a go/no-go task, but with the vocal response "bonk". Digits therefore appear to be verbal stimuli and to yield an RVF advantage.

## Orientation of Stimuli

In an attempt to minimise lateral scanning patterns elicited by verbal stimuli, these have been presented in a vertical orientation in a number of experiments. The results have yielded an RVF advantage just as for conventionally presented words, for recognition (Bryden, 1970; Day, 1977, 1979; Mackavey *et al.*, 1975) and for the recognition of single letters in a string (Hannay and Boyer, 1978). McKeever and Gill (1972a) found the RVF advantage, although it was smaller than for horizontal words, and this finding was also that of Lambert and Beaumont (1981a). Hannay and Malone (1976a) employed vertical words to be matched to a subsequent central word and again found the RVF superior, although only when there was a delay between the lateral and central stimuli. Pairs of words to be matched when presented one above the other also produced superior performance in the RVF.

Even when stimuli are reversed, the RVF advantage is to be observed, whether alphanumeric characters (Cohen, 1975a) or 3-letter words (Isseroff *et al.*, 1974). Bilateral mirrored words have produced an RVF advantage when presented either with or without a central Landolt ring, although the normal words only yielded this advantage when the central ring was present.

## Bilingual Stimuli

Experiments in which the stimuli and the subjects are bilingual are a special field, and are accompanied by a special set of problems (Carmon *et al.*, 1972; Carmon *et al.*, 1975; A. S. Cohen, 1977; Endo *et al.*, 1978; Hardyck *et al.*, 1977, 1978; Hatta, 1976b, 1977a, b; Honda, 1977; Kershner and Jeng, 1972; Sasanuma *et al.*, 1977; Silverberg *et al.*, 1979; Tzeng *et al.*, 1979; Walters and Zatorre, 1978). In view of the recent detailed and thorough review by Albert and Obler (1978), no further review will be attempted here. They have concluded that even fluent and balanced bilinguals may vary in their neuropsychological performance associated with the two languages. The implied cerebral lateralisation may thus also differ for the two languages and both age of acquisition and language-specific factors may play a part together with other factors. The results of DVF studies are therefore complex, and must be associated with unusual difficulties in interpretation, particularly when inferences about cerebral organisation are to be drawn.

## Miscellaneous Studies

Bryden and Allard (1976) have shown that if the characteristics of verbal stimuli become more script-like in their appearance, then the normal RVF advantages may be reversed, although their attempt to isolate the confounding effects of difficulty was not altogether successful. Investigators have also tried to reverse or modify the RVF advantage by presenting non-verbal stimuli as well as verbal stimuli in a mixed task (Hines, 1975; Klein *et al.*, 1976; Pirozzolo and Rayner, 1977), but without any radical effect upon the RVF superiority. Similarly, a nominal match between words and pictures revealed an RVF advantage (Tomlinson-Keasey and Kelly, 1979b).

Stroop colour-words have been used as stimuli in two recent experiments (Schmit and Davis, 1974; Tsao *et al.*, 1979) and both showed greater interference in the RVF. Stroop-type letters composed of letters were presented by Martin (1979), who reported an RVF advantage for local processing of the stimulus elements, but no asymmetry for global processing. Alivisatos and Wilding (1980) essentially support this conclusion, with similar stimuli.

Finally, plotting the letter-ring metacontrast function showed a displacement of 13 ms, being shorter with RVF presentation (McKeever and Suberi, 1974); the enumeration of English, but not Greek, letters was found to be superior in the RVF (White, 1971a); semantic judgments of size and pleasantness of imageable nouns were performed better in the RVF (Lambert and Beaumont, 1981b); and, perhaps most surprisingly, reading musical chords was associated with an RVF advantage for trained musicians (Segalowitz *et al.*, 1979).

## Tasks

### Identification

The previous section dealing with variations in the experimental stimuli which can be regarded as verbal has reviewed most of the literature concerning simple identification or recognition. As the most direct form of response, it has been most commonly employed. As has been seen, the published evidence is for a general and stable RVF advantage across a broad range of stimulus types presented within a variety of experimental paradigms. Even when the verbal stimuli are mixed with non-verbal forms, within or across trials, the RVF advantage is still to be observed (Dee and Hannay, 1973; Hellige, 1978; Hellige and Cox, 1976; Hellige *et al.*, 1979; Hines, 1975; Pirozzolo and Rayner, 1977).

Identification responses have also been used when particular processing strategies were to be induced. Scheerer (1974), in a particularly interesting experiment, presented letter strings and elicited selective processing by indicating the letter to be reported by an arrow or number. Exhaustive processing was implied by asking for the location of a target letter, or the first of the string alphabetically. He found the predicted RVF superiority for selective processing when the arrow indicated the letter for report, and an LVF advantage for the alphabetical, exhaustive processing task. There were additional complex results attributable to the nature of the stimulus and other factors.

The results of many other studies have been interpreted within the serial-parallel or analytic-holistic dichotomies as characterising hemisphere specialisation, and which are discussed in Chapter 5.

## Matching: Words and Letter Strings

Again, much of the evidence has appeared above, and indicates a clear RVF advantage, as in Gross (1972). Similar effects were found with a 2 s delay between stimuli (Tomlinson-Keasey and Kelly, 1979b), effects which were found when the stimuli were also pictures if the task was classified as difficult and sequential. The way in which tasks are classified within this study is, however, open to debate.

It should be noted, though, that Bradshaw *et al.* (1977b) found an LVF advantage for matching easily discriminable names, and Bradshaw *et al.* (1977a) for discriminating words when the first or last, but not one of the middle, letters differed.

The results for letter strings are similar, although with bilaterally presented strings through fixation an LVF advantage has been reported (Schwantes, 1978; White, 1969b). With easy tasks, particularly with respect to end positions, the LVF has been superior, although increasing task demands or lengthening the string produced an RVF advantage (Umilta *et al.*, 1972; Wolford and Hollingsworth, 1974).

## Matching: Letters (Physical)

Matching letters has been performed both as a direct task and within experiments where both physical and nominal matches have been required. When no explicit instructions are given to subjects, identity matches may be performed on either a physical or a nominal basis, and different strategies may be adopted by different subjects or across the experiment by a single subject. This undoubtedly accounts for the differing results which have been reported.

When nominal and physical matches have been deliberately manipulated by the experimenter, physical identity matches may yield superior performance in the LVF, at least for "same" responses (Cohen, 1972; Davis and Schmit, 1973), although some studies have found no lateral asymmetry (Ledlow *et al.*,

1978b; Segalowitz and Stewart, 1979). Where the trials are mixed the LVF advantage has also been reported (Geffen *et al.*, 1972; White and White, 1975), although it should be noted in the Geffen *et al.* study that the lower-case letters were as large as the upper case, which may have increased the spatial-perceptual difficulty of the task.

With a delay introduced between central presentation of the first stimulus and lateral presentation of the second, Wilkins and Stewart (1974) found an LVF advantage for short delays and an RVF advantage for a longer delay, as did Kirsner (1979) with delays over 50 ms. McCarthy (1980), however, found a more stable LVF advantage for single-letter physical identity matching, and essentially no lateral bias for double-letter stimuli.

When subjects were relatively free to adopt a strategy, superior performance for identity matches of single letters was found in the RVF by Egeth and Epstein (1972) and Haun (1978), but in the LVF by Umilta *et al.* (1972). Asked to judge whether the letters in a string were all identical, "same" responses were associated with better performance in the RVF (Cohen, 1973).

## Matching: Letters (Nominal)

When nominal matching of letters is demanded, the result is in almost every report an RVF advantage (Cohen, 1972; Davis and Schmit, 1973; Geffen *et al.*, 1972; Hellige, 1976; Hellige *et al.*, 1979; Ledlow *et al.*, 1978b; Niederbuhl and Springer, 1979; Segalowitz and Stewart, 1979). This is true for "same" responses in each of the above studies, although for the response "different" some workers have found an LVF superiority (Davis and Schmitt, 1973; Geffen *et al.*, 1972) when the trials were mixed, or no lateral asymmetry (Hellige, 1976). In the last study, the RVF advantage for the response "same" only emerged over the series of trials following an initial LVF advantage. Hellige *et al.* (1979) also reported that addition of a concurrent memory load extinguished the RVF superiority.

The only study to stand against this general conclusion is that of White and White (1975) where the trials were mixed and where a string of two to four letters were presented for matching. The result observed was a weak advantage for the LVF. The processing demands of this task clearly differ from those generated by single- or double-letter matching.

The introduction of a delay between the initial central and the lateral test stimulus has also yielded an RVF advantage, at least with interstimulus intervals beyond 50 ms (Kirsner, 1979; McCarthy, 1980; Wilkins and Stewart, 1974). With an interval of just 50 ms Wilkins and Stewart reported no lateral asymmetry, although as a substantial number of their subjects failed to demonstrate a clear physical identity advantage at this interval, the validity of an interpretation based upon a visual code defined by the physical identity: nominal identity ratio must be questioned.

## Lexical Decision

The superiority of performance when stimuli are presented in the RVF is almost uncontested for lexical decision tasks. A clear result has been obtained in a number of studies (Bradshaw and Gates, 1978; Bradshaw *et al.*, 1979; Bradshaw *et al.*, 1977b; Day, 1977; Leiber, 1976). However, Bradshaw and Gates noted that the asymmetry was less consistent than that for overt naming, and Day found the effect only for abstract and not for concrete nouns which showed no lateral asymmetry. Leiber, nevertheless, saw the effect for both high- and low-frequency words, but it was absent for both pronounceable and non-pronounceable non-words.

Shanon (1979) did not find any asymmetry for lexical decision for concrete or abstract nouns or verbs, despite a close replication in part of the study by Day (1977). The only explanation offered was in terms of the number of different stimuli employed, following the hypothesis of Hardyck *et al.* (1977, 1978). As there must be doubts about the validity of this hypothesis (see below), the reason for Shanon's failure to find the effect remains unclear.

## Phoneme Matching

Phoneme matches have been required in four studies with unclear results (M. Martin, 1978; Moscovitch, 1973, 1976; Umilta *et al.*, 1972). Asking subjects to match for "ee" sounds, Moscovitch (1973) found an RVF asymmetry for "same" responses unless the stimuli were identical, in which case the LVF was superior. "Different" responses yielded no asymmetry. The later 1976 study, also involving a successive binaural–visual match, reported that for "same" responses, non-identical stimuli which matched phonemically showed the RVF advantage, but that identical stimuli showed an LVF advantage. These results were not supported, however, in Martin's study. Umilta *et al.* reported an LVF advantage for matching vowel sounds, but an RVF advantage for the more similar, and therefore more difficult, stop consonant discriminations.

## Semantic Processes

Day's (1977) study included asking subjects to make category judgments about nouns following the central presentation of a category noun. In accord with his other findings, he found an RVF advantage for "abstract" categories ("months" or "feelings" for example) but not for concrete categories ("animals", "clothing" etc.).

Category names were also used for semantic priming by Klein and Smith (reported in Moscovitch, 1979) in matching pairs of words, and the effect of semantic priming was found to be greater for words in the RVF than in the LVF.

Perhaps a little surprisingly, M. Martin (1978), in two experiments, found no lateral advantage for semantic selection (plant–animal names; house–people categories), while observing an RVF advantage for physical selection (short–long words; the presence of a double letter). Semantic judgments of size and pleasantness of pairs of nouns have, however, been reported to show the RVF advantage.

Coding effects have also been reported. The instruction to employ an imagery strategy was found to give an LVF advantage by Seamon (1974; Seamon and Gazzaniga, 1973) whether the probes were words or pictures, while a rehearsal strategy gave an RVF advantage with pictures, but an LVF advantage with word probes. These were not the findings of Metzger and Antes (1976) who found no clear effect of manipulating coding strategy. Word probes were not associated with any lateral asymmetry, while pictures gave an RVF advantage with rehearsal or imagery strategies.

The interference observed with Stroop stimuli has already been referred to, with evidence for local interference having a greater effect in the LVF (Alivisatos and Wilding, 1980; Martin, 1979). This conclusion would not be supported by the Schmit and Davis (1974) study, and that of Tsao et al. (1979) using colour words, who found greater interference in RVF performance. Beaumont (1974) reported no lateral differences associated with these stimuli. The interference effect of accompanying a picture to be named with a briefly presented word was shown to be greater, for naming latency, by Underwood (1977).

## Miscellaneous Tasks

Relatively non-verbal tasks have been set for subjects, but using letter stimuli. Cohen (1975) found that judgments of letters as normal or reversed under different rotations produced an LVF advantage, but that cueing by name and rotation led to a greater reduction in response latency in the RVF. Easy and difficult perceptual discriminations between letters were demanded by Jonides (1979). The easy task produced an RVF effect, but the hard task and one of mixed difficulty showed LVF superiority.

Numerate abilities have also been studied. The expected RVF superiority has been reported for number-magnitude judgment (Besner et al., 1979) and for the enumeration of English, although not Greek, letters (White, 1971a). In a calculation task, an LVF advantage was reported by Dimond and Beaumont (1972c), but it is possible that this finding reflects a perceptual matching process rather than a true calculation ability.

Learning abilities have been studied by Dimond and Beaumont (1974b, c). They found no difference between the hemispheres in incidental learning or paired-associate learning of vowel–consonant duograms, but did demonstrate an RVF advantage for the paired-associate learning of digits with key symbols. LeFebvre and Kubose (1975) in a discrimination-learning paradigm discovered no asymmetry on verbal learning, but found an RVF advantage with reversal learning.

Klatzky and Atkinson (1971) presented words or pictures to their subjects and asked that the initial letter of the word, or of the name of the object depicted, be matched to a letter set held in memory. The picture-test stimuli produced shorter response latencies when in the RVF, and the letters in the LVF, reflecting the results noted above, obtained with rather similar paradigms to examine the effect of coding strategies.

Verbal and directional stimuli were employed in a novelty decision task by Salmaso (1979), and decision-theory analysis revealed greater sensitivity in the RVF for both types of stimuli. Umilta *et al.* (1976) examined the stimulus-repetition effect upon response latency, but found no lateral asymmetry of the effects which they observed. Finally, word associations were elicited by stimuli in the LVF and the RVF (Dimond and Beaumont, 1974b), and while there was no difference between the visual fields in speed of response, more common associations, according to established norms, were elicited by RVF presentation.

## Presentation Condition

### Stimulus Eccentricity

The vast majority of studies have employed standard tachistoscopes and, perhaps as a result, stimuli have generally been presented 2–5° from fixation. While, as discussed in Chapter 2, the precise extent of overlap, if any, at the vertical meridian is uncertain for the human visual system, and the implications of the bilaterally integrated ambient visual system (Trevarthen, 1974a), which operates more peripherally, have not been fully explored, it is generally accepted that stimulation of this region of the visual field will result in lateralised cerebral input. There are no clear grounds on which to question studies which have employed eccentricities from visual fixation out to the limits of satisfactory acuity, but it is worth noting atypical presentation conditions, and enquiring whether they yield unusual results.

In fact, the results of studies which have involved stimulus presentation beyond 5° of visual angle have elicited the expected RVF advantage for verbal identification (Berlucchi *et al.*, 1974; Carmon *et al.*, 1972; Kershner and Jeng, 1972), for the identification of digits (Carmon and Nachshon, 1973), in verbal coding (Davis and Schmit, 1973), and in phonemic, although not identity, letter-matching (Moscovitch, 1976). Curiously, in the Carmon and Nachshon study, an effect was present at 8° 30' which was not found at 3°. The several studies of Dimond and Beaumont (Dimond and Beaumont, 1974b), using a larger-scale apparatus, found essentially the expected pattern of results for relative performance in the two visual fields.

Stimulus eccentricity has been treated as a variable in a number of studies, and certainly over the normal range of presentation positions, precise eccentricity had no significant effect (Curcio *et al.*, 1974; Fudin and Kenny, 1972; Haun, 1978; Worrall and Coles, 1976). McKeever and Gill (1972b) found less asymmetry with presentation at 3·9° than 1·6°, but this may be an effect of acuity mediated by relative difficulty. Superimposed upon the RVF advantage, at least in their difficult task, Wolford and Hollingsworth (1974) observed an effect of eccentricity which showed a marked drop in performance to 1·5° followed by a more gradual decline.

Within letter strings, Lefton *et al.* (1978) found that retinal location interacted with serial position, in that letters in the middle positions were primarily affected by retinal location. This could have important implications for the presentation of words in which different elements will differentially transmit information which is used for identification. Haun (1978) reported asymmetries in recognition with eccentricities as small as 5·2' to 20·7', although his method of allowing subjects to judge optimal fixation and initiate trials has yet to be clearly validated.

The studies of McConkie and Rayner (1976; Rayner, 1978a) showing the asymmetrical distribution about fixation of available information when reading are certainly relevant in this context.

## Stimulus Location

Stimuli have been presented almost without exception on the horizontal meridian, or if vertically oriented, then symmetrically about it. One recent study (Worrall and Coles, 1976) has, however, presented letters at various "clockface" positions around fixation. The RVF advantage which was to be expected with these stimuli was only found for stimuli on the horizontal meridian. It is perhaps also worth noting that the experiment of Bradshaw *et al.* (1977b), which found an LVF asymmetry for name matches, presented the two stimulus items in a vertical array.

## Stimulus Duration

Again, as discussed in Chapter 2, it is difficult to be sure just how long exposure durations may be before there is a possibility of gaze deviation to the item presented. The currently accepted conservative value seems to be 180 ms, although on the basis of not very firm evidence. Studies employing longer exposures should be treated with caution, particularly if exposures exceed 200 ms and there is no independent monitoring of fixation maintenance. Studies with long stimulus durations include Bradshaw *et al.* (1977b; 200, 265 ms); Cohen (1975b; 180 ms); Geffen *et al.* (1971; 160 ms); Higenbottam (1973; 195 ms); Hines and Satz (1971, 1974; 170 ms); Klatzky and Atkinson (1971; 400 ms); M. Martin (1978; 225, 200 ms) and Segalowitz *et al.* (1979; up to 200 ms).

Exposure duration treated as a variable was found to have no significant effect on asymmetry, within the usual range of values, by Gill and McKeever (1974), and Mackavey *et al.* (1975). Hines *et al.* (1973) examined the effect of durations up to 330 ms, and found no significant effect. This was, however, within Hines' paradigm of a series of stimulus pairs, one central one lateral, with the central items to be reported first.

Very brief exposures have been employed by Bradshaw *et al.* (1979) and Charman (1979), with opposite conclusions as to the asymmetry implied. The establishment of the threshold and precise stimulus variables need more careful control in "subliminal" perception before conclusions may be reached. The Kemp and Haude (1979) study presented the display for 1 ms, but it is unclear whether the task was in any sense a verbal one, and no asymmetries were observed.

The importance of exposure duration, mediated by accuracy, for laterality indices has been pointed out by Holmes and Marshall (1974b).

## Fixation Control

It is not clear whether methods of fixation control have had any effect upon the outcome of DVF experiments with verbal stimuli. The issue of unilateral or bilateral presentation is relevant, but will be discussed more fully below. It has generally been considered wise to use random presentation to the two visual fields, rather than blocked presentation, although Geffen *et al.* (1972) found no difference between blocked and random conditions. They did, however, directly monitor eye movements and reported failures of fixation on only 0·5% of trials, equally distributed right and left. Carmon *et al.* (1972) and Ledlow *et al.* (1978b) found that the verbal RVF superiority effect disappeared when stimulus location was known, and this is the result which has generally been anticipated.

It is worth noting that in the study of Klatzky and Atkinson (1971), subjects were directed to look to the extreme right or left of the display in order to achieve lateralisation of the stimulus which appeared in the centre of the display. This may account in part for their unusual results. By the use of some other unusual methods, the Haidinger's Brush phenomenon (Gibson *et al.*, 1972) gave an LVF advantage for word-matching but the requirement to fuse a fixation stimulus in a stereoviewer (Carmon *et al.*, 1975) appears not to have modified the RVF advantage.

## *Prestimulus Conditions*

Apart from the debate concerning a concurrent central stimulus for initial report and experiments in which memory is explicitly or implicitly involved (see below), there has been little interest in prestimulus variables. This is surprising in view of the interest in attentional manipulation. Most experiments have placed a small dot or cross at fixation in the prestimulus field which has served to orient fixation, and as a warning stimulus. The implications of providing a fixed period warning stimulus, particularly for gaze deviation, seem not to have been explored.

The effect of a verbal or non-verbal auditory warning stimulus has been assessed (Bowers and Heilman, 1976). Right-hand responses were affected by the nature of the warning stimulus, while left-hand responses were not; a result which is not entirely clear. Pitblado *et al.* (1979) have reported that a bright pre-exposure field produced a greater number of "blank" responses and was associated with an RVF advantage, while a dim pre-exposure field produced neither effect. This is an interesting report, the significance of which is difficult to evaluate as few papers provide sufficient detail about the brightness of the relevant fields employed. Haun (1978) and Orenstein and Meighan (1976) allowed subjects to initiate their own trials.

The effect of various types of cue has been found to modify lateral asymmetries, particularly by Cohen (1975a, b, 1976). Advance information about the name and rotation of a letter produced an RVF advantage in judging letter orientation, as did cueing by alternatives in letter recognition. The same was not true of words, which yielded an RVF advantage whether cued by alternative or class. When words were mixed with digits and dots, precueing the stimulus type modified the lateral asymmetries observed, producing an RVF advantage for the words, a tendency towards an RVF advantage for the digits and an LVF advantage for the dots. In a partial report paradigm, precueing led to a larger partial report advantage in the RVF. However, Hellige (1978) found no effect upon the pattern of lateral asymmetries of a pretrial cue of stimulus type, and M. Martin (1978) found no interaction of the effect of pre- or postcueing categories with the VF asymmetry.

## Unilateral v. Bilateral Presentation

This is really the only topic to have stimulated any heated debate over the past decade. In about 1970, the reviews of the literature suggested that unilateral presentation of verbal stimuli yielded an RVF advantage. Bilateral presentation would also yield an RVF advantage, but only if fixation was carefully controlled and efforts were made to restrict the operation of scanning tendencies associated with left-to-right reading habits. To these were attributed the LVF superiorities observed in earlier experiments, and indeed they have not been entirely dismissed as an explanation of the RVF advantage. Those interested in this debate should certainly read the reviews of Bryden (1978) and Harcum (1978), as well as Chapters 2 and 5 in this volume.

The important development by McKeever and Hines and their coworkers has been the idea of presenting an additional stimulus or stimuli at fixation, usually a digit, to be reported before the lateral material (Hines *et al.*, 1969; Hines, 1972a, b; McKeever and Gill, 1972a, b; McKeever *et al.*, 1972; Parker *et al.*, 1976). The method employed by Hines, over a number of papers, had a series of pairs of stimuli, one of which was at fixation, and the set presented at fixation was to be reported before the lateral stimuli. This method has been less popular than the more general principle popularised by McKeever of simply adding some central stimulus to the bilateral display which might otherwise have been employed. These methods have not been without their critics, who have been concerned that the methods have changed the pattern, rather than countered the contribution, of postexposural scanning tendencies and, perhaps more importantly, that recognising and reporting the central stimulus has had an effect upon subsequent processing of the lateral material. White (1973b) attacked McKeever on this issue, although most of the points seem to be met in McKeever (1974). A further critical paper was published by Fudin (1976).

What is the evidence for the effect of these different presentation procedures on the observed RVF advantage for verbal stimuli and tasks? A number of studies have directly compared unilateral and bilateral presentation. McKeever (1971) showed that both forms of presentation produced an RVF advantage in word recognition, but that this effect was much stronger with bilateral presentation. Hines (1976, 1977, 1978) similarly showed that an RVF advantage could be demonstrated by unilateral or bilateral presentation when the stimuli were words. Essentially similar asymmetries with unilateral or bilateral presentation have been reported also by Hines *et al.* (1976), M. Martin (1978), and Pirozzolo and Rayner (1977), within the context of rather different verbal tasks. There have, however, been alternative findings. Neil *et al.* (1971), with letter stimuli presented independently to single hemi-retinae, found an LVF superiority with bilateral stimuli, but the RVF advantage with unilateral stimulation. The opposite result was reported by Boyle

(1975). The efficacy of fixation control should probably be questioned in both these studies. Carmon and Nachshon (1973) found the RVF advantage both for unilateral and bilateral stimulation with English subjects, although Hebrew subjects showed a reversed advantage for unilateral, though not bilateral, digits.

The bilateral presentation of words, with a digit at central fixation has generally been found to yield an RVF advantage (Gill and McKeever, 1974; Hines, 1975; Klein *et al.*, 1976; Leehey and Cahn, 1979; Marshall and Holmes, 1974; Walters and Zatorre, 1978). Trigrams paired with grids were associated with fewer errors when presented in the RVF (White and Silver, 1975) and Scully's (1978) bilateral matrix with letters showed an RVF advantage on the identity task for females although not for males. Presenting strings through fixation, Wolford and Hollingsworth (1974) observed the RVF advantage for the harder task, although it was only found for the middle positions in the string on the easier task.

Hines (1972a; Hines *et al.*, 1969) had shown that while bilateral presentation of digits or words produced an RVF advantage with a centre digit, but the reverse asymmetry without, studies which have not used a central stimulus have produced rather variable results. Berlucchi *et al.* (1974) presented letter stimuli in a mixed sequence at central or lateral locations, with different groups for left and right lateral stimuli. They found an RVF advantage. By contrast, asking subjects to match a lateral word to one previously presented in central vision has been reported to give an LVF advantage (Gibson *et al.*, 1972). Without any central stimulus, an RVF advantage with bilateral stimuli has been found for paired English and Chinese words (Kershner and Jeng, 1972), for number judgment (Besner *et al.*, 1979) and for performing nominal matches on pairs of letters (Davis and Schmit, 1973). This was also true when report order was controlled, for words (Rosen *et al.*, 1975; Schmuller and Goodman, 1979) for trigrams (Young *et al.*, 1979, 1980) and for picturable nouns, although only on second reports (ibid). White (1973) presented four items in each visual field and asked for recall of the whole string, the items in one hemifield or for single letters. He found in each case, except for total recall of the eight items on bilateral presentation, the RVF advantage.

Against these reports stands the evidence from a number of studies. No lateral asymmetry was to be observed with a string of letters centrally fixated, by Coltheart and Arthur (1971) nor by Smith and Ramunas (1971) who presented stimuli bilaterally and postcued for response between 0 and 2 s following stimulus offset. With eight items presented across fixation, an LVF advantage was reported by White (1969b) for whole report, and by Schwantes (1978) for both whole and single-item report. Orenstein and Meighan (1976) found an LVF advantage for bilaterally presented words which they contrasted with the previous findings of McKeever. This drew a reply from McKeever (1976) and another in turn from Orenstein (1976). It seems likely, as

McKeever pointed out, that the absence of the central stimulus was the most important factor in producing the divergent results, although the reason why this should be so is still a matter open to debate.

Interestingly, Hirata and Bryden (1976) have shown that the presence of a gap in a bilaterally presented string, about fixation, enhances any RVF superiority. This emphasises the care that must be taken in designing experimental stimuli, and the number of factors which may influence lateral asymmetries.

To return to the central stimulus presented at fixation, there have been studies which have directly examined the effect of its presence. The studies of Hines with colleagues have already been mentioned. McKeever, with Suberi and VanDeventer (1972), carried out a thorough study of the effects of the central stimulus, which was a digit, upon unilateral and bilateral stimuli and when the appearance of the central stimulus was predictable and unpredictable. They report a consistent finding of the RVF superiority, and no interaction of the presence of the digit with the lateral asymmetry. They concluded that the use of a digit at fixation does not materially affect subsequent processing, except of course to ensure accurate lateralisation of stimuli. This finding is substantially supported by the study of Mackavey *et al.* (1975), where incidentally the strength of the left-to-right report tendency was found to correlate negatively with the magnitude of the RVF advantage.

Non-verbal stimuli have been concurrently presented at fixation by Caplan *et al.* (1974), Hines (1978), Kaufer *et al.* (1975) and Schmuller and Goodman (1979). It is difficult to know whether the five non-verbal symbols used by Caplan *et al.* contributed to the rather complex results obtained in their study, but Hines made a direct comparison of a verbal and non-verbal central fixation stimulus and found no effect of the central stimulus type upon word recognition. A Landolt ring was presented centrally in the Kaufer *et al.* study, and subjects had to report the position of the gap in the ring before the lateralised material, which was words. An RVF advantage for the words was reported with the rings present, but an LVF advantage without. However, if the words were mirrored, then the RVF advantage was to be observed with or without the central ring. Although it was not to be reported, Schmuller and Goodman (1979) presented an arrow concurrently at fixation to indicate the stimulus for first report. They found the RVF advantage.

The evidence on bilateral presentation is not unanimous, but it would appear that given adequate fixation control, generally by a central stimulus concurrently presented, and with report order controlled, the RVF advantage is to be observed on similar tasks and with similar stimuli as unilateral presentation. Without the concurrent fixation stimulus, the results are rather less predictable. While some doubt must remain about the effect of the presence and nature of the central stimulus, there is no clear evidence that it does significantly bias the nature of subsequent processing.

## Stimulus Set Size

It has been proposed by Hardyck *et al.* (1977, 1978) that reliable visual field asymmetries are only to be observed where there is a limited number of different stimuli employed. They based this conclusion on a series of experiments on verbal matching within and between English and Chinese characters by English and Chinese subjects. They found that asymmetries were only to be found when a very restricted stimulus set was used, and attributed this to the role of mnemonic factors. They suggested that the subjects must in effect know the range of stimuli, or rapidly deduce it from the early trials, and then adopt a strategy which involves "referencing a table of known values". They argued that examination of the literature supported this conclusion in that experiments with small stimulus sets have found an RVF advantage with verbal stimuli, but where new information is presented on each trial, no such effect has been found. They have not to date published an analysis of the relevant literature.

Examination of the studies with verbal stimuli does not seem to support their argument as unanimously as they suggest. Although there are some studies with a large stimulus set (e.g. Dimond *et al.*, 1972) which have not found the expected RVF advantage, there are a number of studies which have obtained a clear visual field asymmetry with a large range of stimulus examples. Bradshaw *et al.* (1977a) used 85 different words; Bradshaw and Gates (1978) 144; Bradshaw *et al.* (1979) 56 different stimuli; Day (1977) 64; Gill and McKeever (1974) 96 words; Marshall and Holmes (1974) 40 words; Silverberg *et al.* (1979) 48 stimuli. In an experiment involving English and Chinese words, with 36 stimuli of each type, Kershner and Jeng (1972) found evidence for an RVF advantage. Segalowitz *et al.* (1979) had 56 different examples of their musical chord stimuli. Even in a novelty task (Salmaso, 1979) the visual field asymmetry has been observed. In a number of different laboratories, with a range of different tasks and experimental paradigms, the RVF advantage has been found for verbal stimuli with relatively large stimulus sets. While not denying that a small stimulus set size may well play a role in determining the subject's processing strategy, and in some tasks play a role in determining hemisphere asymmetries, it cannot be a sufficient explanation for all the visual field asymmetries reported in the literature.

## Response Factors

### Response Mode

The mode and form of response is a fundamental problem in any DVF experiment which draws inferences about cerebral specialisation. There is every reason from clinical evidence to believe that response output is asymmetrically controlled, especially if the response is spoken. When the hands are used for manual response, it is unclear whether the control is bilateral, contralateral, or flexibly organised depending upon other task demands. A significant variable is certainly whether the movement required involves fine and accurate motor control, in which contralateral control seems more important than with more gross and coarser response movements. These issues are discussed in more detail elsewhere in this volume. The important point is that response mode is inextricably confounded with other aspects of the task, and it is not possible to change the response without to some degree changing the task.

Despite these difficulties, most workers in the DVF field have been content to assume that response systems are relatively independent of other systems involved in task performance, and there has been little direct study of their role in determining visual field effects. When using a manual response, most workers have balanced the hands across the conditions of the experiment, although some workers have felt confident that it was unnecessary (e.g. Cohen, 1972). Others have employed a simultaneous bimanual response (e.g. Dimond and Beaumont, 1972c; Bradshaw *et al.*, 1977a), even though there is no clear model of how such a response might be generated by the cerebral hemispheres. Where the effects of the hand employed have been analysed and the results reported, there has been no clear general result. Some workers have found an interaction between the hand of response and the visual field asymmetry (Besner *et al.*, 1979; Day, 1977; Moscovitch, 1976, Exp.I), while others have not (Moscovitch, 1973; Segalowitz *et al.*, 1979). Umilta *et al.* (1972) found the effect for accuracy, but not for response latency. These experiments cover a wide range of tasks and stimuli which, together with precise details of the response demanded, must determine the complex relationship between output and other aspects of task execution.

In comparing manual with vocal responses, White (1973a) found the RVF advantage to disappear when the manual response was demanded in a go/no-go paradigm. This contrasts with the reports of Geffen *et al.* (1971, 1973) who established that vocalisation *per se* did not contribute to the RVF advantage, which was also produced with a meaningless vocal response, again in a go/no-go paradigm. Gross (1972) found the RVF effect with both a manual and a meaningless vocal response. Bradshaw and Gates (1978), however, did report that the RVF advantage was more consistent with overt naming than with a manual response following lexical decision, although the interaction between task and response cannot be ignored here.

As has been seen, go/no-go responses have produced the expected RVF superiority (and see also Isseroff *et al.*, 1974; Rizzolatti *et al.*, 1971). Multiple choice recognition has also been employed and yielded the advantage (Hannay and Malone, 1976a; Klein *et al.*, 1976), although in both these experiments the effect was not present in every condition.

It is also worth noting the response-mapping of Polich (1978) who assigned four digit responses to four stimuli and found an LVF advantage, because, it was argued, this form of response involved a higher degree of spatial complexity. Smith and Ramunas (1971) ingeniously used a vibrotactile cue to indicate the stimulus to be reported, but found no visual field asymmetry.

## *Report Order*

Especially, although not exclusively, with bilateral presentation the effects of report order of the elements of the stimulus array must be carefully controlled. This, however, has not always been the case, and Lambert and Beaumont (1981a), for instance, have shown that previous reports of the effect of imageability upon the RVF advantage are artefactual and may be attributed to the failure to control report order. They also showed that in free report, subjects with a left-to-right bias obtained an LVF advantage and those with a right-to-left bias, an RVF advantage. However, Schmuller and Goodman (1979) found an RVF advantage for both first and second reports with words, as did Young *et al.* (1979, 1980) with nonsense trigrams although not with picturable nouns which gave the RVF advantage on second reports only. Schmuller and Goodman had, however, found a stronger RVF superiority for words on the second reports. McKeever (1971) found the RVF effect and no effect of report order, as did Smith and Ramunas (1971), although as no RVF effect was observed in this last study, the significance of the report is unclear.

The requirement to report non-verbal stimuli, for example faces, before reporting the verbal stimuli has been shown not to prevent an RVF superiority being observed (Klein *et al.*, 1976). This is probably also supported by the Hines (1975) study, although Hines failed to control the order of report systematically in this experiment.

No interaction between report order and the position of fixation in random-letter arrays was reported by Boyle (1975), despite a significant main effect of both variables. With right-to-left report, he also observed a superiority in recognition in the RVF with bilateral presentation, but an LVF advantage with unilateral presentation. Schwantes (1978) found an LVF advantage with eight-item letter strings presented bilaterally, and a delay in the postcue for partial report resulted in an increase in the LVF superiority for this task. As Schwantes found greater lateral asymmetries under whole rather than single report, he argued for an important contribution of a report-order bias effect, although the VF asymmetry effects were still to be observed under balanced single report.

## Memory

The discussion of report order as a contributor to visual field asymmetries raises a more general question which has not been satisfactorily resolved in the experimental literature: what is the role of memory? It is of course impossible not to find some role for memory in any experiment, even if it is only for the instructions about performance which precede the experimental trials. Several writers (Fudin and Masterson, 1976b; Hardyck *et al.*, 1977, 1978; Hines *et al.*, 1973; Metzger and Antes, 1976; Seamon, 1974) have argued for, or tried to demonstrate, a more fundamental role for memory in DVF experiments.

Many experiments have, of course, introduced a delay between stimuli, especially when some form of verbal match has been required. Within short time intervals, McKeever (1971) and McKeever and Huling (1971a) found that stimulus-onset asynchrony did not affect the RVF advantages observed. Rather longer delays have also tended to produce the same effect as no delay (Day, 1977; Tomlinson-Keasey and Kelly, 1979b), although Hannay and Malone (1976a), requiring that nonsense words be matched, found the RVF effect only when a delay had been introduced. Coney and Kirsner (1976) also found an advantage for delayed matching of digits in the RVF over pairs presented in the LVF. This was not the result of Beaumont and Dimond (1973a), who included within- as well as between-hemisphere matching effects for letters within their design. They found various effects in between-hemisphere matching, depending on which hemisphere received or transmitted the targets or probes, but found no significant difference betwen the hemispheres in within-hemisphere matching. Hatta (1976a, b) found left followed by right presentation to lead to more errors than the reverse order.

Many of these designs raise the question of masking effects, especially as Miller (1975) has shown masking effects of two stimuli homotopically presented in the two visual fields. A word on the right followed by a mask on the left was associated with poorer performance than a word on the left followed by a mask on the right. The study of Nice and Harcum (1976) as well as that of McKeever and Gill (1972b) undoubtedly involves very complex mutual masking effects which make interpretation of the results difficult.

The studies of Kirsner (1979), McCarthy (1980) and Wilkins and Stewart (1974), which introduced a delay into physical or nominal letter-matching, have already been noted when the tasks were discussed. Attempts to examine the generation of visual and semantic codes by this strategy within the DVF paradigm have not met with clear success, and the results are probably mainly determined by the field of presentation of the second stimulus. It is also worth noting an intriguing report by Kroll and Madden (1978), using a similar experimental strategy, that performance was linked to Verbal Scholastic Aptitude Test scores, low VSAT scorers showing an advantage for probes in the RVF and vice versa. This is certainly not what might have been predicted.

Memory has been more explicitly involved where either a target item, or a target set, has been held in memory while subsequent probe stimuli are presented. As is so commonly the case with verbal stimuli, such experiments have generally, but not exclusively, yielded an RVF advantage. Positive results have been reported by Bradshaw *et al.* (1977a), Haun (1978) and Isseroff *et al.* (1974), although no effect was reported by White (1970). Following one or six letters presented binaurally, Moscovitch (1973) found an LVF advantage for probes to be matched to the single item, but an RVF advantage when six items were held in memory, a result which he attributed to the visual strategy adopted in the single-item condition, and this conclusion was supported by later results (Moscovitch, 1976). The study of Klatzky and Atkinson (1971), in which the probes were the initial letters of objects depicted or were letters, and in which the RVF superiority was found for the pictures, but not the letters, and the study of Gibson *et al.* (1972) in which an LVF advantage was found for matching a lateral word to a previously presented central word, both illustrate that the inclusion of an element which requires memory for verbal material does not inevitably yield an RVF advantage.

The problem is, of course, to know what kind of strategy a subject will employ in retaining verbal information. It is clear that information might be retained in one or more of a variety of forms, and the possibility that a verbal item may be semantically coded does not imply that it cannot be treated in terms of its spatioperceptual elements. Seamon (1974) and Metzger and Antes (1976) have tried to address this problem by directly manipulating subjects' strategies, but without entirely coherent results. The first study found that a word probe, even with rehearsal instructions, led to an LVF advantage probably indicating a perceptual match. A picture probe, however, yielded an LVF advantage with the imagery instructions but an RVF advantage under rehearsal instructions. The second study replicated the effect for picture probes under rehearsal instructions, but not the effect with word probes.

It is undoubtedly clear that memory effects are involved in the performance of DVF tasks, and in some paradigms more than others (particularly in the Hines and Satz paradigm, which gives very strong asymmetries: 1971, Hines *et al.*, 1973, 1976). On the other hand, in view of the range of evidence, including tasks with a relatively minor memory component, and those with a larger component but anomalous effects, it seems unreasonable to attribute the major part of DVF asymmetries to this aspect of cognitive processing. Until it is possible to determine unequivocally the form of memory-coding employed within a task, and avoid *post hoc* rationalisation determined by the asymmetries observed, then it will not be possible to determine the precise significance of memory factors in DVF effects.

## Additional Tasks

The addition of secondary tasks to be performed simultaneously with the task relating to material presented in the DVF paradigm has been employed as a method of "loading" the processing system and as a way of observing activation and interference effects between various elements of the system.

Dimond and Beaumont (1971a, 1972a, b, 1974) presented pairs of digits for recognition and at the same time asked subjects to perform a manual sorting task. It was expected that the spare capacity available in each hemisphere system while the primary recognition task was being performed could be observed in performance of the sorting task. With concurrent bimanual sorting, an RVF advantage was found on both tasks, although it was stronger on the recognition task. Unimanual sorting was associated with weaker effects on both tasks, suggesting that the control of hand performance can be flexibly allocated between the hemispheres, and that there was a degree of inteference between the two tasks being performed. The sustained performance study of digit identification with infrequent responses, however, suggests limits to the flexibility of task organisation between the hemispheres.

The effects of interference, and the corollary effect of activation, have been more recently studied as a method for investigating hemisphere processes. In some paradigms these effects have been considered to operate through the mediation of attentional control. A good discussion of these strategies as well as the evidence which they have educed is to be found in Kinsbourne and Hicks (1978). The addition of a concurrent verbal task to a verbal DVF task has been found to reduce or reverse the RVF advantage to be observed on the DVF task. Geffen *et al.* (1973) found an RVF advantage in a digit-identification task when presented alone, which was preserved with the addition of a secondary music task. Adding a secondary verbal task, however, reversed the asymmetry observed. An RVF advantage was observed over all their conditions by Hellige and Cox (1976), but with the requirement to hold a number of words in memory during performance, the visual field asymmetry decreased. Similarly, Hellige *et al.* (1979) found no effect of concurrent non-verbal memory on word recognition, but the addition of verbal memory load to a name-matching task deleted the RVF superiority otherwise observed.

The evidence from such studies is, however, not unanimous. Hellige (1978) found that an RVF advantage was still to be found when nouns to be held in memory were added as a second task. McCarthy (1980) found an effect of concurrent verbal shadowing on the RVF superiority in double successive physical and nominal matching, and Honda (1977, 1978), although using Japanese letters and subjects, with the attendant problems of interpretation, found verbal load to increase the RVF advantage and non-verbal load to decrease it.

Cohen (1979) has cogently pointed out the considerable difficulties in interpreting dual task studies in her critical paper on Hellige *et al.* (1979). She points to the difficulty of distinguishing shifts in the allocation of attention from changes in the strategies employed by subjects, and demonstrates that the effect of concurrent load is uncertain. Any model which predicts opposite effects, in this case activation or interference, on the basis of parameters which are ill-defined and imperfectly quantified, is bound to be unsatisfactory in its explanation of the effects of what must be most complex interactions.

## Practice

It has frequently been suggested that practice may have an effect upon observed visual field asymmetries, and that the number of experimental trials, which has varied considerably among the different paradigms employed, may play an important role in determining the effects observed. Most studies report that subjects are given a few practice trials, without precise details being given, and the approach to this problem has been unusually casual. Sometimes more formal procedures are reported, like the requirement made by Bradshaw *et al.* (1977a) that subjects write the target five times before each experimental block. Where an unnatural or complex motor response has been demanded a period of teaching the subject to respond accurately has preceded the experimental trials.

A few studies have examined the effect of practice, deliberately, as an aspect of the experimental design. Not all have found a positive effect of practice on the visual field asymmetry observed. Carmon *et al.* (1972) and Jonides (1979) examining practice across four and six separate sessions respectively found an effect of practice upon task performance, but in neither case did this interact with the visual field asymmetry observed.

Other studies have found an effect of practice, which has most commonly been seen as a shift from an initial LVF advantage to a later RVF advantage (Bradshaw and Gates, 1978; Gordon and Carmon, 1976) or as the emergence of an RVF advantage from no asymmetry on early trials (Fennell *et al.*, 1977a).

This general pattern of a rightward shift in the asymmetry was observed as an increase in the RVF superiority across sessions in another condition of the Bradshaw and Gates (1978) study, and across the early sessions of the study by Hellige (1976). Hellige, however, continued his study across nine sessions, and while an LVF advantage was present in session 1 which changed to an RVF advantage on sessions 3 to 5, no asymmetry was to be observed on sessions 6 to 9.

The observation of a decline in the RVF superiority over a period of practice has been observed elsewhere. Shine *et al.* (1972a, b) found that their RVF advantage declined across trials, and Ward and Ross (1977) report that the advantage present on day 1 of the experiment was not to be seen on days 2 or 3.

These reports together suggest a complex effect of practice which is dependent on a range of factors including the nature of the stimuli and task, the difficulty of the task, the familiarity of the material and the experimental paradigm, the compatability of the response, the pattern of trials and rest pauses, and so on. However, there are perhaps two important elements at work. One is the evolving familiarity of the subject with the stimuli and the task, from which follows the adaptation of the subject by the regulation of cognitive strategies. Hence, perhaps, material which is unfamiliar may initially be processed with attention to its spatial and configurational properties (yielding an LVF advantage) which later evolves into a processing mode with important verbal and semantic components (and an RVF advantage). This effect would find a parallel in the report of Silverberg *et al.* (1979) that with degree of experience in a second language there is a similar shift in visual field asymmetry. The second element is an increasing adaptation to the unnatural process of attending to strongly lateralised presentation. One component of this effect is the reduction in task difficulty which inevitably accompanies practice in the task typically employed, but it may also reflect a more fundamental adaptation and rearrangement by which the relatively lateralised nature of the processing systems is modified to compensate for the asymmetry in performance in the two visual fields. The interaction of these two basic elements in the effects of practice goes a long way to explain some of the very complex effects reported (e.g. Klein *et al.*, 1976), but more systematic study is needed before the parameters of the elements of the practice effect can be accurately specified.

## Failures of the Assumption

We began by making the assumption that with tasks which employed verbal stimuli or were of a verbal nature, unilaterally presented to the visual fields, an RVF advantage would be observed. The studies reviewed have shown that despite a great deal of inconsistency, this assumption is reasonable and may also be extended to appropriately controlled bilateral presentation. It is, however, finally worth considering those studies which have not supported our assumption, to ask whether there is some element, or elements, common to them.

Probably the most important single factor is the possibility that although the experimenter regards the stimuli as verbal, the subject processes them by a more direct perceptual strategy. The findings with physical as against nominal matches (Ledlow *et al.*, 1978b; White and White, 1975; Wilkins and Stewart, 1974) as well as the results of Moscovitch (1976), all demonstrate that letters may be processed in this way and be associated with an LVF advantage, or no asymmetry, because of bilateral processing or the interaction of effects attached to both RVF and LVF advantages. Other studies which could be explained by subjects adopting a perceptual processing strategy perhaps include Cohen (1973, 1975b), Gibson *et al.* (1972), Jonides (1979), Metzger and Antes (1976), Seamon (1974) and Umilta *et al.* (1972). That both Metzger and Antes and Seamon found that the RVF advantage could be seen for picture probes, but not for word probes, applied to the retention of previously presented words is entirely in line with this suggestion. Also linked to this explanation are the studies in which the perceptual difficulty or perceptual elements have been deliberately emphasised by the design of the experiment (Bryden and Allard, 1976; Polich, 1978). This manipulation successfully negated the RVF superiority.

Less directly, but also probably associated with the perceptual processing factor, are the findings of Tomlinson-Keasey and Kelly (1979b), which they interpret in terms of the holistic–sequential dichotomy which may in turn be an aspect of the verbal–perceptuospatial distinction. Similarly, Bradshaw *et al.* (1977b) in the results for "same" matches of names, and LeFebvre and Kubose (1975) in initial verbal discrimination learning may have reflected the operation of this kind of strategy.

The second factor is present in experiments which have presented a task of marked perceptual difficulty (Kemp and Haude, 1979) or have presented stimuli which were perceptually degraded (Hellige and Webster, 1979; McGrane, 1977). There is a considerable perceptual component in each of these experiments which may have been of overriding importance. Linked to these studies are three in which unusual presentation displays have not yielded the expected effects. Pitblado *et al.* (1979) found the visual field asymmetry to disappear if a dim pre-exposure field was employed, and Worrall and Coles (1976) found it only at the horizontal meridian and not at other positions in the RVF. Lastly, and most curiously, Marzi *et al.* (1979) found the RVF advantage for letters arranged in an arc about fixation, but not when they were arranged in a matrix. Whether any of these last results are determined by perceptual difficulty is hard to determine, although differential acuity may play some part, as may unusual patterns of scanning the stimulus array.

Thirdly, there are those studies in which scanning of the display may be considered to play a primary role in determining the results. Most of these studies have presented stimuli bilaterally and include Schwantes (1978); Smith and Ramunas (1971); White (1969b, 1973a) and Wolford and Hollingsworth (1974). These findings have already been discussed in the general context of unilateral and bilateral presentation and illustrate the influence of post-exposural scanning patterns, and possibly failure of fixation control within the bilateral presentation paradigm, which may result in no RVF advantage being found. The studies of Boyle (1975) and Klatzky and Atkinson (1971) both, for different reasons, raise some doubts about the adequacy of fixation control and as a consequence less confidence can be placed in their results.

Fourthly, it is worth noting that there are undoubtedly subject variables which influence visual field asymmetries. Sex effects have been reported in some experiments (Hannay and Malone, 1976a; Kail and Siegel, 1978; Scully, 1978) and will be discussed more fully in Chapter 8. The influence of a variable indexed by Verbal Scholastic Aptitude Test scores has already been noted (Kroll and Madden, 1978) and Zoccolotti and Oltman (1978) found no asymmetry for field-dependent subjects, although it was shown for the field-independent subjects. It would be premature to try to assess the extent or significance of such effects. Handedness has been much studied as a variable, presumed to reflect different patterns of cerebral organisation, in the DVF paradigm with most complex results, to be examined in Chapter 9. The influence of practice, and particularly the possibility that asymmetries may disappear with extended practice, has been discussed above.

This leaves a number of studies which do not fit readily into one of the above categories, and in which the failure to find an RVF advantage remains more or less puzzling. It is possible to point to methodological points in each, but not ones peculiar to these studies. It is tempting to fall back upon the possibility of Type I errors and the sampling distribution of results which is to be expected. This is too easy an explanation, although it may be a real factor in some cases. It remains difficult to see why Scheerer (1974) found an effect when cueing with a bar but not with a letter, although concurrent task effects (Hellige *et al.*, 1979) could be invoked. The studies of Amadeo *et al.* (1977), Day (1977), Dimond *et al.* (1972), Hardyck *et al.* (1977, 1978), C. M. Martin (1978), Michaels (1973), Moscovitch (1976), Shanon (1979), White (1970) and Young *et al.* (1979, 1980) all include conditions in which an RVF advantage might have been expected to be produced by verbal stimuli presented for the performance of a fairly clearly verbal task. It seems unlikely that there is any single factor which has yet to be conceived which would provide a single explanation for these failures. The results of DVF experiments are determined by a complex interaction of factors, some yet to be described, and it must be accepted that at present our knowledge of these factors is far from satisfactory. There are, and will continue to be, results which are more or less puzzling, and which may be pointers to the clarification of just what does produce the RVF advantage with verbal stimuli or in verbal tasks.

## Conclusion

The preceding summary of the experimental findings of the past decade fails to do justice to most of the studies to which reference is made. To take only the most highly abstracted findings of a study without attention to the finer points of the experimental design and analysis, the intentions of the experimenter, or the precise theoretical context in which it was conceived is an unreliable and dangerous procedure. I have elsewhere tried to show (Beaumont, 1981) how, in a related area, excessive summarisation has led to invalid conclusions being adopted about that area. However, given that violence has no doubt been done to many of the studies mentioned above, I hope that the relatively confused state of the literature, the paucity of good reviews in depth, and the difficulty of access following the extent of the literature, all justify the kind of summary which has been attempted here.

Given the kind of caution which I think is proper, the following general conclusions seem to be justified:

1. Words, letters, digits, letter strings and nonsense words are all generally associated with an RVF advantage. Semantic and linguistic parameters have not been clearly shown to be related to this effect. The effect is found with horizontal or vertical presentation.
2. The RVF advantage is found for identification, recognition and nominal matching. With physical (or simple identity) matching this effect is not always found and depends upon the cognitive context. The results of high-level lexical and semantic tasks are unclear.
3. Bilateral presentation, given adequate fixation control and control of report order, gives the same results as unilateral presentation. There is no firm evidence that the central item for first report materially effects later processing.
4. The stimulus- and task-dependent asymmetries are to be found with a variety of responses. The RVF advantage is not dependent upon a vocal or right-hand response. Insufficient attention has been paid to the importance of report order.
5. Memory processes are implicated in some, but not all DVF experiments. Memory is undoubtedly an important aspect of DVF asymmetry, but it cannot be the basis for all the effects reported. Similarly, stimulus set size

may be relevant but not fundamental in interpreting the asymmetries observed.

6. Practice is a variable which deserves more study. Sufficient familiarity with the stimuli and task appear important for the RVF advantage to appear, but lengthy practice serves to diminish the magnitude of the asymmetry.

7. There are a host of other relevant variables which contribute to visual field asymmetries. The extent to which perceptuospatial features of the stimulus or task are relevant, or may be used by the subject, may be seen in the reduction or reversal of the RVF advantage. Postexposural scanning of the stimulus array must also be considered, as well as a variety of subject variables.

Undoubtedly the greatest problem attached to all these studies, and one which has not been explored here, is the definition of "verbal" in the nature of the stimuli and the tasks. Attempts to resolve the problem by investigating higher-level linguistic or semantic parameters have not met with clear success, and the essence of the tasks and stimuli which allows them to be classed as "verbal" remains the single greatest question to be explored. Little progress can be expected until some advance towards an answer to this question has been found. Together with the methodological issues which attach to all DVF research, this problem must be resolved before any valid inferences can be drawn about the real significance for models of cerebral organisation of divided visual field asymmetries. Some of the inferences which have been drawn, and the support which they can command, will be discussed in the next chapter.

# 5

## THEORETICAL INTERPRETATIONS OF LATERAL ASYMMETRIES

*Gillian Cohen*

## Introduction

THE PURPOSE of this chapter is to attempt a critical assessment of the various theories of cerebral organisation that have been proposed to account for the many observations of performance asymmetries that are rapidly accumulating. The need for a sound theoretical framework within which to sift, evaluate and interpret these findings, and as a guide for future research, is acute. Yet the construction of an adequate theory becomes more difficult and more complicated as the observed asymmetries ramify. As a first step, therefore, we start by considering the general conditions which a theory of cerebral organisation should fulfil and the criteria by which it should judged.

## *Explanatory Adequacy*

Any theory should be able to account for that subset of observed asymmetries that prove to be reliable, valid and non-trivial. This obvious truth has to be emphasised, at risk of appearing platitudinous, because much of the data which potentially forms the basis for theorising is conflicting. The reasons for the conflicts are not easy to discern. We may suspect that many findings are not replicable, yet it is hardly ever possible to be sure that this is so. Exact replications are rarely undertaken, since the path to glory as a researcher does not lie that way, and the partial replications which are more common are difficult to interpret. When a partial replication conflicts with the original experiment it is often hard to identify the source of the conflict. We do not know whether to discard or to qualify the original observations; whether they were simply wrong, or whether they only hold good for the particular task characteristics, stimulus parameters and subject population employed in that instance. Thus the reliability of a given observation is not easy to assess. Over a period of time support may either build up (as converging partial replications accumulate), or crumble away (as progressive qualifications render the original observation trivial). Until these processes are complete, assessments of reliability are largely intuitive, with the result that the theorist has too much freedom to select those observations that fit neatly into the particular theoretical framework he favours, and to ignore those that do not conform.

Even when observations appear reliable the conclusions drawn from them are not necessarily valid. For instance, sensory and response asymmetries can produce effects which are wrongly attributed to asymmetrical representation of the cognitive functions involved in the task. If a theory is designed as a description of the cerebral organisation of cognitive functions these are not relevant, and must be identified and discounted.

Finally, some of the asymmetries are trivial from the point of view of theory construction because they are uninformative. Typically, these trivial observations arise out of one-shot experiments which simply record a laterality effect for a given task, instead of showing how the laterality effect interacts with characteristics of the task. What is needed, but rarely available, is a careful series of experiments in which laterality effects are observed when each of the relevant variables is systematically manipulated in turn, with the other variables held constant. In the absence of this kind of data, the theorist must collate the findings of similar experiments independently carried out, and try to judge how far it is legitimate to combine the results.

A satisfactory theory, then, must be able to explain the occurrence of performance asymmetries that are seen as reliable, valid and important. Moreover, it should be able to account for the non-occurrence of asymmetries whose absence has been reliably and validly established—a point that is often overlooked.

Over the last decade it has also become increasingly evident that a theory must account not only for the existence of asymmetries, but also for their variability. Left–right differences between the cerebral hemispheres appear to be extremely labile. It is the task of the theorist to distinguish between spurious variability (produced by experimental artefacts) and lawful variability produced by factors which influence performance asymmetries in regular and lawful ways. For any given left–right difference the theory must explain its existence, its direction, its magnitude, and how, why and when it is liable to shift.

Several sources of variability can be identified. First, there is variability between individuals such that different subjects show different patterns of asymmetry. Laterality effects have been reported to vary with the age, sex and handedness of the individual (e.g. Lake and Bryden, 1976), and this kind of variability is generally interpreted as reflecting structural differences in cerebral organisation. Rather more speculatively, individual differences are sometimes attributed to cognitive style—that is, a disposition to adopt a particular processing strategy which effectively changes the cognitive demands of the task. So, for example, individuals who are good readers or high in verbal ability may be supposed to perform a task differently from poor readers or those low in verbal ability. This kind of hypothesis provides a useful catch-all to explain differences between individuals of the same age, sex and handedness. In fact it is quite common to find that, in an apparently homogeneous group of subjects, several individuals show laterality effects opposite to those predicted, or show no asymmetries at all. The custom of publishing group data, rather than individual data, masks the prevalence of these puzzling discrepancies and encourages researchers to ignore them. When attempts are made to explain the performance of these non-conformist individuals, differences in processing strategy are usually invoked, but should not be uncritically accepted without independent evidence for their existence.

A second source of variability stems from differences between experimental paradigms. Asymmetries can shift with small changes in the nature of the stimulus, the difficulty and type of judgment required, the kind of response, and so on. These shifts can usually be reconciled with an existing theory by incorporating the shift-producing factor as an additional element. The theory is expanded to include that factor as a principle that determines the operating of the mechanism. Successive expansions of this kind have led to a great increase in complexity, with the result that theories have become difficult to conceptualise and to apply.

A third kind of variability may occur over time within the same experimental paradigm, and within the performance of the same individual. The observed asymmetries may shift from trial to trial, from block to block and from session to session. To account for this kind of variability it is necessary to assume that factors such as practice, familiarity and fatigue, that are subject to temporal variation, induce changes in either the type of processing performed, or the operation of the mechanism that performs it.

Theoretical accounts of cerebral organisation must do more than conform with the behavioural data. A model of hemisphere asymmetry is essentially a neurological model. While there may sometimes be justification for the common practice of building models of psychological processes (such as memory, or language) without relating them to the neurology of brain mechanisms, a model that is specifically designed as a description of cerebral organisation cannot be at such a level of abstraction. As will be clear in later sections of this chapter, although some current theories place more emphasis on process and some on structure, all of them include either explicit or implicit assumptions about neurological structures, about neural transmission, and about neural mechanisms. These assumptions must therefore conform to the known facts of neurophysiology and neuroanatomy. A theory of cerebral organisation cannot posit mechanisms which violate or omit these facts.

## Predictive Power

Besides accounting for the existing data, an ideal theory should be able to predict the visual field differences and the changes in these differences which would occur under any specified set of conditions. To the extent that a theory fails to do so it is either wrong or incomplete. In practice, the problem is to decide which. So far, theories of cerebral asymmetry are sufficiently loose and imprecise to be easily amended or modified so as to account for findings that run counter to their predictions without sacrificing the theory altogether. The terms of the theory can be redefined, or the experimental conditions re-described, so as to exclude the discrepant results from the scope of the theory. Or the theory can be extended by additional assumptions. In the long run, however, a theory should be capable of disproof. It ought to achieve a degree of precision and completeness such that the terms do not admit of further redefinition and there are no loopholes for further assumptions to be added, so that the theory can be conclusively confirmed or disproved. Psychological theories rarely attain this ideal state, and instead there comes a point in the life-span of a theory when it ceases to be improved by modifications, and begins to disintegrate from excessive tinkering. It is an unfortunate general characteristic of psychological theories that explanatory adequacy seems to be achieved at the expense of predictive power, and this trend has been particularly marked in the development of theories of cerebral organisation.

In the light of these general conditions which a satisfactory theory ought to fulfil, we can go on to examine some particular models in detail. Models of cerebral asymmetry fall mainly into two classes. There are fixed structural and dynamic process models, and these exist in different versions and combinations. The models that are predominantly structural will be considered first.

## Structural Models

### General Characteristics

According to the structural models, asymmetries of cognitive function arise because the brain structures that mediate that function are lateralised to one hemisphere rather than the other. Each hemisphere is specialised for processing certain kinds of material, or performing certain kinds of cognitive operations. Stimuli presented to one side of the body project directly to the contralateral hemisphere (the hemisphere of entry) and, accordingly, performance is superior when the hemisphere of entry is the locus of the structures specialised for the kind of processing required. The job gets done best when it is fed directly into the right machinery. These assumptions are common to all versions of a structural model. It is worthwhile, therefore, to consider some of the general implications of this class of models before considering the particular implications of specific versions.

Structural models imply the existence of anatomical differences. So where anatomical differences can be discerned, these would tend to confirm the existence of a structural basis for performance asymmetries. The evidence is rendered much more powerful if it can be shown that individuals with reversed performance asymmetries (such as some left-handers display) also have reversed anatomical asymmetries. Left–right anatomical differences have been reported for some brain areas that are not obviously related to functional asymmetries. However where (a) neuroanatomical asymmetries are found in brain areas known to be crucial for functions that exhibit performance asymmetries (such as language tasks), and (b) the pattern of anatomical asymmetry is correlated with some factor such as handedness, which affects functional asymmetry, there is strong support for a structural model. The evidence presented by Geschwind and Levitsky (1968), and reviewed by Witelson (1977d), showed that in the temporal lobe the planum temporale is about 40% larger in the left hemisphere in 70% of individuals. This region is part of Wernicke's area which is critically involved in language comprehension. Moreover, measurements of this area by means of arteriograms showed strong correlations with handedness (Hochberg and LeMay, 1975), and with speech lateralisation as indicated by sodium amytal testing (Ratcliff *et al.*, 1978). There is good reason, therefore, to claim that these structural neuroanatomical differences are linked with, and may causally determine, functional asymmetries.

Structural models can be divided according to the *degree* of specialisation and according to the *nature* of the specialisation that is postulated. The degree of specialisation may be either absolute or relative. The nature of the specialisation hypothesised also varies. The difference between the hemispheres may be conceptualised in terms of specialisation for different classes of stimuli, specialisation for different processes, or specialisation for different stages of processing. Structural models generate different implications depending on the degree and nature of specialisation postulated (see Fig. 1).

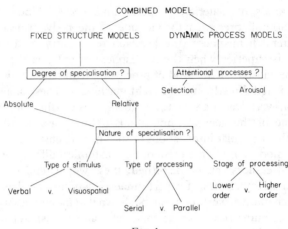

FIG. 1.

## *Degrees of Specialisation*

### A. The absolute specialisation model

According to the absolute specialisation model, lateralisation of a given function is complete. Only the hemisphere specialised for that function can perform it. A number of predictions follow from this assumption.

(i) Following hemispherectomy the functions lateralised to the excised hemisphere should be completely lost.

This prediction is subject to several qualifications, however. The after-effects of hemispherectomies performed in childhood, or resulting from traumas incurred in childhood, must be excluded from consideration since atypical reorganisation of function can occur in these cases. Also, we cannot exclude the possibility that after any hemispherectomy residual functions may be reflecting the operation of subcortical mechanisms.

(ii) Following commissurotomy, a task could be performed only if the stimuli are presented directly to the hemisphere specialised for that task, but again, this prediction is subject to the same qualifications as (i) above.

(iii) In normal subjects, performance should invariably be faster and/or more accurate when the stimuli are channelled directly to the appropriate hemisphere.

(iv) The difference between the time taken for a given task when the stimuli are channelled directly to the specialist hemisphere, and when stimuli are channelled to the inappropriate, non-specific hemisphere, represents the time taken for the stimuli to be transmitted across the corpus callosum—the interhemispheric transfer time (IHTT). This difference should be fairly constant, and of a magnitude consistent with neural transmission time.

(v) Physiological measures of ongoing brain activity should reveal increased activity within the hemisphere specialised for a given task during performance of that task without a concomitant increase of activity in the other hemisphere.

It is not the intention of this chapter to review evidence in detail, but merely to indicate the kind of evidence that is crucial, and to cite a few instances of it. However, before we can decide how well the predictions are borne out, we must specify the nature of the specialisation—we must define the functions that are supposed to be absolutely lateralised. For the purposes of argument, we will consider the version of the structural model which characterises left and right hemispheres as specialised for verbal and visuospatial functions respectively. In terms of this version of the model, how do the predictions fare?

(i) Although it is true that the effects of left and right hemispherectomies are clearly dissociated, with left hemispherectomy producing severe impairment of language abilities while leaving non-verbal visuospatial skills intact, it is nevertheless not true that the language function is always completely lost. The residual language ability that may be retained in right-handed adults may represent the performance of the right hemisphere (RH), but in most of these cases childhood traumas could have caused abnormal reorganisation. Voluntary speech is mostly confined to single words or short phrases, and the production of propositional speech is very limited, but has been observed (Zaidel, 1973). Comprehension is less severely impaired than production. Patients may be able to follow verbal instructions, and to give yes/no answers to questions (Gott, 1973). On this evidence, a model whereby the language function, globally defined, is completely reserved to the left hemisphere (LH) appears unlikely.

(ii) A similar conclusion is enforced by the evidence of RH language ability in split-brain patients. When verbal stimuli are presented to the RH, the patient can pick out objects corresponding to names or descriptions (Gazzaniga and Sperry, 1967). The RH is apparently able to recognise some concrete nouns and adjectives though comprehension of verbs, function words and syntactic relations is much more limited. Nevertheless, Milner et al. (1968) reported instances of the left hand carrying out instructions presented to the left ear. While the disconnected RH appears incapable of producing spoken responses and performing phonological matching tasks, it cannot, on this evidence, be characterised as totally alinguistic. But again the reservation must be made that these cases most probably involved abnormal reorganisation of the brain prior to the commissurotomy (see also Chapter 10).

(iii) In normals, the predicted right visual field (RVF) superiority for verbal material is usually, but not invariably, obtained. In divided visual field (DVF) studies it is estimated that only 70% of individuals who appear to have LH dominance for language on the basis of sodium amytal tests, exhibit the predicted RVF advantage, and in dichotic listening studies only between 65 and 85% of such subjects shown a right ear advantage (REA) (Searleman, 1977). Furthermore, although the scores of a given individual may yield a statistical advantage for the RVF over an experimental series, the visual field (VF) superiority may fluctuate from trial to trial, and from block to block. The performance asymmetry is not uniform across subjects and not constant within subjects. Laterality shifts within subjects (e.g. Ward and Ross, 1977, and Klein *et al.*, 1976) cannot be accounted for by a fixed structural model. While the model can handle between-subject variability where this takes the form of opposite asymmetries, it cannot account for graded differences between individuals.

(iv) Problems arise if differences in reaction time for left and right stimulus presentation are attributed solely to IHTT. First, the obtained differences tend to be too large. Estimates of neural transmission time using neurophysiological methods range from 3 to 15 ms. Ledlow (1976) recorded the onset latencies of evoked potentials for direct and indirect projection. The direct–indirect difference, which corresponds to IHTT, averaged 15 ms. In DVF studies the reaction-time (RT) difference for behavioural responses is commonly much larger, often in excess of 50 ms. These large left–right differences must therefore be reflecting factors other than IHTT. It is also difficult to reconcile the variability in left–right RT differences with a crossing-time explanation. It has been suggested that crossing-time need not be constant, but may vary with the complexity of the stimuli to be transmitted, but experimental data do not give much support for this assumption. For example, Cohen (1973) reported results from an experiment where the stimulus consisted of either 2, 3 or 4 letters, but the left–right difference diminished as stimulus complexity increased (114 ms for 2 letters, 63 ms for 3 letters, 33 ms for 4 letters). It has also be suggested by Carmon *et al.* (1972) that IHTT may vary with the degree of eccentricity of lateralised stimuli, since more peripheral stimuli project to areas connected by less densely innervated interhemispheric paths. Carmon *et al.* tested this claim by systematically plotting RTs for stimuli presented at locations ranging from 1° to 8° from fixation, but found no change in the left–right difference. In short, the absolute specialisation model has difficulty in accounting for left–right differences in reaction times.

Another problem also arises out of the assumption that stimuli entering the inappropriate hemisphere are transferred to the other hemisphere for processing. The model is incomplete in that some important aspects of this job-allocation mechanism are left vague and unspecified. Logically, there are several possibilities. (a) Automatic Transfer—all incoming stimuli are automatically transmitted to both hemispheres: first to the hemisphere of entry, and then to the other hemisphere via the corpus callosum. Both hemispheres receive the input but only the specialised hemisphere can perform the task. (b) Conditional Transfer—a sorting mechanism exists whereby incoming stimuli are classified and directed to the appropriate hemisphere. Again, only the specialist hemisphere attempts the task. (c) According to another version of Conditional Transfer, the hemisphere of entry processes as far as it is able, and transfer to the other hemisphere takes place if and when it fails to complete the task.

The different alternatives listed above carry different implications. While in version (a) performance asymmetries have a precategorical locus, in versions (b) and (c) they are necessarily postcategorical in origin. Version (c) involves some wasteful duplication of effort since the non-specialist hemisphere attempts tasks it cannot perform. Version (b) involves some duplication of mechanisms, since each hemisphere must be equipped with a mechanism of classifying incoming stimuli and routeing traffic accordingly. Version (c) requires some mechanism for deciding when processing has failed. In both (b) and (c), where transfer is not automatic, RT differences may reflect not only crossing time but "decision-to-transfer" time as well, which may explain why the left–right difference is larger and more variable than would be predicted from crossing-time alone.

It is important to consider these various alternatives when trying to analyse left–right differences in error incidence. The general finding is that errors increase when the hemisphere of entry is not the appropriate hemisphere. It is often claimed that these errors arise because information transmitted across the callosal path suffers degradation in transit, so that the input the specialist hemisphere receives from the indirect path is noisy or degraded. However, it is not altogether plausible to suppose that stimuli can travel intact from the sense organ to the cortex, but not from one hemisphere to the other. An alternative explanation of the error asymmetry is that these errors are the output of the non-specialist hemisphere responding on the basis of precategorical or in-complete processing. These alternatives and their consequences are spelt out in some detail here to show how the usefulness of a model is vitiated when it is incomplete or has areas of vagueness.

(v) Physiological measures of brain activity include monitoring EEG pat-terns, measuring evoked potentials and blood-flow changes. Several studies have shown that alpha activity increases relatively more in the non-specialist hemisphere during performance of a given cognitive task (e.g. Morgan et al., 1974), and that the magnitude of the right–left ratio can predict the level of performance achieved (Furst, 1976). Similarly, visually evoked responses have been shown to differ in left and right hemispheres depending on the nature of the task (e.g. Wood et al., 1971; and see Chapter 7). Recent methods of monitoring regional changes in cerebral blood flow (rCBF) during perfor-mance of a cognitive task (described by Lassen et al., 1978) have produced evidence of asymmetrical functioning. Blood flow increases differentially so that, for instance, during verbal reasoning blood flow increases in both hemispheres with a relatively greater increase in the LH. A non-verbal perceptual task produced the opposite pattern with a greater increase in the RH (Risberg, 1980). However, a common feature of these results is that the non-specialist hemisphere is not wholly inactive. Lassen *et al.* found that, during speaking and reading, RH activity mirrored LH activity though on a smaller scale. That is, corresponding regions of both hemispheres became active, but the increase above the base resting level was smaller in the RH. We cannot be certain, though, whether the increased blood flow in the non-specialist hemisphere reflects cognitive activity, or whether it is simply a by-product of symmetrical vascular organisation.

Although not conclusive, there is a considerable weight of evidence against a model which assumes that globally defined functions such as verbal processing or visuospatial processing are exclusively performed by one hemisphere.

## B. The relative specialisation model

According to this type of model, the degree of specialisation of function is not absolute but relative. Cognitive functions are not wholly lateralised to one hemisphere or the other. Both hemispheres can perform a given function, but one hemisphere is more efficient (faster and more accurate) than the other. Again we must define the nature of the hypothesised specialisation before we can assess the model. If specialisation is defined in terms of verbal functions and visuospatial functions, the following predictions can be made.

(i) Following hemispherectomy the functions of the missing hemisphere should not be wholly lost, but inefficient performance mediated by the remaining hemisphere should be retained.

(ii) In the split-brain patients, the non-specialist hemisphere (that is, the hemisphere normally inferior for a given task) should be able to perform, although inefficiently.

(iii) In normals, performance should be faster and more accurate when stimuli are channelled to the specialist hemisphere, and slower and less accurate when stimuli are directed to the non-specialist hemisphere. According to this model it is usually assumed that a task is performed within the hemisphere of entry, and the difference in measures of performance represents the difference in levels of efficiency, not the effects of crossing over. It follows that the magnitude of the difference may vary as a function of task difficulty; the more difficult the task the more inadequate the performance of the non-specialist hemisphere, and the greater the observed asymmetry.

(iv) Individuals may vary in the extent of the difference in efficiency between hemispheres. Genetic and maturational factors could produce varying degrees of specialisation, just as individuals vary in their ability to use the non-preferred hand, with consequent differences in between-hand measures.

It is not easy to determine how well the findings fit these predictions. In general the model appears to be imprecise, rather than to be conclusively disproved.

(i) and (ii) As already noted, the RH of a split-brain or of a left-hemispherectomised patient is not just worse at language tasks in an overall sort of way. Rather it appears capable of performing some language tasks (mainly comprehension), while other language abilities such as the production of propositional speech, and naming of words and objects may be completely absent.

(iii) The assumption that a task is performed within the hemisphere of entry, a No Transfer model, may not be justified. If transfer is automatic, the specialist hemisphere may "race" the non-specialist hemisphere, and output the response if its superiority is sufficient to compensate for the delay imposed by transfer. Alternatively, conditional transfer might take place if and when the hemisphere of entry fails to complete the task. In DVF studies with normals, the prediction that observed asymmetries should vary when aspects of the task that affect the difficulty are manipulated, receives some support. The clearest effects have been obtained from manipulations of stimulus quality. Several experiments have reported that VF differences are produced, or enhanced, when the stimulus is degraded by masking. Moscovitch et al. (1976) reported an LVF advantage in a face-recognition task in a masked condition, with little or no VF difference when the faces were unmasked. Hellige (1976) obtained very similar results in a study where subjects had to recognise polygon shapes under masked and unmasked conditions. Ward and Ross (1977) noted that the RVF superiority for recognition of degraded single letters disappeared as subjects became more practised at the task, which may reflect progressive reduction of difficulty. Manipulations of stimulus duration (e.g. Rizzolatti and Buchtel, 1977) have shown similar effects, with VF differences more marked at shorter stimulus durations. However, not all task manipulations that might be expected to increase the difficulty of the task have the effect of increasing the performance asymmetry. Patterson and Bradshaw (1975) examined asymmetries in a same/different face-discrimination task. When the faces differed on 3 features (an easy discrimination) there was an LVF advantage, but when the task was made more difficult by having the faces differ on only one feature, the asymmetry shifted instead of increasing, and an RVF advantage was obtained. And, as already noted, in Cohen's (1973) experiment, increasing the number of stimulus elements may reduce, rather than enhance, the VF difference. Similarly, Hardyck et al. (1978) found that VF differences are larger for a small set of frequently repeated stimuli than for a large set of infrequently repeated stimuli, although the latter ought, surely, to be more difficult. These contrary results underline the fact that "task difficulty" is an ill-defined concept. For all the manipulations considered above, it is arguable that what is changed by the manipulation is not the level of difficulty, but the nature of the task. So, for example, stimulus degradation may necessitate a different kind of processing such as the extraction of higher-order features, involving the operation of the specialised letter-feature, or face-feature processors which are asymmetrically represented. So we must conclude that the evidence is equivocal, and this ambiguity may be impossible to resolve. To date, at least, it has not been conclusively shown that the superiority of the more efficient hemisphere is more evident as task difficulty increases.

(iv) While the model can explain individual differences in asymmetries as due to differing degrees of specialisation, the low correlations obtained between various measures of lateralisation (such as handedness, VF differences and dichotic listening) (Bryden, 1965) are hard to explain. Fixed structures specialised to perform particular cognitive functions at fixed levels of efficiency should yield more highly correlated results.

Furthermore, the model has difficulty in accounting for within-task trial-to-trial variability. Although, as we have noted in section (iii) above, changes in laterality patterns that occur progressively, over extended series of trials, may perhaps be attributed to changes in the subjective difficulty of the task, the kind of back-and-forth fluctuations that are often observed cannot be explained in this way.

On the whole, then, the findings do not conclusively refute the relative specialisation model, but neither do they conform at all closely to its predictions. A major difficulty arising out of relative specialisation models is that only the No Transfer version allows us to infer which hemisphere performed the task. Neither the Automatic Transfer, nor the Conditional Transfer versions permit such an inference. Neither the absolute nor the relative version of the structural model appears to be wholly satisfactory. However, both can be radically altered if different *kinds* of specialisation are entertained. Instead of degrees of specialisation for verbal and visuospatial processing, a number of other forms of specialisation have been proposed.

## Forms of Specialisation

### A. Specialisation for types of processing

The ideal that each hemisphere is specialised for a characteristic type of processing, irrespective of the nature of the stimulus, has gained some credence. LH-processing is variously characterised as sequential, serial, temporal or analytic; RH-processing as parallel, gestalt or holistic. There has been a tendency to treat these distinctions as much of a muchness, which of course, they are not. There has also been a tendency for researchers to employ the self-validating technique of classifying processes as, say, analytic or holistic, so as to make an obtained laterality pattern fit the theory without any independent evidence that the classification is valid. Some of the empirical evidence is therefore unconvincing. (See Bradshaw and Nettleton, 1981, for a detailed review.)

Several researchers (e.g. Efron, 1963a; Lomas and Kimura, 1976 and Carmon and Nachshon, 1971) have obtained results showing LH mediation of judgments of temporal order and the production of temporal sequences. This form of specialisation ties in neatly with LH superiority for language skills, since temporal ordering is crucial for those language abilities, such as production and syntax, that are most clearly under LH control. It is still unclear, however, whether these language skills depend on temporal processing, or whether temporal processing depends on language, so we cannot say which form of specialisation derives from the other. The LH superiority as a temporal processor does not appear to extend to haptic information (since, for example, braille is usually read better with the left hand; Hermelin and O'Connor, 1971), or to music where a left-ear superiority is often found.

Experiments which examine the pattern of RT asymmetries when varying numbers of features need to be processed have sometimes yielded results consistent with the characterisation of the LH as a serial, analytic processor and the RH as holistic, parallel or gestalt. Cohen (1973) found that for letter arrays (but not for shape arrays) LH RTs showed a typical serial processing pattern increasing with the number of elements to be processed, while RH RTs did not, but this result has proved difficult to replicate. Patterson and Bradshaw (1975) found an LH advantage for judging two faces to be different when only one feature differed. Since "same" responses were slower than "different" responses, they concluded that the LH carried out serial, analytic feature-matching terminating when a difference was detected, or when all the features had been matched. Thus, in their study there is at least some independent evidence for the hypothesised type of processing. Note, however, that when studies reflect a serial/non-serial dichotomy, it is not necessarily an analytic/holistic one, since RH performance could be parallel rather than holistic, and parallel processing is still feature-analytic.

As evidence that the RH is a holistic processor it has been pointed out that in patients with unilateral lesions of the LH, drawings of objects typically preserve global outline but lack detail. Nebes (1971) has also found that subjects were better able to guess the shape of an entire form after palpating a segment with the left hand than with the right hand. How legitimately "holistic processing" can be inferred from these findings is doubtful. They do indicate differences in the way items are remembered and reconstructed from memory, but the exact nature of the difference is difficult to capture.

Support for the classification of processes as analytic or holistic is similarly inadequate in a study by Bever and Chiarello (1974). They found that musically trained subjects showed opposite ear asymmetries to musically naive subjects in recognising musical sequences. They argued that the RH advantage of the naive subjects reflected holistic or gestalt processing, while the trained subjects perceived the sequence analytically and so displayed an LH advantage. As evidence for this interpretation they pointed out that only the musically trained subjects could recognise single tones from the sequences, but their explanation is weakened by the fact that these subjects showed no ear asymmetry for single-tone recognition. In another study, Bever *et al.* (1976) claimed that the finding of an LH advantage for recognition of an initial phoneme, but not for a whole CVC syllable, stems from the fact that analytic processing is required to identify an initial phoneme, but syllables are recognised holistically. The fact that the syllables were detected faster than the phonemes was taken as evidence that they were processed holistically, while the phonemes were said to require analytic decomposition. This interpretation is not the only possible one. The target phoneme was a stop consonant and it is common to find laterality effects for stop consonants, but not for vowels (Darwin and Baddeley, 1974). Although the target syllable could not be identified solely by its vowel, the presence of the vowel might still have influenced the laterality effect.

Attempts to make all the evidence fit a characterisation of left and right hemispheres in terms of serial, analytic or parallel holistic processing leaves many performance asymmetries unaccounted for. While this model is consistent with some degree of between-subject variability, and between-task variability, it does not predict within-task variability unless additional assumptions about strategy changes are made.

B.  Specialisation for stages of processing

Another class of models postulates that the two hemispheres are specialised for particular stages of processing, rather than for types of processing, or for types of stimuli. These models seek to identify the locus of specialisation by establishing the presence/absence of laterality effects at different stages. There are again different versions of the stage model. These are the Component Operations model (suggested by Cohen, 1977); the Information Processing Model (associated with Moscovitch, 1979); and a Levels of Processing Model which is very similar to the Information Processing one. The major difference between these versions of the stage model is along a specificity–generality dimension. The Component Operations model relates to the processing operations specific to a particular task, such as visual analysis, phonological analysis and semantic analysis in word recognition. The Information Processing model distinguishes between stages such as perception, categorisation, memory and response that are common to most tasks. The Levels of Processing version is also general in that it seeks to allocate asymmetries to higher (or deeper) levels of processing, as opposed to lower (or shallower) levels. An unsatisfactory aspect of all these models is that they implicitly or explicitly endorse a sequential, hierarchical, view of processing, in which asymmetries arise at some point in the sequence, and are transmitted to subsequent stages. This view is at variance with current models of cognitive processing which emphasise the heterarchical, interactive nature of cognitive organisation. Moscovitch (1979) acknowledges this difficulty, but appears to believe it is possible to reconcile stage models with heterarchical organisation, while giving little idea of how this could be achieved. It seems evident that if asymmetries actually do originate at a given stage, but may (on the heterarchical model) be transmitted upwards and downwards, a clear localisation of the point of origin is not to be expected. This difficulty constitutes a serious weakness in stage models, since they cannot be tested unless stages are functionally separable.

(i)  The Component Operations Model partly escapes this criticism since no assumptions are necessarily made about order of processing. Asymmetries are considered to arise because a particular operation which is a component of the total task is lateralised to one hemisphere or the other. The model is not concerned with specifying whether a given operation occurs early or late in the chain of processing, or whether it is a higher-order or a lower-order process. Simply, overall asymmetries are seen as the product of component asymmetries which may, in a multistage task, accumulate or cancel out. It is clear, however, that overall asymmetries cannot be predicted from component asymmetries unless the pattern of interaction, and the relative contribution of different stages, is known. The best evidence for component-operation asymmetries comes from letter- and word-recognition studies where, to a limited extent, techniques exist for achieving some degree of functional separation of stages. A number of studies have yielded converging evidence that judgments based on physical characteristics (e.g. matching for visual identity) show little asymmetry, while judgments based on nominal analysis, or phonological analysis (e.g. naming, name comparison, rhyming judgments) yield evidence of LH lateralisation (see, for example, Cohen, 1972; Geffen et al., 1972; Cohen and Freeman, 1978). The relationship between hemispheric asymmetry and semantic analysis is more variable. LH superiority is usually apparent (Bradshaw, 1974; Klein and Smith cited in Moscovitch, 1979), but semantic disorders may arise with right-sided lesions (Lesser, 1974), and split-brain patients can make some semantic judgments about stimuli presented to the RH.

The Component Operations model of specialisation, whereby hemispheres are specialised for particular stages of verbal processing, appears more convincing than a model which assumes that all aspects of verbal processing are lateralised to the same hemisphere and to the same extent. Different component stages may be lateralised to a greater or lesser degree and the degree of lateralisation may vary between individuals. The model can explain between-task variability as reflecting changes in the contribution of the components to the overall asymmetry. But lateralisation of stages cannot explain within-task variability without invoking changes of strategy—a feature of the dynamic models discussed below.

(ii) Information Processing and Levels of Processing models are sufficiently similar to be treated together. These models rely on techniques designed to identify the locus of specialisation by decomposing tasks into successive stages or levels. The accuracy of the conclusions therefore depends on the precision with which the technique can isolate the stages, as well as the evidence for asymmetry. The general trend has been to assign asymmetries to late, but not early stages of processing; to memory, but not perception; to postcategorical, but not precategorical stages; to higher-order, but not lower-order processing. These distinctions do, of course, partly overlap.

The claim that asymmetries are absent in purely perceptual tasks, but originate in memory-dependent operations, receives some empirical support but is weakened by the difficulty of partitioning perceptual and memorial stages. Experiments have shown that asymmetries are absent in simultaneous matching tasks, and in successive matching when the target stimulus precedes the test stimulus by only a very brief interval, but emerge in successive matching over longer intervals (Moscovitch *et al.*, 1976). It is argued that in simultaneous comparisons the role of memory is minimal, and in successive matching across brief intervals the test stimulus is compared with a visual trace of the target still available in iconic storage (a sensory representation), rather than with a memory representation. However, not all experimental results have conformed to this pattern. A more conservative conclusion, that asymmetries increase with greater memory involvement, might be easier to justify than the claim that they are confined to memory processes. It is in any case impossible to disentangle increasing memory involvement from increasing task difficulty (see p. 97) and it may be the level of difficulty that is crucial in producing performance asymmetries.

Other stage distinctions that have been offered overlap both with the perception/memory distinction, and with each other. Stages characterised as perceptual may also be classified as early, precategorical and lower-order. Evidence suggests that performance asymmetries are usually absent or weak for judgments based on sensory features such as colour, brightness or pitch (Berlucchi *et al.*, 1971), although contrary results are reported by Davidoff (1975a, 1976). Identification of vowel sounds, and simultaneous comparisons of letters and shapes are similarly considered to be precategorical, and based on lower-order physical information. In contrast, recognition of letters and consonant phonemes depend on higher-order categorical features, invoke memory representations, and exhibit performance asymmetries. Tasks designed to interrogate early stages of processing such as iconic storage by means of a partial report technique have produced conflicting results, probably attributable to differences of experimental design. Cohen's (1976) experiment showed signs of slightly superior iconic persistence in the RH, but Marzi *et al.* (1979) found no evidence of this. They found an LVF partial report advantage for lines, and an RVF advantage for letters, but decay rates were similar for both VFs, so the asymmetries were attributed to the later stages of categorisation, or rate of encoding from the icon, while the characteristics of the icon itself showed no lateral asymmetry.

Several experimenters have demonstrated that peripheral masking, which disrupts early, precategorical, stages of processing, does not produce asymmetrical effects, while central masking, which interrupts higher-order, categorical processing, does produce asymmetries (e.g. Moscovitch *et al.*, 1976; Ward and Ross, 1977). According to their interpretation, these higher-order processes are asymmetrically represented, and therefore the critical SOA (stimulus onset asynchrony), at which the stimulus escapes the mask, is shorter in the specialist hemisphere because processing is completed faster. While the RH is specialised for processing higher-order features of faces and shapes, the LH is specialised for higher-order features of letters and words, so the direction of the asymmetry revealed by masking should depend on the nature of the stimulus. Moscovitch *et al.*, found that central masking of face stimuli did produce an RH advantage, and Hellige (1976) reported that in a polygon-matching task, masking induced a similar shift to RH superiority. Hellige, however, also found that superiority shifted to the RH when letters were masked in a letter-recognition task. In contrast with the position adopted by Moscovitch *et al.*, he concludes that higher-order features of all visual stimuli are asymmetrically represented in the RH. Hellige's results conflict with those obtained by Ward and Ross, since they found that masking produced an LH superiority in a letter-recognition task. A further puzzle is raised by their results, since they found that the mask-induced LH advantage disappeared with practice, although it would be expected that extraction of higher-order features should improve with practice. Since changing the set of target letters failed to reinstate the waning superiority of the LH, it is difficult to interpret the initial asymmetry in terms of differential ability to utilise critical features.

These inconsistencies are impossible to reconcile at present. Masking effects could, anyway, be due to increased difficulty instead of a change in the nature of the feature processors employed. The claim that mask-induced asymmetries reflect a shift towards higher-order processing requires evidence of a qualitative change, such as a change in the kind of confusion errors, if it is to be substantiated. Although the information-processing approach appears to offer precision in the characterisation of hemisphere specialisation, the results so far obtained are too inconsistent to be very illuminating. Three reasons can be suggested for the inconsistency of the findings. First, it may be misguided to envisage cognitive processes as divisible into discrete stages. Secondly, even if this approach were theoretically justified, technical methods may be inadequate to allow separate interrogation of the stages. And, thirdly, the conceptual distinctions being made are perhaps insufficiently well-defined.

## Dynamic Models

### General Characteristics

It is the contention of this chapter that no version of a fixed structural model can adequately account for the observed variability of performance asymmetries, especially the trial-to-trial variability that occurs within a given subject's performance on a given task. To extend the power of the structural model so as to explain this kind of variability, it is necessary to postulate some form of dynamic mechanism which controls or influences the functioning of fixed structures. Dynamic models therefore represent an extension or amplification of structural models, rather than a distinct alternative. Although an increase in explanatory power is achieved by marrying structural and dynamic models, there is a corresponding loss of predictive power because the principles which govern the dynamic mechanism are not at present sufficiently well specified.

Some researchers (e.g. Hellige *et al.*, 1979) have tended to divide dynamic models into two different kinds: attentional models and strategy models. It seems preferable, however, and more in line with current theories of attention, to incorporate strategy selection within an attentional model rather than regarding it as a completely different mechanism. According to this formulation there are two different kinds of attentional processes which can interact with hemisphere specialisation, and influence resulting performance asymmetries. Processes of selection govern the allocation of capacity, and processes of arousal, or activation, govern the amount of capacity available. The two factors are not independent since the particular strategy selected may dictate how much capacity is available for a particular operation, and the amount of capacity available may, in turn, dictate the optimal strategy.

### The Attentional Model

An attentional model of lateral asymmetries has been proposed by Kinsbourne (1970, 1973, 1975), and has undergone some modifications. Although this model is incomplete in several respects, it is still sufficiently well-defined to generate predictions which have been tested in numerous experiments, so that an empirical assessment of the model can be undertaken. Experimental testing has also served to reveal those areas where the model is vague or equivocal.

The attentional model recognises that the observed asymmetries derived from structural specialisation should be small and constant. It accounts for the greater magnitude and variability that is generally observed in terms of the fluctuation of attention. Increased allocation of attention to a given hemisphere induces perceptual selection for contralateral stimuli projecting to that hemisphere, and enhanced power, or processing capacity within that hemisphere. The asymmetries imposed by structural specialisation may therefore be increased, diminished, cancelled or even reversed, depending on the relative allocation of attention between the hemispheres. Such a combined structural–dynamic model clearly has the explanatory power to accommodate any observed pattern of asymmetry, or change in asymmetry. If it is to have predictive power, however, it must state the laws that govern the allocation of attention. Some of these laws have been formulated and tested. For example, several factors are supposed to prime or activate a given hemisphere by increasing the allocation of attention to it.

(i) *Priming for Stimulus Location.* Experimental subjects may focus attention on a particular stimulus source. In dichotic listening, for example, a subject can selectively attend to left or right ear inputs. Similarly in DVF experiments, subjects can orient attention towards the LVF or RVF (see Posner, 1980, for a review of evidence for attention shifts in the absence of eye movements) and improve performance in the attended field. If stimulus location is predictable, subjects orient attention to the predicted location. Even if location is unpredictable, subjects may adopt a strategy of orienting toward the most difficult VF in order to optimise overall performance, thereby reducing VF asymmetries due to structural specialisation. Although this possibility has not been formally investigated, informal reports of subjects suggest it may be prevalent.

(ii) *Priming for Stimulus Type.* Several experimental results (e.g. Cohen, 1975b; Spellacy and Blumstein, 1970) support the assumption that foreknowledge of the type of stimulus to be presented can prime the appropriate hemisphere so that, for example, an LH superiority for words and letters is more marked if verbal stimuli are expected, and a verbal "set" has been formed. How this improvement is achieved is not clear. There are several possibilities. Expectancy for a particular type of stimulus may allow preselection of an appropriate processing strategy such as the use of critical features, holistic matching, or covert naming, which engages functions that are asymmetrically represented. Or it may increase the power and processing capacity by arousing the hemisphere appropriate for the type of stimulus. Or, as Kinsbourne suggests, it may produce a perceptual orientation to the VF contralateral to the appropriate hemisphere. It has not proved easy to devise ways of testing between these alternatives, so the exact nature and locus of the priming effect is still not well understood. Kinsbourne's theory, locating the effect at a peripheral stage (perceptual orientation) predicts that the VF contralateral to the activated hemisphere should yield best performance, and there should be a gradient of diminishing attention across the whole VF, with poorest performance in the ipsilateral VF, and an intermediate level of performance in the central visual field (CVF). Although Kinsbourne himself reported results conforming to this pattern, Hellige *et al.* (1979) found CVF trials were superior in both primed and unprimed conditions, a result more consistent with a central priming effect operating at later stages of processing.

Questions as to how far priming is under conscious voluntary control, and how far it is an unconscious and automatic process likewise remain unanswered. Insofar as priming affects selection of strategy, it may be voluntary, but insofar as it affects capacity by arousal mechanisms, it is more likely to be automatic.

Although the model predicts that when none of the factors that produce asymmetrical distribution of attention are present any observed VF asymmetry can only be due to structural specialisation, and should be negligibly small, this has not always been the case. Berlucchi *et al.* (1974) found an RH advantage for face recognition and an LH advantage for letter recognition in a mixed series of faces and letters where no expectancy for type of stimulus could be formed. Goodglass and Calderon (1977) also obtained simultaneous opposite asymmetries for superimposed tones and digits. So significant asymmetries do sometimes emerge which cannot be explained by an attentional model, and which suggest that the contribution of structural factors is larger than attentional theorists allow.

Testing of the model is made more difficult by the fact that manipulation of expectancies may not be successful if subjects fail to form the appropriate set. In addition to a laterality shift, some independent evidence that an effective set has been established is required.

Studies of priming effects generally make the assumption that the hemisphere of entry performs the task. Although, as we have noted already, this assumption may be unjustified, alternative versions render the interpretation of priming effects even more complex.

(iii) *Priming by Practice.* The effects of practice on lateral asymmetries are very variable. Asymmetry may be initially absent and appear with practice (Perl and Haggard, 1975); it may change direction so that the initial asymmetry reverses with practice (e.g. Sidtis and Bryden, 1978, who found ear superiority for *tones* reversed from right to left, while ear superiority for *words* reversed from left to right); or asymmetry may wane with prolonged practice and disappear (Kallman and Corballis, 1975; Ward and Ross, 1977). It is quite possible to claim that these shifts represent the development of a strategy, a change of strategy, or a change in the level of activation with arousal or fatigue. However, as yet no clear principles have emerged which allow the direction of the practice effect to be predicted, and, consequently, any explanation offered is *ad hoc*.

(iv) *Priming by Concurrent Task*. A further principle of the attentional model is that the level of activation in a hemisphere may be increased by a concurrent task which engages or loads that hemisphere, and that performance asymmetry in the primary task will be enhanced in favour of the loaded hemisphere. The clearest evidence in support of this prediction comes from Kinsbourne's (1973) study in which subjects who were required to detect the location of a gap in a square showed an RVF advantage when the LH was loaded by a concurrent task (holding a string of words in memory), and an LVF advantage when the RH was loaded (by holding a melody in memory). Other studies have confirmed the priming effect of a verbal memory load (e.g. Hellige and Cox, 1976), but some have produced conflicting results, raised new questions, or suggested necessary qualifications.

Evidence of RH-priming by non-verbal concurrent tasks has generally proved harder to obtain. Hellige *et al.* (1979) failed to elicit a priming effect by imposing a spatial memory load, and suggested that priming effects may be confined to the LH. In contrast, Hines (1978) found that a non-verbal central fixation stimulus slightly increased LVF superiority for recognition of faces, while a verbal fixation stimulus had no priming effect on recognition of words. He concluded that "attentional set is at best a minor influence on RVF asymmetry for words". Klein *et al.* (1976) studied priming effects in face recognition and word-naming by looking at performances on the second block of trials. They found that a first block of face-recognition trials affected asymmetries on a second block of word-naming trials and vice versa. However, their results showed that priming operated by improving the performance of the inferior hemisphere so that, for example, RVF performance on face recognition was improved by the prior word-naming block. This finding suggests that priming produces a general, non-specific improvement within the primed hemisphere which could stem from perceptual orientation, or from general arousal, but is not consistent with priming of task-specific cognitive mechanisms.

Another controversial aspect of the attentional model concerns the effect of priming one hemisphere on the performance of the unprimed hemisphere. Kinsbourne (1975) states that the two cerebral hemispheres are in reciprocal balance so that an increase in activation of one results in a decrease in activation of the other, and a see-saw effect on performance is predicted. Not all priming studies exhibit this pattern of results (see Hellige and Cox, 1976, and Hellige *et al.*, 1979, for a detailed account of obtained shifts under various priming conditions). Sometimes the performance of the unprimed hemisphere is unchanged, while the primed hemisphere shows improvement. This pattern of results is difficult to reconcile with a perceptual locus of priming, since orientation to the contralateral VF should produce poorer performance in the ipsilateral VF, but could arise from selective activation of the cognitive functions of the primed hemisphere. Sometimes priming produces improvement of performance in both VFs, with a relatively greater improvement in the VF contralateral to the primed hemisphere. This pattern of results has been speculatively attributed to the combined effect of selective and general arousal. Alternatively, it might be explained by a combination of selective activation and absolute specialisation, with all responses being mediated by the primed hemisphere. This version predicts that responses to contralateral stimuli will show facilitation from priming, and responses to ipsilateral stimuli will also show the priming effect minus the crossing-time lag. The variable nature of priming effects when changes in the performance of both hemispheres are taken into account, and the difficulty of predicting the pattern of these changes, reveals the inadequacy of the present state of the model.

(v) *Interference Within a Hemisphere.* A crucial aspect of the priming effect appears to be the size of the concurrent load, or difficulty of the secondary task. Instead of priming performance on the primary task, a secondary task can depress performance if it absorbs too much capacity. The two tasks may compete for processing capacity, and interference results instead of facilitation. Selective interference effects have been obtained by increasing load size. Hellige and Cox (1976) found that LH performance on a form-recognition task improved with a concurrent memory load of 2 or 4 words, but worsened when the load was increased to 6 words. With a memory load of more difficult low-frequency words, the flip-over from facilitation to interference occurred with a smaller number of words. If the primary task is word recognition, rather than form recognition, so that it engages the same mechanisms as the secondary task, then even the smallest verbal memory load constitutes interferences. Size of load effects have varied from one experiment to another, so that a 6-word load may sometimes prove depressing (Hellige and Cox, 1976; Gardner and Branski, 1976), and sometimes facilitating (Kinsbourne, 1973; Davidoff, 1977). While it is clear that a complex interaction of processing demand and capacity is involved, the model is powerless to predict the magnitude, or even the direction of the resulting laterality shift.

Again, when overloading a given hemisphere produces interference with the performance of that hemisphere, there are variable effects on the performance of the other hemisphere which may improve, decline, or remain unchanged. And, again, *ad hoc* explanations can be advanced for whatever pattern of results is found. Sometimes more than one explanation can be offered for the same pattern of shift. When a decline in the performance of an overloaded LH is accompanied by an improvement in the performance of the RH, this could be due to a reciprocal balance mechanism. Alternatively, Hellige *et al.* (1979) suggested that both hemispheres might benefit from general arousal, but the gain is cancelled in the LH by selective interference so that there is a net loss in that hemisphere.

Some of these complex patterns of overload effects can equally well be explained as redistribution of processing occasioned by a change of strategy, and it is quite plausible to suppose that imposing a secondary task might induce a change of processing strategy on the primary task, so as to reduce competition for the same resources, but as yet there is no evidence of qualitative changes in performance to support this interpretation.

Interference effects have also been studied in dual task paradigms, when motor and cognitive tasks are combined. The two tasks may create mutual interference when they compete for the same functional space, so manual and verbal tasks may interfere with each other when both are controlled by the same hemisphere. Yet this type of interference does not seem to produce quite the same effects as the imposition of a secondary cognitive task. The general finding is that, in right-handers, concurrent verbal tasks disrupt performance of the right hand on tasks such as finger-tapping (Lomas and Kimura, 1976), or dowel-balancing (balancing a wooden rod upright on one finger) (Kinsbourne and Cook, 1971). The explanation offered is that the neural structures controlling both tasks overlap within the LH. The performance of the left hand has been variously reported as enhanced, unchanged or disrupted to a lesser extent than the right hand. Lomas and Kimura's findings suggested that only sequential manual tasks were liable to be asymmetrically disrupted. Although concurrent verbalisation may induce right-hand gesturing and rightward eye movements (Kinsbourne, 1978), it does not appear to facilitate right-hand performance on manual tasks, even when the verbalisation is very simple and undemanding. Different kinds of verbalisation appear to produce similar amounts of right-hand disruption, although the nature of the verbalisation task does affect the extent to which interference is bimanual (Bowers et al., 1978). It is paradoxical that a large concurrent memory load is necessary to produce interference on a primary cognitive task, while the simplest forms of concurrent verbalisation (or even humming, according to Hicks, 1975) can disrupt a manual task. Since the degree of neuronal overlap should be greater for cognitive–cognitive dual tasks, than for cognitive–motor dual tasks, the former should be more easily disrupted. This paradox underlines the fact that the attentional model has not succeeded in specifying the mechanisms governing facilitation and interference with sufficient precision.

It is possible to explain individual differences in performance asymmetries in terms of attentional factors in addition to, or instead of, structural differences. Individuals may differ in preferred strategies, in capacities, and also in the incidence of self-imposed priming and interference. This latter phenomenon may occur if an individual's performance of a primary task is accompanied by subvocalisation (activating the LH), or by imaging (activating the RH), but this suggestion has not been formally tested.

Adoption of a combined structural–dynamic model of hemisphere asymmetries solves some of the problems that arose from a purely structural model. The combined model can explain the variability of observed asymmetries both within and between individuals and tasks. Its weakness is that it too easily accommodates any pattern of results that may be obtained. It is too difficult to predict a result and too easy to explain an unpredicted one. The model itself it too unconstrained and imprecise, but the research techniques employed in its service are also at fault. Researchers too readily attribute effects to attentional shifts without independent evidence that any such shift has occurred. One way to remedy this is to devise experiments in which qualitative changes in the nature of the judgmental processes can be monitored more carefully. Another is to examine physiological indices of activation in conjunction with performance measures.

## Conclusions

The conclusions of this chapter can be briefly summarised as follows. Models are divided into fixed structural models and dynamic models. Of the structural models, the absolute specialisation version, whereby a given cognitive function is completely lateralised to one hemisphere, is not well-supported. A relative specialisation model, whereby a given cognitive function is performed preferentially, better or more efficiently by one hemisphere than the other, is more consistent with empirical findings. Within the relative specialisation model several different accounts of the form of specialisation are discussed. The version which proposes that specialisation is for particular stages of processing, or particular operations, is considered plausible, but difficult or impossible to verify experimentally.

All versions of fixed structural models are considered inadequate in that none can account for the variability of observed asymmetries satisfactorily. Combining a structural model with a dynamic model, by incorporating attentional factors, can overcome this weakness. This combined model attributes performance asymmetries to a complex interaction of numerous factors, and proves to be flexible and accommodating. At the present stage, however, the model is seriously underdetermined. In consequence, we are in the position of explaining results (which we often cannot predict) in terms of mechanisms (which we do not fully understand) and factors (which we have failed to define) and hypothesised operations (for which there is no independent validation).

If the present chapter has concentrated on exposing the muddles in the models, its conclusions are by no means pessimistic. We have been able to jettison some oversimplified interpretations of cerebral organisation, to recognise and confront its complexity, and, with the adoption of the combined structural–dynamic model, to move a short way in a promising direction. New research techniques are becoming available. We have hardly begun to explore the potential usefulness of measurements of regional cerebral blood flow. We have so far neglected the possibility of using computer simulation to test models of hemisphere asymmetry, which could be of great value in making them more precise and increasing their predictive power. To acknowledge that current theories are still inadequate does not mean that the outlook for future progress is unhopeful.

# 6

# DEVELOPMENTAL
# ASPECTS

*J. Graham Beaumont*

INVESTIGATION of the developmental aspects of cerebral lateralisation has tended to employ the experimental strategy of dichotic listening, together with the study of other performance asymmetries, rather than divided visual field presentation. The vigorously conducted debate about the ontogenetic course of cerebral lateralisation has therefore principally drawn evidence from these other areas of experimentation, together with that derived from studies of traumatic and surgical brain lesions in children.

There has, however, been some study of DVF performance in children, although much has been directed to the study of dyslexia and other learning disabilities. Nevertheless, the normal control groups generally employed in such studies are also a source of useful evidence, and allow us to examine the various theoretical positions on the development of lateral asymmetry with reference to lateralised presentation in the visual modality. There have been two notable reviews to date: Witelson (1977c) and Young (1981). Witelson's review, while a most impressive, stimulating and wide-reaching paper, does not include the sizeable amount of data which has appeared since its publication, and Young's review, while also excellent, does not include studies of children in the second decade of life. Also to be noted is the provoking pair of papers by Corballis and Morgan (1978) on the maturation of cerebral laterality which, together with the associated commentaries and replies by the authors, form a lively introduction to a whole range of topics in this area. Hécaen (1978) has also reviewed the clinical evidence from lesions in childhood, and Harcum (1978) studies reported before 1970.

The earliest theories, derived principally from clinical evidence and its

113

emphasis on the plasticity of the immature brain, assumed an initial bilateral-isation of function which gradually evolved by progressive lateralisation to the adult pattern of mediation by unilateral structures at the time of puberty or thereabouts (for example, see Buffery and Gray, 1972). This position is still maintained in the theory of Corballis and Morgan (1978) and their concept of the maturational gradient. It is not exactly clear in their papers just how the maturational gradient hypothesis might be expressed in higher-level func-tions, and they have not regarded criticism of their model on this aspect as important to the status of the model as a whole, but they appear to propose that cerebral lateralisation develops in accord with the maturational gradient and that LH specialisation precedes RH specialisation. Challenged on the evidence for this in the commentaries by Beaumont, Bertelson, Geffen and Whitaker, among others, they accept that the evidence does not entirely support this position, but reply that there may not be a clear correspondence between performance observed and the underlying functional processes, and also that there will be variability with respect to specific tasks. Requiring qualification of this kind, the theory loses much of its power in explaining the asymmetries observed in human performance studies.

The most extreme critic of the progressive lateralisation model has been Kinsbourne (1975b, 1976a, b). He has critically reviewed the evidence, both from clinical and human-performance studies, and raised a number of objec-tions to the earlier interpretations. He points out, first, that inferences cannot be drawn directly from performance asymmetries to individual patterns of cerebral organisation. The poor correlation among different indices of cerebral laterality and the very different estimates of the primary RH representation of language from performance studies, from the study of groups with different degrees of manual preference and from the study of aphasic patients, clearly demonstrate the validity of this point. Secondly, there is the difficulty that the child's conception of the experimental task may not be the same as that of the experimenter. In Kinsbourne's terms, this is likely to be expressed in attention being biased in unexpected ways. Although Kinsbourne makes these points with particular reference to dichotic listening, they apply with equal validity to DVF studies. He also points to the evidence then available that in dichotic listening studies, studies of lateral eye movements and of tapping perform-ance, there was evidence of lateralisation by the age of 5, and evidence from a variety of other sources of anatomical, electrophysiological and motor asym-metries from birth. Kinsbourne concluded that there was no evidence at all to support the progressive lateralisation hypothesis, and that lateralisation must be present from the start, while only abilities, and the expression of lateralisa-tion through performance, develop.

Other theorists have adopted a position between these two extremes, al-though most have tended to maintain some aspect of developing lateralisation, with the exception perhaps of Young (1981). Both Galin (1977) and Brown (1979) accept that there is evidence both for "prewiring" and for gradual bias in lateralisation, but both suggest processes by which the development of lateralisation might be achieved. Galin proposes competition between the hemispheres, seeded by an initial advantage of one hemisphere, which by progressive shaping, by competition for shared sensorimotor systems, or by reciprocal inhibition, would lead to progressive lateralisation. Brown sees progressive lateralisation as the ontogenetic expression of an evolutionary progression from generalised cortical function through focal representation to true contralateral organisation. He proposes that the differentiation of focal zones within the cortex of the LH matures through childhood, and may indeed continue into late life.

In contrast, Witelson (1977c) makes no proposals about the mechanisms which might be operative, but adopts a middle position incorporating pre-programmed potential and the operation of some degree of specialisation in infancy, with a gradual realisation of lateralisation which may be modified by environmental factors. Moscovitch (1977) had adopted a similar position, and emphasises the difficulty of deciding between the more extreme alternatives on the basis of the present evidence.

We shall return to review these theoretical positions after summarising the evidence from DVF studies, but it is reasonable to enquire before doing so just what evidence is required in order to be able to conclude that lateralisation does develop. It is first necessary to assume that performance on DVF and similar tasks does reflect underlying cerebral organisation. This may, as indicated elsewhere, be an unwarranted assumption, but if it is not made then the evidence becomes quite irrelevant. It is unreasonable to accept the data and yet imply that the performance measures have no clear functional interpretation (as do Corballis and Morgan). The evidence must be accepted, even though clearly with associated error, or rejected as not relevant. We must also pass over the methodological problems associated with DVF studies in children, although these will be discussed below, and are by no means trivial.

Supposing, then, that we had good valid indices of cerebral organisation based upon DVF performance, what would constitute evidence of the matura-tion of cerebral lateralisation? It would be necessary to have data from a task which could be performed adequately across a wide range of ages, which in matched or parallel forms could assess the relative specialisation of the right and left hemispheres, and in which the cognitive variables of attention and strategy could be controlled. Without such a task, no comparisons can be made across data derived from individuals at different ages. If different tasks are to be used at different ages, or if different accuracy rates are typical of different age groups, then either the nature or the difficulty of the task will be con-founded with the maturational changes. If exactly parallel forms, matched in difficulty as well as in other relevant aspects of task performance (notably response factors), are not available then no comparison can be made between the status of the two hemispheres. Much of the confusion in this area has in fact been generated by comparisons being made between the degree of lateralisation being exhibited on quite unmatched "right-hemisphere" and "left-hemisphere" tasks. Lastly, the tasks must not only appear similar across the different ages, but also must not be distinguished by the operation of different cognitive variables. If subjects were to perform the same tasks, but by different cognitive strategies, at different ages, then the variable of maturation would be inextricably confounded with the change in cognitive function.

It is, of course, the case that no task of this kind has yet been devised, and it is unlikely that it is possible to devise such a task. The root of the problem is that any change of the pattern of lateralisation is bound into a whole range of other changes in ability and cognitive processing. As a consequence, it is impossible to extricate the hypothesised biological maturation of lateralisation from the factors which mediate its expression in performance. For this reason, with current methodology, employing lateral performance measures, the question of cerebral maturation is unanswerable. We are properly able to do no more than state whether performance asymmetries are to be observed on a particular task at a certain age, and certainly not at present to draw inferences about the developing brain organisation upon which this performance is founded.

## Methodological Issues

All of the methodological difficulties previously discussed in the context of experiments with adults also apply to studies with children. While experiments with children pose no unique methodological problems, certain difficulties become more acute, in particular the problem of ensuring stable central fixation. It is probably this difficulty which discouraged much early use of the DVF technique with children. There is no *a priori* reason to believe that children are less able to fixate than adults, but there has been a constant suspicion that they would be unable to carry out instructions to do so. Despite this suspicion, extra steps have not in general been taken to ensure fixation maintenance, although electrooculography has been used (Gross *et al.*, 1978; Jablonowska and Budohoska, 1976), as well as the ingenious requirement that performance on lateral stimuli should be no better than on the central stimuli which were included among the trials (Young and Ellis, 1976; Young and Bion, 1979). However, these studies are the exception, and most have failed to include even visual monitoring. Young (1981) in his review discards all studies which have not carefully monitored fixation (including, a little unfairly,

Reynolds and Jeeves, 1978a, b in which monitoring of the kind used by Young and coworkers was partially employed). While this caution seems proper, it does rule out the bulk of studies which are worthy of some consideration. Incidentally Young considers that lack of fixation, presumably random, is likely to lead to the reduction of observed asymmetries. This seems an unwarranted assumption. Failure of fixation may well be associated with a tendency to look to one visual field rather than the other, and may therefore accentuate the asymmetry in performance. The outcome of fixation failure is at present quite unpredictable.

Pirozzolo (1979) gives data on the latency for saccadic movement to various lateral positions from central fixation, with a mean of around 200 ms for 11-year-old children. This means that studies which have employed exposures of this duration (for example, Butler and Miller, 1979) must be viewed with added caution.

The strategy of adding a central item to be reported first has also been used with children, the item being a number (McKeever and Huling, 1970b; McKeever et al., 1976), or the symbols "+" or "−" (Kershner, 1977; Garren, 1980). It has been shown, however, by Kershner et al. (1977) and by Carter and Kinsbourne (1979) that the verbal or non-verbal nature of the central item may have an effect upon the asymmetries observed for the lateral stimuli, even entirely reversing the visual field advantage, and this must be taken into account in these studies.

Response factors may also present unusual problems in studies with children. Response latencies may be unusually long with young children, and the response itself may add variance to the response latency which masks any visual field effects. This is almost certainly the cause of the failure to find a significant asymmetry in the youngest group in the study by Reynolds and Jeeves (1978a). In addition, the effects of response compatibility, and the tendency to respond on the side of stimulation, may introduce errors with young subjects (Barroso, 1976; Reynolds and Jeeves, 1978a).

The question of whether the tasks presented at different ages should be adjusted to compensate for differences in difficulty is a thorny one. Many studies have individually titrated exposures for individual subjects, and have used different exposure durations for different age groups (Miller and Turner, 1973). Alternatively, the problems may be made a little easier for younger groups (Carter and Kinsbourne, 1979). This manipulation is not always successful in equating the overall performance of the different groups, but the alternative where widely different accuracies are achieved (from 40% to 100% for example in Carmon et al., 1976) also creates problems of analysis. Neither strategy seems in fact acceptable. If comparisons are to be made across age groups then an independent measure of the difficulty of the task, together with an appropriate quantitative adjustment in either the material, the parameters of presentation, or in the analysis, is required. This, however, does not seem to have been attempted, and the result is an analysis in which the effects of difficulty are confounded with the performance measures being examined.

Subtle task effects are no less present in studies with children as, for example, the experiments of Turner and Miller (1975) clearly demonstrate. An additional variable, which may be important, is whether the individual subjects show an order bias in the reporting of stimuli. Aaron and Handley (1975) found that a performance asymmetry was only found among those of their subjects who had previously been shown to exhibit a right-to-left bias.

Lastly, there is the obvious question of comparisons with adult asymmetries. A number of studies have included adult samples, and others have used tasks on which the adult asymmetry can reasonably be predicted. However, the adult pattern cannot always be predicted with confidence, and it is often unreasonable simply to assume that a certain pattern of results would be obtained. In describing the cerebral organisation of children by comparison with the mature adult pattern, this consideration should be carefully borne in mind.

It should be noted that Witelson in her 1977 review was led to conclude that "not one tachistoscopic study of left hemisphere specialisation in children is free of methodological dificulty or provides unequivocal results", and this is echoed by Young (1981).

## The Studies

### Words

The most natural way in which to divide the studies is by the stimulus material employed. Most studies have used very simple tasks requiring identification or simple matching. The most common stimulus material has been words.

Amongst the older children tested the result has been an almost unanimous finding of an RVF advantage with word stimuli, irrespective of the precise nature of the task or of the stimuli employed. Studies which have included children aged 11 and over and have found this effect include: Carmon *et al.*, 1976; Forgays, 1953; McKeever and Huling, 1970b; McKeever and VanDeventer, 1975; McKeever *et al.*, 1976; Miller and Turner, 1973; Olson, 1973; Pirozzolo, 1979; Pirozzolo and Rayner, 1979; Reitsma, 1975; Tomlinson-Keasey *et al.*, 1978; and Tomlinson-Keasey and Kelly, 1979a, b. The conclusion in the study by Forgays must be modified in that while he found an overall RVF advantage across the age groups tested, it is evident from the graphical presentation of the results that the advantage is greater for the older children. It is not clear from the analysis whether the difference between the visual field scores is significant for the 11-year-old group as well as the 13- and 15-year-olds.

Only one study with older children has failed to find the RVF advantage, that of Yeni-Komshian *et al.* (1975). They found no visual field asymmetry in a group aged between 10 and 12. Their task was, however, a little unusual in that a series of vertically oriented digit names were presented in the left or right visual fields, intermixed with digits at central fixation. Report followed presentation of the five-item series. While this strategy has been used with adults and has produced the expected RVF advantage, and while performance was at an acceptable level (around 75%) in this study, it may be that the delay between presentation and report for the earlier items, or the intermixing of digits and digit names, acted to remove the RVF effect. The exposure duration of 189 ms was also uncomfortably long.

A similar picture emerges when the studies with younger children are examined. The RVF advantage with word stimuli has been found in studies with children aged 10 and below, from age 6 (Turner and Miller, 1975), from age 7 (Butler and Miller, 1979; Marcel *et al.*, 1974; Marcel and Rajan, 1975; Olson, 1973), from age 8 (Garren, 1980; Kelly and Tomlinson-Keasey, 1977; Leehey, 1976), from age 9 (Miller and Turner, 1973) and at age 10 (Carmon *et al.*, 1976; Kershner, 1977; Koetting, 1970; Pirozzolo, 1979; Reitsma, 1975). Three of these studies included a younger age sample which did not show the RVF advantage. Carmon *et al.* (1976) examined 6- and 8-year-old groups and did find the RVF asymmetry but only for 2-letter and bilaterally presented words, not for 4-letter words. Miller and Turner (1973) also had a 7-year-old group who did not show the RVF advantage, but this may well have been due to a floor effect. Reitsma (1975), in a study very similar to that of Miller and Turner, also failed to find the RVF effect in an 8-year-old group. None of these studies reported a significant change in the RVF advantage with age, with the exception of Turner and Miller (1975) who reported the RVF superiority to increase with age for identification, although not for discrimination, of words. Tomlinson-Keasey *et al.* (1978) classified their children at age 8 as having an individual RVF or LVF advantage and found an excess of children with an RVF advantage at both ages, but the excess was not very marked at age 8 (40% as against 33%) and increased considerably at age 13 (69% to 16%).

Aside from these studies, two others have failed to find an RVF superiority with word stimuli in children under 11. The study of Yeni-Komshian *et al.* (1975) has already been discussed. The study of Forgays (1953) also failed to find a visual field asymmetry among the younger children, although this is discussed by Forgays within the context of the development of postexposural scanning, rather than the development of cerebral asymmetry.

The balance of evidence is therefore clearly in favour of an RVF advantage being observed with words for children as young as those that have been tested. Of the reports of a failure to find this advantage, mostly among the younger children, there is nothing to mark these studies as being more methodologically sophisticated. There is also no evidence to indicate a change in the RVF advantage with increasing age. It can be concluded, within the methodological limits discussed above, that there is an RVF advantage which is invariant with age.

Despite the variety of word stimuli employed, there has been little systematic study of the variables of these stimuli. A similar effect was found for both upper- and lower-case characters by Pirozzolo and Rayner (1979), although Kelly and Tomlinson-Keasey (1977) report that the RVF advantage was stronger for low-imagery words. Young (1981) points out that a difference between verbs and concrete nouns may have been a confounding effect in the differences between 3- and 5-letter words in the studies by Butler and Miller (1979) and Turner and Miller (1975) where these aspects of the stimuli were not directly controlled, and in which some differences between the shorter and longer words were reported. (There is also the general problem of the asymmetrical lateralisation of the initial letter with horizontal words, which is greater for longer words.) Marcel *et al.* (1974) also used verbs and concrete nouns but report no differences between them.

Butler and Miller (1979) also used approximations to English together with words as stimuli, but the effect of increasing approximation only appeared to be significant with the older children. Carmon *et al.* (1976) used Hebrew words as their stimuli, with Hebrew speakers, but the results are not notably different from studies with English words. Silverberg *et al.* (1979) also found an RVF advantage for Hebrew words with adolescent Israelis, but for English words there was an initial LVF superiority which changed to an RVF superiority over the years of study of English as a second language. Tomlinson-Keasey and Kelly (1979b) used sequential and holistic word tasks (although the nature of these tasks seems most unclear from their report), and found the RVF advantage only for the sequential task. Incidentally, Ellis and Young (1977), and Young and Bion (1980b) found no age-of-acquisition effect on later testing for the asymmetry associated with words, but reading attainment has been shown to be a significant variable in the observed asymmetry (Garren, 1980; Kershner, 1977; Tomlinson-Keasey and Kelly, 1979a). The relation of visual field asymmetries to reading performance will be discussed below.

## Letters

The results of experiments which have used letter stimuli are more difficult to interpret, as discussed in Chapter 4, because it is clear that these stimuli may be processed either as graphemic units or purely according to their configurational characteristics. This has not generally been recognised in the research with children, although Witelson (1977b, c) discusses her data retrospectively in regard to this issue. Most studies have assumed that letters must represent verbal stimuli, an assumption which is not well-founded, especially among young children, who in learning to read must pay particular attention to the configurational properties of individual graphemic components. In this context, whether the task requires the child to name or simply to match the letter stimuli may well be important.

It is not surprising, therefore, that the results of studies with letter stimuli are more varied, and that among the younger children evidence of an LVF advantage has been found (Broman, 1978, at age 7; Carmon *et al.*, 1976, at age 6; Jablonowska and Budohoska, 1976, at age 5 although not significant). Broman (1978) found in general no asymmetry, and his stimuli were vertically oriented pairs drawn from a small set requiring a go/no-go response, which might be expected to enhance spatial as against verbal processing of the stimuli. Similarly, Carmon *et al.* (1976) found no asymmetry after age 6, although an asymmetry for words had been found for the same subjects. Amongst slightly older children, Jablonowska and Budohoska (1976) found an RVF advantage, but they did require that their subjects name the stimuli. Reynolds and Jeeves (1978a) found no visual field difference for their 7- to 8-year-old group, but as suggested above, this may be due to the variance in response latency exhibited by this group. By contrast, Witelson (1977b, c) found a significant RVF superiority for 6- to 7-year-old children which disappeared for an 8- to 9-year-old sample. Witelson emphasises the dual hemisphere processing likely to be involved in the perception of letters as against words. Aaron and Handley (1975) found the RVF advantage, although subjects were required to choose between the stimulus array and its mirror image, surely a more spatial than verbal task, but only among those subjects who had previously shown a significant right-to-left response bias.

The findings are no more clear among the rather older children. Crosland (1939) found an overall LVF advantage for children aged 10½ and older, but other studies have tended to find an RVF advantage (Keefe and Swinney, 1979, at around 10½; Phippard, 1977, 11½- to 14½-year-olds; McKeever and VanDeventer, 1975, at around 12¾ and in subsequent retest one year later; Reynolds and Jeeves, 1978a, 13- to 14-year-olds). Other studies have failed to find a significant asymmetry (Gross *et al.*, 1978, 10- to 13½-year-olds; Richardson and Firlej, 1979, 11- to 15-year-olds).

The results of these studies do not have a clear conclusion. As in the studies with adults (Chapter 4) there is a tendency to find an RVF advantage, but a considerable proportion of studies find the reverse, or no, asymmetry, particularly among younger children. The sensible conclusion seems to be that letters may be processed in a variety of ways and that the precise nature of the experimental stimuli, and particularly the task instructions, explicit and implicit, play a part in determining how the stimuli will be treated. There are, in addition, individual differences which will be in operation. Studies with letter stimuli cannot be considered to throw light upon cerebral organisation without further understanding of these task and subject variables.

## Digits

The few studies which have used digits as stimuli have similarly variable results. Carmon *et al.* (1976) report an RVF advantage for 10- and 12-year-olds, but not for 6- and 8-year-olds. Reitsma (1975), however, found an RVF advantage for 6-year-olds, but not for 7- and 8-year-olds. Kershner *et al.* (1977) also found the RVF superiority in children aged 5½ to 6½, but only with a verbal item at central fixation. The asymmetry was reversed by a non-verbal fixation stimulus for first report. Similarly, Carter and Kinsbourne (1979) found an RVF advantage in their study of children aged 5, 6, 9 and 12, but this was also reversed by inducing a spatial set through presentation of a non-verbal item at fixation. Malatesha (1976) reports an LVF superiority for children aged 6 to 8 and 11 to 13, as do Beaumont *et al.* (1981) for children aged 8½ to 11½.

Once again, it is tempting to conclude that there is evidence for a slight though unstable right field advantage for digit stimuli. This seems, however, hardly warranted by the evidence. It seems unclear how children might process digits as stimulus items, and in particular how the concept of number as taught to the younger children may influence the results. Children are now commonly taught to treat numbers in terms of sets and the ordered "number line", and this must surely have an important influence on the cognitive processes which underlie recognition and subsequent processing of number stimuli. The present data are too meagre for satisfactory conclusions to be drawn.

## Miscellaneous Verbal Studies

Three studies might be regarded as involving verbal processing but are not easily classifiable above. Barroso (1976) asked subjects to match a spoken word to a simple figure and found the expected RVF superiority among 10- and 12-year-olds, although not at 6 and 8. Buffery (1976), in a complex study, also required auditory–visual matching, using easy-to-verbalise (EV) and difficult-to-verbalise (DV) stimuli. He found that the best performance for EV stimuli was obtained when the auditory word was presented to the LH and the figure to the RH, but when both stimuli were presented to the LH for DV stimuli. This can probably be best interpreted in terms of stimuli being directly presented to the "appropriate" hemisphere for the processing to which they are best suited leading to the best performance. Buffery also argues that the data reveal evidence of progressive lateralisation across the ages (5 to 9) examined. The interpretation of this study is, however, difficult.

Vellutino *et al.* (1978) used a paired-associate task with Chinese ideographs and English words, a task previously shown to be easily mastered by the 7- to 8- and 11- to 12-year-old children studied. An RVF advantage was found for both groups of children.

## Figures

The studies which have employed representational figures as stimuli, like the studies with letters and digits, reveal no clear pattern of asymmetry, and probably for the same reasons.

Kelly and Tomlinson-Keasey (1978) found an RVF advantage for concrete pictures, their subjects being on average about 8½, while Witelson (1977a, b, c) found the opposite asymmetry for children aged 6 to 7, 8 to 9 and 12 to 14, although there was no asymmetry for the 10 to 11 age group. Neville (1975) found no asymmetry, although a conceptual match between different drawings of the same object was required, and it is possible that the task was rather difficult for the children to whom it was given. Barroso (1976), as with his verbal stimuli, found an LVF superiority at ages 10 and 12, but not at 6 or 8.

To further complicate the picture, Tomlinson-Keasey *et al.* (1978) found evidence of an RVF advantage for correct matches, but an LVF advantage for correct responses to unmatched stimuli. The effect was, however, rather stronger for the adults examined than for the children. The Tomlinson-Keasey and Kelly (1979a) study in which the subjects were classified by individual field preferences found no change between ages 8 and 13. An equal proportion of subjects with left and right advantage was found at both ages (when the misprint in their published Table I has been amended). The sequential and holistic tasks studied by these workers (1979b), although showing an interesting pattern of asymmetries with word stimuli, showed no asymmetry for the juvenile groups with picture stimuli, although an RVF advantage was found for the adults.

The data for picture stimuli is limited, the involvement of verbal mediation in coding the stimuli is uncertain, and the general conclusion is quite unclear.

## Shapes

Aaron and Handley (1975) report an LVF advantage with shapes for children aged 5 to 7, although again only for those showing a previously established preferred right-to-left report order. Turner and Miller (1975) found an RVF advantage for children aged 6 to 9, and for college students, with no change in asymmetry attributable to age.

## Faces

Faces have been a little more popular as stimuli in studies with children, possibly because it is believed that these stimuli lead to a stable LVF effect. This belief would find some support from the childhood studies.

The LVF advantage has been found in a number of studies: Broman (1978), although *post hoc* comparisons revealed the effect only at 7 and 10 and not at 13 years; Leehey (1976), down to age 8 for highly familiar faces but only down to age 10 for unfamiliar faces; Pirozzolo and Rayner (1979) for subjects aged about 12½; Reynolds and Jeeves (1978b) for 13- to 14-year-olds; Young and Ellis (1976) for ages 5½ to 12; Young and Bion (1980a) for ages 7 to 13, although only for upright faces. Young and Bion (1981a) found the same effect, with no change in asymmetry across age for faces known to the subjects. An LVF asymmetry was also reported by Marcel and Rajan (1975) in terms of lower thresholds for face identification in the LVF. There are, however, some particular methodological problems in this study relating to the control of exposure durations and the number of trials employed. The results are none the less generally in line with others using face stimuli.

No studies have reported an RVF advantage with face stimuli, although no asymmetry has been reported in two studies, besides the 13-year-old group of Broman. Reynolds and Jeeves (1978b), while finding the effect with 13- to 14-year-olds, did not find it for 7- to 8-year-olds, although as with the verbal stimuli in their 1978a study, the younger children gave more variable and longer response latencies which may have introduced an error which masked the underlying asymmetry. Phippard (1977) also failed to find any asymmetry with normal subjects aged between 11½ and 14½, although the expected effect was found with college students using the same paradigm.

It can be concluded that face stimuli, presented laterally to children, are generally associated with superior performance in the LVF. There is no clear evidence of any change in this asymmetry over age.

## Miscellaneous Non-verbal Studies

Unstructured visual stimuli were used by Jeeves (1972) and he found that with right-handed children, as with adults, there was a significant LVF advantage. This was interpreted as resulting from the combined effects of the advantage of direct pathways with the advantage of right-hand response, and this seems a sensible interpretation.

Dots have been used as stimuli in a few studies. These studies have tended to find an LVF advantage (Malatesha, 1976, ages 6 to 8 and 11 to 13; Young and Bion, 1979, ages 5 to 11; Witelson, 1977c, an almost significant result for children aged between 6 and 14). McKeever and VanDeventer (1975) failed to find this asymmetry, as did Dyer and Harcum (1961) with preschool children presenting binary patterns. Braine (1968), using Israeli subjects, found an RVF advantage for binary patterns for 8-year-old children which shifted at about age 12 to an LVF advantage. The results were partly, but not entirely, determined by an order-of-report effect.

Colour-naming was investigated by Grant (1980), and while there were differences between the 5-, 7- and 10-year-olds tested, the greatest LVF advantage was for 5-year-olds and the smallest for 7-year-olds. Different stimulus sets and exposure durations were used at each age, however, and the implications of the study are not entirely clear.

The orientation of lines, or orientation within an array, has also been studied. Phippard (1977) found the expected LVF advantage at the ages 11½ to 14½, although Reitsma (1975) with younger children aged 6 to 8 did not find a visual field asymmetry. An interesting result was reported by Schaller and Dziadosz (1976). They found no asymmetry among preschool children, but they did find an RVF advantage for the 8-year-olds studied. This compared with an adult pattern of about one-third showing an RVF advantage, and two-thirds an LVF advantage. The significance of this result is unclear, although it is tempting to link it to the development of cognitive strategies, and in particular the processes being developed in children who are learning to become fluent readers.

With all these studies, the results are of interest, but the body of evidence is insufficient, bearing in mind the methodological problems associated with each study and the variability of the findings, for clear conclusions to be drawn. The results do not deviate far from the pattern of results which might well be found with a similar group of studies carried out with adult subjects.

## Handedness

Handedness has been little studied as a variable in tachistoscopic studies with children, one exception being Jeeves (1972). Jeeves found that the pattern of asymmetry typical of right-handed adults was also to be found for right-handed children, but that left-handed children differed from left-handed adults.

## Sex Differences

The issue of sex differences in performance is treated in Chapter 8 and will not be discussed here. The reader interested in sex differences in childhood performance should consult the papers of Buffery (1976, 1978), Buffery and Gray (1972), Carter and Kinsbourne (1979), Marcel et al. (1974) and Young and Bion (1979, 1980a) amongst others. It should be remembered, however, that many of the studies with children have included in their design equal numbers of boys and girls, and have either incidentally reported no difference between the sexes, or have failed to comment upon this variable at all, perhaps because the results were inspected and no effect of the variable believed to be present.

## Pathological Groups

There have been a number of studies of deaf subjects which are outside the scope of this chapter (except that data from their normal controls have been included above) but again the interested reader is advised to consult Kelly and Tomlinson-Keasey (1977, 1978); Manning *et al.* (1977); McKeever *et al.* (1976); Neville, 1975; Phippard (1977); Ross *et al.* (1979); Scholes and Fischler (1979); and Virostek and Cutting (1979). An interesting discussion of the implications of such studies for the education of the deaf is to be found in Kelly (1978).

Curtiss (1977) has also reported the results of DVF examination with "Genie", the severely deprived girl who developed in isolation and confinement until 13½ years old. The findings in the visual modality are, however, rather inconclusive.

## Reading

The association between DVF performance and reading, and in particular the performance on DVF tasks of the reading disabled, is an important topic, but one which cannot be treated here. Good reviews of neuropsychological investigations of dyslexia are to be found in Benton and Pearl (1978), Knights and Bakker (1976), Myklebust (1978), and Pirozzolo (1979) and these include the results of investigations using the DVF technique. Particular discussions of results using this experimental strategy are also to be found in Beaumont and Rugg (1978), Naylor (1980), and in Young and Ellis (1981).

As indicated above, many of the studies reported in this chapter were designed to investigate the cerebral organisation of the reading disabled, or to contrast good with poor readers. Where the results of such studies have been summarised above, the results are those of the normal controls, or only of readers within the normal range of attainment. Those interested in the results of these studies with reference to the backward readers should, however, consult one of the above reviews or the studies themselves (Beaumont *et al.*, 1981; Crosland, 1939; Garren, 1980; Gross *et al.*, 1978; Jablonowska and Budohoska, 1976; Keefe and Swinney, 1979; Kershner, 1977; Malatesha, 1976; Marcel *et al.*, 975; Marcel and Rajan, 1975; McKeever, 1977; McKeever and VanDeventer, 1975; Olson, 1973; Pirozzolo, 1979; Pirozzolo and Rayner, 1979; Satz, 1976; Tomlinson-Keasey and Kelly, 1979a; Vellutino *et al.*, 1978; Witelson, 1977a, b; and Yeni-Komshian *et al.*, 1975). There is, however, no reason to amend the conclusion drawn by Beaumont and Rugg in their 1978 review that there is evidence, albeit not entirely clear, that dyslexic subjects do not show the RVF advantage for language-related stimuli which is to be found among children who are attaining normally in reading. This is in contrast to the evidence from dichotic listening, where the normal right-ear advantage does seem to be found among dyslexics. It is possible to construct a neuropsychological model of the dyslexic deficit from these conclusions, as Beaumont and Rugg have shown.

Reading may, however, be an important variable within the normal range of attainment. It has already been noted that some studies have demonstrated this effect upon visual field asymmetries for word stimuli. This is hardly surprising, for two reasons. It is, first, reasonable to believe that observed asymmetries are at least in part linked to postexposural scanning processes, and these are likely to develop in association with learning to read, and may well be more powerfully developed among the more able readers. Related to these, there may also be gross lateral biases of attention which are more powerfully developed among more able and practised readers (Beaumont, *et al.*, 1981). Postexposural eye movements have also been shown to facilitate recognition in the lateral visual fields (Mandes, 1980), and may occur with unequal frequency to the left or right, in association with reading habits.

Secondly, if the process of learning to read is accomplished by a series of stages in which different cognitive processes are of particular importance (Pirozzolo, 1978), as is widely accepted, then different developmental stages would be coloured by the dominance of these cognitive processes. This might well be reflected in the cognitive performance observed at the relevant stages, and find expression in the pattern of visual field asymmetries recorded. Future investigations might therefore profit from more systematic attention being paid to the variable of reading attainment.

## Conclusions

Despite the smaller number of studies, and the additional methodological problems attendant upon studies of DVF performance in children, a number of conclusions can be drawn, which do not differ greatly from the conclusions to be drawn from studies with adults.

1. There is evidence that an RVF advantage is observed when words are employed as stimuli. With other "verbal" stimuli, and in particular with

letters, the results are rather less clear, owing to the variability of the cognitive processes which are entailed in task performance.

2. With "non-verbal" stimuli, only faces have been found to yield a consistent asymmetry, with superior performance being associated with LVF presentation. Results of studies with other stimuli are either too meagre or too variable for clear conclusions to be formed.

3. Reading attainment may well be an important variable, and deserves further study, particularly for the light it may throw upon the cognitive processes involved in determining visual field asymmetries.

4. Within the limits of the methodology of the studies there is no evidence, taking the body of evidence as a whole, for any progressive change in the pattern of asymmetries with age. Asymmetries are to be observed among the youngest children studied, and in studies which have examined groups at different ages, there is, in general, no evidence for progressive lateralisation.

These conclusions do not differ from the conclusions of the earlier review by Witelson (1977c) or that of a broader body of evidence by Young (1981).

There is one interesting last point which may be made, which returns to the theoretical issue of the development of cerebral lateralisation. The failure to demonstrate progressive lateralisation in the DVF studies may mean that studies of DVF performance do accurately reflect cerebral organisation, and that the underlying cerebral mechanisms upon which performance is based do not develop by progressive lateralisation.

However, it may alternatively mean that the DVF asymmetries which have been recorded do not reflect underlying cerebral organisation at all, and while they may apparently be associated with it in adult performance, the asymmetries during childhood are in fact determined by other factors which are independent of the development of cerebral organisation. Such factors may be suspected, but cannot be clearly identified at the present time.

Finally, and this implication is not unconnected with the last, it may well be that within current paradigms, as argued above, it is not possible to draw inferences about the development of cerebral organisation from performance studies with children, and that we should not consider that the studies with young subjects yield evidence relevant to the question of cerebral maturation. The data on asymmetries in performance is of course of importance in its own right, but it cannot be assumed that inferences may be made validly and directly to the neuropsychological substrate of cerebral organisation. This is a challenge which neuropsychological investigations using the DVF technique will have to face if significant progress is to be made within this field of enquiry.

# 7

# ELECTROPHYSIOLOGICAL STUDIES

*Michael D. Rugg*

## Introduction

THE possibility of obtaining data from normal subjects which complements purely behavioural indices is an attractive prospect for neuropsychology. The development, over the last two decades, of techniques and associated hardware allowing the recording and analysis of averaged evoked responses (AERs) has resulted in these phenomena becoming widely regarded as filling such a role. The use of AERs to investigate psychological and neuropsychological issues has grown enormously in the past few years and such studies now cover a wide field of enquiry, as the perusal of any of a number of recent books on the subject will indicate (see, for example, Begleiter, 1979; Callaway *et al.*, 1978; and Lehmann and Callaway, 1979). A substantial number of studies have employed AER techniques to investigate hemisphere asymmetries and many of these will be found summarised in one of several recent reviews (Donchin *et al.*, 1977b; Hillyard and Woods, 1979; Marsh, 1978). It is the intention in the present chapter to review a subset of this literature and to discuss in some detail those studies which have utilised electrophysiological indices in experimental paradigms employing divided visual field (DVF) presentation of stimuli. The studies reviewed are concerned exclusively with the recording and analysis of the visual evoked response (VER).

The typical experimental paradigm used in the behavioural investigation of DVF stimulus presentation is relatively easy to adapt so as to allow the collection of concurrent electrophysiological data. For example, the use of transient, well-controlled stimuli presented accurately in the lateral visual fields (VFs) is a precondition of a successful behavioural as well as electro-physiological experiment, and the use of relatively large numbers of stimulus presentations is also a common feature of both techniques. For reasons such as these it might be expected that this area of study would be fertile ground for the amalgamation of behavioural and electrophysiological data. As will become apparent as this chapter progresses, however, this has yet to occur.

As with behavioural experiments it is convenient to divide the studies carried out in this field into those utilising relatively simple unstructured stimuli (e.g. light flashes), the processing of which might not be expected to engage lateralised cognitive functions strongly, and those studies which have employed more complex stimuli (e.g. letters) in response to which lateralised functions might be expected to become operative. It is also possible to further divide these studies into those in which subjects were required actively to process the stimuli used to elicit VERs, and responded on the basis of such processing, and those in which subjects were not given a task explicitly associated with the eliciting stimuli. Prior to discussing these various experiments, it is necessary to discuss briefly the nature of the VER and to note a number of pertinent methodological issues.

## VERs

Whilst it is not possible in this chapter to provide a detailed account of the nature and methodology of the VER, some discussion is necessary. Further coverage of the morphology, topography and methodology of AERs can be found in numerous sources (see, for example, Regan, 1972; Thompson and Patterson, 1974).

### Morphology and Topography

AERs are formed by averaging samples of EEG time-locked to the occurrence of some definable event, usually the onset of an external stimulus. They consist of plots of voltage against time over a period of around 500 ms, the various peaks and troughs making up the AER waveform being labelled according to their polarity and latency or order of occurence (e.g. "$P_{120}$" would be a positive peak occurring with a latency around 120 ms; "$N_1$" would refer to the first measured negative component). The morphology and topography of the VER varies considerably according to a number of factors, the most notable of which are the nature of the eliciting stimulus (e.g. contoured/non-contoured), the recording montage, and the instructions given to the subject (e.g. to pay attention or ignore a particular class of stimulus). AER components are often characterised by the labels "exogenous" and "endogenous" (Donchin, 1975).

Exogenous components are those elements of the waveform which are reliably elicited by a stimulus independently of the cognitive state of the subject (e.g. the auditory brainstem potentials). They are strongly influenced by the properties of the eliciting stimulus and generally occur relatively early ($<$ 100 ms) in the AER waveform. Endogenous components are considered to be relatively modality non-specific and to be influenced almost entirely by the cognitive processes of the subject. These occur late in the AER ($>$ 250 ms) and are more diffusely distributed over the scalp than the earlier components. A good example of an endogenous component is the intensively investigated $P_{300}$ wave, the amplitude of which appears to be determined to a very large extent by the factors of stimulus probability and task-relevance (Donchin et al., 1978).

With respect to VER studies of DVF stimulation, the majority of investigators have analysed components in the latency range 60–250 ms, the so-called "middle latency" components, which exhibit the properties of both exogenous and endogenous components in that they are influenced both by stimulus and cognitive variables. Analysis of these waveforms has proceeded by a number of methods, the most common of which has been to measure the latency and amplitude (either from a prestimulus baseline or as a peak-to-peak measure) of individual components, and to subject these to individual analyses. A prescription for the best means of measuring and interpreting AER waveforms is not possible, due to the lack of any consensus as to the neurophysiological significance of the majority of the components observed in AER waveforms. However, in view of the fact that innumerable studies have demonstrated that the various components of a waveform may be differentially affected by experimental variables, it would appear advisable to adopt a means of analysis which allows assessment of the effect of such variables on individual components, avoiding methods of analysis which ascribe characteristics to the undifferentiated waveform. A number of other specific methodological points are also relevant with respect to DVF studies of VERs (for a fuller discussion of the methodological issues surrounding electrophysiological investigations of hemisphere asymmetry see Donchin et al., 1977a).

(a) *Reference electrode.* All biopotentials are the result of voltage fluctuations between two sites. When recording the human EEG it is customary for both of these sites to be on the scalp. It is desirable that only one of these sites should be "active" and the other indifferent or neutral (the reference) so that interpretation of the locus of any changes in activity observed to occur can be unambiguous. As no site on the head is free from EEG activity (including the ear lobes and mastoids, Stephenson and Gibbs, 1951; Lehtonen and Koivikko, 1971), it is necessary to effect a compromise and to place the reference electrode on a site the activity underlying which is unlikely to be affected by the variables manipulated in the experiment. This is particularly important in experiments investigating hemisphere asymmetries as an asymmetrical reference site (e.g. unilateral ear lobe) may be differentially affected by experimental manipulations which are intended to affect the lateral distribution of EEG activity. Perhaps the most appropriate site for VER studies is an active midline site, to which all exploring electrodes are referenced (a common reference). The commonly used references of linked mastoids or earlobes are undesirable because the fact that they are active means that they may give rise to asymmetries in activity which vary with experimental condition, and, unless the impedances of the two sites are closely matched, are an asymmetrical reference in any case (Mowery and Bennett, 1957). Unfortunately, an active midline reference is of no utility when it is intended to elicit the late, endogenous components of the VER, due to their widespread anterior–posterior distribution over the scalp. Under these circumstances it is arguable that a reference placed away from the head (e.g. the balanced non-cephalic reference of Stephenson and Gibbs, 1951) is the only really appropriate solution.

(b) *Artefact rejection.* AERs are notoriously liable to contamination from extracerebral artefacts. The most common of these are electro-oculographic (EOG) potentials, particularly those arising from blinks. It therefore behoves investigators to ensure that EEG records containing such artefacts are not entered into an average. This is particularly the case when eliciting ERs containing late slow components (i.e. $P_{300}$ etc.) as these are extremely sensitive to ocular artefact.

(c) *Control of cognitive set.* It is now reasonably well-established that subjects' cognitive activity will influence the amplitude of VERs evoked by "simple" stimuli such as flashes. For example, Galin and Ellis (1975) reported that when subjects were required to engage in verbal tasks, VERs elicited by flashes in central vision were asymmetrical, being smaller on the left side, and that this asymmetry was reversed when subjects performed visuospatial tasks. Other investigators have reported similar findings (Papanicolaou, 1980; Rasmussen *et al.*, 1977). It is important to bear the results of these studies in mind when assessing the reasons for the asymmetries reported in VERs in studies in which no attempt was made to control subjects' cognitive set by imposing an explicit task. In such circumstances it is conceivable that subjects will construct their own tasks. At the least, this will give rise to increased intersubject variance in the VERs obtained under such conditions, and at the worst, if the adopted cognitive set should be consistent across subjects (e.g. covert verbalisation), will result in a confounding factor which may affect VER asymmetries in an undetectable fashion.

(d) *Assumptions underlying the use of averaging.* An AER only forms an accurate representation of the activity elicited by the stimuli if it can be assumed that this activity is unvarying from trial to trial, other than by being combined additively with uncorrelated noise (the background EEG). If, however, single trials are not similarly time-locked to the eliciting stimulus (latency jitter) the resulting average will be a distortion. More importantly, if the degree of latency jitter varies as a function of the experimental variables, differences in the amplitude of the components of the resulting AERs may be erroneously assumed to be present, as, all other factors being equal, components of larger amplitude will be found in those AERs formed from samples having the least latency jitter. To date, no DVF study has employed any of the methods now available for estimating and correcting for latency jitter among single trials (e.g. the Woody filter (Wastell, 1977)), investigators being content to assume that amplitude differences may be ascribed to "genuine" differences in the single trials making up the VER.

In the light of the above remarks, it should be clear that, attractive as AER data may be as a means of complementing behavioural measures, their interpretation is not without problems. These difficulties are exacerbated by the fact that, to date, no single study has fulfilled even the small number of methodological criteria noted above.

## Review of the Literature

### Preliminary Remarks

A crucial assumption behind the studies to be reviewed below is that electrodes placed over homolateral sites detect almost exclusively the activity of directly underlying brain tissue. This has been shown not to hold in at least one set of circumstances. Barrett et al. (1976) reported that the $P_1$ component (latency approx 100 ms) of VERs elicited by chequerboard reversal in one visual half-field was larger in lateral electrodes placed over the hemisphere *ipsilateral* to the VF stimulated. This finding directly contradicted that of Cobb and Morton (1970) who reported the more expected result, that half-field chequerboard stimulation gave rise to larger contralateral VERs. However, these latter investigators employed bipolar occipital–parietal electrode linkages, and Barrett et al., using a common mid-frontal reference, showed clearly that the finding of Cobb and Morton was an artefact of bipolar recording. Barrett et al. argued that the "paradoxical" lateralisation of the VER they observed was a result of the disposition of the human striate cortex on the medial surfaces of the hemisphere, i.e. largely within the calcarine fissure. This has the effect of orienting each striate area such that electrodes ipsilateral to the side of stimulation are best placed to detect contralateral activity. That the ipsilateral VER to this type of chequerboard stimulation is indeed the result of activity in the contralateral hemisphere was demonstrated by Blumhardt et al. (1977) in a patient with a unilateral occipital lobectomy; VERs recorded from over the excised occipital area were larger than those from the intact hemisphere when elicited by ipsilateral stimulation, and absent in the case of contralateral stimulation.

A further series of experiments by this group (reported in Halliday *et al.*, 1979) investigated parametrically the stimulus conditions giving rise to the "paradoxical" lateralisation of VERs. They reported that the $P_1$ component is so lateralised as a result of asymmetrical stimulation of the macular region (up to approximately $2 \cdot 5°$ from the midline) of the VFs. Stimulation extending $15°$ into the periphery, but with no stimulation of the macular region, gave rise to VERs with a prominent positive–negative–positive component which was larger when recorded from contralaterally placed electrodes.

What are the implications of the above findings for studies investigating VERs elicited by DVF stimulation with the assumption that homolateral electrodes are best placed to detect activity in the hemisphere on which they are situated? There are three reasons why these findings most probably do not invalidate this assumption. First, many of the components of interest in DVF studies are, in view of their relatively long latencies, unlikely to originate in the striate cortex but rather in extrastriate regions situated mainly on the lateral surface of the occipital lobe. Assuming Barrett *et al.* (1976) to be correct in their explanation of the lateralisation of the $P_1$ component of the chequerboard response, components originating from cortex outside the calcarine fissure would not be expected to be paradoxically lateralised. Secondly, it may be the case that the Barrett *et al.* result is restricted to a limited range of stimuli. This conclusion is drawn on the basis of the report by Biersdorf and Nakamura (1971) that asymmetrical stimulation of a VF with a flash stimulus (semi-circle with a radius of $7 \cdot 5°$) yielded VERs with an early positive component (latency around 75 ms) which was considerably larger over the hemisphere contralateral to the VF stimulated. Finally, the majority of the studies discussed below used stimuli at eccentricities outside the macular region and thus outside the region of the visual field which when stimulated (at least by chequerboard reversal) gives rise to "paradoxical" lateralisation of VERs.

One exception to these points is the study of Vella *et al.* (1972). These investigators studied the distribution of VERs to flash-illuminated chequerboard stimuli in central vision and when lateralised to each VF separately. They reported that in the case of lateralised stimulation, VERs from the right hemisphere were larger irrespective of the field of stimulation, an effect absent with flash stimuli. However, the electrode montage used in this study consisted of a bipolar chain across left-temporal, left-occipital, midline-occipital, right-occipital and right-temporal sites. In the light of the results summarised by Halliday *et al.* (1979) it is likely that the montage used by Vella *et al.* does not allow any conclusions to be drawn as to the true locus of these effects.

To conclude this section, it is argued that it is only under a rather narrow range of conditions that the assumption that electrodes detect primarily ipsilateral activity does not hold true. Outside of these conditions it might be anticipated that if asymmetrical stimulation of the lateral VFs results in VERs which reflect the anatomical arrangements of the human visual system, then VERs recorded from the hemisphere contralateral to the VF stimulated should reflect the fact that they are detecting activity from the more directly stimulated hemisphere. The results of Halliday *et al.* (1979) and Biersdorf and Nakamura (1971) intimate that this is indeed the case, and the consensus of the studies cited in the review below adds further weight to this conclusion.

## Studies Employing "Simple" Stimuli

One of the first investigators to study the effects of DVF stimulation on VERs was Eason who, in a series of experiments, has studied the distribution of VERs across the occipital areas to asymmetrical flash stimuli. Eason and White (1967) recorded VERs from the right occipital area (referenced to the right ear lobe) of one subject. Stimuli consisted of flashes of a diameter of 1° directed either to the nasal or temporal hemiretina of the right eye. They reported that the initial components of the VER were larger when elicited by stimulation of the temporal hemiretina and suggested that this might reflect the fact that under this condition of stimulation the right hemisphere is stimulated directly, this not being the case when stimuli are projected to the left visual field (LVF). Subsequently, Eason *et al.* (1967a) recorded VERs from both right and left occipital sites (referred to ipsilateral ear lobes) using binocular stimulation in each visual field in three subjects. No clear evidence of an overall difference between VERs from direct and indirect hemispheres was observed, VER amplitudes appearing to interact with handedness and VF of stimulation. In a further experiment Eason *et al.* (1967a) utilised left- and right-handed subject groups. They reported that on comparing the amplitudes (as reflected by the size of a positive component with a latency of around 200 ms) of the VERs recorded from each hemisphere when each was directly stimulated, the right hemisphere was found to give rise to significantly larger VERs than the left in the left-handers, the effect being absent in right-handed subjects. Furthermore, right-hemisphere responses were larger in the left-handed group than in the right-handers.

A similar experiment to that described above was performed by Eason *et al.* (1967b), the difference being that groups of right-handed subjects differing with respect to sex were employed. Amplitudes of VERs were in this case assessed by taking the mean of the peak-to-peak amplitudes of a negative–positive–negative complex extending over the latency range 180–260 ms. In this study it was reported that the directly stimulated hemisphere gave rise to larger VERs although this effect was not significant in females for RVF stimulation. In addition, it was reported that the mean latencies of the components analysed were shorter in the directly stimulated hemisphere although no quantitative data are presented in support of this assertion. In addition to the above results, it was reported that the mean amplitude of the VERs elicited by stimulation in the LVF was significantly greater than that due to RVF stimulation in female, but not male, subjects.

Culver *et al.* (1970) report yet another study in this paradigm. In this case right- and left-handed females were employed, and the dominant and non-dominant eye stimulated separately. The amplitudes of the resulting VERs were obtained in a somewhat bizarre fashion, the largest deflections from an extrapolated baseline in each of five 100 ms segments being summed to produce an overall measure of "amplitude". No effects of handedness were observed and only when subjects were stimulated in the LVF did a direct v. indirect hemisphere difference occur. These results are to some extent in accord with those previously reported by the Eason group in that Eason *et al.* (1967b) failed to find a significant hemisphere asymmetry in VERs elicited by RVF stimulation in females.

A number of methodological inadequacies make the interpretation of the above series of studies difficult. In all of the studies described the description of the means of analysis of the VERs is vague and the presentation of quantified data minimal. Asymmetric reference sites were utilised (ipsilateral ear lobes), giving rise to problems of interpretation of the VER differences observed (see p. 131). In no study is any mention made of the instructions given to subjects, giving rise to the possibility of the VERs being contaminated with the effects of an uncontrolled cognitive set (p. 132). Finally, although stimuli were presented to each VF in a blocked fashion, their location therefore being predictable, no report is made of any attempt to monitor fixation to ensure that systematic deviations did not occur.

These inadequacies are all shared by a further study conducted in a paradigm similar to that used by Eason's group by Gott and Boyarsky (1972). Subjects consisted of right- and left-handed males, in whom occipital VERs were recorded to flashes (size unspecified) directed to points of 38° eccentricity in each visual field. A particularly odd aspect of this study was that stimulation was via the right eye only for LVF stimulation, and the left eye for RVF stimulation. Whilst individual components of the resulting VERs are labelled in a figure in the experimental report the amplitudes and latencies of these appear to have been averaged prior to analysis. One aspect of the results of this study is of interest in that it accords with the findings of Eason *et al.* (1967b). As with those authors, Gott and Boyarsky report that comparison of the directly stimulated hemisphere reveals an asymmetry for left-handers, the amplitude of the VERs being greater in the right hemisphere, and an absence of such an asymmetry in right-handers. A number of other effects are also reported, the most notable of which is that the hemisphere contralateral to the preferred hand gave rise to VERs with longer latencies than did the ipsilateral hemisphere.

Whilst the studies of Eason *et al.* (1967a, b), Culver *et al.* (1970) and Gott and Boyarsky (1972) are methodologically deficient in many ways, two aspects of their results are intriguing. These are the findings that in both left-handed males and females the amplitudes of the VERs from the hemispheres when directly stimulated give rise to an asymmetry (right > left) which is absent in right-handed males. This is unexpected in view of the fact that the strongest hemisphere asymmetries might be expected to be observed in the most homogeneously lateralised group, right-handed males, and not in groups who might be expected either to be heterogeneous with respect to functional lateralisation, i.e. left-handers (Hardyck and Petrinovich, 1977), or to be lateralised to a lesser extent, i.e. females (McGlone, 1980). It would be of interest to know to what extent these findings are replicable in a well-conducted study, and if so whether they reflect differences principally in some structural aspect of the brain organisation of these groups, or in their preferential mode of cognitive processing.

Andreassi *et al.* (1975) report two experiments in which VERs were elicited by a stimulus (a small cross) projected on to the fovea and at varying eccentricities in either VF (1·33°, 2·67° and 4·00° in their experiment 2). VERs were recorded from left and right occipital areas referred to the left ear lobe and subjects were required covertly to count the occurrence of each stimulus in each block of trials, which were blocked with respect to VF of stimulation. In both experiments it was observed that the peak latencies of the components selected for analysis ($P_1$, around 120 ms; $N_2$, around 170 ms; and $P_2$, around 260 ms) showed no asymmetries to midline stimulation but were asymmetric when stimuli were projected into the lateral VFs. These latencies were observed to be shorter in VERs recorded from the hemisphere contralateral to the site of stimulation. Similarly, the peak-to-peak amplitudes of the $P_1$–$N_2$ and $N_2$–$P_2$ components were significantly greater in VERs from the directly stimulated hemisphere, a finding in agreement with several of the studies reviewed above.

The explanation offered by Andreassi *et al.* for these results centred, as might be expected, on the anatomical arrangements of the geniculo-striate visual pathways. They proposed that the latency differences between homologous components in the VERs recorded from directly and indirectly stimulated hemispheres results from the time taken for the information arriving at the directly stimulated hemisphere to cross the corpus callosum and activate the opposite hemisphere. Likewise, the relative attenuation of the VER from the indirectly stimulated hemisphere presumably reflects the degradation of information as it is transferred. In this context it is relevant to note that the mean latency difference between directly and indirectly stimulated hemispheres (averaged over VFs and conditions) in Andreassi *et al.*'s experiment 2 is 19·3 ms for the earliest component measured, $P_1$, which had a latency of around 110–140 ms. The significance of this delay will be discussed below.

Buchsbaum and Drago (1977) reported an experiment employing right-handed females in which VERs were recorded from homolateral occipital and "Wernicke's area" (posterior temporal) sites, referred to ipsilateral ear lobes. Stimuli consisted of flashes (size unspecified) centred 2° either to the left or right of fixation. In contrast to the studies reported so far in this section, blocks of trials consisted of stimuli appearing unpredictably in either VF. Four experimental conditions were employed, one in which subjects engaged in mental arithmetic (while fixating appropriately), and three requiring attention to be paid to the eliciting stimuli so as to detect the occurrence of various stimulus combinations. VERs were analysed by averaging the amplitude of time bands considered to contain prominent components, these being 76–112 ms, 116–152 ms and 168–248 ms respectively, and reported as encompassing a positive, a negative and a further positive peak; no latency data were presented. In the three conditions requiring attention to the stimuli, the directly stimulated hemisphere gave rise to VERs which were significantly greater in amplitude than that indirectly stimulated, this effect occurring for both hemispheres at both electrode sites and in all time bands. Moreover, on comparing the two hemispheres when each was directly stimulated, the left hemisphere was found to give rise to VERs with the greater amplitude, a result directly contradicting that of Culver *et al.* (1971). The effect of requiring subjects to engage in mental arithmetic was to depress the amplitude of all VER time bands, particularly that encompassing the $N_{140}$ component, and to abolish the hemisphere asymmetries related to direct/indirect stimulation observed in the other conditions.

The results of Buchsbaum and Drago (1977) further confirm the expectation that the structural arrangements of the visual system are reflected in VER asymmetries to DVF stimulation. They indicate, however, that such effects may not be accounted for solely by assuming that visual information suitably directed along the visual pathways necessarily results in asymmetries in VERs; when subjects were not required to attend to the eliciting stimuli, these effects disappeared. This finding emphasises the need to view critically the results of studies in which task or attentional set has not been controlled, and suggests that VERs may reflect the anatomical asymmetries of the visual system only under some minimal condition of stimulus-processing.

Ledlow *et al.* (1978a) reported an experiment in which a go/no-go RT task was utilised, target stimuli being small squares containing a cross, and non-targets empty squares. The stimuli subtended a visual angle of 1° and were exposed 2·5° in one or other VF. Separate VERs were formed to targets and non-targets in each VF with respect to hand used for response and known v. unknown (i.e. blocked or randomised) stimulus localisation. Recordings were from left and right occipital sites referred to linked mastoids. Whilst all the experimental variables had some effect on the RT data, only that of the VF of the eliciting stimuli affected the asymmetries of the VERs. Five components were reported as being analysed ($N_{70}$, $P_{130}$, $N_{170}$, $P_{240}$ and $P_{300}$) although data for only two of these ($P_{130}$ and $N_{170}$) are presented in the analysis of VF effects. It was reported that the latencies of $P_{130}$ and $N_{170}$ were significantly shorter in the directly stimulated hemisphere, the mean difference between the $P_{130}$ components of the VERs from directly and indirectly stimulated hemispheres being 18 ms, a figure in good agreement with Andreassi et al. (1975). This VF effect on component latencies was accompanied by the finding that the amplitude of $P_{130}$ was smaller, and $N_{170}$ larger, in the directly stimulated hemisphere. This finding of a smaller component in VERs elicited by direct stimulation is inconsistent with previously reviewed studies. Inspection of Ledlow et al.'s Fig. 2 suggests that the cause of this effect may lie in the fact that in the directly stimulated hemisphere this component (i.e. $P_{130}$) was influenced to a greater extent by the following $N_{170}$, which occurred at a shorter latency than in the indirect hemisphere, and therefore had the dual effect of shortening the latency and decreasing the amplitude of the preceding $P_{130}$ component. Also of interest is the fact that in four subjects on whom a further condition was imposed, that of not being required to respond to the stimuli, the hemisphere asymmetries described above were not obtained. This finding is reminiscent of that of Buchsbaum and Drago (1977) who reported that lack of attention to the eliciting stimuli abolished hemisphere asymmetries in the resulting VERs.

What conclusions may be drawn on the basis of the results of studies requiring active processing of the eliciting stimuli? It would seem clear that under such circumstances the asymmetries observed in VER amplitude are congruent with the notion that a hemisphere is, initially at least, activated to a greater extent when it is stimulated directly rather than indirectly by a visual stimulus. That this may reflect more than just the flow of information along the visual pathways in such stimulus conditions is indicated, as mentioned previously, by the finding that DVF stimuli fail to elicit such asymmetries when they do not require attention (Buchsbaum and Drago, 1977; Ledlow et al., 1978a). This example of an interaction between structural and cognitive factors in the processing of relatively simple stimuli is of great interest, and deserves further research.

Also of interest is the finding in the studies of Andreassi et al. (1975) and Ledlow et al. (1978a) of systematic latency differences in the initial components of VERs arising from directly and indirectly stimulated hemispheres. The question arises as to whether such differences reflect the time taken for information to cross the interhemispheric commissures, as suggested by Andreassi et al. (1975). Ledlow et al. (1978a) reject this notion on the grounds that (i) they detected no latency differences in homologous components in VERs from directly and indirectly stimulated hemispheres until a latency of around 120 ms, and (ii) those differences which are observed disappeared when active processing of the stimuli was not required. For these reasons, they argued, interhemispheric transmission must occur without detection, and the latency and amplitude asymmetries reflect, when they occur, the slower or less efficient processing of visual information in the indirectly stimulated hemisphere. To these reasons may be added one more against the view that such latency asymmetries reflect in any straightforward way interhemispheric transmission time (IHTT). Studies of manual simple reaction times to DVF stimuli consistently report an advantage for the ipsilateral over the contralateral hand of around 2·5 ms, and this has been taken as an estimate of the time taken for information to cross the additional, presumably callosal, pathway involved in contralateral responding (see Rizzolatti (1979) and Chapter 3 for discussion of these experiments). This estimate of IHTT is almost an order of magnitude smaller than that given by Andreassi *et al.* (19·3 ms) or Ledlow *et al.* (18 ms), a massive inconsistency.

It should be noted that it has recently been argued (Milner and Lines, 1982) that the IHTT deduced from studies of manual reaction times reflects transmission time across callosal fibres connecting the motor cortices, and not those at the level of the visual cortex. Milner and Lines (1982) argue that estimates of IHTT based on differences in vocal RT to ipsilateral and contralateral stimuli, which are in the order of 5–12 ms, are more likely to reflect IHTT between the visual cortices. These estimates are still less than the "IHTT" suggested by the studies of Andreassi *et al.* (1975) and Ledlow *et al.* (1978a). Thus, if it is the case that VER latency differences in DVF studies do give an estimate of IHTT, it is unlikely to be related to the information required for a simple behavioural response, and reflects a somewhat slower process.

## *Studies Employing "Complex" Stimuli*

A number of studies have used rather more complex stimuli and tasks than those described in the previous section, with the hope of obtaining information regarding material- or task-specific asymmetries of function.

The first of these studies was performed by Buchsbaum and Fedio (1970). These investigators elicited VERs from occipital placements (referred to ipsilateral ear lobes) with computer-generated stimuli consisting of either 3-letter words or nonsense patterns of the same size and photic intensity. The stimuli subtended an angle of 1° and were displaced with an eccentricity of 2° 20' to one or other side of the visual midline. The subjects were not required to engage in any task, but simply to fixate and observe the stimuli. Analysis of the VERs proceeded by computing the cross-correlation between homologous time points of each possible pair of waveforms within and between hemispheres and thus no information was presented about either the amplitude or latency of individual waveforms. Significant differences between waveforms were found for VERs elicited by direct and indirect stimulation and for the VERs elicited by the two types of stimuli. This latter effect was strongest in the directly stimulated left hemisphere, a finding in agreement with Buchsbaum and Fedio (1969), who reported that with midline stimulation these stimuli elicited more dissimilar VERs from the left hemisphere. In an identical experimental design to Buchsbaum and Fedio (1970), Fedio and Buchsbaum (1971) investigated VERs in a group of patients with unilateral temporal lesions. They reported that VERs from each hemisphere when directly stimulated were more stable than those elicited by indirect stimulation and that, in the group with right temporal damage, VERs from the left hemisphere differentiated the verbal and non-verbal stimuli. A further finding was that the left temporal group produced VERs to the verbal stimuli which, independently of visual field of stimulation, were less stable than those from the right temporal group, this effect being reversed with respect to the VERs elicited by the non-verbal stimuli.

The above studies suffer from a number of methodological deficiencies, most notably the use of large numbers of pairwise comparisons in evaluating waveform differences (giving rise to the risk of type I error) and the lack of any control over subjects' processing of the eliciting stimuli. In spite of these problems, the results suggest that VER waveforms may, in a DVF paradigm, discriminate between verbal and non-verbal stimuli in a way congruent with expectations derived from the results of behavioural studies.

Gott et al. (1977) investigated VERs to DVF stimulation in normal and commissurotomised subjects. Stimuli consisted of words and geometric shapes, which were presented either unilaterally or bilaterally, and the respective associated tasks were rhyme detection or shape-matching. VERs were recorded from occipital and parietal electrodes referenced to the left ear, and were formed only from trials associated with correct behavioural responses. Analysis of VERs took the form of comparison of cross-correlations between pairs of waveforms and was centred mainly on assessment of the differences between VERs recorded from each hemisphere when bilaterally stimulated as opposed to those elicited by direct unilateral stimulation. It was reported that in both normals and the patient group, VERs from each hemisphere were more similar when elicited by bilateral stimulation. Group differences were observed, however, in that patients' VERs from occipital sites in response to direct stimulation with verbal stimuli were more dissimilar than normals, while bilateral stimulation gave rise to VERs which were significantly more similar. A number of other results are also reported, perhaps the most interesting of which is that verbal stimuli gave rise to an asymmetry in an $N_2$–$P_3$

component, in VERs from both groups, when the left hemisphere was directly stimulated. This and other results are, however, difficult to evaluate due to the lack of quantitative data presented.

Unfortunately, Gott *et al.* (1977) do not compare VERs evoked from each hemisphere under conditions of unilateral stimulation, i.e. a direct v. indirect comparison. Were such a comparison to have been performed, the expectation would be that the VERs recorded from the patients would differ more than those of the normal group, in view of the lack of forebrain commissures in these patients. Inspection of Gott *et al.*'s Fig. 4, however, suggests the intriguing possibility that the absence of such commissures does not prevent the production of VERs in an indirectly stimulated hemisphere which are morphologically similar to those from the hemisphere receiving the stimulus information directly. Further investigation is required to determine the extent to which this similarity is a result of the contribution of activity at the common reference employed, the left ear. If a consistent result, it calls into question the assumption that the information required for the emission of a VER in an indirectly stimulated hemisphere is transferred via the forebrain commissures.

An experiment involving normal and congenitally deaf children has been reported by Neville (1977). VERs were elicited from left and right posterior temporal regions (referred to linked ear lobes) in response to stimuli consisting of line drawings of common objects (3°–7° in visual angle) projected with their inner edges 2° left or right of fixation. The task of the subjects was to match the picture of the object exposed to the correct one on a test card. VERs were formed separately to correct and incorrect responses, although only those to correct responses are reported. Three components of the VERs were analysed, $P_{270}$, $N_{900}$ and $P_{970}$. For all three peaks in the VERs from the hearing children, latencies were shorter and amplitudes greater in the right hemisphere, irrespective of visual field of stimulus presentation (no quantitative data pertaining to peak latencies are presented, however). In contrast, in the deaf children, VER asymmetries interacted with VF of presentation such that the directly stimulated hemisphere gave rise to larger and earlier responses. Breaking down this group of subjects on the basis of whether they employed sign language revealed that signing children showed larger VERs from the left hemisphere, non-signers exhibiting no VER asymmetries.

These intriguing results suggest that later components of the VER may be influenced more by functional hemisphere asymmetries than the site of initial stimulus registration, and that deaf and hearing children may differ with respect to functional cerebral organisation.

Lehmann and Julesz (1978) elicited VERs from left and right occipital areas (referred to a midline occipital placement) with lateralised "dynamic random dot stereograms". Such stimuli appear, when viewed monocularly, to be random visual noise; viewed binocularly, however, they are observed to pulsate in depth and VERs were formed from EEG samples time-locked to this appearance of depth. With stimulation in either VF the directly stimulated hemisphere was found to give rise to VERs with larger middle-latency components than those from the indirectly stimulated hemisphere. No other hemisphere asymmetry was observed, and Lehmann and Julesz argued that these findings offered no support for the view that the processes mediating stereopsis were lateralised predominantly in the right hemisphere, as suggested by Carmon and Bechtoldt (1969), and Durnford and Kimura (1971).

Rugg and Beaumont (1978) report two experiments in which VERs were elicited by lateralised letter stimuli (subtending 1°) exposed at an eccentricity of 4°. Recordings were made from occipital areas referred to a central midline reference. Both experiments required subjects to perform a go/no-go RT task, responding in experiment 1 to letters, the names of which contained an "ee" sound, and in experiment 2 to those letters containing a right angle. In both experiments the latencies of components $P_1$ and $N_2$ (occurring around 130 ms and 180 ms poststimulus) demonstrated a VF-by-hemisphere interaction of the type described by Andreassi et al. (1975) and Ledlow et al. (1978a). The mean direct/indirect difference in the latencies of the earlier of these components, $P_1$, averaged over hemispheres and experiments, was 15·2 ms. None of the latencies of the components analysed differentiated between the different tasks involved in the two experiments. On the other hand, the finding in experiment 1 that $N_1$–$P_2$ amplitude was greater in each hemisphere when directly stimulated did not occur in experiment 2. In this experiment the amplitude of $N_1$–$P_2$ from the left hemisphere did not differ with respect to visual field of stimulation, an effect possibly attributable to the relative lack of the involvement of the left hemisphere in the task requirement of the second experiment.

It is of interest to note that in neither experiment 1 or 2 of Rugg and Beaumont (1978) did hemisphere differences in peak-to-peak amplitude of the earliest measurable VER components, $P_1$–$N_1$, interact with VF of stimulus presentation. This finding, combined with the lack of such an interaction in the amplitude of $N_1$–$P_2$ in the left hemisphere in experiment 2, adds further weight to the suggestion than an important determining factor of VF-dependent asymmetries in VERs is the processing demands associated with the stimuli; they do not *necessarily* follow as a result of DVF stimulus presentation.

Ledlow et al. (1978b) performed a study similar in many respects to that of Rugg and Beaumont (1978). VERs were recorded from occipital areas (referred to linked mastoids) in response to stimuli consisting of letter pairs. These pairs consisted of letters either of the same or different cases and subjects were required to make same/different responses on the basis either of physical or name matches. The stimuli subtended a visual angle of 0·6° and were presented at an eccentricity of 2·5°. A formidable number of experimental conditions were involved, namely, stimulus location (central, left or right of fixation), knowledge of location (blocked or unblocked), letter combination (upper case, lower case or mixed), blocking v. non-blocking of letter combinations, type of match, and responding hand. These conditions interacted in a complex fashion with respect both to RT data and those derived from the concurrently recorded VERs. Of principal interest in the present context are the findings that the latencies of the components $N_{70}$, $P_{130}$ and $N_{170}$ were apparently all shorter under conditions of direct stimulation (unfortunately no data are presented relating to this effect and so the magnitude of these differences is unknown). Furthermore, the amplitude of $P_{130}$ was reported as being smaller under direct stimulation and that for $P_{300}$ larger. The finding with respect to $P_{130}$ is in agreement with that reported by Ledlow *et al.* (1978a), and may be explicable in similar terms (see page 139). Further analysis of the amplitude of $P_{300}$ revealed that this direct/indirect difference was larger in the left hemisphere when name matches were performed, and in the right hemisphere during performance of physical matches. This finding is of particular interest as it is one of the very rare occasions on which the $P_{300}$ component has been demonstrated as showing task-dependent cerebral asymmetries (see Friedman *et al.* (1977) and Rugg and Beaumont (1979) for further discussion of this issue).

The results of the above experiment of Ledlow *et al.* (1978b) are of much interest, and reinforce the view that VERs may be used to index cerebral asymmetries of processing. Lack of presentation of much potentially relevant data (e.g. peak latencies), however, is unfortunate, and hampers a more detailed evaluation of their results.

To conclude this section, it is suggested that the experiments reviewed above indicate that VERs elicited by stimuli whose processing engages lateralised processes are sensitive both to the locus of such processing and VF of stimulus presentation. The asymmetries in the VERs recorded under such conditions appear to be the result of complex interactions between these two factors.

## Conclusions

The conclusions that can be drawn on the basis of the above review are limited. Whilst ample evidence exists that DVF stimulation gives rise to VER asymmetries broadly congruent with what would be expected on anatomical considerations, it is clear that an unknown number of other factors act to influence the magnitude and direction of these asymmetries. One of these factors is the nature of the processing associated with the eliciting stimuli, and it is perhaps encouraging that several studies have produced evidence suggesting that task-dependent VER asymmetries are congruent with expectations derived from behavioural studies of DVF stimulation. A number of problems, however, prevent studies of this type making an independent contribution to the understanding of hemisphere function. A major handicap is that because of the relative paucity of knowledge of the neurophysiological and cognitive concomitants of AERs it is rarely possible to make crucial predictions allowing the testing of specific hypotheses; to date, the inferences which have been made from AER data with respect to cerebral asymmetries have been on a *post hoc* basis.

It is, however, premature to dismiss VER techniques as a means of investigating cerebral asymmetries, both in DVF and other paradigms, as very few well-conducted studies have yet been reported. The possibility that such data may allow the elucidation of problems proving obstinate when tackled by purely behavioural means still exists, but this question will not be resolved until the results of a substantial number of well-conducted experiments are available for assessment.

## Summary

Following a brief review of some relevant aspects of methodology, studies investigating hemisphere differences in VERs elicited by DVF stimulation are reviewed. The first section of the review concentrates on studies the results of which challenge the assumption that homolaterally placed electrodes mainly detect activity emanating from the hemisphere on which they are sited. It is concluded that violations of this assumption occur only in a narrow range of conditions.

Studies employing relatively simple stimuli are then reviewed, and particular emphasis given to those furnishing data regarding latency differences between homologous components of VERs recorded simultaneously from directly and indirectly stimulated hemispheres. Such differences do not concur with behavioural estimates of interhemispheric transmission time, and the possibility that such latency differences do not directly reflect the time taken for information to cross the corpus callosum is discussed.

The final set of studies reviewed are those employing more complex stimuli and, in some cases, responses requiring processing which might be expected to be lateralised. Whilst the results of these studies can be interpreted so as to be reasonably consistent with behavioural studies employing DVF stimuli, they do not at present offer new insights into the processing of such stimuli.

The general conclusion reached is that, although promising, too few well-conducted studies have been carried out in this area to permit an evaluation of its potential as a means of increasing knowledge of the cerebral basis of the processing of DVF stimuli.

# 8

## SEX DIFFERENCES: LITTLE REASON FOR FEMALES TO PLAY MIDFIELD

*Hugh Fairweather*

                                                        i would

suggest that certain ideas gestures
rhymes, like Gillette Razor Blades
having been used and reused
to the mystical moment of dullness emphatically are
Not To Be Resharpened.
                                        (e.e. cummings)[1]

THIS REVIEW will be structured as follows. First we shall consider some of the "background" arguments—if sex differences in visual half-field studies are to be a piece in a jigsaw, what sort of assurance do we have that a picture will emerge? Notably these arguments centre around two issues: that of sex differences in overall cognitive ability, and that of the effects of unilateral lesions. Much of the argumentation with respect to the latter has been aired in McGlone's recent (1980) paper and the attendant discussion. With respect to the former, most of the ground rules have been laid down in Fairweather (1976) and the present discussion will very much follow that in both tone and intent—essentially a companion piece. In both cases we shall be highlighting the broad themes and updating and expanding the evidence where available and where appropriate.

---

[1] From *Complete Poems* by E. E. Cummings (Granada Publishing Limited), with permission.

147

Having established our general texts we shall then move on to the specific enterprise—that of logging and classifying all studies in which sex has been both a factor either discussed or analysed, and a word which has not evaded the author's visual search. We shall dwell at length upon two case studies which currently excite interest, and which also clearly illustrate most of the present contentions. These are, from within the verbal domain, lexical decision (be it noted against a background of extremely few positive findings), and from within the non-verbal domain, that of face recognition (against a background of comparatively frequent positive findings, mostly indicating more clear-cut asymmetries in males).

One further remark might perhaps be made before we embark. The area of sex-difference research is bedevilled, not to say constipated, by an extraordinary proclivity for the erection and elimination of straw men, both empirical and (less justifiably) theoretical. For those absorbed by such pastimes the two general texts will serve as orientation, and almost any of the currently available books or review chapters as illustration. In what follows we shall try to establish as unfussily as possible the simple state of the game.

## Clinical Background: Aphasia, Crossed Aphasia, Non-aphasia, and Prosopagnosia

McGlone (1980) contends, briefly, that the male brain is both functionally and anatomically more asymmetrically organised than the female brain. She supports this contention by claiming that females are less susceptible to unilateral cerebral insult, as evidenced by a preponderance of male aphasics (though not crossed aphasics) and patterns of cognitive (verbal/non-verbal) test performance.

It now seems extremely unlikely that more males than females are liable to become aphasic as a result of strokes in the left hemisphere: the slight absolute preponderence of males in the largest samples matches almost exactly the slight preponderance of males suffering strokes *with whatever outcome,* typically in a ratio of about 1·3:1 (Kertesz and Sheppard, 1981). This latest study is notable not only in that it concerns geographically the same catchment area as that of McGlone, but also that it involves a much larger sample (114 males, 78 females) and finds no distinction between the male and female groups in terms of education, lesion size, age and scores on the various subtests of the Western Aphasia Battery. The broad findings of this report are further echoed in communications from centres in Italy (De Renzi *et al.*, 1980; Miceli *et al.*, 1981).

If right-handed males are in general presumed to have no (or very little) language in their right hemispheres (or alternatively there are presumed to be very few males with right-hemisphere dominance for language), there is no *a priori* reason to expect that there should be any (or certainly, comparatively few) male crossed aphasics (male right-handers aphasic as a result of a right-hemisphere lesion). This is clearly not the case, either in McGlone's original survey, or in our own additional search (see Table 1).

It is also not difficult to find crossed aphasics amongst patients with missile wounds, a fate most usually restricted to males (Newcombe and Ratcliff, 1973). McGlone, arguing from the female viewpoint, says that such a finding is not incompatible with the "suggestion that right hemisphere *dominance* is not more common in females than males" (p. 218). This is true, but that would

TABLE 1

*Reports of Crossed Aphasia in Male and Female Adult Right-handers*

| From McGlone (1980) | Sex | Additional cases | Sex |
|---|---|---|---|
| Angelergues *et al.* (1962) | Female | Anastasopoulos (1959) | Male |
| Barraquer-Bordas *et al.* (1963) | Female | April and Han (1980) | Male |
| Botez and Wertheim (1959) | Male | April and Tse (1977) | Male |
| Brown and Wilson (1973) | Female | Assal *et al.* (1981) | Male |
| Clarke and Zangwill (1965) | 2 Females | Carr *et al.* (1981) | 3 Males |
| | | | 1 Female |
| Denes and Caviezel (1979) | Male | Chesher (1936) | Male |
| (NB. See formal report, 1981) | | Claude and Schaeffer (1921) | Female |
| Ettlinger *et al.* (1955) | Male | Fernández-Martín *et al.* (1968) | Male |
| Foroglou *et al.* (1975) | Male | | |
| | | Ito (1980) | Male |
| Hécaen *et al.* (1971) | Male | Kertesz and Sheppard | 1 Male |
| Holmes and Sadoff (1966) | Male | (1981) | 3 Females |
| Kennedy (1916) | 1 Male | Lovell *et al.* (1932) | Male |
| | 2 Females | Mendel (1914) | Female |
| Marinesco *et al.* (1938) | Male | Pillon *et al.* (1979) | 2 Males |
| Milner *et al.* (1964) | Male | Rothschild (1931) | 1 Male |
| Solomon and Taylor (1979) | Male | | 1 Female |
| Stone (1934) | Male | Senator (1904) | Female |
| Urbain (1978) | Female | Souques (1910) | Male |
| Wechsler (1976) | Female | Subirana (1952) | Female |
| Weisenburg and McBride | Male | Weisenburg and McBride | Female |
| (1935) (Case 20) | | (1935) (Case 10) | |
| | | Zangwill (1979) | 2 Males |
| Total | 12 Males | | 18 Males |
| | 9 Females | | 10 Females |
| Grand total | 30 Males | | |
| | 19 Females | | |

hardly seem to be the suggestion she wants to make anyway, since it would be incompatible with her own claims regarding the overall incidence of aphasia (and, incidentally, would not square with her own later argument that "an acute lesion should produce an equivalent or somewhat higher incidence of verbal impairments in females compared to males (since a lesion in either hemisphere may depress verbal scores in females)" (p. 253)). McGlone could only win this particular battle by losing the war. The argument is not in any case terribly compelling, principally because the positive instances would have to be assessed against the negative instances (non-occurrence of aphasia despite unilateral lesion)—data which is less readily available. (Apropos of which, McGlone appears to be alone in finding right-hemisphere female non-aphasics with comparative ease, at least with respect to the studies by Weisenburg and McBride (1935) and Kertesz and Sheppard (1981).) It is also extremely doubtful whether very many of the cited cases would count as "pure" cases of crossed aphasia, in the sense of being uncontaminated by hints of ambidexterity, familial sinistrality, early damage and bilateral dysfunction (see table in Ettlinger *et al.*, 1955; comments in April and Han, 1980; and individual case notes). At all events, probably not compelling enough to continue the exercise with conviction.

Let us now turn to the nub of McGlone's thesis, which concerns precisely those patients not rendered aphasic by stroke to one or the other hemisphere. It is important here to remind ourselves that the patients we are discussing fall into two main categories—those who have suffered strokes, and those with cerebral tumours. The latter group typically accounts for the minor proportion of aphasic patients (a quarter in Weisenburg and McBride, 1935), probably because tumours are of much earlier origin, and compensation may have been possible. It is also not contended that this group, when not aphasic, show any sex-related patterns of cognitive test performance according to side of lesion. This is true both in McGlone's own (1980) data and also in that in a far larger sample from the National Hospital in London, England, comprising 114 male (68 left-hemisphere, 56 right) and 83 female patients (46 left-hemisphere, 37 right) (Shallice and Evans, unpublished data). No significant sex-by-side of tumour interactions were found for age-corrected scores on the WAIS Block Design, Picture Completion and Digit Span.

The clinical evidence for greater functional asymmetry in males, then, presently rests almost entirely[2] on McGlone's series of stroke patients reported in most detail in 1977, but also in 1978 and, with some additions, in the 1980 review. Numbers vary from report to report depending on changes in testing

---

[2] Other studies, even in this context, have been either anecdotal in terms of numbers, or idiosyncratic in terms of tests (or both): see discussion, e.g. of Lansdell's series, in the general texts.

schedules, but at most the core pool comprises 34 males (22 left-hemisphere, 12 right-hemisphere) and 20 females (11 left-hemisphere, 9 right-hemisphere), with an additional 25 patients (aetiology unspecified) mentioned in 1980. Only males show a specific reduction in Wechsler Verbal IQ and Verbal Memory scores consequent upon left-hemisphere damage, right-hemisphere patients performing much as controls. In females both groups show an equal impairment, scoring roughly midway between the two male groups. In contrast to the Verbal IQ results, a pro-rated Performance IQ score (missing out the Digit Symbol subtest because of handwriting problems with some left-hemisphere patients) failed to differentiate the four groups. However, data on tests of mental rotation and memory for faces (undetailed), presented in 1980, showed left-hemisphere males to be selectively spared on the former, and (less significantly) right-hemisphere males to be selectively affected on the latter.

Whilst these findings are viewed with much scepticism[3] from within the clinical ranks, it remains that no substantial (published) voice has been heard in denial (or support). If it did indeed turn out to be the case that it was very much more difficult to demonstrate hemisphere-related cognitive deficit in female stroke patients then we should have to ask the following question: "What is it about a stroke to males' left hemispheres that fails to render them aphasic, yet still selectively reduces their Verbal IQ?" The possibility discussed by McGlone (see section on "Vascular Asymmetries" in the 1980 paper) is that strokes in males may have more profound effects, both in terms of precise site and extent, and with a tendency to be more damaging in the left. Thus far the grosser measures have not been seen to be systematically related to language function, and it remains to be seen whether finer-grain measures would be more successful.

One intriguing piece of information that has so far failed to permeate the mainstream of the discussion, is that it appears extremely difficult to locate females suffering from prosopagnosia, a loss of the ability to recognise faces (Mazzucchi et al., 1977). A compilation of 49 published cases included only 8 females. Almost two-thirds of the lesions were vascular in origin (i.e. strokes). In over half the cases the critical lesion was bilateral (although only one female fell in this category); all but three of the remainder fell in the right-hemisphere category. Whiteley and Warrington (1977) add three further patients to the

---

[3] A scepticism fuelled in part by uncertainties regarding localising signs of the lesions: McGlone (1977) reports that lateralisation was "determined on the basis of positive signs reported in at least two of the following independent investigations: neurological examination, angiogram, EEG, brain scan, air study or computerised transaxial tomography" (p. 776). However no precise numbers are reported. There are two points to note: (i) signs do not always agree; (ii) some signs are generally considered more accurate than others. Brain scans are usually given priority in this respect, and Kertesz and Sheppard (1981) report that for 169 out of their 206 cases lateralisation was established in this way.

list: one bilateral male, and two right-hemisphere females. Such findings may be (somewhat tantalisingly) juxtaposed with asymmetries in the normal population to be discussed later.

TABLE 2

*Incidence of Prosopagnosia in Males and Females (from Mazzucchi et al., 1977)*

| Sex | N | Side of lesion | | |
|-----|---|-------|-----------|------|
|     |   | Right | Bilateral | Left |
| Males | 41 | 15 | 25 | 1 |
| Females | 8 | 5 | 1 | 2 |

## Normative Background

The tacit answer to the tacit question "Why asymmetry of function?" is that the more asymmetric the division of function, the better the overall performance for any given function. Otherwise we would indeed have had to invent it. In which case, if female brains were in fact less asymmetrically organised for a variety of functions, we should expect them to be, as a group, disadvantaged for all those particular functions. Not even the archest anti-feminist would subscribe to that, since even they would "concede" female advantages on some verbal skills. The ontological argument, whilst naively attractive, is in any case overly simplistic: first, there may be a number of skills (face recognition and lexical decision being apposite candidates) that would benefit from bilateral representation; and second, the cognitive capabilities of each of the hemispheres are much more interchangeable (at least in the normal population) than a clear division would dictate. There is no *a priori* reason to expect that the level of a particular cognitive skill should be related to the particular index of cerebral organisation known as "cerebral lateralisation". It may indeed not be very easy to fashion a direct correlation, although researchers have been slow to capitalise on perhaps the only two examples that would be both easy to test and that we might confidently include among the literal handful of tests giving consistent sex differences—namely mental rotation and spelling (a basis for lexical decision?).

There are also other reasons for being wary of the argument, in whichever direction it is mounted. Endemic to the methodology of psychology is the urge to match *differences* to *differences*, in this case (and some others) in terms of patterns of cognitive test scores to indices of cerebral organisation, and vice versa. Now *differences* necessarily beget *deficiencies:* one group necessarily has to possess less of a certain commodity than another. And deficiencies begin, subtly, to acquire the undertones of values: one group, one hemisphere is *better* or *worse* than another. When these groups have easily identifiable social roles, we are fast moving towards inviting recipes for discrimination. The methodology swamps the sum of its parts and the hemispheres, as the sexes, are seen to have just as stereotyped roles. The facts of the matter turn out to be remarkably parallel: both the sexes and the hemispheres are in equal parts advantaged for a very small number of idiosyncratic skills practised in idiosyncratic circumstances. In which case we might be much better advised to adopt the strategy of Hardyck (1977), in reviewing the analogous case of right- and left-handedness, and ask not how such possibly different patterns of cerebral organisation underpin possibly dissimilar cognitive capacities, but rather how they underpin such certainly similar cognitive capacities.

The intrusion of normative considerations into the present discussion, then, seems at best thoroughly unhelpful, and at worst, divisive. The notion of hemisphericians looking over their shoulders for validation of intricate interactions is akin to builders of houses of cards scrabbling for prime sites on sand.

## The Divided Visual Field Studies

### General Remarks

In an exercise of this kind one inevitably develops a mental checklist of criteria against which each individual study is assessed: the column headings in Table 4 essentially reflect these preoccupations. In what may be taken as a pessimistic sign, the early and indeed the majority of items on this list have to do with basic experimental design: the precise nature and "parentage" of the stimulus, and the operation(s) that have to be performed with it; the response; the measure; the numbers of practice and test trials; the numbers and nature of subjects (handedness, familial handedness, age); the statistics. Here, as elsewhere, these considerations are important because they determine the outcome of the experiments; and they may all, independently or in combination, interact with sex.

Laterality effects are tied to the difficulty of the task (whether expressed in terms of the operation, or the stimulus on which it is performed). Some effects may only appear to occur with particular responses, which may themselves be lateralised, unwittingly or otherwise (e.g. vocal responses, or manual responses confined to one hand). Some effects may occur only at certain practice levels, and in turn interact with difficulty and overall performance level. Small numbers of trials produce unreliable findings: Berenbaum and Harshman (1980) point out in the case of dichotic listening that reliability over

30 trials is only of the order of 0·6 or 0·7, but rises to 0·9 over 240 trials. This means that a "substantial proportion of subjects are probably providing scores that do not accurately reflect their underlying neurological organisation" (p. 210). The situation is unlikely to be different for divided visual field studies (e.g. Hellige, 1976; Ward and Ross, 1977). Fewer than half the studies reviewed have employed more than 100 trials, and only a third more than 240.

If the measure is reaction time, then one has to know the error rate: an error rate of 20% (quite common in laterality experiments) may allow a completely different strategy from that of 5% or under (the standard sort of rate for "pure" reaction-time experiments). Similarly, if the measure is accuracy, then one has to be assured that the overall level is comfortably above chance. The value of the statistic employed (the most appropriate of which is taken to be an analysis of variance allowing assessment of a sex-by-visual-field interaction) may be obscured by the inclusion of more than one task (often from both the verbal and non-verbal domains), and/or of different handedness and age groups; or even by the sexes not being analysed together under the same statistic.

Those then are the considerations at the outset obstructing the quest for a grand design. That grand design might consist in finding a cluster of positive results not merely dominated by one of the more esoteric aspects of methodology, but rather by an aspect of the material or the task that would allow us to generate a plainly psychological hypothesis. Readers are urged to consult Table 4: here is the madness in the method, and the grist of this review. What follows is a brief commentary on these findings.[4]

## Verbal Material

It may be as well to underscore again here that the distinction between our two main classifications—"verbal" and "non-verbal"—is in terms of material rather than operations. Thus under the aegis of "letters" come studies involving the recognition of rotated letters, degraded letters, and the disembedding of constituent letters from an overall (letter-like) pattern, all of which might very properly be deemed "spatial". In which context, those entertained by the possibilities of the reduction of overall cognitive capacities to patterns of cerebral lateralisation might note three recent laboratory demonstrations of a male facility to rotate both verbal and non-verbal stimuli (Kail *et al.*, 1979; Petrusic *et al.*, 1978; Tapley and Bryden, 1977). This particular and peculiar capacity seems to be the only and essential factor distinguishing the sexes on

---

[4] The commentary is restricted to studies with adults. Developmental studies were considered too sparse to merit lengthy consideration: they are tabulated for information in the Appendix (and see Chapter 6). The generally negative nature of the findings in children for visual stimuli is broadly in line with that for the more numerous studies on dichotic listening (see Witelson, 1977c; McGlone, 1980).

TABLE 3

*Summary of Sex Differences in Divided Visual Field Studies
with Adult Right-handers*[5]

| Material | Sex more lateralised | | |
| --- | --- | --- | --- |
| | No difference | Males | Females |
| *Verbal* | | | |
| Digits | — | 2 | — |
| Letters | 18 | — | 1 |
| Letter strings | 5 | 1 | — |
| Words | 12 | 1 | — |
| Names: categorisation | 1 | — | — |
| Lexical decision | 6 | 1 | 1 |
| Total | 42 | 5 | 2 |
| *Non-verbal* | | | |
| Dots: detection | 8 | 1 | 1 |
| localisation | 10 | 2 | — |
| enumeration | — | 1 | — |
| Line orientation | 2 | 1 | — |
| Illusions | 1 | — | — |
| Figures: irregular | 1 | 1 | 1 |
| regular | 6 | 1 | — |
| Common objects | 2 | 1 | — |
| Colours | 2 | — | — |
| Faces: famous | 1 | — | — |
| familiar | 2 | 1 | — |
| unfamiliar | 6 | 3 | 1 |
| categorisation | — | 1 | — |
| emotions | 4 | — | 1 |
| Total | 45 | 13 | 4 |

more general tests of spatial ability, but it has so far failed to attract a
sex-related placement across the cerebral hemispheres.

Quite unexpectedly, certainly for McGlone (1980) and probably many
others, is the almost total lack of positive findings for verbal material (see Table
3). Of the handful that do present themselves, the two on digits are both highly
idiosyncratic and attract considerable adverse comments. The one for letters
and the one for words are offset by the abundance of negative findings; and the
one on letter strings by the inclusion of familial sinistrals and a failure to
replicate. This leads us to the most difficult of the tasks involving verbal
material—lexical decision (deciding whether a series of letters is a word or not a
word).

[5] See footnote p. 189.

TABLE 4

Sex Differences in Divided Visual Field Studies with Adult Right-handers

| Study | Sex more lateralised | Task details | Response | Measure | Trials | Ns M:F | Comments |
|---|---|---|---|---|---|---|---|
| **Verbal** | | | | | | | |
| *Digits* | | | | | | | |
| Kail and Siegal (1978) | Males (see Comments) | Immediate recall, 4 of 9 (in grid); position and/or identify information (three conditions). Central fixation letter or form. | Manual (written) | Accuracy | $4^P + 16^T$ (per condition) | 18:18 | Sex effect for identity, not position. No overall ANOVA, sexes separately. Performance only just above chance level. |
| Milstein et al. (1979) | Males (see Comments) | Single-digit multiplication with 5 types of distractors (inc. same or different multiplication in opposite VF. Exposure 300 ms. | Vocal | Accuracy | $100^T$ | 10:10 (varying in age from 19 to 60 years!) | Ill in both design and (uncomfortably near-sexist) intent: distractors included male/female nudes—"we had expected that males would be most affected by slides of nude females. . .". |
| *Letters* | | | | | | | |
| Bryden (1965) | ND | Identify 1 of 16. Exposure 25 ms, 20 ms. | Vocal | Accuracy | $64^T$ | 10:10 | L-handers included in (NS): from raw data interaction for R-handers looks unlikely. |
| Bryden (1973) | ND (see Comments) | Recognise 1 of 4. Exposures 10 ms. | Vocal | Accuracy | $48^T$ | 8:8 | Handedness, familial handedness further factors in ANOVA (NS): no raw data given. |

| Study | Sex diff. | Task | Response | Measure | Stimuli | N (M:F) | Comments |
|---|---|---|---|---|---|---|---|
| BRADSHAW et al. (1976a) | ND | Exp. 3. Classify 2 groups of 2; blocked by orientation (mirror, correct), 150 ms. | Key-press (bimanual) | RT—2 choice 5% errors | $32^P + 128^T$ | 12:12 | Slightly unsatisfactory: 4 subjects replaced (NM sex) because very small VF differences with correctly oriented letters |
| | ND | Exp. 4. As per 3, mixed orientations | Key-press (bimanual) | RT—2 choice 5% errors | $32^P + 128^T$ | 12:12 | Again, 4 subjects replaced. For both experiments together "no sex differences were apparent". |
| HELLIGE (1976) | NS | Exp. 1. Simultaneous matching (Posner), set of 10, upper- and lower-case. Central and lateral presentation of pairs. 30 ms. | Key-press (two hands) | RT—2 choice 8% errors (lateralised stimuli) | $18^P + 270^T$ (each of 3 days) | 6:6 | RVF advantage on *same* responses for trials 181–450 only. Error rate 16% for trials 1–180. |
| McKEEVER and VAN DEVENTER (1977) | Females | Identify 2 of 10. Bilateral, masked, 30 ms. | Vocal | Accuracy | $40^T$ | 17:27 | Separate analyses: RVF advantage for F only. |
| WARD and ROSS (1977) | NS | Identify 1 of 5. Backward masking. | Vocal | Threshold (20 ms plus) | $10^P$ | 8:8 | |
| MARTIN, C. M. (1978) | NS | Categorisation: curve/no curve; "ee"/not-"ee", 100 ms. | Key-press (two hands) | RT—2 choice 10% errors | $10^P + 112^T$ (each condition) | 6:6 | Three-way interaction with decision type, but monster individual differences (range of 700 ms for F). |
| HELLIGE and WEBSTER (1979) | ND | Identify 1 of 5. Forward and backward masking, two types of mask. 7 ms at 5·2°. | Vocal | Accuracy | $210^T$ (each of 4 conditions) | 8:8 | |

TABLE 4 (*continued*)

| Study | Sex more lateralised | Task details | Response | Measure | Trials | Ns M:F | Comments |
|---|---|---|---|---|---|---|---|
| SEGALOWITZ and STEWART (1979) | NS | Matching: 1 central, 1 peripheral. 100 ms. | Key-press (bimanual) | RT—2 choice (difference scores) NM errors | $16^P + 96^T$ | 30:30 | |
| MARTIN, M. (1979) | NS | Stroop-type task: letters made up of letters. Task to identify "global" letter shape, or its "local" letter constituents. 100 ms; masked. | Vocal | RT—2 choice 9% errors (but 0–48% over response classes.) | $12^P$ $+ 72^T$ (local) $72^T$ (global) | 8:8 | Overall RVF advantage, and for local decisions in all response classes |
| UMILTA et al. (1980) | NS | *Exp. 1.* Simultaneous matching (Posner), both letters lateralised. Printed letters (B,C,D,G,P,T). 100 ms. | Key-press (one hand) | RT—2 choice 4% errors | $P+288^T$ | 6:6 | Subjects 1–6 male, 7–12 female in Table 1. No overall field effects for either *same* or *different*. Physical matches in LVF (more consistent in females?), name matches in RVF. |
| | | *Exp. 2.* As per 1, letters in script | Key-press (one hand) | RT—2 choice 9% errors | $P+288^T$ | 4:4 | Subjects 1–4 male, 5–8 female in Table 2. VF-by-type of same match interaction accentuated. Discarded subjects failed to make practice criterion. (Personal communication.) |
| MILLER and BUTLER (1980) | NS NS | Identification: 1 of 4 (10 ms) 1 of 11 (15 ms) | Vocal Vocal | Accuracy Accuracy | $8^P + 60^T$ $8^P + 60^T$ | 10:10 10:10 | |

| Study | Sex | Task | Response | Measure | Exposure | Ratio | Comments |
|---|---|---|---|---|---|---|---|
| KIRSNER (1980) | NS<br>NS | 1 of 26 (20 ms.)<br>Recognition memory (Sternberg): 6 letters, upper- and lower-case; set size 1, 2, 3. 200 ms. Bilateral probes (2). | Vocal<br>Key-press one hand—"go/no-go" for single positive only. | Accuracy<br>Search rate (slope of items/RT) 6% errors. | $8^P + 60^T$<br>$1188^T$ | 10:10<br>10:10 | |
| HELLIGE (1980a) | NS | *Exp. 1.* Recognition memory (Sternberg): 10 letters (upper- and lower-case); set sizes 2, 3, 4, 5. Degraded and ungraded probes. 100 ms. | Key-press (two hands) | RT—2 choice 6% errors | $20^P + 960^T$ | 10:10 | For negative trials, overall LVF advantage. For positive trials, degradation produces slope changes in LVF, not RVF. |
| | | *Exp. 2.* As per 1, upper-case letters only | Key-press (two hands) | RT—2 choice 7% errors | $20^P + 960^T$ | 10:10 | |
| *Letter Strings*<br>HANNAY and MALONE (1976a) | Males (see Comments) | Delayed matching at 0, 5 and 10 s (nonsense CVCs) 5-25 ms (from central PT) | Vocal | Accuracy | $64^{PT} + 96^T$ | 15:15 | Laterality effect significant for males at 5 s, 10 s delay. Five females FS+, but no males. Fifteen additional FS— females showed significant laterality effect at 5 s delay (Hannay and Malone, 1976b). |

TABLE 4 (*continued*)

| Study | Sex more lateralised | Task details | Response | Measure | Trials | Ns M:F | Comments |
|---|---|---|---|---|---|---|---|
| SASANUMA et al. (1977) | NS | Recognition of Japanese *Kana* and *Kanji* nonsense words. 25–76 ms (from P). | Vocal | Accuracy | $50^P + 100^T$ | 12:12 | |
| ANDREWS (1977) | ND | Identification of 3-letter words, pronounceable non-words, CCCs, VVVs. 70–130 ms. | Vocal | Accuracy | $PT + 160^T$ | 24:24 | Correlations run with familial handedness |
| LEVY and REID (1978) | NS | Identification: nonsense CVCs (60), 90–180 ms. | Vocal | Accuracy ÷ exposure | $12^P + 120^T$ (plus pretest for exposure) | 12:12 | |
| HANNAY and BOYER (1978) | NS | Recognition of "nonsense" CVCs, 1 of 10 (see Comments). 11–23 ms. | Vocal—number of stimulus from response card of twenty alternatives | Accuracy | $PT + 40^T$ | 56:56 | Only example of "nonsense CVC" is "VEX" (*sic*) |
| SMITH and MOSCOVITCH (1979) | NS | Identification of nonsense CVCs (30). 40–130 ms. | Vocal | Accuracy | $PT + 60^T$ | 8:7 | Analysis includes two groups of L-handers (inverted and non-inverted writers) |

*Words*

| | | | | | | | |
|---|---|---|---|---|---|---|---|
| MARSHALL and HOLMES (1974) | Males | Naming CVCs: 20 concrete nouns, 20 verbs by high/low frequency. Lower-case, horizontal, 80 ms. | Vocal | | $80^T$ | 24:24 | Overall RVF effect, males marginally more lateralised. Groups of FS+ (R-handers, L-handers) included in analysis (NS). |
| METZGER and ANTES (1976) | NS | Recognition memory: 3-letter concrete nouns, rehearsal and imagery instruction conditions, set size 2. 100 ms probe. | Key-press (two hands) | RT—2 choice 4% errors | $12^P + 32^T$ | 5:5 (per condition) | |
| | NS | As above, but with picture probe, 3- and 4-letter words, and pretest with no instructions (word probe). | Key-press (two hands) | RT—2 choice 4% errors | $12^P + 20^T$ | 5:5 | |
| BRADSHAW *et al.* (1977a) | NS | Matching to memorised target (4-letter words: non-targets differ on one letter only). 150 ms. | Key-press (bimanual) | RT-2 choice 12% errors | $16^P + 256^T$ | 8:8 | Overall RVF advantage (but no difference when different letter first or last) |
| | NS | As above, but non-targets differ on 4-letter/position combinations, and letter shape controlled | Key-press (bimanual) | RT—2 choice 4% errors | $32^P + 512^T$ | 8:8 | Overall RVF advantage (no difference on "first-and-last" or "all-four" combinations—i.e. easier conditions?) |

TABLE 4 (*continued*)

| Study | Sex more lateralised | Task details | Response | Measure | Trials | Ns M:F | Comments |
|---|---|---|---|---|---|---|---|
| BRADSHAW and GATES (1978) | NS | *Exp. 3.* Naming 3-, 4-, 5-letter words: abstract/concrete, high/low frequency | Vocal | RT 3% errors | 32$^P$ + 288$^T$ | 12:12 | Overall RVF advantage; no interactions |
| | NS | *Exp. 4.* Naming of 4-letter words, homophonic non-words, non-homophonic non-words (readable/legal) | Vocal | RT 3% errors | 32$^P$ + 192$^T$ | 12:12 | |
| LEEHEY et al. (1978) | NS | *Group 1.* Report word/part of word. 4-letter high-frequency nouns. 80, 100 or 120 ms (from practice trials). Bilateral presentation (pairs). Central fixation digit. This group also tested on upright faces. | Vocal | Accuracy | 8$^P$ + 18$^T$ | 16:16 | Initial ANOVA combines tasks. Overall RVF advantage. Extraordinarily few trials; and performance very poor. Hardly worth reporting. |
| | NS | *Group 2.* As per 1, except also tested on inverted faces | Vocal | Accuracy | 8$^P$ + 18$^T$ | 20:19 | |
| LEEHEY and CAHN (1979) | NS | *Exp. 1.* As above (Leehey et al., 1978). This time mixed with recognition of familiar and unfamiliar faces. | Vocal | Accuracy | 8$^P$ + 18$^T$ | 16:16 (each group) | Initial ANOVA combines tasks, groups |

| Reference | | Stimulus / Task | Response | Measure | Exposure | N | Comments |
|---|---|---|---|---|---|---|---|
| BRADSHAW and TAYLOR (1979) | NS | Naming of mono-syllabic, 4- and 5-letter words, homophonic non-words, non-homophonic non-words. 150 ms. | Vocal | RT 8% errors | $40^P + 400^T$ | 12:12 | Grand ANOVA including groups of familial and non-familial L-handers. Overall RVF greatest for R-handers, unaffected by stimulus type |
| SCHMULLER and GOODMAN (1979) | NS | Naming 4- or 5-letter high- and low-imagery words ($N=40$). Bilateral, order of report cued by arrow. Exposure always less than 60 ms. | Vocal | Accuracy | $PT + 40^T$ | 4:4 | RVF advantage for R-handers. For L-handers, LVF advantage for FS+, no difference for FS−. All groups included in ANOVA. Males show greater decrement for second report. |
| PIAZZA (1980) | NS | Recognition of 4-letter high-frequency words ($N=6$). Bilateral, side of report cued by arrow. | Vocal (report number on response card containing only stimuli) | Accuracy | $PT + 60^T$ (see Comments) | 8:8 | Methodology misleading: only 30 possible correct responses per VF |
| *Names: Categorisation* | | | | | | | |
| BRADSHAW et al. (1977a) | NS | *Exp. 2.* 3-letter male and female names (e.g. TIM, DOT) for simultaneous matching as same or different sex. Lateralised pairs, 165 ms. | Key-press (bimanual) | RT—2 choice | NM (24 *same* pairs, 32 pairs) | 8:8 | VF-by-decision interaction: LVF for *same*, RVF for *different* |

TABLE 4 (continued)

| Study | Sex more lateralised | Task details | Response | Measure | Trials | Ns M:F | Comments |
|---|---|---|---|---|---|---|---|
| *Lexical Decision* | | | | | | | |
| DAY (1977) | NS (see Comments) | *Exp. 1.* Abstract/concrete, 4- and 5-letter words v. non-words formed by changing 1 letter. Printed vertically, in capitals, 100 ms. | Key-press (one hand) | RT—"go/no-go" 25% false positive errors, 16% false negative errors | $16^P + 128^T$ | 8:6 | Significant sex-by-hand-by-field interaction (reanalysis by Pring, see below): possible interpretation females less lateralised |
| | ? | *Exp. 2.* Semantic categorisation: abstract/concrete central superordinate followed by lateral instances (100 ms at 1 s delay). | Key-press (one hand) | RT—"go/no-go" 9% false positives 3% false negatives | $16^P + 128^T$ | 8:8 | |
| | ? | *Exp. 3.* As per Exp. 2, simultaneous matching, 150 ms. | Key-press (one hand) | RT—"go/no-go" 7% false positives 23% false negatives | $16^P + 128^T$ | 8:8 | All three experiments show RVF advantage for abstract nouns only: of 6 atypical individuals (LVF advantage) 5 were females |
| BRADSHAW *et al.* (1977a) | Males | *Exp. 1.* Monosyllabic, 4-letter words v. *either* homophones *or* consonant strings (2 conditions). 200 ms. | Key-press (bimanual) | RT—2 choice 5% errors for homophone condition, 4% for non-homophones | $32^P + 128^T$ (each condition) | 12:12 | Grand ANOVA includes group of L-handers (FS+): only R-handed males show RVF advantage |

| Study | Sex difference | Task | Response | Measure | Stimuli | M:F | Comments |
|---|---|---|---|---|---|---|---|
| BRADSHAW and GATES (1978) | NS (see Comments) | *Exp. 1.* High/low frequency 3-letter words v. legal non-words formed by changing 1 letter. Horizontal, lower-case, 150 ms. | Key-press (bimanual) | RT—2 choice 7% errors | $32^P + 576^T$ | 12:12 | Highly significant practice effect: females attain RVF advantage only in second half of trials |
| | NS (see Comments) | *Exp. 2.* Homophone decision tasks: 4-letter legal non-words. | Key-press (bimanual) | RT—2 choice 19% errors | $32^P + 128^T$ | 12:12 | Fewer males, consequently high error rate and high variance: 9 males with RVF faster, but only 3 females. Trend to RVF advantage increased with practice. |
| BRADSHAW *et al.* (1979) | NS | *Part 1.* 3-letter words v. non-word rearrangements (same letters) at subthreshold (20 ms). | Vocal | Signal detection analysis | $56^T$ | 24:22 | Slight LVF advantage for hits. Familial handedness factor in ANOVA: presumably some FS+ subjects. |
| | NS | *Part 2.* As per Exp. 1, pre- and post-threshold (14, 17, 23, 26 ms). | Vocal | Signal detection analysis | $28^T$ (per exposure) | 22:22 (Same Ss as Part 1) | Advantage tends to move to RVF (NS) |
| PRING (1981b) | Females (see Comments) | *Exp. 1,* 4-, 5-, 6-letter words high/low on abstractness and imagery v. non-words formed by changing 1 letter. Horizontal, lower-case, 150 ms. | Lever switch (one hand to/fro) | RT—2 choice 12% errors (6·9–23·9% across ANOVA cells) | $24^P + 96^T$ (each hand) | 16:16 (all FS⁻) | RVF advantage greater for females for words alone |

TABLE 4 (*continued*)

| Study | Sex more lateralised | Task details | Response | Measure | Trials | $N$s M:F | Comments |
|---|---|---|---|---|---|---|---|
| | NS (see Comments) | *Exp. 2.* As per Exp. 1, but words printed vertically, in capital letters (cf. Day, 1977) | Lever switch to/fro | RT—2 choice 18% errors (10·6–29·85 across ANOVA cells) | $24^P + 96^T$ (each hand) | 8:8 (all FS⁻) | Significant 3-way effect for words alone indicates only females show hand-by-field interaction (cf. Day, 1977, above) |
| BARRY (1981) | NS | 4-letter homophones, other words v. pseudo-homophones, 1-letter changes (16 in each of four classes). Horizontal, lower-case. 150 ms. Two groups: R-hand responders; L-hand responders. | Lever switch (one hand to/fro) | RT—2 choice 16% errors (10·9–23% across word classes). | $16^P + 128^T$ | 4:4 (per group: 17 yrs, FS⁻) | Clear RVF advantage for both words and non-words; no interactions |
| **Non-Verbal** *Dot Detection* | | | | | | | |
| KIMURA (1969) | NS | *Exp. 3.* Two square frames corresponding to response grid presented with stimulus. | Vocal | Quasi-threshold (ms) | | 14:14 | No overall field effect |
| | NS | *Exp. 6.* Circular Frame—no blank trials. | Vocal | Accuracy | $2^P + 48^T$ | 10:10 | No overall field effect |
| | NS | *Exp. 7.* Circular frame. | Vocal | Quasi-threshold (Pts. for ms steps) | | 16:16 | No overall field effect |
| McKEEVER *et al.* (1975) | NS | *Exp. 1.* Single position: half blank trials; feedback on hi–lo RTs in blocks; exposure 100 ms at 1·3°. | Vocal | RT—2 choice: presence/absence NM errors | $120^P + 120^T$ | 8:8 | No overall field effect |

| Study | | Description | Response | Measure | Trials | Ratio | Results |
|---|---|---|---|---|---|---|---|
| BRYDEN (1976) | NS | *Exp. 3.* As per Exp. 1, plus report of central fixation digit. | Vocal | RT—2 choice: presence/absence NM errors | $120^P + 120^T$ | 8:8 | No overall field effect |
| | NS | *Exp. 3.* Various positions: rectangular grid for response. One half blanks. 6 ms at 1·5° to 2·8°. | Vocal | Sensitivity and bias (non-parametric) | $144^T$ | 10:10 | No field effect for detectability but LVF bias in false alarms |
| | NS | *Exp. 4.* As per Exp. 3 except that fixation card contained two outline rectangles delimiting frame of reference (cf. Kimura 1969). One third blanks. | Vocal | Sensitivity | $108^T$ | 10:10 | No field effect for detectability; tendency to LVF bias only in females |
| DAVIDOFF (1977) | Males (see Comments) | Single position, one third blank trials. Rectangular dot, eight levels of contrast, for 10 ms at 4·5°. Report central fixation digit before detection. | Vocal | Accuracy | $50^P + 192^T$ | 12:12 | Separate ANOVAS: RVF advantage for males only |
| ALLARD and BRYDEN (1979) | Females (see Comments) | *Exp. 2.* As per Bryden (1976, Exp. 4) 10 ms, but with concurrent verbal loading condition. | Vocal | Sensitivity and bias (parametric) | $108^T$ | 16:16 | Marginal sex-by-field-by-condition interaction: males reduced VF difference in control condition, for detectability. Overall LVF |

TABLE 4 (continued)

| Study | Sex more lateralised | Task details | Response | Measure | Trials | Ns M:F | Comments |
|---|---|---|---|---|---|---|---|
| | | | | | | | advantage, but RVF bias in false alarms, more pronounced in females (contra 1976 results). |
| SMITH and MOSCOVITCH (1979) | NS | Exp. 1. 150 ms, half blanks. | Key-press ("go/no-go", L hand only) | RT | $10^P + 200^T$ | 8:7 | Analysis includes two groups of L-handers (inverted/non-inverted writers). LVF advantage. (Compatibility effect?). |
| Dot Localisation | | | | | | | |
| KIMURA (1969) | Males | Exp. 1. Square grids precede each stimulus. 10 ms. | Vocal (report position number from response card above tachistoscope) | Accuracy | $50^T$ | 19:19 | No overall sex effect in any experiment. LVF advantage for males only. |
| | NS (see Comments) | Exp. 2. As per 1, different measure. | Vocal | Quasi-threshold | | 23:23 | Separate analyses show LVF advantage significant only for males |
| | NS | Exp. 4. Circular pre-exposure field | Vocal | Accuracy | $2^P + 48^T$ | 17:17 | Overall LVF advantage |
| | NS | Exp. 5. Replication of Exp. 4—different experimenter. | Vocal | Accuracy | $2^P + 48^T$ | NM | Overall LVF advantage |
| BRYDEN (1973) | NS (see Comments) | Rectangular grid for response presented in tachistoscope | Vocal | Accuracy | $60^T$ (48 scored) | 8:8 per group | Overall ANOVA on all groups (handedness by sinistrality). Slight RVF advantage emerged with practice as LVF score deteriorated markedly. |

| BRYDEN (1976) | NS | Exp. 1. Response grid either in or above the tachistoscope (two groups of Ss). 10 ms. | Vocal | Accuracy | $60^T$ (48 scored) | 10:10 (per group) | Overall accuracy improved for response card in tachistoscope |
| | NS | Exp. 2. As per Exp. 1 except that two outline rectangles corresponding to response grid presented with stimulus. | Vocal | Accuracy | $48^T$ | 10:10 (per group) | Effect of response card location insignificant |
| | NS | Exp. 3. Signal detection procedure (to unconfound detection and localisation): one half blanks. 6 ms. No frame of reference. | Vocal | Accuracy | $144^T$ | 10:10 | |
| | NS | Exp. 4. As per Exp. 3, except frame of reference and one third blanks. | Vocal | Accuracy | $108^T$ | 10:10 | For all experiments: no overall laterality effect, no overall sex difference (tendency for men to be more accurate, women to produce more false alarms) |

TABLE 4 (*continued*)

| Study | Sex more lateralised | Task details | Response | Measure | Trials | Ns M:F | Comments |
|---|---|---|---|---|---|---|---|
| LEVY and REID (1978) | Males | Frames of reference; report central fixation digit. 25–100 ms, followed by mask. | Vocal | Accuracy ÷ Exposure | PT + 40$^T$ | 12:12 | LVF advantage for males only, but also had shorter exposures. N.B. curious measure—why not straightforward threshold expt? |
| SMITH and MOSCOVITCH (1979) | NS | Single rectangle with stimulus. Forward mask. Central digit. 20–115 ms. | Vocal | Accuracy | PT + 40$^T$ | 8:7 | Again, analysis swamped with two groups of L-handers. LVF advantage. |
| NICOLETTI and FAIRWEATHER (1979) | NS | Matching the position of a dot relative to a word describing its possible position (right or left) | Key-press (two hands): "true"/ "false" | RT—2 choice | 160$^P$ + 320$^T$ (plus 320$^{PT}$ in central vision) | 12:12 | RVF advantage for the word *sinistra* ("left" in Italian) restricted to males |
| *Dot Enumeration* | | | | | | | |
| McGLONE and DAVIDSON (1973) | Males (see Comments) | Three to ten dots for 70–80 ms, out to 3° 50' | Vocal | Accuracy (max. 10) | 20$^T$ (presumably) | 41:38 (inc.44 L-handers) | Methodology unclear, statistics poor (chi square only on numbers revealing/not revealing 1-point difference between fields; L-handers included). N.B. Kimura (1966) finds laterality effects for females only in enumeration of dots (Exp. 2) and forms (Exp. 3) but not letters, and types of letters or forms (Exp. 3). |

### Line Orientation

| Study | Sex diff. | Task | Response | Measure | Exposure | N | Findings |
|---|---|---|---|---|---|---|---|
| SCHALLER and DZIADOSZ (1975) | NS | Horizontal v. vertical, 1–12 ms, masked. Presentation within grid of 35 possible positions. | Key-press (R hand only —2 responses) | Accuracy | $80^P + 280^T$ | 16:16 | Ss selected for accuracy: 23 too good, 4 too poor omitted. Overall LVF. Significant three-way interaction: "Females did not show as much decrement in upper corners as did males" (p. 357). |
| SASANUMA and KOBAYASHI (1978) | Males | Eight oblique orientations, at 100 or 150 ms for "majority of Ss" | Vocal | Accuracy | $20–40^P + 160^T$ | 14:14 | Overall LVF, and males alone |
| PITBLADO (1979b) | NS | Judgments of subjective vertical within three frames (one circular, two oblique) using "staircase" of tilts | Key-press (one hand— ipsilateral to VF (blocked)) | RT—2 choice; Accuracy | $36^T$ (per frame) | 12:12 (per group) | L-handers and R-handers. Circular frame gives RVF advantage for RT, LVF for accuracy (final subjective vertical) |

### Illusions

| Study | Sex diff. | Task | Response | Measure | Exposure | N | Findings |
|---|---|---|---|---|---|---|---|
| CLEM and POLLACK (1975) | ND | Muller-Lyer illusion 150 ms at 2°. "Simultaneous" and successive conditions. | Vocal (report whether line within arrowheads "longer" or "shorter" than standard) | Methods of limits | 16 series of 19 trials | 6:6 (per VF, per condition) | LVF for simultaneous, RVF for successive, overall NS. Subsequent unpublished study (S. Holmes, 1974, Ph.D.) using monocular vision found field effects in females only for the successive condition. (Pollack, pers. comm.) |

TABLE 4 (continued)

| Study | Sex more lateralised | Task details | Response | Measure | Trials | Ns M:F | Comments |
|---|---|---|---|---|---|---|---|
| *Figures (Irregular)* | | | | | | | |
| HELLIGE (1976) | NS | Vanderplas figures (6-, 8-, 12-point; $N=10$: simultaneous matching, central and lateral presentation, 30 ms at 3–9° | Key-press (two hands) | RT—2 choice 8% errors (lateral trials) | $18^P + 270^T$ (each of 3 days) | 6:6 | |
| HANNAY (1976) | Males (see Comments) | Vanderplas figures (4-point only; $N=7$: delayed matching (10 s), 9–40 ms | Vocal ("*same*" or "*different*" to single match) | Accuracy | $40^{PT} + 56^T$ | 30:30 | Separate experiments, separate analyses. Marginal RVF effect for males only (0.05). Field effects correlate with Block Design in females, but not males. |
| BIRKETT (1980) | Females | Vanderplas figures (12-point only; $N=20$: delayed matching (10 s), 10 ms | Manual (point to target amongst 5 | Accuracy | $40^T$ | 33:40 (16 to 42 yrs) | RVF advantage for females only, and associated with lower DAT Space scores |
| *Figures (Regular)* | | | | | | | |
| PATTERSON and BRADSHAW (1975) | NS | *Exp. 1.* Schematic faces, successive matching, all three features *same* or *different.* Unilateral and bilateral. | Key-press (bimanual) | RT—2 choice | $32^P + 256^T$ 5% errors | 12:12 | No overall field effect: LVF for *same*, RVF for *different* |

| | | | | | | |
|---|---|---|---|---|---|---|
| NS | *Exp. 2.* Schematic faces: one target stored in memory matched against three non-target faces (all three features different). Single unilateral presentation. | Key-press (bimanual) | RT—2 choice 3% errors | $32^P + 128^T$ | 12:12 | Overall LVF advantage |
| NS | *Exp. 3.* As per Exp. 2, non-targets differing on only one feature. | Key-press (bimanual) | RT—2 choice 14% errors | $32/64^P + 128^T$ | 12:12 | Overall RVF advantage. N.B. Comparatively high error rate (*and* 5M, 3F omitted because too many errors) confounds laterality interpretation (see Fairweather *et al.*, 1981 |
| BRADSHAW *et al.* (1976a) NS | *Exp. 1.* Geometric elements arranged in triangular configuration, either one or two elements changed for *different* (2 conditions). | Key-press (bimanual) | RT—2 choice ("very infrequent" errors) | $24^P + 288^T$ (per condition) | 8:8 | Marginal LVF advantage |
| NS | *Exp. 3.* Geometric figures, matching against memorised target. | Key-press (bimanual) | RT—2 choice | $36^P + 144^T$ | 12:12 | |
| PITBLADO (1979a) NS | Random Dot Stereopsis (Julesz patterns: like superimposed | Vocal (select from | Accuracy | $12^P + 48^T$ (each condition; | 12:12 | Subjects selected for accuracy in central vision. LVF advantage with small |

TABLE 4 (continued)

| Study | Sex more lateralised | Task details | Response | Measure | Trials | Ns M:F | Comments |
|---|---|---|---|---|---|---|---|
| | | rectangles). Identify 1 of 6 patterns. Three dot sizes. 120 ms at $2.2°$–$3.3°$. | response card of 6) | | plus PT for selection) | | dots reverses with large dots |
| BAGNARA et al. (1980) | Males | Triangles and trapezoids: same–different judgments (Posner) | Key-press (two hands) | RT—2 choice 1% errors | $320^T$ | 8:8 | "Mesas-and-buttes" experiment: since base always flat, effectively "pointed–plus–not pointed" for different. RVF for same, LVF for different, significant only for males. |
| *Common Objects* | | | | | | | |
| McKEEVER and JACKSON (1979) | Males (see Comments) | *Exp. 1.* Object-naming, $N=5$ from PPVT (apple, shoe, lamp, clock, moose). Central fixation, digit, 100 ms. | Vocal | CRT—5 choice 1% errors | $30^P + 180^T$ | 10:10 | Overall RVF advantage, but 1 male, 4 females FS + |
| LANDIS et al. (1979) | NS | *Exp. 2.* Simultaneous matching of central cartoon, lateral photo, $N=3$ (corkscrew, key, brush). | Key-press (one hand) | RT—"go/ no-go" 4% errors | $384^T$ | 12:12 | Overall RVF advantage |
| SCHMULLER and GOODMAN (1980) | NS | Recognition ($N=64$). Bilateral, order of report cued by arrow. Exposure less than 60 ms. | Vocal | Accuracy | $PT + 32^T$ | 4:4 (per group) | LVF advantage for R-handed FS–, RVF for L-handed FS+, no effect for other two groups |

| | | | | | | | |
|---|---|---|---|---|---|---|---|
| *Colours*<br>PENNAL (1977) | NS | Discrimination $N=12$. 30 ms at $8°$ on diagonals from fixation. | Manual (press 1 of 24 coloured discs) | Accuracy | $4^P + 48^T$ | 59:66 | Overall LVF advantage |
| McKEEVER and JACKSON (1979) | NS | *Exp. 2.* Colour naming, $N=5$ | Vocal | CRT—5 choice | $30^P + 180^T$ | 12:12 | Overall RVF advantage. Five males, 7 females FS+ (not significant). |
| *Faces: Famous*<br>YOUNG and BION (1981a) | NS | *Exp. 2.* Naming famous faces (all male) with/without list of names (2 conditions). Bilateral, 150 ms. | Vocal | Accuracy | $P + 20^T$ (presumably—unspecified). | 10:10 (each condition) | LVF advantage only when list provided. Essentially trivial ($N$ trials etc.). |
| *Faces: Familiar*<br>UMILTA *et al.* (1978) | Males | Recognition/discrimination of 4 male faces (photos). Opportunity for prior familiarisation (week-end before experimental week) for "familiarity". Four conditions from factors of familiarity and naming (see also "Faces: unfamiliar"). This condition "*Unnamed familiar*". Exposure 100 ms. | Key-press (two hands) | RT—2 choice 11% errors (averaged over all four conditions) | $160^P + 640^T$ (max.) | 12:12 | For ANOVA comprising all four conditions, the familiarity-by-VF-by-sex interaction just fails to reach significance. Subsequent analyses for individual conditions, and sexes apart. RVF advantage for males only ($p<0.01$). No significant VF effects for single days. |

TABLE 4 (*continued*)

| Study | Sex more lateralised | Task details | Response | Measure | Trials | $N$s M:F | Comments |
|---|---|---|---|---|---|---|---|
| | NS (see Comments) | As above, except stimuli named: "*Named familiar*" | Key-press (two hands) | RT—2 choice | $160^P + 640^T$ (max.) | 12:12 | Separate analyses. RVF advantage for males attains significance with 6 extra subjects (all giving RVF effects). |
| LEEHEY and CAHN (1979) | NS | Immediate recognition, faces half-male, half-female. Bilateral presentation (1 pair per trial). Central fixation digit. 60 ms. | Manual (pointing). Response array of 12 faces. | Accuracy | $8^P + 18^T$ | 16:16 | No sex effects in overall ANOVA for familiar/unfamiliar words and faces. Extraordinarily few trials. LVF advantage. |
| *Faces: Unfamiliar* | | | | | | | |
| RIZZOLATTI and BUCHTEL (1977) | Males | Faces from Umiltà *et al.* (1978), same task, different response. "*Unnamed unfamiliar*". Exposure 100 ms. | Key-press (one hand) | RT—"go/no-go" | $640^T$ | 8:8 | Sloppily reported: no details on familiarisation session, errors reported as "few, between 10–15%" (? *sic*). Overall LVF advantage for males only. |
| | Males | As above; "*Unnamed unfamiliar*". Exposure 20 ms. | Key-press (one hand) | RT—"go/no-go" | $640^T$ | 8:8 | Sex effect increased. LVF advantage increased, again only in males. |
| UMILTA *et al.* (1978) | Males | Recognition/discrimination of 4 male faces. Stimuli unnamed: "*Unnamed unfamiliar*". | Key-press (two hands) | RT—2 choice | $160^P + 640^T$ | 12:12 | Separate analyses. Small LVF advantage over all trials, males only ($p<0.05$). |
| | Females | As above, stimuli named: "*Named unfamiliar*" | Key-press (two hands) | RT—2 choice | $160^P + 640^T$ | 12:12 | Separate analyses. Small LVF advantage over all trials, females only ($p<0.05$). |

| | | | | | | |
|---|---|---|---|---|---|---|
| FINLAY and FRENCH (1978) | NS | Recognition memory for 40 female faces. Test *hemi*-faces (80) varied in orientation (mirror/ not) and side. 8 ms exposure only. Fixation at edge of *hemi*-face. | Vocal ("yes-no" plus confidence rating) | Signal detection | $80^T$ | 14:14 | Overall LVF advantage for detectability, NS for bias |
| LEEHEY et al. (1978) | NS | *Group 1.* Immediate recognition of pairs of upright faces (half-male, half-female) presented bilaterally, 120 ms. Central fixation digit. | Manual (pointing: array of 12) | Accuracy | $8^P + 18^T$ | 16:16 | Initial ANOVA includes word-recognition task (see earlier). Overall LVF. |
| | NS | *Group 2.* As for Group 1, faces inverted, 150 ms. | Manual (pointing: array of 12) | Accuracy | $8^P + 18^T$ | 20:19 | No overall field effect |
| LEEHEY and CAHN (1979) | NS | As above (Leehey et al., 1978) mixed with word-recognition task (see earlier). | Manual (pointing; array of 12) | Accuracy | $8^P + 18^T$ (each task) | 16:16 | Initial ANOVA includes word-recognition results. Overall LVF advantage. |
| HANNAY and ROGERS (1979) | NS | *Exp. 1.* Almost immediate and delayed matching (10 s, 20 s), lateral→ central (3 conditions). Two groups of Ss: Block Design Score <11, >11. Exposure 56 ms | Vocal | Accuracy | $2^{PT} + 32^T$ (each condition) | 12:12 (each group) | Overall field effect (LVF) interacts with delay (LVF at 0 s, 10 s, RVF at 20 s). Failure to replicate effect of Block Design Score (Hannay, 1976, earlier). |

TABLE 4 (*continued*)

| Study | Sex more lateralised | Task details | Response | Measure | Trials | $N$s M:F | Comments |
|---|---|---|---|---|---|---|---|
| STRAUSS and MOSCOVITCH (1981) | NS | *Exp. 2.* Photos (3M, 3F from Ekman) simultaneously matched for identity, ignoring variations in expression. Half subjects *same* responders, half *different*. Unilateral, 800 ms (!) | Key-press (one hand) | RT—"go/ no-go", 8% errors | $28^P + 252^T$ (plus 5 min familiarsation) | 6:6 (each condition) | For *different* responders, overall LVF advantage. As with the Rizzolatti and Buchtel (1977) and Umiltà *et al.* (1978) studies, unlikely that these faces would have remained truly "unfamiliar" for very long |
| *Faces: Categorisation* | | | | | | | |
| JONES (1979, 1980a) | Males | Categorise faces as male or female. Signal detection analysis | Vocal | Sensitivity (non-parametric), optimisation | $140^T$ | 12:12 | Females marginally better, but only males exhibit RVF advantage. 1980 paper includes two groups of L-handers (FS+/FS−). |
| *Faces: Emotions* | | | | | | | |
| CAMPBELL (1978) | NS | Briefly delayed matching of chimeric faces, one with left-side smile, one with right-side smile: "which face looked happier?" Both M and F faces. | Vocal | Preference | $40^T$ | 12:12 | Preference for smile in LVF |

| | | | | | | | |
|---|---|---|---|---|---|---|---|
| LANDIS et al. (1979) | NS | Exp. 1. Simultaneous matching central cartoon to lateral photo (1M, 1F, familiar). Three emotions: happy, angry, astonished. 150 ms. | Key-press (one hand) | RT—"go"/no-go/ 24% errors | $384^T$ | 12:12 | Overall LVF advantage |
| LADAVAS et al. (1980) | Females | Matching to memorised target. Photos (3M, 3F, actors). Six emotions: happy, sad, surprised, disgusted, angry, afraid. | Key-press (one hand) | RT—"go"/no-go" 11% errors (3–16% across emotions) | $156^P + 936^T$ | 12:12 | Overall LVF advantage in females only. Emotions listed in descending order of speed, accuracy; ascending order of VF difference. |
| STRAUSS and MOSCOVITCH (1981) | NS (see Comments) | Exp. 1. Photos (3M, 3F from Ekman). Simultaneously matched for one of 3 expressions. Unilateral, 800 ms. Half subjects same responders, half different. | Key-press (one hand) | RT—"go"/no-go" 8% errors | $28^P + 252^T$ (plus 5 min. familiarisation). | 8:8 (per condition) | For same responders, overall LVF advantage. For different responders, field-by-hand interaction: males particularly fast for RVF/R-hand responses. No clear justification for enormous exposure time. |
| | NS | Exp. 3. Same materials, matching to target expression in memory, for either of 2 presented faces | Key-press (one hand) | RT—"go"/no-go" 3% errors | $28^P + 252^T$ (plus 5 min. familiarisation) | 6:6 (per condition) | For positive responders, marginal LVF advantage (for males, only when both faces had same expression). For negative responders, field-by-sex-by-hand interaction: males particularly fast for LVF/R-hand responses. |

TABLE 4 (*continued*)

KEY

*Sex more lateralised*
NS = No significant differences
ND = No differences: stated or observed impression.

*Task details*
Precise stimulus exposure and eccentricity tend to be mentioned either when they fall outside the norm (80–150 ms, at 1–3°) or when a number of studies produce conflicting results (or consistent results over a wide range of conditions).
C = consonant; V = vowel

*Response*
Bimanual = Each response involves one finger from each hand (Bradshaw)
One hand = Each response involves one finger from one hand only
Two hands = Each response involves single fingers, responses shared between hands

*Measure*
RT = Reaction time
NM = No mention (errors, etc.)

*Trials*
P   = Practice
PT  Pretest, often in central vision to determine exposure duration.
T   Test
WU = Warm-up, usually immediately before blocks of test trials.

*N's*
Reference to right-handers with no history of familial sinistrality (FS–), where assessed; and generally to numbers for individual groups rather than totals.

Of the studies that allow a fairly straightforward interpretation, the trend for Bradshaw and Gates (1978) is for females to either take longer to develop a left-hemisphere advantage, or to achieve it in fewer numbers. This trend reached significance in the work of Bradshaw et al. (1977). However this series of findings is precisely counterposed by one of the results from those studies not allowing a straightforward interpretation (Pring, 1981b). The non-straightforwardness of these studies (Barry, 1981; Day, 1977; Pring, 1981b) stems from their use of hand-by-field interactions to assess the localisation of function. This method, pioneered lately by Moscovitch, rests briefly on the contention that a hand-by-field interaction indicates a bilateral representation of function, whereas additive and therefore independent effects of hand and field indicate a lateralised representation of function. Apart from other considerations, this assumes that fine motor responses, of the sort used in most reaction-time experiments, are strongly lateralised. By and large this is the case, and by and large there are no interactions with sex (Kimura and Davidson, 1975; Peters, 1980) although there are exceptions, particularly where some measure of regularity is involved (Peters and Durding, 1979; Wolff et al., 1977). All of the above studies refer to tapping tasks: it has recently been suggested that the preferred hand's superiority is mostly attributable to the reverse portion of the tapping movement (Peters, 1980), a component which presumably would be much less relevant for the sort of discrete response involved in reaction-time measures.

Moscovitch himself has found evidence of sex-by-hand-by-field interactions in two studies of emotions (Strauss and Moscovitch, 1981). Both cases concern negative responses, but in one the interaction derives from males' especially fast right-hand responses to stimuli in the RVF, in the other to stimuli in the LVF. His conclusion is that this pattern "does not conform to the predictions developed from a strict localisation model", and that there is little to uncontrovertibly differentiate the sexes. Pring (1981b), following Day (1977) but using a two-choice lever switch rather than the go/no-go key-press, also found a three-way interaction indicating a greater hand-by-field effect amongst females, for "word" decisions. This might be interpreted as evidence for greater bilateral representation of lexical decision skills in females. It might also be explained by presuming a (verbal) stimulus-processing/motor-organisation imbalance across the sexes, with stimulus-processing factors more paramount for males, motor factors for females. Motor factors might derive from two sources: control of responding hand, and the compatibility relation between hand and visual field ("Simon effect"). Pring himself provides a spirited account of the possibilities and their pitfalls, and it is probably most appropriate to address potential speculators to his discussion.

The effect for Pring is in any case small, and, for Day as well, limited by comparatively few subjects making large numbers of errors. In Strauss and

Moscovitch's case, the result is obscured by the unnecessary and unjustified use of an extraordinarily long exposure time,[6] and the possibility (as in the vast majority of studies) of some subjects being familial sinistrals. It might well be that all three authors, in common indeed with ourselves, might prefer to quietly ignore these rather disquieting findings. However, it may also be that this is the shape of things to come (or indeed as they really are)—namely that no simple story will ever emerge. The other broad hint is that it is well-nigh time that reaction-time studies unable to be performed without incurring high error rates (or "necessitating" over-long exposures) were replaced by studies using signal-detection measures.

## Non-verbal Material

*Dots (detection, localisation, enumeration).* Sixteen of 23 studies here emanate from just two Canadian laboratories, and are generally of less rather than more recent vintage. There are only five positive findings, and of those only two that do not arouse substantial comment. Dot detection is essentially a task in visual acuity, and this capacity would clearly be crucial to localisation, and (the one study on) enumeration. Males appear to have a slight but consistent advantage over a wide age-range: Burg (1966) investigated 17 500 California drivers, and found the sex difference "surprising", adding that "several theories have been proposed, such as differential motivation, and physiological and/or physiognomic differences, [but] no proof of any of them has been brought forth". At least one small-scale study found differences disappeared with practice (Slonim *et al.*, 1975). The story in any case seems unlikely to be a simple one. One of the main protagonists in the area, McGuinness, has recently proposed a tripartite scheme to describe sex differences in the relation between contrast sensitivity and spatial frequency (Brabyn and McGuinness, 1979). Females were found to excel on contrast threshold judgments at low frequencies (0·4 to 0·8 cycles/deg), there was no difference at middle frequencies (1 to 4 cycles/deg), but males had an advantage at high frequencies (6 to 10 cycles/deg). Taking the fairly recent finding of Davidoff (1977) as an example, here the stimulus (0·6° by 0·3°) would correspond to a spatial frequency of a little over 0·8 cycles/deg, towards the "female" end of the spectrum. The result was a left-hemisphere advantage for males (incidentally the only such laterality effect in all these experiments), but no effect for females: the statistics did not allow a

---

[6] Quite what the strength of "Bryden's personal communication" is, one is not privy to; however, it is certainly the case that the use of computerised analysis of eye movements (as in Hardyck's laboratory) makes it abundantly clear that subjects move their eyes considerably. It is also not beyond the realms of possibility that movements in different directions may differ in their alacrity, and that these alacrities may be different for males and females. All in all, a case thus far of the quickness of the eye deceiving the eye?

direct comparison of overall performance. McKeever *et al.* (1975) used stimuli less than half the size of Davidoff's, corresponding to the no-person's land of 2 cycles/deg, and found no differences whatever.

Brabyn and McGuinness speculate that a low-frequency ("female") system would be conducive to "global" processing, whereas a high-frequency ("male") system would be conducive to "analytic" processing. This is clearly much too close to the caricatures of the right and left hemispheres for quietude on the part of hemisphericians, but little direct advantage can be taken in the present absence of fine-grain laterality studies. Interestingly, perhaps, in an experiment on form recognition under conditions of random-dot stereopsis, Pitblado (1979a) found that an LVF advantage moved towards the RVF as dot size increased from the equivalent of a high spatial frequency to a middle-range value. Visual field effects were also more pronounced at the lower of two disparities (13′, 20′). If acuity is at least in part related to eye movements, then one should also be looking here for clues to sex differences.

*Irregular figures* (or more precisely, Vanderplas figures) constitute a very "suitable case for treatment", spanning as they do in the confines of three studies the entire gamut of methodology, stimulus complexity and outcome. Of factors to underline, perhaps that of stimulus complexity might merit the earliest consideration: the three studies concerned used easy, medium and difficult material, and produced VF outcomes biased to males, biased to no one, and biased to females respectively. The demonstration of such a continuum within a single method might contrast interestingly with suggestions regarding another source of difficulty, namely that calling upon acuity.

*Face recognition* provides the highest success rate in terms of the ratio of positive to negative outcomes of any of the reasonably researched groupings of material.[7] All the positive findings here emanate from two Italian laboratories, using the same material, and both being prone to exorbitant error rates in some subjects (undoubtedly not a unique malady, but the author has no such privileged access elsewhere). The studies certainly merit repetition, since the negative instances (with one exception) derive from experiments employing trivial numbers of trials (18–20). In addition there are two associations that tend to make this an especially attractive area for speculation regarding sex differences. The first is the widespread assumption that females excel in general in tasks involving face recognition. This assumption is not as soundly based as one might expect (see Table 5). Albeit six of 24 studies find female

---

[7] Somewhat embarrassingly for the present author, whose name is attached to two of the four positive findings. However it should be pointed out that his relation to three of the four studies in the relevant paper was literary rather than executive, and that to the fourth was suggestive and only partly executive: the fact that this last part of the experiment produced the least embarrassing outcome is surely coincidental.

TABLE 5
*Sex Differences in Face Recognition*

| Study | Advantaged sex | Task details | Subjects M : F | Comments |
|---|---|---|---|---|
| HOWELLS (1938) | | Photos (14M, 28F) presented individually (3 photos per stimulus person). Immediate recognition, one group from 42 groups of three photos. | 13 134 (students) | |
| WITRYOL and KAESS (1957) | Females | Photos-plus-names (12M). Delayed recognition (20 min), match face to given name. | 103:69 (students) | Slight advantage |
| | Females | Live persons-plus-names (half M, half F). Delayed recognition ("later"), match name to given (living) face. | 103:69 | Advantage confined to female faces |
| | Females | Photos-plus-names (10M, 10F). Delayed recognition (5 min), identify foils, name the rest. | 103:69 | Advantage much more pronounced on female faces |
| BROOKS and GOLDSTEIN (1963) | NS | Previously successfully named faces of classmates (upright presented for test (inverted) 1 week later. | 91:86 (3–14 years) | Overall accuracy very high (87%) |
| GOLDSTEIN and CHANCE (1964) | NS | Photos (4M, 4F, three ages). Immediate recognition, forced choice 1 from 5. | 6:6 (5, 8, 13 years) | |
| BENTON and VAN ALLEN (1968) | ND | Photos (half M, half F). Simultaneous matching, single faces; varied angle of view, lighting. | 33:59 (16 to 50 years) | |

| Study | Result | Method | N (M:F) | Comments |
|---|---|---|---|---|
| YIN (1969) | NS | Photos (40 M). Immediate recognition, forced choice, one from pair (24 pairs). Inspection and test series mixed (2 kinds of material from: faces, houses, aeroplanes, men in motion). Upright and inverted. | 13:13 (students) | Second experiment where orientation changed from inspection to test series also produced no difference (cf. Brooks and Goldstein, 1963, for children) |
| GOLDSTEIN and CHANCE (1971) | Females | Photos (14 F). Immediate or delayed (2 days) recognition. Test series singly: "old/new?" | | No differences for similar groups tested on ink-blots/ snow-flakes |
| CROSS et al. (1971) | NS (see Comments) | Photos (half M, half F; half black, half white). Delayed recognition (interviewing task rating faces for beauty). | 40:40 (7,12,17 years) 30:30 (36 years) | Females better overall in all except oldest group (males better); females also significantly better at F rather than M faces (no such effect for males) |
| LAUGHERY et al. (1971) | NS | Photos (both M). Single target for recognition in series of 150 (once only). | 53:75 (students) | Females have higher hit rate |
| | Males | Photos (NM Sex). Similar to above save varied poses in test series also. | 55:73 (students) | |
| | NS | Live target (NM Sex). Only front views. Target appeared twice in test series. | 17:15 (students) | |

TABLE 5 (*continued*)

| Study | Result | Materials/procedure | Subjects | Comments |
|---|---|---|---|---|
| ELLIS *et al.* (1973) | Females (see Comments) | Photos (10M, 10F). Delayed recognition (4 h). | 15:15 (12, 17 years) | Females better only on F faces |
| SHEPHERD and ELLIS (1973) | NS | Photos (all F: $N=27$, high/medium/low on attractiveness). Immediate or delayed (6 days, 35 days). Forced choice pairs of old/new. | 18:18 (graduate students) | |
| SHEPHERD *et al.* (1974) | NS | Coloured photos (half M, half F; half white, half black, $N=20$). Delayed recognition (1 day). | 32:32 (half white adolescents, half black adults). | |
| GOING and READ (1974) | NS | Photos (half M, half F: $N=28$). Immediate recognition. | 40:40 (students) | Again, sex of Ss by sex of photo interaction: only females excel with F photos |
| YARMEY (1974) | Females | Photos (M and F: 4 trials with $N=3$, one sex only). Interpolated task, then pick 3 from 12. | 52:52 (half with M faces, half with F) | Subsequent test for release from proactive interference showed no sex effect |
| McKELVIE (1976) | NS | Schematic faces ($N=9$: high medium/low on labelability, e.g. "innocent", "scheming"). Delayed recognition in sets of 8 (10 min, or 7 days); pre-training either observing or labelling. | 5:5 (each of four conditions) | |

| Study | | Method | N | Comments |
|---|---|---|---|---|
| YARMEY (1979a) | NS | Photos (M and F: $N=30$, high/medium/low on one of attractiveness/feature saliency/likeability). Immediate or delayed recognition (7, 30 days). | 126 (M and F) | |
| YARMEY (1979b) | See Comments | Photos—self-poses as "sociable", "intelligent", "trustworthy". Classified and rated as "best of class" and "real self"—then tested for recognition. | 20:20 | No overall differences, but females remember "best sociable" and "real self" photos better. Presence of F experimenter in somewhat embarrassing experiment felt to contribute to poorer M performance. |
| CAREY et al. (1980) | NS | Photos (all M from Yin, 1969: upright/inverted, $N=20$). Forced-choice recognition in pairs. | 10:12 (6, 10 years) | |
| | NS | Photos (half M, half F, $N=48$). Forced choice recognition in pairs. | 15:15 (at 7,9,10,11, 12, 14 years) | "Dip" in performance at 11 years |
| | NS | Photos, Benton and Van Allen task (see earlier). | 19–23 subjects at each year from 8–14, and 16 years | |

advantages, but three of them require *naming* the faces, (Witryol and Kaess, 1957) which may call upon mechanisms extra to that of recognition *per se*. Additionally, one of the remainder involved only female faces, and another owed the overall advantage solely to females' performance with female faces. Notably, perhaps, there are no sex differences over a wide range on the task most widely used in clinical practice, the Benton and Van Allen test (see Benton and Van Allen, 1968; Carey *et al.*, 1980).

Performance in any case remains confounded with a general memory factor. Achilles (1920) finds that females excel with words and syllables, but not forms, concentrating most subjects in the age range nine to fourteen years, but also including adults. Duggan (1950) reports adolescent females to be better with objects and words, but not with numbers, and adds:

This result is in accordance with the opinions of District Justices D. B. O'Sullivan of Cork, and D. Gleeson, D. Litt of Limerick, also of the Senior Detective Inspector of Union Quay Barracks, Cork; all of whom agree that, where court testimony is concerned, women witnesses usually surpass men in the amount and accuracy of their description in evidence.

In two more recent and less anecdotal accounts of simulated eye-witness testimony, females have in fact been found somewhat more accurate, in terms of the ratio of correct items to all items recalled (Lipton, 1977) and somewhat more suggestible (Powers *et al.*, 1979). This latter study again underlines the importance of the nature of the material: males and females are both more accurate and more suggestible on items deemed to be sex-typed as male or female respectively.

The second association involves the assumption that face recognition is exclusively the province of the right hemisphere, which would at least simplify the theorising. However, this does not appear to be the case, at least in the limiting case of prosopagnosia (Benton, 1980; Mazzucchi *et al.*, 1977). The critical lesion more often than not appears to be bilateral. And, indeed, divided visual field studies have shown that a left-hemisphere advantage can be induced by extended familiarisation, sometimes to the point of fame (Umilta *et al.*, 1978). However, it does remain true that both defects in face recognition, and significant visual field effects for face recognition (whether right *or* left) are more common in males. This is at least a starting argument for greater functional localisation. One can only suppose that face recognition is a multi-component process, and that each of these components (which may be tapped to a greater or lesser extent by particular tasks) may be more definitively located (in whichever hemisphere) in males. Otherwise it remains only to be noted that while "analytic" and "global" have been the adjectives tagged to the recognition of familiar and unfamiliar faces, and to the left- and right-hemisphere advantages they respectively induce, it also seems perfectly clear that both hemispheres are equally capable of these two different sorts of processing (Fairweather *et al.*, 1981).

*Recognition of facial emotions.* There is a rumour abroad that females have a special ability for decoding emotions, and that this ability is specially and exclusively located in the right hemisphere. This rumour may, for the present, be swiftly dispelled. The source review for claims in this area is that by Hall (1978). Considering those studies most analogous to DVF studies, i.e. using the visual mode, adult "senders" and judges of both sexes, and either drawings or photos, the list of possible candidates reduces to five. Of them the only one cited as finding *significant* differences is Izard (1971). Izard (1971, p. 327) in fact comments "since no appreciable differences between the sexes appeared for adult subjects, sex was not considered as a variable in these analyses". Sex was indeed not considered as a variable anywhere in the book. One study, that of Zuckerman *et al.* (1975), not mentioned in the appropriate section of Hall's review, did find a small advantage for females and has been replicated, although in much smaller groups and many fewer trials, elsewhere (Brunori *et al.*, 1979).

## Concluding Remarks

Eighty-seven out of 111[8] divided visual field experiments reviewed here failed to find a significant sex difference in degree of cerebral lateralisation. True enough, few of the experiments were specifically directed towards the study of sex differences, but the incidental nature of the findings has certainly not staunched the flow of theoretical speculation. This speculation itself, however, has most probably served to ignite the few positive results, whilst leaving the negative instances to bury themselves. Within the verbal domain, there are almost no positive findings whatever. Within the non-verbal domain, whilst there are certainly many more findings, they are not found within a rich vein of a single consistent methodology, or between disparate laboratories.

There might be, or have been, a temptation to have selected at the outset some of the more "key" studies, or the more technically adequate, or those with the clearest outcome. This surely would have made a briefer essay. However, so skeletal is the corpus at our disposal that it would have rendered

[8] Since this chapter went to press, a number of studies have either come to light (Hannay, 1979) or appeared anew (Bradshaw *et al.*, 1981; Graves *et al.*, 1981; Pizzamiglio and Zoccolotti, 1981; Pring, 1981a; Ross and Turkewitz, 1981; Safer, 1981; Salis, 1980). Between them they contribute a further 16 non-significant findings, together with two instances of marginally greater male lateralisation—one verbal (Bradshaw *et al.*) and one non-verbal (Safer). The corrected count thus becomes 103 non-significant findings from 129 experiments.

the exercise an essential disservice, That exercise was directed towards two questions. The first was, "Is the incidence of sex differences in divided visual field studies sufficient to warrant its inclusion in any theory of cerebral lateralisation?" And second, "Is that incidence sufficient to warrant the inclusion of cerebral lateralisation in any theory of sex differences?" The answer in both cases is "No".

As for the future, one can confidently predict that some of the larger claims regarding aphasia and the effects of unilateral lesions on verbal and non-verbal skills will be quietly dismantled whilst still (inevitably) retaining popular currency. The attention of neurophilatelists will turn to ever-rarer imprints. How long will it be, for example, before somone notices that the sex ratio for prosopagnosia is matched almost exactly by that for deep dyslexia? As for divided field studies, the important minority (meaning those seriously concerned with the uses and abuses of the technique) will remain largely (and quite rightly) disinterested. The majority (meaning those who might be tempted to look for sex differences) will trundle on much as heretofore: and bearded they will be.

So we shall not end with the feeble clarion call for more of the same. Let us decide now that the issues are too important to be trivialised by slap-happy experimenters and trigger-happy editors. The irony is that the current destratification of the female sex role may at once both focus and then blur the issues surrounding the correlation between behavioural and biological descriptions of sex differences, attendant as that correlation is on both biochemical and spiritual autonomy. Dot Griffiths and Esther Saraga (1979) signpost the cul-de-sac:

. . . it is not possible in a capitalist society to even begin to answer questions about the origins of sex differences. Only in a society where women and men are equals will it be possible to do this, and it *may* be the case that sex differences will be shown to have a biological basis. However, sex *differences* research is unlikely to be a priority in such a society.

APPENDIX

*Sex Differences in Divided Visual Field Studies in Children*

| Study | Sex more lateralised | Task details | Response | Measure | Trials | $Ns$ M:F | Comments |
|---|---|---|---|---|---|---|---|
| *Verbal* | | | | | | | |
| MARCEL et al. (1974) | Males | Naming 5-letter verbs, concrete nouns ($N=40$). Exposure 50–180 ms. | Vocal | Accuracy | $32^P + 40^T$ | 10:10 (7, 8 years; good readers) | ANOVA includes similar groups of poor readers. All groups show RVF advantage, accentuated in boys. |
| YENI-KOMSHIAN et al. (1975) | NS | Memory span for series of 5 digits (3 lateral, 2 central, 189 ms) | Vocal | Accuracy | $64^T$ | 9:10 (11 years) | Similar group of poor readers: only they showed RVF advantage, as did FS+ males in particular (NM numbers) |
| | NS | Memory span for series of 5 words (digits), as above | Vocal | Accuracy | $64^T$ | 9:10 (11 years) | Again, VF difference scores greater for poor readers |
| MARCEL and RAJAN (1975) | NS | Naming 5-letter verbs, concrete nouns ($N=40$); individual exposures (about 80 ms) | Vocal | Accuracy (scored for letters) | $PT + 40^T$ | 10:10 (7–9 years) | Overall RVF advantage smaller in similar groups of poor readers (who had much longer exposure times) |
| TURNER and MILLER (1975) | NS | Recognition of 3-letter words ($N=32$) presented both horizontally and vertically, 12–18 ms at 2° 30′ | Manual (circle correct of 4 in booklet) | Accuracy | $PT + 32^T$ | 6:6 (6, 7, 8, 9 years, plus adults) | Overall RVF advantage |

APPENDIX (continued)

| Study | | Task | Response | Measure | Stimuli | Subjects | Result |
|---|---|---|---|---|---|---|---|
| LEEHEY (1976) | NS | Naming 4-letter words printed vertically in upper case. Bilateral (2 words each trial). At 1° 14′ for 80, 100 or 120 ms. Central fixation number. | Vocal | Accuracy | $8^P + 20^T$ | 20:20 (8, 10, 12, 14 years, and adults) | No interactions in overall ANOVA including data from faces task. RVF advantage throughout. |
| BUTLER and MILLER (1979) | NS | Report 3- or 5-letter arrays (2 conditions): words, and zero- and third-order approximations. 195 ms | Manual (write down letters) | Accuracy | $8^P + 48^T$ | 6:6 (per condition; 7, 8, 9, 10 years) | Overall RVF advantage |
| *Non-verbal* | | | | | | | |
| MARCEL and RAJAN (1975) | NS | Face recognition, N=20, all male | Manual (pointing to correct of 2) | Threshold | | 10:10 (7–9 years) | Overall LVF advantage. Problem artefact: girls needed more trials to criterion (69 v. 52), so faces more familiar. |
| SCHALLER and DZIADOSZ (1976) | NS | Line orientation: horizontal v. vertical, 1–30 ms, masked. Presentation within grid of 35 possible positions, 1.28° at furthest line. | Wand wave (R hand only) | Accuracy | $56^{PT} + 280^T$ | 8:8 (9 years) | Overall RVF advantage |

| Study | | Task | Response | Exposure | Subjects | Results |
|---|---|---|---|---|---|---|
| YOUNG and ELLIS (1976) | NS | Faces: immediate matching lateral and central (70 ms, 50 ms, 40 ms for each age) | Vocal ("same/ "different" to single match) | Accuracy | $6^P + 40^T$ (lateral trials) | $7{:}7$ (5, 7, 11 years) | Overall LVF advantage. Twice as many boys as girls omitted for poor central performance. No details on faces. |
| LEEHEY (1976) | NS | Faces (unfamiliar, half M, half F): immediate recognition. Bilateral (2 faces each trial). At 55' to 4° 46' for 120 ms. Central fixation number. | Manual (pointing to 2 of 6) | Accuracy | $8^P + 20^T$ | $20{:}20$ (8,10,12,14 years, and adults) | No interactions in overall ANOVA including data from words task. LVF advantage at 10, 12 years and adults; *not* at 8, 14 years. |
| YOUNG and BION (1979) | Males | Dot enumeration: 2–6 dots lateral and central, 100 ms, 80 ms, and 80 ms for three groups | Vocal | Accuracy | $PT + 60^T$ | $10{:}10$ (5, 7, 11 years | Overall LVF advantage. Some Ss eliminated for poor central performance. |
| YOUNG and BION (1980a) | NS | *Exp. 1* "Familiar" face recognition, where "familiar" means "member of small set" (N = 4, all female, "difficult"/ "easy" (to discriminate), upright/ inverted: 4 conditions). Bilateral pairs, 150 ms. | Manual (point to 2 of 4 faces) | Accuracy | $8^P + 40^T$ | $4{:}4$ (per condition; 7, 10, 13 years) | Overall LVF advantage but overall performance considerably less than 50%, which ought to be chance level for forced choice |

APPENDIX (continued)

| | | | | | | |
|---|---|---|---|---|---|---|
| Males | *Exp. 2* "Unfamiliar" face recognition. As per Exp. 1 except stimuli members of large set ($N=40$). Hence 2 "different" conditions only. | Accuracy | Manual (presumably: nature of response cards unmentioned) | $8^P + 40^T$ | 8:8 (per condition; 7, 10 13 years) | No overall VF effect: small LVF advantage for boys with upright faces (which only means for 10 faces/trials in each VHF) |
| YOUNG and BION (1981a) NS | *Exp. 1* "Known" faces (classmates, colleagues: half M, half F, $N=20$). Unilateral/bilateral, upright/inverted; 150 ms. | Accuracy | Vocal (naming, though this not always possible (?!)) | $P + 40^T$ | 10:10 (7, 11 years, adults) | |

For Key see Table 4

*Note.* Tomlinson-Keasey *et al.* (1978) report a study on word–word and picture–picture matching in groups at 8, 13 and 27 years. Since, as far as one can make out, for the one age group properly referrable to as children, the table on which the analysis is based (Table 2) comprises cells representing the mean of two (*sic*) reaction times, this study demands to be omitted. The study on face recognition by S. Leehey (1976) has been included in spite of its not being widely available, given the overall paucity of studies, and the fact that it is widely referred to.

# 9

# HANDEDNESS

*Marian Annett*

## Introduction

Bryden (1964) demonstrated a significant difference between handedness groups in divided visual field (DVF) perception when he reported that for 75% of 108 right-handers and for 56% of 27 left-handers accuracy was superior for letters presented in the right visual field (RVF) in comparison with the left visual field (LVF). This initial report exemplifies features which are characteristic of many later ones to be reviewed below. First, the RVF superiority was *not* found in a substantial minority of right-handers. Second, the bias detected in right-handers was reduced but not reversed in left-handers. Third, the difference between handedness groups was not very robust statistically; here the comparison was significant at the 5% level on a one-tailed interpretation of the test.

Bryden's (1964) paper followed soon after Kimura's (1961) demonstration of a right-ear superiority in dichotic listening in patients whose speech hemisphere had been assessed by the injection of sodium amylobarbitone into the carotid arteries, and the evidence that speech hemisphere as assessed by this procedure and handedness are related, though imperfectly (Branch *et al.*, 1964). The theoretical jump from auditory to visual asymmetries was a reasonable one to make and the hypothesis that both types of perceptual asymmetry depend on similar hemisphere mechanisms needed to be tested. It is important to notice, however, that no direct test of the cerebral dominance explanation of DVF asymmetries has been made in patients of known speech hemisphere, as far as I have been able to ascertain. There have been several attempts to validate the hemisphere specialisation explanation of DVF asymmetries by correlating them with dichotic listening asymmetries in normal subjects, all without success (Bryden, 1965; Fennell *et al.*, 1977a, 1977b; Zurif and Bryden, 1969). In two studies (Bryden, 1973; Smith and Moscovitch, 1979) negative correlations were found between auditory and visual asymmetries. There is no ground for linking DVF asymmetries with hemisphere specialisation for speech except through the evidence for differences between handedness groups.

Using handedness as a variable in DVF studies is using one unknown to explore another unknown. Although this does not sound promising as a research strategy, something of value could emerge if correlations between the two unknowns limit the range of possible explanations. The interpretation of the evidence depends on theories of the nature of DVF asymmetries and on theories of the nature of cerebral specialisation in relation to handedness. The numerous theoretical approaches to DVF asymmetries are reviewed elsewhere in this volume (see Chapter 5). The only point to be made here with respect to those theories is that any differences found between handedness groups in DVF perception have structural implications. Whether these differences are enhanced or obscured by attention processes or subjective strategies, significant differences between handedness groups entail a structural factor at some level in the perceptual processes leading to the hemisphere asymmetries.

With regard to theories of cerebral specialisation and its relation to handedness, the first task of this chapter must be to review the models of handedness and cerebral dominance which have possible implications for DVF asymmetries. The majority of findings are reported, it seems to me, as if they were *negative*. Perhaps this is why the same kind of experiments have been repeated so often, sometimes by the same investigators, in a search for "positive" findings, but usually with similar "negative" outcomes. I hope to show that these typical outcomes are not negative, but as predicted by the right-shift theory of handedness (Annett, 1972), and on this theory at least they can be regarded as positive.

Studies treating subject laterality as an independent variable in DVF studies have classified subjects for three main characteristics. First and most often, personal hand preference has been the basis of classification, using a variety of criteria of right- and left-handedness. Second, subjects have been divided for the presence or absence of sinistral relatives. Third, subjects have been classified for the manner of holding the writing implement, either pointed away from or towards the self in the so-called "hooked" or "inverted" postures. The theoretical justifications of these three classifications must be examined. For each of them, the evidence must be summarised with respect to the main types of stimuli presented in the DVF, whether alphanumeric or non-alphanumeric; the latter include non-verbal patterns and simple light stimuli. The chapter will conclude with a brief review of evidence for differences in reaction time to stimuli in the DVF in right- and left-handers.

## Models of Cerebral Dominance and Handedness

Three main types of theory of handedness and cerebral dominance need to be distinguished which I will label the "pathological", "deterministic" and "probabalistic" models. The pathological models assume that left-hemisphere speech and right-handedness are universal human characteristics and that all departures from the norm are due to pathological influences. The idea that the pathologies are due to aberrations of character in the sense of the negativistic personality can be dismissed fairly quickly. Unless it is to be supposed that the negativism of character causing left-handedness also causes a shift in cerebral speech laterality, the pathological personality theory has no predictions to make about hemisphere asymmetries. More seriously, theories which assume that left-handedness is a pathological result of a reversal of cerebral asymmetry, most often due to early physical brain damage, should predict right-hemisphere speech in left-handers. This theory is open to the objections that many left-handers do not have right-hemisphere speech (Goodglass and Quadfasel, 1954); that there are individual differences in physical asymmetries of the brain in areas probably involved in language functions which can be detected from the twenty-ninth week of gestation (Wada *et al.*, 1975); and that speech and the preferred hand may continue to be served by an early damaged hemisphere (Milner *et al.*, 1964). This last paper suggested that shifts of hemisphere dominance for speech do occur in association with early brain injury, but that such shifts do not occur in many cases. Several left-handers continue to depend on the left hemisphere for speech, despite early left-hemisphere brain damage, and in one case a right-handed man continued to speak with the right hemisphere despite early right-sided damage. These observations demonstrate, as did the earlier clinical analyses, that the relations between cerebral dominance and handedness are far from straightforward.

Deterministic models of the relations between handedness and cerebral dominance accept that these relations are not straightforward, but assume that they could become straightforward if we were clever enough to discover the rules. They assume that the relations are fully predictable in principle, if not in present practice, and that aside from the uncertainties due to inadequate tests and errors of measurement, predictions could be made in individual cases if the true "indices" of cerebral dominance could be discovered. The most recent claim to have discovered such an index is that of Levy and Reid (1976, 1978) that holding the pen in the normal orientation for writing indicates contralateral relations between the writing hand and the speech hemisphere, while holding the pen in the inverted position indicates ipsilateral relations between writing hand and speech hemisphere. Other possible indices which have been considered are strength of left-hand preference and familial sinistrality. In my first theory about handedness and cerebral dominance I suggested that very strong sinistrals, who were consistently left-preferent for all unimanual actions, might have predictable right-hemisphere speech; all the unpredictability of cerebral laterality in the majority of left-handers was suggested to be associated with their mixed-hand preferences and capacity to develop speech in either hemisphere (Annett, 1964). My current theory differs from this view only in that I have given up the idea that any left-handers, however strongly sinistral, have determinate cerebral speech. The idea that familial sinistrality might offer an index of possible departure from left-hemisphere speech in right-handers has been accepted in neurological thinking for many years. The theoretical underpinnings of this assumption and the effects of classifying subjects for familial sinistrality will be reviewed below.

The first and most pervasive of the deterministic models hypothesised a contralateral relationship between hand and speech hemisphere, in left- and right-handers. The belief that left-handers "ought to" have a dominant right hemisphere is so compelling that in spite of innumerable demonstrations that left-handers are not equal and opposite to right-handers, popular accounts continue to assert the contralateral rule. In the more serious literature the claim is not made overtly, but it seems to me that results finding left-handers the opposite of right-handers are searched for more vigorously and cited more frequently than the more common findings which are negative for the contralateral rule. The claim that the contralateral rule is true of left-handers, provided they point the pen away from the body during writing, has been eagerly followed up by several investigators, with results to be examined below. To move from an expectation of deterministic and preferably contralateral relations between handedness and cerebral dominance to an expectation of indeterminate and probabilistic ones requires a shift of paradigm in the sense of Kuhn (1970).

The right-shift theory of handedness was developed in a series of papers which cannot be reviewed in detail here (Annett, 1972, 1974, 1975, 1978). The theory assumes that whereas lateral asymmetries in other mammals are due to chance, those of man are due to chance plus a factor which biases the left hemisphere to develop speech and incidentally increases the chances of dextral hand preference. When the biasing factor is absent, as is expected to be the case in 18–20% of the population, there is no systematic bias to either side; handedness and brainedness each depend on chance and on chances which are independent of each other. This postulate of independence can be regarded as a null hypothesis to be refuted by further research if untrue, but for the time being it represents the most parsimonious assumption. Figure 1 illustrates the relationships envisaged. The abscissa represents differences between the hands in measures of skill, as for the peg-moving task in which differences between the hands have been shown to be systematically and reliably related to degrees of mixed-hand preference (Annett, 1976). Those whose differences

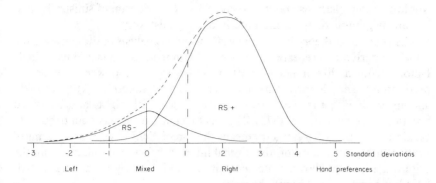

FIG. 1. Hypothesised distribution of the population for differences between the hands in skill, as in speed of peg-moving. There are two subgroups, one having the right-shift factor (RS+) and one lacking the factor (RS–). The mean differences between the hands in skill are 0 for the RS– group and about two standard deviations to the right of 0 for the RS+ group.

between the hands in skill are around 0 are likely to show mixed-hand preferences, whereas those with definite advantages in skill to the right or left are likely to show consistent right- or left-handedness. The larger distribution represents about 81% of the population in whom the right shift or left-hemisphere speech factor is present (RS+) and the smaller distribution represents those in whom the factor is absent (RS–). It is important to notice that both distributions span the full range of hand preferences so that some RS+ are left-handed. The RS– are expected to be about evenly divided between the right and left superior for skill, the proportion being classified as left-handed depending on the criterion of sinistrality adopted.

Expectations for the cerebral speech of left-handers depend on the position of the criterion which may be thought of as moving to the left or the right, along the abscissa, as the criterion becomes severe or lenient. If the criterion is at the extreme left of the mixed group, about 3% of the population who are consistently left-handed would be classified as sinistral. If the criterion is at the extreme right of the mixed group, those with any one left-hand preference would be identified, about 35% of the population. Inspection of the areas under the two curves of Fig. 1 shows that these two locations have very different implications for the proportions of left-handers who are RS+ and have left-hemisphere speech. At the more severe criterion, very few left-handers would be RS+ and the incidence of left-hemisphere speech would fall towards the theoretical minimum of 50%. By the more generous criterion, many left-handers would be RS+ and the majority would have left-hemisphere speech. Conversely, the incidence of right-hemisphere speech in right-handers would be high (perhaps about 8%) given a severe criterion of sinistrality and become negligible on the generous criterion of sinistrality.

The right-shift theory is extremely simple in its analysis of the causes of the biases underlying cerebral dominance and handedness: chance plus a single factor giving a directional bias. It has also proved a powerful theory in predicting the handedness distributions in families (Annett, 1974, 1978, 1979) and in predicting the handedness of dysphasics with right- and left-sided unilateral lesions (Annett, 1975). The fact that chance is a major contributor to the determination of asymmetry means that predictions have to be in terms of probabilities, estimates of the probabilities varying with changes in the criterion as shown above. Statements of the kind, "All right-handers. . ." or "No left-handers. . ." cannot be made.

With regard to DVF and other lateral asymmetries thought to depend on cerebral dominance, the right-shift theory expects left-handers to show little bias to either side when the criterion is strict but to show biases in the same direction as right-handers when the criterion is generous. In all cases, however, trends should be in the same direction as those of right-handers. Given small numbers of left-handers, however, it is easy to see how sampling variations could produce an apparent reversal of the directional bias. Any claim to have discovered an asymmetry in left-handers which is opposite to that of right-handers must be based on a number of cases large enough to test that the contrary bias departs significantly from the expectation of the right-shift theory of no systematic bias to either side.

Evidence of lack of systematic bias of speech functions to either hemisphere in left-handers has been noted in several neurological analyses. Does this imply that in left-handers speech is represented bilaterally as seems to have been the view of Chesher (1936), Conrad (1949) and Hécaen and Piercy (1956) or does it imply that left-handers develop unilateral cerebral dominance with about equal probability of left- or right-sided speech (Bingley, 1958)? The right-shift theory suggests that the laterality of cerebral speech depends on chance in those who are RS– (who are right- and left-handed with about equal chances). A glance at the normal distributions shown in Fig. 1 suggests that if cerebral asymmetry is distributed like manual asymmetry, there may be some individuals who are evenly balanced for cerebral functions in the same way what some have no difference between the hands in skill. In those cases speech functions may develop bilaterally rather than unilaterally. In the majority of RS– cases, however, it seems probable that accidental factors in the course of development will lead to an advantage on one side or other and that speech will be lateralised. The assessments of speech hemisphere reported by Rasmussen and Milner (1977) suggest that bilateral speech does occur in right- and left-handers but it is less common in both groups than lateralisation of speech to the right or the left.

In the DVF literature, as in that for dichotic listening, findings of reduced bias to either side in left-handers have often been attributed to reduced cerebral specialisation or bilateral speech. When only mean differences between sides are given it is not possible to distinguish between the two alternate hypotheses, either bilateral representation or equal chances of right- or left-sided speech. Variances would be expected to be smaller for left- than right-handers on the bilateral representation hypothesis, whereas on the equal distribution hypothesis, variances should be at least as great for left-handers as for right-handers. The DVF studies reporting variances will be considered for their contribution to the distinction between these alternatives.

In summary, this review of models of handedness and cerebral dominance for speech suggests that for any significant lateral asymmetry found in right-handers, left-handers would be expected to show one of the following.

A. *Reversed asymmetry.* This would be expected on:
   (i) the pathological shift of dominance model;
   (ii) the classical contralateral rule hypothesis;
   (iii) modern variants of the classical rule which suggest that contra-lateral hand—speech relations are predictable from indices such as manner of holding the pen in writing.

B. *No significant asymmetry* to either side, with presumably smaller variance than in right-handers, on the bilateral representation model.

C. *A reduced asymmetry* in the same direction as right-handers but with variances as great as in right-handers on the right-shift theory.

Further predictions relating to familial sinistrality and to writing orientation will be reviewed in the relevant sections below.

## DVF Asymmetries and Personal Hand Preference

This section reviews studies of DVF asymmetries which have classified subjects for personal hand preference. Some of the studies may be cited again in later sections if they also classified subjects for familial sinistrality or for position of the writing hand. Studies are included here if the analysis of results makes the findings fairly clear for the total groups of right- or left-handers. Studies vary, of course, in the tasks used, the method of analysis of results and in the criteria of classification of handedness. No attempt will be made to distinguish between studies for these characteristics, except for the broad distinction between those using alphanumeric and non-alphanumeric stimuli. In the following analyses I have made what I hope are reasonable guesses as to the significance of trends in left-handers when this is not specifically reported. The overall picture is consistent enough to make a summary overview useful.

## Alphanumeric Stimuli

Table 1 lists studies according to date but keeping together those by a single investigator or research team. The table gives the numbers of subjects in each handedness group. RVA or LVA indicates a statistically significant advantage for the perception of stimuli presented in the right or left visual field. When the asymmetry was not statistically significant, as in many comparisons for left-handers, the direction of any detectable differences between fields is indicated. In all studies of alphanumeric stimuli listed, significant RVAs were reported for right-handers, and without this finding comparisons with left-handers would probably not have been reported. Despite this redundancy in the table, the column for right-handers is retained in order to show sample sizes and also for uniformity with later tables where significant results for right-handers were not always found.

Bryden (1964) compiled data from several of his previous experiments on tachistoscopic letter recognition. Subsequent experiments (Bryden, 1965, 1973; Zurif and Bryden, 1969) used letter-recognition procedures which varied in details of numbers of letters and manner of presentation. In all cases, the left-handed groups showed no significant differences for either field, the trend being to RVA in at least two of the four studies.

Cohen (1972) found that all of 6 right-handers were able to judge letters as having the same name, despite differences in physical shape (e.g. *Aa* or *aA*), faster in the RVF than the LVF; 4 of 6 left-handers made the judgments faster in the LVF. These findings suggest a difference between right- and left-handers but with these *N*s, it is not possible to judge whether left-handers were significantly biased to the LVF.

McKeever and Gill (1972c) compared letter recognition in the visual fields in a task which was evidently very difficult as the mean correct scores were in most analyses less than 25% of the possible score. The small number of left-handers showed a trend to LVA in comparison with the RVA of right-handers for total recognition scores. Using the same task with slight variations in procedure, the experiments of 1973 and 1975 using larger samples of left-handers found non-significant trends toward RVA. For the large numbers reported in 1977, it is not clear whether the RVA for left-handers was significant overall, the findings having been reported for familial sinistrality groups separately (Table 3 below).

Holmes and Marshall (1974a) compared recognition of 3-letter words in the DVF and found the RVA of right-handers considerably reduced in left-handers. Hines and Satz (1974) tested recognition of digits in the half-fields. The RVA was smaller for left-handers than for right-handers but the difference between handedness groups was not significant. Fennell *et al.* (1977a) reported the performance of right-handers and Fennell *et al.* (1977b) reported

TABLE 1

Handedness and DVF Asymmetries for Alphanumeric Stimuli

| | Right-handers | | Left-handers | |
|---|---|---|---|---|
| | N | Asymmetry | N | Asymmetry |
| Bryden (1964) | 108 | RVA | 27 | NS trend RVA |
| Bryden (1965) | 20 | RVA | 20 | None |
| Zurif and Bryden (1969) | 20 | RVA | 20 | NS trend RVA |
| Bryden (1973) | 32 | RVA | 32 | None |
| Cohen (1972) | 6 | RVA | 6 | NS trend LVA |
| McKeever and Gill (1972c) | 20 | RVA | 9 | NS trend LVA |
| McKeever et al. (1973) | 24 | RVA | 24 | NS trend RVA |
| McKeever et al. (1975) | 20 | RVA | 20 | NS trend RVA |
| McKeever and Van Deventer (1977) | 44 | RVA | 71 | ? RVA |
| Dimond and Beaumont (1974c) | 18 | RVA | 12 | RVA |
| Holmes and Marshall (1974a) | 30 | RVA | 18 | NS trend RVA |
| Hines and Satz (1974) | 60 | RVA | 30 | ? RVA |
| Fennell et al. (1977a) | 16 | RVA | — | — |
| Fennell et al. (1977b) | — | — | 20 | RVA |
| Haun (1978) | 12 | RVA | 12 | LVA |

the performance of left-handers on a task of letter recognition. Significant RVAs were found in both handedness groups, as they were by Dimond and Beaumont (1974c) studying paired-associate learning of digits and symbols.

Haun (1978) tested letter recognition in subjects selected for extreme right- and left-handedness; 66 self-described left-handers were screened to find 12 who were strongly left-handed and who also had a sinistral relative in the immediate family. A significant difference was found between handedness groups and also a significant asymmetry for each group: RVA for right-handers and LVA for left-handers. With regard to individual subjects 11 of 12 right-handers showed some RVF superiority and 9 of 12 left-handers showed some LVF superiority. The right-shift theory expects about a half of strong left-handers to show the opposite asymmetry to right-handers. Haun's result depends on the observation of 9 as opposed to an expected 6 left-handers with LVA. It could be due to sampling factors.

In summary, for the perception of alphanumeric stimuli there is not one convincing finding of an asymmetry in left-handers which is the reverse of that of right-handers. In the majority of studies, the direction of asymmetry in left-handers is the same as that for right-handers but the extent of asymmetry is reduced. The evidence is in full accord with Bryden's (1964) original observations.

Data on individual differences and variances within handedness groups were rarely given in these reports. MacKavey *et al.* (1975) examined DVF word recognition in right-handers. In several experiments 22–28% of subjects did not show RVA. These findings are consistent with Bryden's (1964) observation that 25% of right-handers did not show right-field superiority. In two studies reporting standard deviations (Bryden, 1965; McKeever and Gill, 1972c) the variances of scores in left-handers appear to be at least as large as those of right-handers. This would suggest that the smaller differences between fields in left-handers were not due to lack of differences between fields in individuals as expected on the bilateral function hypothesis. The smaller mean differences probably arise from a more equal division of left-handers between right-superior and left-superior performance.

## Non-alphanumeric Stimuli

Table 2 lists reports of lateralised perception of a variety of non-verbal stimuli in studies comparing right- and left-handers. The studies are grouped for type of task. In the clinical neuropsychology literature it took very much longer to show that the right hemisphere has a special role in some non-verbal activities than to show that the left hemisphere has a special role in verbal ones. Similarly, in the DVF literature for normals, LVAs for non-alphanumeric stimuli in right-handers appear to be more difficult to find and are less robust

TABLE 2
*Handedness and DVF Asymmetries for Non-alphanumeric Stimuli*

| Stimuli | Right-handers | | Left-handers | |
|---|---|---|---|---|
| | N | Asymmetry | N | Asymmetry |
| Geometrical forms | 47 | NS trend RVA | 15 | None |
| Nonsense forms | 32 | None | 32 | None |
| Dot location | 32 | NS trend RVA | 32 | NS trend RVA |
| Abstract shapes | 20 | LVA | 10 | LVA |
| Dot enumeration | 35 | NS trend LVA | 44 | NS trend LVA |
| Dot location | 16 | LVA | 16 | LVA |
| Faces | 34 | LVA | 29 | None |
| Faces | 32 | LVA | 32 | LVA |
| Faces | 130 | LVA | 68 | None |
| Lightness (greys) | 12 | LVA | 12 | RVA |
| Lightness (red/grey) | 12 | LVA | 12 | None |
| Lights for RT | ? 40 | LVA | ? 20 | LVA |
| Lights for RT | 10 | LVA | 10 | None |

Bryden (1964)
Bryden (1973)
Bryden (1973)
Beaumont and Dimond (1975)
McGlone and Davidson (1972)
Smith and Moscovitch (1979)
Gilbert and Bakan (1973)
Gilbert (1977)
Lawson (1978)
Davidoff (1975a)
Davidoff (1975a)
Jeeves and Dixon (1970)
Jeeves (1972)

than RVA effects for alphanumeric stimuli. Bryden's (1964) paper included a summary of findings for the perception of geometrical forms. This was followed by new experiments carefully designed to look for asymmetries in the perception of nonsense forms and the localisation of dots. No significant asymmetries were found for either right- or left-handers. An asymmetry for matching of abstract shapes was however found by Beaumont and Dimond (1975), but did not differ between the handedness groups.

McGlone and Davidson (1972) tested dot enumeration and found no significant differences but trends to LVA in both handedness groups. Smith and Moscovitch (1979) reported significant LVA for dot location in both right- and left-handers.

Tests of face perception by Gilbert and Bakan (1973), Gilbert (1977) and Lawson (1978) found LVA in right-handers. Gilbert (1977) also found LVA in left-handers but the other two studies found no advantage for either side in left-handers.

Davidoff (1975a) compared the DVFs for perception of lightness in one experiment using grey rectangles and in another experiment using grey and red rectangles. Right-handers were found to judge the stimulus on the left as lighter in both experiments. In the first experiment left-handers reversed the directional asymmetry, and in the second, left-handers showed no difference between sides. The RVA reported for left-handers in the perception of lightness is the only report in the table of a significant reversal in left-handers of the asymmetry found in right-handers. As in the study of Haun (1978), the only significant reversal in Table 1, Davidoff's finding rests on 12 subjects of whom 9 gave the reverse asymmetry. This number is insufficient to test for a significant departure from the chance division expected on the right-shift theory.

The report of Jeeves and Dixon (1970) concerns reaction time (RT) to light stimuli presented at various eccentricities in the nasal and temporal retinas of the DVFs. The report is a summary over several experimental conditions and as subjects may have served in more than one condition, a "?" is recorded against $N$. The clear and unexpected finding was that RT was faster to lights presented in the LVF than in the RVF. This was true of about 80% of both right-handed and left-handed adults. In a follow-up study of schoolboys (Jeeves, 1972) the LVA was confirmed for right-handers but no bias to either side was found for left-handers. A series of other studies, employing a slightly different paradigm designed to study the hemispheres operating together or alone, found various lateralised effects in the operation of fatigue, in the transfer of paired-associate duograms, and in colour-naming (Beaumont and Dimond, 1973; Dimond and Beaumont, 1972b, d) but no differences in the pattern of results between right- and left-handers. These studies, with others, are discussed in Beaumont (1974).

## Family Handedness

Table 3 lists studies which have classified subjects for presence of sinistral relatives. Not all studies have tested all possible subgroups, but it is nevertheless useful to include them in a single table to show the overall consistency of results. The majority of studies used alphanumeric stimuli but the few studies using non-alphanumeric stimuli are also listed.

The possible relevance of familial sinistrality (FS) as a variable in laterality studies depends on the supposition that brainedness depends at least in part on genetic factors and that subjects with a left-handed relative (FS+) are more likely to have the sinistral patterns of cerebral dominance than those without such relatives (FS–). Any asymmetries typical of dextrals are expected to be weaker in FS+ right-handers (RFS+) and any contrary biases in left-handers are expected to be stronger in those who are LFS+. These assumptions imply that the sinistral pattern of hemisphere function, whatever that may be, can occur in right-handers and does not occur invariably in left-handers. Brainedness is thus a matter of probability rather than direct correspondence between brain and hand, but no method of calculating these probabilities has been offered, as far as I know, for any genetic theory.

The right-shift theory assumes that the RS factor inducing left-hemisphere speech has a genetic basis and it has been shown that a single gene would be sufficient to account for the distribution of handedness in families (Annett, 1978). The theory does permit the calculation of probabilities, in principle, but the estimates would depend on several variables, such as the incidences of left-handedness in parents, offspring and siblings as well as the incidence of right-brainedness in the general population. Estimates from clinical studies suggest that about 40% of left-handers in the general population are right-brained. On the right-shift theory a maximum of 50% are right-brained but this is reached only in families with two left-handed parents. The presence of one sinistral parent would be expected to give a probability between 40–50%. Clearly, the influence of a sinistral parent on the chances of right-brainedness in a left-hander is not large. Similarly, the presence of one left-handed parent affects the chances of right-brainedness in a right-hander very little. Just as the majority of left-handers occur as the only sinistral in families of right-handers, so the majority of all those who are right-brained occur in the families of two right-handed parents. These considerations suggest that the use of FS+ as a variable in laterality experiments would be expected to make a very small change in the probabilities of right-brainedness for speech.

Table 3 shows that Bryden (1965) was the first to report an analysis of left-handers for FS. In the 4 LFS+ in that first sample there was an LVA for letter recognition. In a second sample (Zurif and Bryden, 1969) LFS– and LFS+ groups differed in that the former showed a significant RVA while the

TABLE 3

*Familial Sinistrality (FS) and DVF Asymmetries for Alphanumeric and Non-alphanumeric Stimuli*

| | Right-handers | | | | Left-handers | | | |
|---|---|---|---|---|---|---|---|---|
| | FS− | | FS+ | | FS− | | FS+ | |
| | N | Asymmetry | N | Asymmetry | N | Asymmetry | N | Asymmetry |
| *Alphanumeric stimuli* | | | | | | | | |
| Bryden (1965) | 20 | RVA | — | | 16 | NS trend RVA | 4 | LVA |
| Zurif and Bryden (1969) | 20 | RVA | — | | 10 | RVA | 10 | NS trend LVA |
| Bryden (1973) | 16 | ?RVA | 16 | ?RVA | 16 | ?NS trend RVA | 16 | ?NS trend RVA |
| McKeever and Gill (1972c) | 13 | RVA | 7 | NS trend RVA | — | | 14 | NS trend RVA |
| McKeever et al. (1973) | 24 | RVA | 24 | NS trend RVA | 9 | NS trend RVA | 7 | None |
| McKeever et al. (1975) | — | | — | | 13 | RVA | 7 | RVA |
| McKeever and Van Deventer (1977) | 44 | RVA | 36 | NS trend RVA | 34 | NS trend RVA | 37 | RVA |
| McKeever and Jackson (1979) | 12 | RVA | 12 | RVA | — | | — | |
| Hines and Satz (1974) | 30 | RVA | 30 | RVA | 28 | RVA | 26 | RVA |
| Higgenbottam (1974) | 32 | RVA | — | | 18 | NS trend RVA | — | |
| Holmes and Marshall (1974a) | 30 | RVA | — | | — | | — | |
| Marshall and Holmes (1974) | 48 | ?RVA | 48 | ?RVA | — | | 48 | ?RVA |
| Bradshaw et al. (1977b) | 24 | RVA | — | | — | | 24 | NS trend RVA |
| Bradshaw and Taylor (1979) | 24 | RVA | — | | 24 | NS trend RVA | 24 | RVA |
| Haun (1978) | 12 | RVA | — | | — | | 12 | LVA |
| Piazza (1980) | 16 | ?RVA | 16 | ?RVA | 16 | ?RVA | 16 | ?RVA |
| *Non-alphanumeric stimuli* | | | | | | | | |
| Bryden (1973) (Nonsense forms) | 16 | None | 16 | None | 16 | None | 16 | None |
| Bryden (1973) (Dot location) | 16 | ?NS trend RVA | 16 | ?NS trend RVA | 16 | ?NS trend RVA | 16 | ?NS trend RVA |
| Piazza (1980) (Faces) | 16 | LVA | 16 | None | 16 | ?NS trend RVA | 16 | None |

latter showed no significant asymmetry, the small trend being to LVA. A third study (Bryden, 1973) found no significant effects for FS in the overall ANOVA and no details of findings were given. The "?" before the results cited in the table acknowledges that they are inferred from the report for right-handers and left-handers when no specific analysis for FS was given.

In the several studies of McKeever and his colleagues, the significant RVAs found for RFS– were reduced in most other groups, although sometimes remaining significant statistically. Looking over the rest of the studies, none reports a significant LVA except that of Haun (1978) already shown above to be based on very small numbers. It is worth noting that Marshall and Holmes (1974) who tested 48 subjects in each of 3 groups found no overall effect of FS and like Bryden did not report detailed results for FS groups. Similarly, Piazza (1980) found no significant effects for groups on the general ANOVA and did not report the significance of biases for FS groups.

Table 3 also lists the three tests of perception of non-alphanumeric material in DVF studies classifying for FS. Bryden (1973) included tests of the perception of nonsense forms and dot location with the study of letter perception referred to above. As for letters, FS was not a significant variable in these non-verbal tasks and no details of scores in FS groups are given. Piazza (1980) found an LVA for her RFS– groups and no differences between fields for the other groups.

In summary, these several studies are remarkably consistent in showing that subdivision of samples for FS adds nothing substantial to the findings for handedness, as seen in Tables 1 and 2. The presence of close sinistral relatives in groups of right-handers is sometimes sufficient to reduce the typical RVA of the RFS– group to a non-significant level. The presence of FS+ in left-handers has sometimes been associated with a trend to reversed asymmetry but never when $N$s were substantial.

## Orientation of the Writing Hand

Levy and Reid (1976, 1978) suggested that the laterality of the speech hemisphere can be predicted if handedness groups are subdivided for pen orientation during writing. Right-normal writers (RN) and left-normal writers (LN) who point the pen away from the body are said to have speech in the hemisphere contralateral to the writing hand, that is, the left hemisphere for RN and the right hemisphere for LN. In left-handers who invert the pen so that it points towards the body (LI) and in the rare cases of right-handers adopting a similar posture (RI) the relations between hand and speech hemisphere are said to be ipsilateral, speech hemisphere being left for LI and right for RI. In all cases it is suggested that the same hemisphere controls both speech and the writing hand and whereas in RN and LN the hand is controlled through the crossed pyramidal tracts, in LI and RI the hand is controlled by uncrossed pyramidal fibres. This last aspect of the theory derives from the Levy and Nagylaki (1972) model of the genetics of handedness and brainedness and it is not strictly necessary to the writing-hand/brain-hemisphere hypothesis since if it were true that the speech hemisphere of LI and RI were ipsilateral to the writing hand, control could be effected via the corpus callosum. The non-speech hemisphere of all groups is expected to serve those non-verbal functions which have been attributed to the right hemisphere of right-handers. Thus, an orderly and fully predictable set of relationships between brain function and handedness has been postulated, provided the orientation of the pen is taken into account. Levy and Gur (1980) reaffirm the belief that "An index of control pathways has been discovered".

There are several reasons to doubt that this new "index" of cerebral dominance offers a trustworthy guide to speech laterality. First, orientation of the writing hand is a variable open to differing interpretations. Observing students writing examination papers under my direct supervision I have found 1·7% of 528 students using the hooked or inverted position; this represents 0·65% of 460 right-handers and 8·82% of 68 left-handers. Other estimates greatly exceed these percentages, ranging from 30–60% in several studies (Peters and Pederson, 1978; Coren and Porac, 1979; McKeever, 1979). If position of writing hand is open to such variability of ascertainment it cannot be a clear index of anything. A second problem is that cerebral lateralisation itself may not be a discrete variable, as suggested by the evidence for bilateral speech. Third, measures of relative EEG alpha suppression between the hemispheres during writing found no differences between LN and LI groups at central and parietal leads (Herron *et al.*, 1979). With a smaller subset of subjects, a difference was found between RN and LN subjects at the occipital leads, suggesting greater involvement of the right hemisphere than the left hemisphere in the LN subjects during reading and writing. This reversal depended on a group of 9 LN subjects. As shown for other studies above, chance fluctuations in the composition of small groups can easily lead to apparent reversals of asymmetry which are not confirmed by larger samples. The LI group mean was unbiased to either side as expected on the right-shift theory.

Levy and Reid's (1978) evidence for opposite asymmetries in LI- and LN-handers depended on comparisons of performance, within subjects, for an alphanumeric and a non-alphanumeric test: nonsense-syllable perception and dot location. Raw data were not reported for either task so that the significance of RVAs and LVAs on these tasks in groups cannot be assessed. The claim to have found data consistent with the hypothesis of contralateral hand–hemisphere speech relations in writers with normal orientation and ipsilateral relations in inverted writers, in 70 out of 73 subjects rests on directions of difference between transformed scores on the two tasks.

Smith and Moscovitch (1979) attempted to replicate the Levy and Reid experiment using similar nonsense-syllable and dot-location tasks as well as a dichotic listening test. They reported means for each VF and also numbers of subjects showing the group trends. On the verbal test the RN and LI groups showed RVAs while the LN group showed a small LVA; the single RI subject also showed an LVA. This pattern of results is as predicted by Levy and Reid. On the dot-location test, all groups and the RI subject showed LVAs. On the dichotic listening test the LN group, predicted by Levy and Reid to show reversed asymmetry, gave a mean right-ear advantage as did the RN and LI groups. Thus, the evidence for a reversed pattern of cerebral dominance in the LN groups rests on a trend whose significance was not established, in 1 out of 3 tests. Inspection of the individual distributions shows that 8 out of 15 LN subjects were right-ear superior; this proportion is fully compatible with the right-shift hypothesis of lack of bias to either ear. With an almost equal number of left-dominant and right-dominant subjects in this group it is not unlikely that chance factors would give a slight LVA on the verbal task.

Bradshaw and Taylor (1979) measured vocal RT to alphanumeric material. Dividing their left-handers into 37 LN and 11 LI, they found that the latter gave a smaller RVA than the former, a difference in the direction opposite to the prediction of Levy and Reid and the observation of Smith and Moscovitch. McKeever (1979) compared LN and LI groups on a colour-naming task previously shown to give a significant RVA in right-handers. Both LI and LN left-handers obtained similar RVAs, smaller than expected in right-handers but with no hint of reversed asymmetry in either group. McKeever and Van Deventer (1980) gave a letter-perception task to 30 LN- and 35 LI-handers and found no differences due to writing posture, both groups showing RVA. Lawson (1978) compared hand-orientation groups for a face-judgment task. She confirmed the findings of Gilbert and Bakan, as shown in Table 2, but found no difference between LI- and LN-handers.

These several attempts to test the hypothesis of contrary cerebral specialisation between those with inverted and normal orientation of the pen when writing have all proved negative except for the trend on the verbal task of Smith and Moscovitch. Other attempts to follow up the Levy and Reid hypothesis of ipsilateral cortical hand control have been made using reaction-time studies. These are considered in the next section.

## Handedness and Reaction Time to Light Stimuli in the DVF

Comparisons of the DVF for perception of briefly exposed stimuli such as spots of light have been made using measures of manual RT. Before the recent interest in writing postures and the possibility of ipsilateral cerebral motor control in those with inverted writing, few studies compared handedness groups (see Table 2). In view of speculation generated by the inverted writing hypothesis and renewed attempts to calculate transmission times between the hemispheres, it is important to analyse what facts have been established about

    (i)    DVF asymmetries in RT to light stimuli;

    (ii)   the effect of using same versus different VF–hand combinations;

    (iii)  any effects of handedness on these asymmetries.

It is also important to distinguish between simple RT where only one response is made to stimuli which may appear in either VF and choice RT where different responses are made to stimuli in each VF. In the choice situation, RT is greatly influenced by the spatial compatibility of stimuli and responses. In the simple RT situation the spatial location of the responding hand with respect to the location of the stimulus seems not to be a significant variable (Anzola *et al.*, 1977). The following account concerns simple RT unless choice is specifically mentioned.

The classic study of RT to simple stimuli which could appear in either VF was that of Poffenberger (1912) whose aim was to estimate the time for callosal transmission. This was to be done by subtracting the time taken for stimuli and responses to be processed by the same hemisphere (RVF and right hand or LVF and left hand) from the time taken for stimuli and responses to be processed by different hemispheres (RVF and left hand or LVF and right hand). He found in two subjects differences of 5·6 ms and 6·0 ms. Replication of this experiment by Berlucchi *et al.* (1971) in two groups of 6 and 8 subjects found differences of 3·3 ms and 2·1 ms between the same VF–hand v. different VF–hand combination. Anzola *et al.* (1977) confirmed that the faster response in the former is not due to spatial compatibility effects by having subjects cross their arms while making the simple RT with one hand. Anzola *et al.*'s experiment found a significant effect due to the "anatomical" connection but inspection of the data as shown in Fig. 2 of their paper suggests that the difference was even smaller than for Poffenberger and Berlucchi *et al.*, and of the order of 1–2 ms. The anatomical basis of these small differences is, of course, unknown. Berlucchi *et al.* (1971) showed that it is unlikely to be due to a simple extra callosal synapse since the time difference was roughly constant for stimuli presented from 5°–35° across the horizontal meridian of the VF; commissural connections between the striate areas of the two hemispheres seem to be restricted to the central visual field. It is necessary to emphasise the uncertainty as to the size and the origin of the time differences for crossed and uncrossed RTs, in view of the temptation to neurophysiological speculation about ipsilateral and contralateral pathways prompted by the hypothesis of ipsilateral control in inverted writers.

The second main fact which has been established about DVF and RT to simple stimuli is that response tends to be faster to stimuli in the LVF. The

Jeeves and Dixon (1970) report listed in Table 2 summarised findings from several experiments designed to estimate callosal transmission times; the major and unexpected finding was faster response to LVF stimuli, irrespective of the responding hand. Faster response to LVF stimuli was also evident in the data of Anzola et al. (1977), even when the responding hand was held across the other, showing that the effect cannot be due to stimulus-response compatibility. A left-sided stimulus bias has also been noted for *choice* RT by Bradshaw and Perriment (1970) and by Annett and Annett (1979). Faster perception of stimuli on the left has been found in other experimental situations (Braine, 1968; Sekuler et al., 1973).

The Levy and Reid (1978) hypothesis of ipsilateral cortical control of the hand in inverted writers suggests that any anatomical advantage there may be for same VF–hand over different VF–hand combination in RT might be reversed in LI and RI subjects. As we have seen above, the differences are expected to be very small and their origin is unknown. Previous studies also suggest that one of the main effects should be an LVA irrespective of responding hand.

Smith and Moscovitch (1979) included an RT task with the DVF and dichotic listening tasks discussed above in their study of writing orientation. In a first experiment, all subjects used the left hand to respond. RT was faster to stimuli in the LVF in RN- and LN-handers, but in LI response was faster to RVF stimuli. In a second experiment all subjects used the right hand to respond but now the direction of differences was reversed; RN and LN groups responded faster to stimuli in the RVF, and the LI group responded faster to stimuli in the LVF. These results follow the pattern expected for contralateral hand–hemisphere control in normal writers and ipsilateral hand–hemisphere control in inverted writers, but before accepting this simple interpretation it must be noted that the results are extraordinary in several respects. First, reversals of VF asymmetries for RT to simple stimuli with responding hand have not been observed in previous studies of right-handers (Jeeves and Dixon, 1970; Anzola et al., 1977). Second, the size of mean differences reported by Smith and Moscovitch (1979) are 5–33 ms, very much larger than in any previous study of "anatomical" differences. Third, previous work suggests a strong tendency to LVA in all groups, whereas RVAs were reported here for normal orientation right- and left-handers.

Moscovitch and Smith (1979) reported RTs to lateralised tactual, auditory and visual stimuli in inverted and normal right- and left-handers. For tactual and auditory stimuli, all groups responded faster with the right hand to right-sided stimuli and with the left hand to left-sided stimuli. On the visual task, this was true for RN and LN groups. A reversal of VF differences was reported for the 12 LI and 1 RI subjects with faster responses by the right hand to left-sided stimuli and by the left hand to right-sided stimuli. As in the Smith and Moscovitch (1979) report, mean differences tended to be much larger than in previous experiments and the RVA for right-hand responding was extremely large. The sources of these differences from previous work are unclear. One possibility is that the very large number of blank trials (50%) changed the nature of the task, in comparison with the usual simple RT experiment where fewer blank trials, if any, are included.

McKeever and Hoff (1979) measured simple RT to light stimuli presented in either VF and without blank trials in LI and LN groups. For both groups and both hands responses were faster to stimuli in the LVF. The difference was negligible for the right hand of LN-handers and about 5–6 ms for other comparisons. The LVA is compatible with previous experiments reviewed above. There was no evidence of reversal of directions of differences between hands or between normal and inverted writers.

## Summary

This chapter has reviewed studies of DVF asymmetries in which subjects have been classified for personal hand preference, presence or absence of sinistral relatives and for orientation of the pen during writing. For those tasks finding significant asymmetries for right-handers, RVAs for alphanumeric and LVAs for non-alphanumeric stimuli, findings for left-handers range between reduced differences in the same direction as right-handers, no asymmetries to either side, and weak trends in the direction opposite to right-handers. On balance the evidence suggests that in left-handers there are no significant biases to either side and the trends are predominantly in the same direction as the asymmetries of right-handers. There is no evidence of a reversed directional asymmetry in any left-handed group where $N$s are large enough to give confidence in the result. Distinctions between subjects for familial sinistrality and for orientation of the pen in writing make no significant addition to the original classification for hand preference.

Attempts to follow up neurophysiological speculations about ipsilateral and contralateral control via the pyramidal pathways in inverted and normal writers through reaction-time studies have been shown to be subject to many problems. The only studies reporting reversals of asymmetry between hand-orientation groups differ substantially from other RT studies in methods and findings.

In so far as DVF asymmetries are related to cerebral asymmetries for speech, the evidence for handedness groups suggests that asymmetries may occur in right-handers but not in left-handers, when the latter are classified on strict criteria of sinistrality. There is no substantial evidence that any group of left-handers, whether classified for strong sinistrality and presence of sinistral relatives, or classified for normal orientation of the pen in writing, is typically right-brained for speech. The findings of DVF studies are fully compatible with expectations of the right-shift theory, that biases are unidirectional and more likely to found in right-handers; when absent, there are no systematic biases to either side.

## Acknowledgment

This chapter was written during the tenure of a grant from the Medical Research Council.

# 10

## THE SPLIT-BRAIN STUDIES

*J. Graham Beaumont*

THE STUDY of patients who have undergone cerebral commissurotomy, or the "split-brain" operation as it is more popularly known, has a special place in contemporary neuropsychology. The dramatic nature of the operation and its effects, as projected in particular by Roger Sperry, captured the scientific imagination of many workers in the mid 1960s, and has attracted the attention of a wider audience in the ensuing years. Whatever the scientific value of the data collected from these patients is, and it is my view that the data should be approached with a great deal of caution, the studies acted as a significant stimulus to the development of experimental human neuropsychology, and the techniques developed by Michael Gazzaniga have proved fruitful within a much broader neuropsychological context.

Although there had been an earlier series of commissurotomy patients operated on by Van Wagenen in the 1940s, and studied by Akelaitis and Smith, it was not until the preliminary reports of the Vogel and Bogen series began to appear (Gazzaniga *et al.*, 1962; Sperry, 1964a, b, 1966) that the significance of the commissurotomy operation in man was realised. In the commissurotomy operation, performed to control severe and intractable epileptic seizures, the forebrain commissures (the corpus callosum, the hippocampal commissure, the massa intermedia when present, and the anterior commissure) are sectioned. The exception to this procedure is in the more recent series of Wilson (Wilson *et al.*, 1975; Wilson *et al.*, 1978) in which, except for the earliest patients, the anterior commissure is spared. The anterior commissure was also variably sectioned in the Van Wagenen series. All three series have also included a number of patients with only partial commissurotomies, and

217

the literature also contains a number of cases in which parts of the callosum and other commissures have been removed in the course of other surgical procedures.

The significance of complete commissurotomy is that the operation severs all direct communication between the cerebral cortex of the two hemispheres. By presenting information in one half-field of sensory space, it is possible to observe the performance of either hemisphere operating independently from its partner, and to address questions about hemisphere specialisation and competence, which cannot be studied so readily in the intact brain with its normal opportunities for interhemispheric integration, cooperation and mutual inhibition.

Before proceeding to examine the evidence obtained with divided visual field (DVF) presentation in commissurotomy patients, it is important to note two major difficulties which characterise many of the studies. The first is the nature of the subjects. The number of patients who have undergone the operation is small, probably no more than 25 from the two recent series, and of these the number suitable for investigation is a minority. The number of patients for whom there is any extensive data is only seven, of whom just two provide the majority of the data. Not only are the numbers small, but the variation among the patients in terms of both their performance and their neurological status is very great. As might be expected, most of the patients have a relatively severe degree of extracallosal cerebral pathology which undoubtedly contributes to the deficits which have been observed. A discussion of this problem, with a most helpful tabulation of the patients, is to be found in Whitaker and Ojemann (1977), although it is not always possible to identify which subjects are being reported, particularly in the earlier studies. The patients do not comprise a single group about which clear generalisations can be made, despite the attempts of a number of writers to draw such conclusions (see Beaumont, 1981). However, when the results from individual patients are treated independently, and the variation clearly observed (a good example being the papers of Levy and Trevarthen 1976, 1977), then the difficulty of handling the data in a rigorous manner also becomes apparent.

The second difficulty to be considered in assessing these studies is the degree to which these patients develop ingenious strategies which, despite the experimental paradigm, allow the stimulus presented to be transferred across the midline. Gazzaniga has been particularly astute in identifying some of these "cross-cueing" strategies, and in demonstrating their operation (Gazzaniga, 1969, 1970; Gazzaniga and Hillyard, 1971; Johnson and Gazzaniga, 1969). The strategies have included postexposural gaze deviation with bilateral feedback of eye movements; eye movements to indicate the vertical extent of stimuli; focusing on a plane behind the plane of presentation; differentiating "0" and "1" in terms of two and one vertical elements; headshakes, emotional reactions and the effect of admonishment; and in more recent studies, the use of finger-tracing. The patients must clearly be adept at developing more general cognitive strategies which can compensate for their disability in every-day life, particularly as they seem so little handicapped in a normal free environment, and such strategies must also carry implications for their per-formance within the laboratory. To construct an experimental paradigm which prevents all possibility of the employment of cross-cueing strategies is a difficult task, and the possibility of their operation must be examined when considering the results of any of the split-brain studies.

The studies will now be reviewed, in so far as they have employed DVF presentation, in order to assess their contribution to neuropsychological models of cerebral organisation, and to enquire whether the results throw light upon the results of DVF studies with normal intact subjects.

## Ipsilateral and Contralateral Identification and Matching

### Verbal Response

The general view concerning verbal identification, particularly since the publication of Gazzaniga's influential *The Bisected Brain* in 1970, has been that stimuli projected in the right visual field (RVF) can be identified, but that left-visual-field (LVF) stimuli cannot be reported through speech, although other forms of response indicate that the stimuli are correctly perceived and comprehended in the right hemisphere (RH). Gazzaniga, summarising a series of earlier papers with Sperry and others, reported this finding for geometric symbols, letters, numbers, pictures of objects and words. This general con-clusion, supported by more recent papers (Gazzaniga *et al.*, 1975, 1977), has been taken to indicate that the right hemisphere has no access to the cerebral mechanisms by which speech is generated.

A number of papers suggest, however, that this general conclusion must at least be qualified. Gazzaniga and Hillyard (1971) reported a study of verbal reaction time to numerical stimuli. They found longer reaction times associ-ated with LVF presentation, but not a complete failure of performance. They attributed the RH performance to a strategy which involved counting up by the LH until the count was interrupted by a non-verbal signal transmitted by the RH, indicating the correct response. They supported this interpretation by demonstrating that the reaction time increased with the number of items in the response set. Nevertheless, they still found the effect when using the two stimuli "2" and "4", although the strategy is not entirely inappropriate to this condition.

Above-chance performance by the RH in verbal response accuracy was also reported by Teng and Sperry (1973) in a task using both letters and digits as stimuli. They also found a superiority of RVF performance, but LVF performance at about 20% was above chance, and increased to 30% if a rather laxer scoring criterion was employed.

Another example of a study which failed to demonstrate a total deficiency of the RH in verbal response is the chimeric stimuli study of Levy *et al.* (1972). The chimeric studies will be discussed in more detail below, but involve a bilateral stimulus configuration composed of two half-stimuli, one of which appears to each side of the vertical meridian. In examining vocal naming responses to a variety of figural stimuli, they found the expected preference for reporting the stimulus associated with the RVF elements, but a significant number of LVF responses (36%, 23%, 36% and 16% for face, "antler", drawing and pattern stimuli).

More general indications of verbal activity associated with RH activity have also been reported. Evidence of verbal description of objects presented in the LVF is available for at least one patient (Preilowski, 1979), although the possibility that this was achieved through finger-tracing by the left hand, or some other cross-cueing strategy, remains. More definite reports of verbal response to a wide variety of forms of LVF stimulation, including the detection of visual change, altered direction of change, rhythm of motion, enumeration, parallax changes, colour changes, shapes and the identification of objects by shape, have also appeared (Trevarthen and Sperry, 1973). There are complex differences between the abilities of different patients, and performance associated with each type of stimulus was not always at a very high level, but definite, if variable, signs of some degree of ability were present. The startling evidence of general social knowledgeability (Sperry *et al.*, 1979), demonstrating "characteristic social, political, personal and self awareness" in manual and verbal response to LVF stimuli, also seems relevant here.

A final point relating to verbal response concerns the neglect of LVF stimuli, and indeed their denial, despite accurate left-handed selection of a stimulus match. This phenomenon has been clearly reported (Gazzaniga, 1967; Kinsbourne, 1974; Trevarthen and Sperry, 1973). This raises the question, expressed by Joynt (1977), of why there are not more reports of left-field inattention in everyday behaviour for these patients. It may well be that the independence of hemisphere systems from subcortical systems which integrate and regulate higher performance has been overemphasised (Beaumont, 1981), and that everyday behaviour is subject to the effects of a system which binds together the activities of the two hemispheres, even in commissurotomy patients. However, it may also be that the disconnection of the RH from speech processes has also been overestimated, and while the access of the RH to speech mechanisms is restricted in the split-brain patient, a total disconnection is not to be assumed in all of the cases.

## Visual–Visual Matching

Early reports, derived principally from the first three or four patients of the Vogel series, suggested that interhemisphere matching of verbal stimuli was not possible (Gazzaniga, 1970). This conclusion was extended to the matching of colour and of brightness. As with verbal responses, subsequent reports have tended to modify this view in favour of a relative difficulty for interhemisphere matching. The position is, however, much less clear as there are few studies which have demanded simple matching between visual stimuli in the two lateral visual fields.

Gott *et al.* (1975, 1977) studied visual evoked responses, but also reported performance on behavioural measures. They demanded rhyme matches for flashed words, and matches for rotated shapes, one of the stimuli being at the fixation location. The results were complicated by considerable differences among the 5 patients studied, but at least 3 performed above chance with the LVF verbal stimuli, attaining a mean 65·5% correct, although this was inferior to RVF performance. With the spatial stimuli, only 3 patients performed above chance, 2 with both hemispheres.

Direct visual matching of rotated "L" forms has been reported in a patient with partial (centre section) commissurotomy, an increase in errors of inter-hemispheric matching, relative to the intrahemispheric conditions, being observed following surgery (Dimond *et al.*, 1977).

The picture has been recently complicated by the demonstration that when the anterior commissure is spared at surgery, then visual information can be transferred via that route (Gazzaniga and LeDoux, 1978; Risse *et al.*, 1978). This applies whether the response is in the form of a verbal response, or in direct visual matching, and a number of patients (varying with the precise task, but approximately 4 of 5 examined) have shown good interhemisphere transfer via the anterior commissure. This emphasises the importance of being aware of the precise extent of surgery in any given patient, and of making a distinction between patients of the Vogel series, whose anterior commissure was cut, and several patients in the Wilson series, for whom it was spared. The finding also raises the question of why posterior section of the corpus callosum should affect the reading of verbal stimuli if the anterior commissure is available for the transfer of such visual stimuli. In patients for whom this has been reported, the possibility of extracallosal damage has not been resolved (Gazzaniga and LeDoux, 1978), and the question remains, as a result, an open one.

## Manual Response

Again the situation is more complex than indicated by the early reports, which suggested that in order to retrieve pictorial matches, to draw shapes or to adopt hand and finger postures, then the stimulus and response must be on the same side of the body (Gazzaniga, 1970). The first complication is that a distinction must be made between responses which can be executed by relatively gross arm movements, and those which demand control of fine distal musculature. It seems clear that a substantial degree of ipsilateral control exists for the relatively gross arm movements. It is often difficult to distinguish the two types of movement in particular studies. The demonstration of visual transfer by an intact anterior commissure also applies when a manual response is demanded.

In measurement of motor reaction time, Gazzaniga and Hillyard found no clear differences with a go/no-go paradigm (1971), although with foreperiod reaction time with a lateralised warning stimulus (1973) they found significantly slower responses with the LVF–right-hand combination, a result which was also suggested by the earlier study.

With bilateral stimuli, an LVF bias in the selection of response, with either hand pointing, was found for the faces, "antlers", drawings and patterns employed by Levy *et al.* (1972), and this finding was supported by Nebes (1973, 1974b) using arrays of dots and a go/no-go finger response. Both these studies may well demonstrate the possibility of ipsilateral control of the manual response. Bilateral stimuli, as well as unilateral presentation of digits and letters, were used by Teng and Sperry (1973), ipsilateral response being required in the bilateral conditions. They observed some LVF neglect in the presence of an LVF stimulus, and a general RVF advantage. With digits as stimuli, there was no interaction between the RVF advantage and the superiority of performance in the unilateral condition, but with letters as the stimuli, the RVF superiority was greater under bilateral presentation than under unilateral presentation conditions. Again, this suggests a relative degree of proficiency, possibly mediated by preferential access of the LH to general regulatory systems, interacting with the association of differential processing strategies within the hemisphere systems, rather than a model based upon absolute failure of communication between the two hemispheres. None of the evidence is, however, entirely incompatible with the latter model, given the possibility of ipsilateral response control.

A further illustration of the role of cross-cueing strategies is also provided in this context, following the observation (Sperry *et al.*, 1969) that left-hand printing of words presented in the LVF was indeed possible, but only after left-hand spelling of the word. This has been observed as a spontaneous strategy in later patients.

Some further studies with bilateral letter stimuli might have been expected to provide important evidence, but present particular difficulties of interpretation because of the differences between individual patients. Gazzaniga presented 4-letter arrays in one or both visual fields (1968, 1970; Gazzaniga and Hillyard, 1973; although it should be noted that some differences are present in these descriptions of the same experiment). The patients were asked to point with the left hand. The split-brain patients showed an improvement in performance when shown stimuli bilaterally, an effect not observed in normal controls, although their "improved" performance was still well below that of the control subjects. Of the two patients tested, one reported stimuli from both visual fields, but with the LVF stimuli reported first, while the other reported more from the RVF, and these tended to be reported first. Some rather similar experiments have been described by Kinsbourne (1974, 1975a). Employing upper-case letters, targets presented to the left of a bilateral probe elicited no response or a left-hand response after a long latency, while right-side targets elicited right-hand latencies equal to those observed with a single-letter probe, leading to the inference of a right-side bias in performance. Letter search similarly produced a right-side advantage when stimuli appeared in both visual fields, for two patients, despite differences between them when unilateral stimuli were presented. An alternative visual search task with bilateral targets supported the idea of relative independence between the hemispheres, responses sometimes favouring each of the hemispheres, in a pattern similar to that observed with unilateral targets. In general, unimanual responses with the right hand were found to accentuate any RVF advantage, while left-hand responses attenuated an RVF superiority.

Little can be firmly concluded from the studies employing manual response, particularly in isolation from the details of individual cases. Some patients have difficulty, or even a complete failure of performance, in responding to visual stimuli with the contralateral hand. Where a significant degree of performance has been observed, it is not possible to distinguish between explanations based upon ipsilateral response organisation, some degree of transfer within the brain or externally between the hemispheres, and the contribution of relative specialisation and attentional mechanisms linked to the performance of individual hemispheres.

## Verbal Functions

Research has been directed more profitably towards assessing the verbal competence of the separated hemispheres. The critical question has, in fact, been the degree to which the RH possesses verbal functions, the assumption being that no dysfunction of verbal abilities is to be observed for the LH performing alone.

As suggested above, there has been general agreement that the RH is unable to generate speech, although it may produce automatic utterances, swear and sing. Nevertheless, it has always been clear that the RH has a degree of verbal ability, albeit at a level below that of the LH. Gazzaniga (1967, 1970) had reported that the split-brain patient was able to select objects semantically related to stimuli which were presented in the LVF, and to read letters, numbers and short words. This was accomplished more easily if the verbal material was nominal, with noun-object words being the easiest stimuli. Adjectives followed in difficulty, and performance with verbs was extremely limited. The difficulty associated with verbs also extended to nouns derived from verbs, such as "locker" or "teller". That the difficulty with verbs was a true comprehension difficulty is supported by the observation that patients could readily carry out actions signalled by pictures presented in the LVF, although not when the commands were written. This evidence is supported by Levy (1970; reported in Nebes, 1974a) who describes that when verbs were presented to the LVF, patients could not perform the actions, but could select a pictorial match with about 50% accuracy, and could reliably retrieve an associated object. This is, however, essentially the same data, from the same patients, as the reports of Gazzaniga.

Gazzaniga and Hillyard (1971) adopted a slightly different approach, presenting a picture to the LVF, and administering a spoken two-choice question relating to the actions or relationships depicted. The patients were unable to distinguish simple relational expressions of the form "the boy kisses the girl" from "the girl kisses the boy", to recognise the future tense or to distinguish singles from plurals. Affirmation and negation were, however, understood in relating the verbal statement to the picture, within the RH.

A considerable advance in our appreciation of the verbal abilities of the RH has been made by Eran Zaidel (1976, 1977, 1978a, b, c, 1979). He has employed an ingenious technique involving contact lenses and a collimator (Zaidel, 1975), to allow prolonged exposure of test materials in the lateral visual fields. This has allowed standard psychometric procedures to be administered to the LH and the RH independently in the commissurotomy patients, and the results to be compared with performance in free vision. Although the technique has not been clearly validated as a method of lateralising stimuli, and while it must be remembered that the nature of the apparatus inevitably limits the performance of the patient by comparison to a test performing under normal conditions, the findings are coherent, possess a degree of face validity, and are valuable in that they are derived from within-subject hemisphere comparisons.

The tests administered by Zaidel have included the Peabody and Ammons Full-Range Picture Vocabulary Tests, the Token Test, elements of the Illinois Test of Psycholinguistic Abilities, Raven's Progressive Matrices, the Benton Visual Retention Test, the Carrow Test, and elements from several aphasia batteries. The results are of course extensive and complex, particularly as there are different findings for different patients, but have greatly extended the range of verbal functions which can be attributed, at some level of competence, to the RH. In the early reports there was a tendency to characterise the RH performance in terms of age-norm comparisons, finding the RH vocabulary to be at about the 11-year-old level and auditory comprehension comparable to 4-year-old children. Zaidel has properly recognised the problems of using "mental age" comparisons to describe data of this kind, and the limited value of such a comparison. In addition, it is important to bear in mind the direct comparison with LH performance, because while the RH performance was in almost all cases inferior to LH performance, and the RH was often performing well below the adult level, the LH alone was also found to have a performance inferior to free-field performance, at a level not greatly in advance of the RH. To describe RH performance without reference to LH performance is to artificially deflate estimates of RH performance.

Despite these qualifications, Zaidel has shown the RH to possess a rich auditory picture vocabulary, to recognise diverse semantic relations, and only to experience difficulty with long non-redundant sentences in which order is important, or where assistance is not provided by contextual cues. Zaidel suggests (1978b) that the RH has a rich lexical structure, but access to a severely limited verbal short-term memory and neither phonetic encoding nor grapheme–phoneme correspondence rules. He argues that this competence could be acquired by non-linguistic cognitive mechanisms. The RH possesses a remarkable degree of language ability but it does not incorporate specialised language mechanisms for phonetic and syntactic encoding and analysis, as are to be observed in the performance of the LH.

## Spatial Functions

There has been no investigation of spatial functions to parallel the examination of verbal functions in the separated hemispheres. For the most part, the evidence is a series of isolated and relatively unconnected observations, which have concentrated on relatively basic perceptual processes rather than higher spatial functions.

In a patient with the posterior part of the callosum sectioned (this region, the splenium, is responsible for primary interhemispheric connection between the visual cortices), light-detection thresholds were found to be raised, but to be increased equally in the LVF and the RVF (Levine and Calvanio, 1980). In the same study, an RVF advantage was found for naming and matching colours, although Levy (1978) had reported wide variation in dominance for colour perception among 5 total commissurotomy patients examined. Similarly, variable results were found when patients were asked to name or select the typical colour for an object depicted in black outline. The Stroop colour-word test produced rather more coherent results in the two patients tested, however, the RH being superior at identifying the ink colour, and the LH at pointing to the black name of the ink colour or the colour named. Levy concluded that the two hemispheres process colour by verbal (LH) or imagistic (RH) strategies, and that the LH is poor at generating colour images.

Dimond studied vigilance performance (1976, 1978a, 1979a) and found a gross depletion in vigilance in patients with complete section of the callosum. In addition, the LH performance was characterised by gaps or "holes" in performance, and he concluded that sustained attention depends upon hemispheric cooperation. These results were partially supported by Ellenberg and Sperry (1979).

Rather surprisingly, in a study of enumeration, with identification of a numeral as a control, no difference was found between the two visual fields, and no interaction between visual field and unilateral or bilateral presentation (Teng and Sperry, 1974). In this, and other studies, it has been difficult to assess the importance of the transfer of relatively elemental attributes by midbrain visual systems. Sperry *et al.* (1969) pointed to this possibility, citing evidence from a number of earlier studies, and Trevarthen in particular has developed the idea (Trevarthen, 1974a, b, 1975; Trevarthen and Sperry, 1973). Trevarthen, by employing a variety of stimuli not previously investigated, and using an apparatus which allowed presentation at greater degrees of visual angle out into the "ambient visual field", demonstrated a degree of hemisphere cross-integration not previously suspected. Studies of active reaching; of a range of basic perceptual processes such as the detection of visual change, motion perception and parallax changes; the location of a midpoint between targets in opposite visual fields; the judgment of alignments; all pointed to the integrated perception of stimulation in the ambient visual field by either hemisphere, presumably mediated by subcortical visual systems.

The importance of the location of stimulation within the entire visual field, as well as the mode of response, is emphasised in the studies of Trevarthen. He observed that incomplete figures presented near fixation would be reported as complete, either verbally if in the RVF or by drawing if in the LVF. Further, the operation of completion was also balanced by the presence of neglect. Patients experienced difficulty in using the contralateral hand to mark the geometric centre of a figure, even including verbal reports of its perceptual disappearance from the RVF when the left hand moved to cross the midline to make a response. These reports underline the lack of sophistication which often characterises perceptual and spatial studies of neurological patients, our lack of a good model to understand how these functions may be subsumed by the hemispheres, and our lack of empathy for the strange visual perceptual distortions and abnormal phenomena which these patients may experience.

## Chimeric Figures

Some of the most elegant and inventive studies have been undertaken by Jerre Levy and coworkers using "chimeric" figures (Levy, 1974a, b, 1978; Levy and Trevarthen, 1976, 1977; Levy et al., 1972; Trevarthen, 1974a). In these stimuli, two half-figures are presented simultaneously, one on each side of the fixation point, to be matched to whole figures presented in central vision, using left- or right-hand pointing or vocal responses. The commissurotomy patients, of course, do not recognise the ambiguous nature of the stimulus configuration. As noted above, with figural stimuli, an LVF bias was observed with manual pointing with either hand, and an RVF bias, although it was less clear, with a vocal response.

Undoubtedly the most impressive of these studies was the one which employed a set of stimuli which could be matched either according to holistic figural characteristics ("appearance" matches) or according to the semantic associations of the objects depicted ("function" matches). Free matches could be made, or the two types of match could be demanded in the instructions given to the patient. Unfortunately, the findings are particularly complex when considered across the four patients investigated, but some broad conclusions seem to be justified. Most importantly, there was evidence that appearance matches were made preferentially in the RH, and function matches in the LH, and Levy and Trevarthen ascribe this to the operation of "metacontrol" systems which are linked to cerebral specialisation. Nevertheless, strategies and hemispheres were not found to be consistently associated, and dissociations between hemisphere and strategy were not uncommon. This evidence seems valuable in pointing to at least one level of description of whatever fundamental processes form the basis of hemisphere specialisation as observed in split-brain or in normal subjects. It also serves to emphasise that the relative dichotomy between right- and left-hemisphere processes is not based upon the unique access of a particular hemisphere to certain elementary processes, but upon the relative modes or styles or strategies of performance adopted by each hemisphere. It is possible that there is a rigid dichotomy between the hemispheres, which because of the variety of mechanisms which may be employed in the execution of a high-level task, never finds clear expression when complex tasks are studied, but in the absence of evidence for such a clear dichotomy (except perhaps in the control of speech) it does not seem reasonable to assume that it must exist.

The chimeric figures technique was also directed to the perception of words, to semantic decoding and to phonetic similarity. With a spoken response, the RVF word was reported, but when pointing, there was a strong bias to the LVF word, even when pointing with the right hand. However, when pictures were to be selected to match the words, an opposite RVF bias was observed in every subject with either hand, the effect being stronger for the left hand. Similarly with rhyming (phonetic similarity), even with the left hand pointing, there was a clear bias to respond to the stimulus presented in the RVF. The RH was therefore observed to be dominant in the visual recognition of words, providing that semantic or phonetic decoding was not required, but the LH assumed control for semantic matching and for rhyming. The RH however, although showing little ability for rhyming, appeared to be competent at semantic matching, but failed to gain control of response when in competition with the LH.

It is perhaps relevant to note that the findings with chimeric faces, of a significant LVF superiority with a manual response, have been replicated in normal subjects (Milner and Dunne, 1977; Schwartz and Smith, 1980). The findings are also in accord with the earlier double-stimulation studies reported by Gazzaniga (1970) and Gazzaniga and Hillyard (1973), which had found the preferential report of an RVF stimulus with a vocal response. The reports of Jeeves (1979; Jeeves et al., 1979) concerning two partial commissurotomy patients with the splenium intact, presented with chimeric faces, are also broadly in support of the findings outlined above.

## Miscellaneous Findings

The reports of simultaneous reaction-time performance, which have been taken by some to show that independent engagement of the hemispheres allows a doubling of task performance (Gazzaniga, 1970), have attracted much attention. However, although the split-brain patients did not show a normal decrement following the addition of a second task, their performance under both conditions was so dramatically below the level of normal subjects, that to suggest that commissurotomy allows a doubling of mental capacity seems quite unreasonable.

Gazzaniga, with Johnson (Gazzaniga, 1970, 1972; Johnson and Gazzaniga, 1969), carried out some investigations on learning in one patient, and found evidence for learning being lateralised to the hemisphere in which it was established. There was, however, clear evidence of the transfer of response-cueing by non-cognitive mechanisms to allow apparent bilateralisation of learning. These investigations find closer parallels in the animal neuro-psychology literature than in human studies.

Electrophysiological evoked-response parameters have been reported (Gazzaniga and Hillyard, 1973; Gott et al., 1975; Hillyard, 1971). The results are of interest, but because of inherent methodological difficulties, the low levels of behavioural performance, inconsistencies between patients and differences between the studies, no clear conclusion has emerged. Psychophysiological variables were measured by Preilowski (1979), but the results really only point to the difficulties of research in this area.

Reports of one complete and one partial commissurotomy patient who were both left-handed are to be found in Levy *et al*. (1972) and in Gazzaniga and Freedman (1973) and Gazzaniga (1975a). A bilingual Spanish–English-speaking patient was described by Dimond (1979b).

## The Development of Ideas About the Effects of Commissurotomy

It seems appropriate to reconsider the Akelaitis and Van Wagenen series of patients operated upon in the 1940s. The principal conclusion at the time was that there were no clear cognitive deficits to be observed, in marked contrast to the more recent series of cases. Explanations of the discrepancy have tended to concentrate upon both the difference in surgical technique and upon a lack of sophistication in the methods of investigation employed by Akelaitis and the psychologist associated with the studies, K. U. Smith (for example, see Moscovitch, 1973). It is true that the Van Wagenen operation was performed in stages, and that the anterior commissure was also generally spared. A contemporary report (Bridgman and Smith, 1945) also suggests the possibility of the accidental sparing of some splenial fibres. These differences might well account for differences between the Akelaitis and the Bogen patients.

It seems a little unfair to dismiss the studies on the grounds of being unsophisticated. Certainly, Akelaitis (1941, 1943, 1944) did not use a tachistoscope, but he did carefully present objects in the lateral visual fields and monitor fixation, used a variety of stimuli, and yet observed no deficit. An LVF deficit for verbal stimuli had been reported by Tresher and Ford (1937) following partial commissurotomy, and Akelaitis specifically considered this in his reports, concluding that his patients presented no evidence of this phenomenon and attributing the earlier result to extracallosal damage, as had in fact been discussed by Treshner and Ford. Smith's reaction-time study (1947) was certainly not unsophisticated, and he manipulated visual field and responding hand independently to yield crossed and uncrossed responses. He found evidence for slowing in both crossed and uncrossed left-hand responses (although there was no differences between the hands in simple reaction time), but no difference between crossed and uncrossed responses. The role of the intact anterior commissure must be suspected in this result (although one patient with a cut anterior commissure performed as the others), and we can only speculate what would have been found if more complex stimuli than simple lights had been used as stimuli.

The development of ideas from the early papers of the Sperry group in the 1960s to the wider range of reports in the last decade repays study, although there is insufficient space here to illustrate its course. A discussion of this development is to be found, with reference to consciousness, in Beaumont (1981), and more generally in Bogen (1979) and Joynt (1974). What is clear is that there was a considerable influence of the first case to be reported, particularly upon the writings of Sperry, and it is unfortunate that this patient now seems not to have been entirely typical of the group as a whole, in so far as there is any typical pattern of deficits. Much was made of the first three cases, and perhaps rather excessive generalisations of the data, and inferences about their significance, were made. It has become increasingly clear that the patients differ in their response to the surgery, and that their performance cannot be considered without reference to extracallosal abnormalities and general neurological status. There was a regrettable tendency to neglect these factors in early reports, to present the split-brain phenomenon as if it were an experimental preparation, and to overestimate the degree of specialisation and independent operation of the separated hemispheres. This view has been increasingly modified, and an examination of Gazzaniga et al. (1962, 1965); Sperry (1968a, b); Gazzaniga and LeDoux (1978); and Sperry et al. (1979) will illustrate this development.

Finally, it is worth noting the influence of the recent case of "P.S." who underwent complete section at the age of 15, and has been followed closely over two years from surgery (Gazzaniga et al., 1977, 1979; Gazzaniga and LeDoux, 1978; LeDoux et al., 1977). The importance of this case has been the degree to which P.S. has developed RH linguistic abilities over the period following surgery, and the way in which the acquisition of LVF naming, spelling and description has been charted. It now seems that this facility may be in part attributed to early left-temporal-lobe damage in this patient, resulting in atypical lateralisation of language, but nevertheless the demonstration of this capacity, and the concept that developmental changes occur following operation, has had an important influence on current thinking about the effects of commissurotomy. It also highlights a previously neglected observation of Sperry (1968b) concerning improvements in cross-integration observed in a patient at that time, and previously attributed to the development of subtle cross-cueing strategies that were extracerebral, rather than to essential changes in neuropsychological organisation.

## Conclusions

Before stating some general conclusions, it should be noted that much of the discussion about partial commissurotomy has not been treated here, although

DVF presentation has been employed with partial split-brain patients in several studies (Gordon *et al.*, 1971; Jeeves, 1979; Levine and Calvanio, 1980; Sugishita *et al.*, 1978, 1980). The evidence from individuals with agenesis of the corpus callosum, while difficult to interpret, is relevant and has been well reviewed (Jeeves, 1979; Milner and Jeeves, 1979).

Readers interested in the issues raised by the evidence from commissurotomy patients are also recommended to see, apart from the volumes by Gazzaniga (1970), Dimond (1972) and Gazzaniga and LeDoux (1978), the reviews and discussions to be found in Gazzaniga (1975b), Nebes (1974a), Searleman (1977), Trevarthen (1975), and Zaidel (1978c).

Some general conclusions can be stated about the performance of commissurotomy patients presented with DVF stimuli:

1. Most of the patients experience a relatively severe difficulty in responding by speech to material presented in the LVF. The evidence suggests that the RH has only very restricted access, if any, to the mechanisms which control speech.
2. A range of arm and hand movements can be regulated by ipsilateral as well as contralateral projections, and this makes interpretation of studies employing a manual response difficult. There is evidence for a deficit in crossed visual–manual performance providing the movement required involves fine, and preferably skilled, distal control.
3. The extent to which some degree of crossed visual matching may be possible is unclear. If the anterior commissure is spared then interhemisphere visual integration may take place by this route.
4. The language abilities of the RH have in general been underestimated. It is possible that the RH does lack access to mechanisms for phonetic and semantic analysis and encoding, but the level of linguistic competence, speech apart, is relatively great.
5. No clear conclusions can be drawn about spatial or perceptual abilities.
6. It would appear that the most appropriate model of cerebral organisation to account for the split-brain data is one based upon hemisphere differences in cognitive strategies or styles, or modes of processing, linked to differential access to common systems of response control, rather than one based upon independence of the hemisphere systems with functions allocated to one or the other of these relatively autonomous entities.
7. All of the above conclusions are subject to extensive qualification, as a result of differences between the data derived from individual patients, and because of the problems of recognising and controlling extracerebral lateral transfer strategies.

The most important point to bear in mind about the split-brain studies is that the data, while valuable, present considerable problems of interpretation, and many fundamental inconsistencies. It may be said to be largely in accord with the data collected in DVF studies of normal subjects. There are certainly no profound disagreements. The same may be said of parallels between the split-brain and clinical evidence (although some discrepancies have been discussed: see Gazzaniga, 1975b; Gazzaniga *et al.*, 1973). The quality of the results (although not the ingenuity and elegance of many of the studies) should not be overrated, and findings in commissurotomy patients should be treated with some caution. Perhaps the major contribution of these studies has been in providing such a dramatic stimulus to human experimental neuropsychology, in fostering the development of experimental techniques, and in capturing the imagination of scientists who have made considerable advances in various fields of psychology, psychiatry and even philosophy, as well as within the neurosciences in particular.

# 11

## DIVIDED VISUAL FIELD STUDIES OF PSYCHIATRIC PATIENTS

*Christopher J. Colbourn*

## The Background

### History

This chapter concerns an area of research which uses the divided visual field (DVF) technique, as one of a number of experimental paradigms, to study the cerebral organisation of psychiatric patients. The notions that the brain is the seat of the mind and that mental disorders result from damage to the brain have a history extending back to at least Hippocrates' era in the fourth century BC. However, such views about mental illness have waxed and waned in popularity throughout the centuries and modern interpretations have differentiated functional psychiatric disorders where no cerebral pathology is detectable from those disorders that are consequent upon such pathology (see e.g. Kräupl Taylor, 1966; Wing, 1978a). Nevertheless, there has been a continued interest among an increasing number of psychologists and psychiatrists in the notion that at least some of the functional psychiatric disorders, particularly those classified as psychopathological states (i.e. the psychoses), are associated with subtle neurological disorders (Gur *et al.*, 1977; Mirsky, 1969; Reitan, 1976) and with disturbances in lateralisation of function in particular (e.g. Zangwill, 1960). Progress in this research seemed very slow at first, perhaps as a result of the rather stultifying atmosphere of American clinical neuropsychology (Luria and Majovski, 1977), which concentrated on the concept of "organicity" (see e.g. Heaton *et al.*, 1978); and a lack of agreement on whether cognitive deficits actually exist in a characteristic form in psychotic illness (e.g. Venables, 1978).

Dramatic changes occurred with the explosion of interest in cerebral hemisphere asymmetries of function, largely because the experimental paradigms developed were non-invasive, and therefore relatively easy to use, and the interpretation of the data seemed easily framed in terms of neurological organisation, in particular a rather gross form of localisation of function, i.e. allocation of cognitive functions to the left or right hemisphere (LH or RH) of the brain.

The history and development of these so-called "laterality" studies has been documented earlier in this volume, and so it remains here to illustrate the reasoning connecting psychiatric disorders and hemisphere function (or dysfunction as the theories put it). The arguments have originated both from a consideration of psychiatric symptoms and from known lateralised neurological disorders and extended to their counterpart in the putative relation. For example, in schizophrenia, commonly observed symptoms include disruption of propositional speech, verbal hallucinations, and body-image disturbances (e.g. Shimkunas, 1978; Wing, 1978b). The functions underlying these have been found to be lateralised within the brain from observations made on patients with unilateral focal brain damage (e.g. Hécaen and Albert, 1978; McFie, 1969). However, it is clear that the actual functional disorders manifest in schizophrenic patients do not entirely resemble the similar disorders following destruction of brain tissue, at least not for the more thoroughly investigated language disorders (e.g. Critchley, 1964; Pavy, 1968). A recent clinical study using various linguistic performance tasks demonstrated clear differentiation between aphasic patients and schizophrenic patients (Rausch *et al.*, 1980). Critchley commented that the similarities between aphasic and schizophrenic speech were only superficial and concluded from his survey that the latter patients' speech disorder resides in an underlying thought disorder rather than in the linguistic inaccessibility which characterises asphasic language.

Similarly, Erwin and Rosenbaum (1979) observed that patients with parietal lobe syndrome and schizophrenics showed a somewhat similar pattern of neuropsychological deficit with respect to parietal function, although only the schizophrenic group showed unusual body experiences. The authors suggested that this pattern was consistent with the notion that neurological bases for the proprioceptive deficit shown by both types are quite different.

Thus, although aspects of the symptomatology of psychotic illness are related to lateralised functions, the nature of the disorders is not the same as that found in brain-damaged individuals showing deficits in those same functions. Another recent study compared behaviourally significant schizophreniform symptoms encountered in various neurological diseases with the various sites of subcortical damage associated with them. No clear-cut relation was found when the area of the lesion had been controlled for except that damage to the basal ganglia seemed to have a higher degree of involvement than expected (Bowman and Lewis, 1980). The true significance of this association between schizophrenia and basal ganglia damage must await further study although it clearly does not fit in easily with the types of dysfunction theory with which we are concerned. However, it does seem clear from Bowman and Lewis' study that an association of this psychiatric state with cortical damage is far from obvious. Such findings for a study of this nature are not perhaps surprising since any obvious parallels between psychiatric and neurological disorders would have been noticed by now. Clearly such cerebral damage or disorder as might exist in functional psychiatric illness must be much more subtle, and disorders of lateralisation would seem to fit this conclusion admirably.

## A Laterality Hypothesis of the Endogenous Psychoses

The approach of looking at psychiatric symptoms concomitant with cerebral abnormalities has been explored in depth by Flor-Henry (e.g. 1969; 1974; 1976) using the clinical picture provided by patients with temporal-lobe epilepsy. In a retrospective study, Flor-Henry (1969) found an association between schizophrenic psychoses and epileptic foci in the dominant left temporal lobe, and between manic-depressive (the so-called "affective") psychoses and non-dominant right-temporal-lobe foci. Similar analyses of the literature and other medical records broadly confirmed these trends relating lateralised organic brain disease and psychopathology (Davison and Bagley, 1969; Lishman, 1968; 1973), although a recent study in India only found an association between right temporal foci and neurotic disorders (Shukla and Katiyar, 1980). Earlier studies of this kind were largely instrumental in spawning this "laterality hypothesis of the endogenous psychoses" (Flor-Henry, 1979). Other authors reviewing the intersection of psychiatric and neurological disorders arrived at similar conclusions, with particular emphasis on the nature of schizophrenic illness (e.g. Dimond, 1978b, Chapter 8; Galin, 1974; Jaynes, 1976). The sources of this illness have proved elusive to brain and behavioural scientists and this latest explanation in terms of laterality seemed at first just another straw in the wind, but interest still grows in the notion that some disturbance in the functional organisation of the brain, particularly with respect to functions known to be lateralised in the cerebral hemispheres, may be a concomitant of, or even a basis for psychotic illness, especially schizophrenia. In general, the hypothesis considered is that schizophrenia involves a left-hemisphere dysfunction of some unspecified, or even generalised, type (e.g. Gur et al., 1977; Jaynes, 1976; Shimkunas, 1978). In addition, defects in interhemispheric communication along the lines of a disconnection syndrome (especially as found in "split-brain" patients) have been proposed as concomitants of schizophrenia (e.g. Butler, 1979; Dimond,

1978b; 1979). Strangely enough, this echoes in part Wigan's (1844) theory that mental health depended on an intimate union of man's two brains, although of course Wigan's idea was based on the equality of the two cerebral hemispheres, a hypothesis we now know to be untrue.

## Research Directions

The past decade has seen intensive and still-continuing research into these hypotheses using a variety of different experimental techniques and measures, e.g. neuropathological, psychophysiological (skin conductance and electro-encephalographic indices) and behavioural (hand preferences, visual, auditory and tactile laterality in cognitive performance). Detailed compilations and evaluations of this work have only recently appeared in the literature, providing rather cautious conclusions on the whole (e.g. Gruzelier, 1979, 1981; Gruzelier and Flor-Henry, 1979; Wexler, 1980).

Much of the evidence is, of course, equivocal with regard to its support for the hypothesis in question, particularly neuropathological findings (e.g. Johnstone *et al.*, 1976; Luchins *et al.*, 1979; Rosenthal and Bigelow, 1972) which have been much-beloved by behavioural researchers as providing "substantive" support for their own findings. Both Marsden (1976) and Gruzelier (1981) have cautioned against over-hasty conclusions from such data, and Butler (1979) provided a very cogent demonstration of the subtle and complex relation that must exist between any neuropathology of interhemispheric pathways and behaviour. Another body aimed at supporting the relation between abnormal laterality and psychiatric illness is that on hand preference patterns (e.g. Fleminger *et al.*, 1977; Gur, 1977; Lishman and McMeekan, 1976) where certain psychiatric diagnoses (especially psychotic states) have been found to be associated with an increased incidence of sinistrality relative to general population norms. A recent study of hand preferences has, however, reached the opposite conclusion and associated an increased incidence of dextrality with schizophrenia (Taylor *et al.*, 1980). The main inference from such data is, however, that part, not even a majority, of a *subset* of the psychopathological population is involved. This may be important since it seems quite likely that a number of factors underlying these disease states may combine in different ways. Since there is an association between handedness and other forms of laterality (although not clearly defined: see Chapter 9 this volume; Levy and Reid, 1978; Satz, 1979) we need to take this into account when making between-group comparisons.

However, the key aspect of the laterality phenomenon lies in the cerebral organisation of cognitive processes, especially with regard to their distribution between the two cerebral hemispheres, and it is on this data that much attention has been focused and we shall concentrate.

## DVF Studies

One of the earliest contemporary reports of a DVF experiment on psychiatric patients came from Beaumont and Dimond (1973b). They claimed a demonstration of the impaired capacity for cross-matching visual information fed separately to the two hemispheres in schizophrenic subjects as compared to another psychiatric control group and normal patient controls. Their findings were interpreted in terms of a corpus callosum dysfunction in the psychotic patients, drawing on the neuropathological findings of Rosenthal and Bigelow (1972) for support. Although this DVF study report was relatively brief, as it has become a much-quoted piece of research in this area it is worth scrutinising the quite complex findings.

The three groups of 12 subjects tested (active schizophrenics; psychiatric controls who were patients suffering from anxiety, affective and personality disorders; and normal controls who were patients in hospital for systemic disorders) each performed five different tasks presented via a divided-field apparatus. This apparatus utilised back-projection tachistoscopic principles (i.e. 150 ms exposures) and masking screens to achieve separate stimulation of the visual half-fields of each eye (see Dimond, 1970, for a full description of this apparatus). This apparatus allowed stimuli, either singly or in pairs, to be presented to either hemisphere, and in the case of pairs to both hemispheres simultaneously. The subjects' required tasks were identification and "same–different" matching of letter, digit, and shape stimuli, using vocal responses.

Error data (both incorrect and failure-to-respond types) were analysed, and with respect to the two identification tasks (letter and digit stimuli), there were no differences in performance between the groups of subjects, although it was observed that overall the RH was somewhat superior at identifying digits (not an expected result). However, the performance on the matching tasks varied as a function of both subject group and hemisphere stimulated. For the condition where both hemispheres were stimulated, requiring interhemisphere communication to evaluate the match between the two stimuli, the schizophrenic group performed significantly worse than either of the two control groups for both letter and shape stimuli, although this effect was not evident for digit stimuli. These results seem broadly consistent with a deficit in interhemisphere communication, but in addition there were intergroup differences in the performance under intrahemisphere matching conditions. On letter-matching where stimulation was directed at the LH, schizophrenics made significantly more errors than normals whereas RH stimulation was not associated with group differences. For both digit- and shape-matching tasks the schizophrenic group performed at a lower level than the psychiatric controls when stimuli were directed at the RH. In these latter cases the normal group performed at a level intermediate to the other two groups, and LH stimulation was not associated with any group differences.

The authors' conclusion from the intrahemisphere findings was that there was some "small" specific hemisphere deficit for the schizophrenic patients. Unfortunately, the lack of a clear-cut difference between the schizophrenics and both control groups on all the types of processing represented makes such a specific conclusion rather speculative. In addition, there is the problem of which hemisphere shows a deficit since this depends on where one believes the relevant processing takes place, and how each set of stimuli is presumed to be dealt with. Letter-matching could be executed via a phonemic code, i.e. by name (an LH method) or via a visual code (an RH method) (see Cohen, 1972; Geffen *et al.*, 1972; Wilkins and Stewart, 1974). Similar arguments for the other types of stimuli used here (e.g. see Birkett, 1978, with respect to shape stimuli) show that a number of different models of hemisphere function (e.g. Cohen's automatic/conditional/no-transfer trichotomy, see Chapter 5 of this volume) could be used to specify almost any or all types of hemisphere deficit for these psychotic patients. This interpretational problem will, of course, be present in many of these types of experiment but it particularly reaches a head in Beaumont and Dimond's complex findings. Dimond (1978b, 1979c) has pointed out that the interpretation of schizophrenics' performances in laterality tasks requires converging operations using other paradigms and modalities, which he and his colleagues have done, particularly in the tactile modality (see e.g. Carr, 1980; Dimond *et al.*, 1980). However, in general these merely compound the problem since they do not provide true convergence because these other techniques involve similar interpretation problems.

Following Beaumont and Dimond's initial study, a number of conventional tachistoscope experiments involving separate stimulation of the left and right visual fields has been carried out using psychiatric patients. In order to avoid, if possible, the complications of the handedness-cerebral laterality relation (see Chapter 9 this volume), researchers have selected all their subjects for right-handedness using one of the well-documented questionnaire assessment techniques (e.g. Annett, 1970). Although providing a degree of consensus in favour of the left-hemisphere deficit for schizophrenics rather than the inter-hemisphere dysfunction considered previously, there are a number of anomalous results and the interpretation of these studies is not always as clear as their authors would have us believe.

Gur (1978) described a well-controlled experiment (which included a fixation task) comparing the performance of 12 paranoid and 12 non-paranoid medicated schizophrenics with 24 matched normal controls on two tachistoscopically presented identification tasks. These tasks were related to putative LH processes in one case (consonant–vowel–consonant syllables) and RH processes in the other (dot location). Accuracy was the dependent variable and Gur reported an overall LVF advantage for the dot-location task, as expected from earlier research. Although the schizophrenic group performed significantly more poorly than the controls, they showed the same asymmetry of performance. However, the syllable-test results showed a dissociation in the performance of the two subject groups with schizophrenics showing an LVF advantage—i.e. against the expected LH basis for this task—while normals produced the usual RVF advantage for this type of material. The *post hoc* comparisons indicated that LVF performance was not different between the groups but RVF performance was significantly higher for the controls. Unfortunately, the statistical reliability of the visual field advantages was not reported and it appears that while the schizophrenics' LVF advantage in the syllable task was significant, there was no field advantage for the control group in the same task.

Nevertheless, this data suggests that even according to very conservative methodological criteria (Colbourn, 1978, 1979), the laterality of performance differs for the two groups. Gur concluded that her data support a hypothesis of left-hemisphere dysfunction being associated with schizophrenia and argued further that this deficit occurred in the initial stages of visual processing. This latter conclusion was based on the reasoning that the right hemisphere is "totally incapable" of the phonetic analysis required in the syllable task. In view of research demonstrating considerable RH ability in processing verbal material, albeit on a non-phonetic basis, this conclusion can be seriously questioned (e.g. Coltheart, 1980b; Marcel and Patterson, 1978; Searleman, 1977). On the other hand, these results clearly do not support a deficit in interhemisphere communication for the schizophrenics, since the vocal response required was most likely to be produced by the LH irrespective of which hemisphere received the stimulus initially.

Connolly *et al.* (1979) reported similar findings in a more extensive experiment involving a wider range of psychiatric patients and using reaction time (RT) as the dependent variable. They, like Gur, used two tasks but they were of a match-to-sample type. One task involved alphanumeric stimuli and was assumed to demand LH-processing capabilities, while the other involved dot patterns and RH capabilities. Connolly *et al.* compared the performances of 15 schizophrenics, 6 patients with affective disorders (depressives) who were considered psychotic, 14 non-psychotic psychiatric cases, and 20 normal controls. All subjects showed the expected LVF (RH) advantage for the "spatial" task involving dot patterns and in general the RTs were longer for this task than for the one involving alphanumeric stimuli. Performance on this latter task, however, discriminated between the psychotic patients (both schizophrenics and depressives) and the two control groups (non-psychotic psychiatric patients and normals) in that the latter groups showed no reliable asymmetry in their performance as a function of the visual field stimulated. The psychotic groups, however, also demonstrated a significant LVF (RH) advantage on this task. From the data presented, this pattern of results seems to stem largely from the intersubject consistency of performance asymmetries (or inconsistency in the case of non-psychotics and the "verbal" task).

As in the case of Gur's experiment, a vocal response was used by Connolly *et al.* and hence an interpretation of the psychotic groups' performances in terms of a deficit in interhemispheric communication is less likely than one in terms of a specific hemisphere deficit. There are, however, several complications in relating these findings to the laterality hypothesis of the endogenous psychoses.

## Revision of the Hypothesis

First, as Connolly *et al.* (1979) point out, the performance of the affective disordered group (pointing to an LH deficit on the conventional interpretation of asymmetries in this paradigm) is somewhat at odds with Flor-Henry's (1976) original work briefly outlined in an earlier section. However, in a more recent formulation Flor-Henry (1979) has amassed a range of clinical observations which point to laterality shifts in bipolar psychotic illness such that mania is associated with an LH disorder, and depression with an RH disorder. Connolly *et al.* evaluated their rather small group of affective patients in terms of mania and depression at the time of testing and noted that four out of the six in this group were manic and showed the LH deficit while the remaining two were depressed and showed no asymmetry of performance. This, they suggested, was consistent with Flor-Henry's revised hypothesis, although the present author feels that this conclusion must be tentative in view of the small number of subjects and lack of support from other DVF studies (e.g. Colbourn and Lishman, 1979).

With respect to the association between schizophrenia and an LH deficit, this has been replicated by Connolly and Gruzelier (1980) using similar match-to-sample tasks involving symmetrical letter stimuli and dot patterns, but using unimanual responses. In the case of both types of stimuli there was an LVF (RH) advantage in RT for both the left and the right hand. Although control groups have not been tested yet, it would be expected, on the basis of earlier research using normal subjects, that the letter and dot stimuli would be associated with RVF (LH) and LVF (RH) advantages respectively. Thus again the LH deficit hypothesis of psychosis seems to have been supported.

## Interpretational Complications

However, the problem with the hemisphere deficit explanation is that many information-processing tasks offer more than one method of solution, as suggested earlier. This seems to apply particularly in the case of alphanumeric stimuli where a specific type of processing, e.g. name matches, is not enforced.

Thus Connolly *et al.*'s results may reflect a bias toward RH processing strategies in psychotic illness rather than a dysfunctional LH. In view of the substantial differences in performance levels on both the "lexical" and the "spatial" tasks between the subject groups (i.e. normals had the shortest RTs and the two psychotic groups the longest, the difference being some 150–200 ms for equal levels of accuracy across the other variables), and the finding of no overall asymmetry for the verbal task in normal subjects, this "bias" explanation seems as likely as the "deficit" explanation. Nevertheless, it is interesting that Coltheart's (1980b) cogent argument that deep dyslexia involves a lesion which abolishes access to the LH lexicon from orthography, thereby implying that reading (silent and out loud) in such patients comes from their RHs, leads to the prediction, which Coltheart clearly states, of an LVF advantage in reading tasks for deep dyslexics. Although taking a slightly different theoretical stance on the nature of deep dyslexia, Saffran *et al.* (1980) provided some evidence in support of the LVF advantage prediction for three such patients, using a lexical decision task which generally produces an RVF or no VF advantage in normals (e.g. Cohen and Freeman, 1978; Day, 1977; Leiber, 1976). In the perspective of the DVF studies of psychiatric patients, such findings can be taken as (perhaps) support but, more importantly, they question the capacity of the paradigm to discriminate between markedly different mental disorders. We shall return to these difficulties again a little later, but first let us complete our survey of the DVF studies involving psychiatric patients.

## Further Studies

In another RT paradigm where subjects had to decide whether a pair of horizontal arrows pointed in the same or opposite directions by making a bimanual response, Hillsberg (1979) reported that her five schizophrenic subjects showed an overall LVF advantage while the normal controls ($N=10$) showed no such performance asymmetry. In addition to the two lateral VFs the stimulus sequence involved presentations of the arrow pairs to the central fixation area and to both visual fields (BVF) simultaneously (i.e. one arrow in the LVF and the other in the RVF). The rationale for the latter condition was to evaluate any interhemisphere communication deficit, since a decision on such stimuli would require such communication. However, although overall performance was poorer for the schizophrenics compared to the normals, BVF presentation was associated with similarly longer RTs for both subject groups, indicating that the schizophrenics did not show any interhemisphere communication deficit relative to normals. Thus again, the interpretation was in terms of an LH dysfunction in schizophrenia, although here the task used did not appear to be hemisphere-specific in normals. Consequently the processing-bias explanation advanced above would be equally viable.

Colbourn and Lishman (1979) reported a similar study to Connolly *et al.* where groups of schizophrenic, manic-depressive, and non-psychotic psychiatric patients were compared with normal subjects on a word-recognition task and a shape-recognition task, using unilateral, mixed-list tachistoscopic stimulus presentations. Unfortunately, the shape-recognition task, involving a five-alternative forced-choice procedure and pointing responses, failed to reveal asymmetry of performance in any subject group despite the expected LVF advantage found during pilot studies. However, similar observations have been made by Hellige (1978) and the task is unlikely to be hemisphere-specific as originally thought. The word-recognition task, based on McKeever's procedure (e.g. McKeever, 1971) was associated with an RVF (LH) advantage for all subject groups although for *male* schizophrenics and non-psychotic psychiatric patients this was not significant. Little importance can be attached to the performance of the latter group of subjects since they had considerable general difficulties with all the tasks, and showed very variable performance. This was partly attributable to the heterogeneity of their symptoms and small size of the subject sample. Comparisons across groups by visual field showed that LVF performance was not reliably different for all the subject groups tested but RVF performance did vary as a function of group, largely due to the superior performance in this visual field of normals relative to patients. In addition analyses of the distribution of subjects showing asymmetrical performance, using a categorical scale of laterality (Colbourn, 1978, 1979), revealed a majority of all subject groups showing an RVF or no advantage on the word-recognition task, and no advantage on the shape-recognition task. Thus the evidence here is slender for concluding that any hemisphere deficits were manifest in psychotic patients, and the data from affective patients were not consistent with Connolly *et al.*'s findings. However, the suggestion that the male schizophrenic subgroup may have an LH deficit is further supported by similar observations on some of the same patients using hemisphere-specific dichotic listening tests reported by the same authors. In the dichotic tests, left-ear advantages were shown by all groups on an RH task, while again the male schizophrenics (or at least a large subset of them) failed to show the right-ear advantage on an LH task which was manifest in the other subjects.

With respect to Colbourn and Lishman's DVF results we can argue that word recognition is an LH task and therefore we can interpret a lack of asymmetry as a hemisphere deficit. However, if we take note of Saffran *et al.*'s (1980) studies and theory we might be hesitant to even consider word recognition as hemisphere-specific and therefore, again, the "bias" explanation might be more appropriate.

Another study which failed to reveal any performance asymmetries in schizophrenics or controls was reported by Clooney and Murray (1977) who used a same–different judgment task with manual key-press responses and letter-array stimuli. The latter were presented unilaterally in the LVF, RVF and also in the central fixation field. The 12 normal subjects responded with shorter RTs than the 24 schizophrenic patients and while performance did not change appreciably with the size of the letter array (2, 3, or 4 letters being used) the authors reported that the paranoid schizophrenic subgroup ($N=12$) made progressively longer RTs as the array size increased. This was interpreted as the dependence of these patients on serial LH-processing rather than parallel RH-processing. However, the authors failed to explain why, if this were the case, there were no interactions of array size with VF or responding hand.

Where positive findings in favour of the laterality hypothesis have been reported they generally indicate an LVF advantage which has been interpreted as an LH deficit. None of the above studies has reported evidence of RH deficits in psychiatric patients relative to normal controls. However, Pic'l *et al.* (1979) describe data from a dot-enumeration task which they interpret in terms of a spatial (RH) deficit in non-paranoid schizophrenic patients. However, relative to control subjects there was also a verbal (LH) deficit for both paranoid and non-paranoid patients, which, the authors claimed, could be attributed to educational achievement, although Gruzelier (in press) has pointed out that there do not appear to be educational differences between the controls and the paranoid patients at least. Since these findings are idiosyncratic it is difficult to know what to make of them until they are replicated.

## The Influence of Drugs

All of the studies described above have involved psychiatric patients who were maintained on medication (or at least the majority of the patients were) and Gruzelier (1979) commented that Colbourn and Lishman's negative findings may have been associated with this, or with the fact that a number of the psychotic patients were outpatients. He argued that "If so this would imply that the [hemisphere] deficit in visual processing is an accompaniment of the illness rather than a genetic trait detectable when symptoms were in remission" (p. 653). However, since both positive and negative findings were associated with medicated patients this consideration seems hard to justify.

Nevertheless, Eaton (1979) reported a DVF study where the presence and absence of drug treatment was used as an independent variable. In the initial studies she carried out using same–different manual RT tasks and letter (name-matching), digit and form stimuli, the results indicated that unmedicated acute schizophrenic patients ($N=51$) had the same RVF advantage on the verbal task and LVF advantage on the form- and digit-matching tasks as normal control subjects ($N=18$) for an accuracy measure but not RT. In addition, it was observed that overall accuracy was lower for the schizophrenic group on the verbal task but performance did not differ between the groups on the other two tasks. Eaton argues that this pattern of results, in itself, suggests an LH deficit for schizophrenics on the assumption that the name-matching task is hemisphere-specific.

In a second phase of this study, 24 acute schizophrenic patients were tested on the same tasks as described above, both during their admission to hospital, before they were receiving specific drug therapy for their illness, and after an average of 24 days of chemotherapy with neuroleptic drugs. All patients showed at least mild improvement on various psychiatric and clinical rating scales, which may well explain the overall improvement in their performance on the tasks, both in terms of shorter RTs and increased accuracy. However, the differentials between the tasks were maintained and lateral asymmetries in performance were not found in the RT data, only in the accuracy data.

Essentially, the schizophrenics showed an RVF advantage on the name-matching task prior to antipsychotic medication which all but vanished after treatment. The source of this effect was found to be increased accuracy on LVF (RH) trials while RVF (LH) performance remained at the pretreatment level. For the digit-matching task a reversal of asymmetry was observed from an LVF advantage before treatment to an RVF advantage after treatment—an effect attributed to improved RVF (LH) rather than LVF performance, which did not change. The form-matching task showed the same LVF (RH) advantage irrespective of treatment, although performance on both VFs improved with medication.

Eaton's results are not easy to interpret, and while the effects described above were reported to be statistically reliable, the actual size of some of them, particularly the asymmetries, was very small. In order to reconcile the disparate aspects of her findings, Eaton conveniently ignores her initial assumptions about the hemisphere specificity of the tasks used and argues that there was no specific LH deficit in schizophrenics observed here but a "specific cognitive deficit for verbally mediated processing". This conclusion was based on the overall differences between the performances of the acute schizophrenics and the normals tested initially. With respect to the pre- v. posttreatment comparisons, it can be seen that the neuroleptic treatment was associated with an improvement in performance in the *non-specialised* hemisphere (i.e. in terms of the original assumptions about the tasks), which Eaton takes to indicate that antipsychotic medication facilitates the shifting of activity between the two hemispheres in terms of Kinsbourne's (1974, 1978) model. Implicit in this argument is the notion that such "shifting" is impaired in acute schizophrenia. Apart from the fact that Kinsbourne's dynamic model of hemisphere function has been seriously challenged by empirical evidence contrary to its predictions (e.g. Geffen *et al.*, 1972; Hellige, 1978; Goodglass and Calderon, 1977), it is impossible to distinguish between any particular model on the basis of Eaton's data. The one sure conclusion is that the chemotherapy used did not transform the schizophrenics' performance into that shown by the normal group. However, it has been reported that chronic schizophrenics treated with chlorpromazine, one of the original antipsychotic medications still in use, showed improved LH performance on both auditory temporal discriminations and auditory RT tasks, compared to their perform-ance when given placebos. The tasks used were not hemisphere-specific and, in the case of the discrimination task, normals showed no asymmetries while the schizophrenics showed a left-ear advantage (RH) when on placebos (Gruzelier and Hammond, 1979; Hammond and Gruzelier, 1978).

While these studies indicate that medication does interact with asymmetries of performance in psychotic patients, there does not seem to be a clear pattern of change, and it is difficult to relate the results just discussed with those considered earlier where different patterns of asymmetries from those found in normal subjects were observed in medicated psychotic patients. It seems quite feasible that patterns of laterality may alter at various stages of psychotic illness, as recently reported by Wexler and Heninger (1979) for dichotic listening performance, and therefore it may be very important to take careful account of the symptoms manifested by patients at the time of testing—an approach currently being tested by Gruzelier et al. (1980).

## Other Psychiatric Groups

The studies surveyed above have largely concerned investigations of psychotic patients, particularly schizophrenics. While other psychiatric groups have been tested on various DVF tasks as controls for these experiments, they were usually not selected to be a particularly homogeneous group with respect to psychiatric diagnosis. Thus, neurotic disorders, personality disorders, obsessional and anxiety states were all represented in classifications termed "non-psychotic psychiatric control group". In general such groups did not show patterns of lateralisation which were different from normal subjects, a feature of the data to support the hemisphere deficit/dysfunction hypothesis of specifically psychotic illness. However, the level of performance of these groups was often quite poor in comparison to normals (see e.g. Colbourn and Lishman, 1979; Connolly et al., 1979). The small numbers of homogeneous diagnoses with such psychiatric control groups made detailed analysis of diagnostic categories rather unproductive although the trend, if different from normal, was towards a lack of asymmetrical performance.

There have been few other studies in the literature looking specifically at other psychiatric groups in terms of a laterality hypothesis, except for those using neuropsychological test batteries. Zangwill (1960) noted an apparent association between various neurotic and behaviour disorders and disturbances of lateralisation (particularly as indexed by hand and eye dominances) and a recent report from Yeudall and Fromm-Auch (1979) suggested that both children and adults showing behaviour disturbances were more likely to demonstrate left-hemisphere deficits on neuropsychological test batteries. However, such patterns of deficit are not markedly different from those reported for schizophrenic patients being given similar types of tests (e.g. Gruzelier and Hammond, 1976; Krynicki and Nahas, 1979; Taylor *et al.*, 1979), although Kronfol *et al.* (1978) observed right-hemisphere deficits in patients with depressive psychoses. Again the logic of such studies depends on assuming the hemisphere specificity of the tasks employed. However, while the verbal and performance tests of such batteries as the WAIS clearly correlate with hemisphere function, they do not adequately define it.

With regard to experiments using DVF techniques, Hare (1979) reported an attempt to relate psychopathy and lateralised cerebral dysfunction using a word-recognition task, with stimuli presented briefly in the left and right visual fields. Subjects from a prison population were rated for psychopathy and three groups of subjects were selected (high, medium and no psychopathy) and tested. However, the findings were simply of an overall RVF advantage unrelated in size or pattern to the severity of psychopathy.

Another, more peripheral, study attempted to relate "state anxiety" in undergraduate subjects to different patterns of lateralised performance on two DVF tasks (Tucker *et al.*, 1977). Anxiety was manipulated by the experimental situation and measured by questionnaire. Laterally displaced, tachistoscopically presented stimuli were used in a verbal antonym-judgment task and a shape-matching task. While no overall asymmetries were observed, a comparison of high- and low-anxiety subjects indicated that errors in the RVF were greater for the high-anxiety classification, while LVF errors were unrelated to anxiety. The authors interpreted these results as demonstrating that anxiety places a high processing load on the LH. However, this interpretation begs the question of why this was the only significant result, given that there were two very different tasks which were expected to produce asymmetrical performance with respect to the VFs. It is possible that intersubject consistency was not very high in this study since, despite 80 subjects being tested, only 8 were classified as showing high anxiety. The other problem is, of course, whether such a result could have implications for psychiatric disorders. State anxiety in normals cannot be directly compared to psychiatric anxiety disorders.

## Conclusions

The majority of DVF studies carried out on psychiatric patients have been in order to test the laterality hypothesis of the endogenous psychoses, which was described in the introduction to this chapter. Although the number of these studies is relatively small, the interpretation of results offered by their authors has generally been in support of the hypothesis, particularly with respect to the left-hemisphere deficit/dysfunction believed to be associated with schizophrenic patients. However, it was argued here that some of these interpretations were equivocal since the possibility that psychotic patients and normals (or other comparison groups) may have used different strategies or processes from one another was not taken into account. In fact, in some cases it was not clear that the control groups showed internal consistency in their approach to the experimental tasks (e.g. Connolly *et al.*, 1979; Hillsberg, 1979). Thus it was suggested that a processing/hemisphere-bias explanation of psychotic performance in these studies was as viable as the dysfunction/deficit interpretation. In addition, there were often substantial overall performance differences between the psychiatric groups and the normal controls making comparisons of laterality between the groups rather difficult, as discussed by Birkett (1977), Colbourn (1978, 1979) and Richardson (1976).

Young and Ellis, in a review of DVF studies on poor readers, concluded that it may be fruitful to search for cases where the same lateral asymmetries are shown by both normal and poor readers, on the grounds that it would then be reasonable to infer the same cerebral organisation in these groups for the given circumstances. Such mapping would provide a useful context from which to view the differences, and clearly this would be equally true in the case of psychiatric patients. Perhaps studying laterality through the course of the illness, as mentioned earlier, would provide a starting point for such an approach.

Nevertheless, as Saffran *et al.* (1980) commented, the DVF experiment can never be entirely conclusive with regard to hypotheses of hemisphere function, even when it is methodologically sound, and this is equally true for other laterality paradigms. If we are to gain further insight into the cerebral organisation of psychiatric patients using such procedures as DVF, dichotic listening, or other methods, we shall need to gain more knowledge of the cognitive tasks we use, as Marshall (1973) pointed out. One way to attempt this is to take a very comprehensive and detailed look at individual subjects and patients along the lines of current research into deep dyslexia (e.g. Coltheart *et al.*, 1980). Clearly we need to move away from the sort of syllogistic inference which seemed to underlie the original laterality hypothesis considered here, i.e. schizophrenia is a disorder of rational thought; LH dysfunction is a disorder of rational thought; therefore schizophrenia is an LH dysfunction! Such reasoning suggests the common predicate fallacy which has been considered typical of the thought disorders of schizophrenics themselves (e.g. Matte-Blanco, 1965). It is the impression of the present author that this move is beginning to happen, perhaps fostered by methodological discussions such as that included in the present chapter and Young and Ellis (1981), and also by cautionary looks at the laterality phenomenon from an evolutionary perspective (e.g. Corballis, 1981).

# 12

## CONCLUSIONS

*J. Graham Beaumont*

## The Findings of DVF Research

The reviews of the literature presented in this volume show that there are a number of stable findings which have emerged from DVF research. Whether these are more or less than might be expected is a matter for debate, but certain stimuli and tasks have been shown to yield a left or right visual field advantage within the DVF paradigm. What is interesting is that, with either verbal or non-verbal stimuli, the visual field asymmetries seem to be associated with relatively "low-level" stimuli and tasks: colour and orientation perception, the matching of faces, the matching and identification of words, nonsense words, letters and digits. While a true cognitive component is involved in most of these tasks, once the tasks require more sophisticated cognitive manipulations the lateral asymmetry appears to become less stable. This may be because there are fewer of such studies reported, or it may be because such studies are more difficult to control experimentally, but it is tempting to conclude that the basis for lateral asymmetries, in so far as there is a single underlying factor, is not at the highest levels of cognitive processing.

A note of optimism is also to be detected in the foregoing pages. There still seems to be a feeling that if only we can gain a better understanding of the cognitive structure of the tasks employed, and can control subject variables and cognitive strategies, then clearer and more stable effects will emerge. This, linked with increasing clarification and closer specification of the theoretical models, will lead to significant advances in our understanding of the lateral specialisation of the cerebral hemispheres. This may, or may not, be the case but it is certainly clear that until we can make progress in these various aspects of the research, we shall not know whether the advances can be made or not.

249

In contrast, there are negative tones. The review of electrophysiological studies points to the paucity of the contribution which they have made to date, whatever the promise that they may hold, and the evidence from the split-brain patients has turned out to be less incisive and illuminating than was once thought. It also appears that commonly held views about the relevance of sex and handedness turn out to be mistaken. The sex differences which are often assumed may not exist at all, and the differences which do exist between right- and left-handed groups may not be those which are often described.

Caution is expressed with respect to the interpretation of developmental studies, in particularly with respect to any conclusions about the ontogeny of lateralisation, although the performance asymmetries to be observed in children seem to run roughly in parallel with those found in adults. A similar wariness is evident with respect to the studies of psychiatric patients, although here there does seem to be the promise of a real association between visual field asymmetry and schizophrenic psychoses, whatever the interpretation of that may be.

If any consistent recommendations seem to emerge, then one of the clearest must be to increase the attention given to methodological factors. As clearly stated in a number of chapters, where the inferences being drawn are very long and where a great many artefacts may intervene in the chain of inference, it is especially important that the most scrupulous care be taken over experimental methodology. In addition, attention to the cognitive factors involved in the performance of experimental tasks, and a reformulation of the working models employed in terms of cognitive processes, seems to be sound advice. Some authors have also suggested the more intensive investigation of individual subjects, perhaps across periods of time as well as across various tasks, and this seems likely to make a significant contribution. Gillian Cohen's suggestion (Chapter 5) that computer simulation might be explored as an aid to theory development seems a valuable proposal. Finally, each chapter has emphasised the care that must be taken in interpreting DVF studies, and the problems of moving from any description of performance to explanations in terms of the function of the brain.

## Applications

If there were to be any disappointment with the current state of the field, I think it should be that more progress has not been made with applications of the DVF technique. This has not been because of the frustration of attempts, but rather a lack of interest in developing useful test instruments based upon the DVF paradigm. Beaumont and Dimond (1973c) described, some years ago, an apparatus which was designed to be portable, and which was used in the studies of psychiatric patients. The design of this apparatus has been made obsolete by the advent of the inexpensive and versatile microcomputer,[1] but the principle of designing tasks which would reveal relative hemisphere performance, based upon DVF methodology, and which could be readily administered in a variety of locations, has not been pursued.

It would be counter to the spirit of this book to underestimate the methodological and practical problems raised by such a venture. It is clearly not easy, although certainly not impossible, to find a task which should be capable of yielding reliable estimates of at least some aspects of lateralised cerebral functions. The practical aspects of designing the apparatus and tasks in a form suitable for widespread and varied administration should present no insurmountable problems. I suspect that the task of testing the validity of such an instrument and collecting the necessary normative data appears unexciting and unrewarding to many investigators.

While studies employing tests of hemisphere function have begun to appear (e.g. Gordon, 1980), the batteries which they employ often work by inference from performance on verbal contrasted with spatial tasks, which are presented in free vision. While inferences of this kind may be valid, they are even more problematical than those which derive from the relatively more direct DVF studies, and it would seem that a better strategy would be to work with DVF, as well as dichotic listening (Geffen *et al.*, 1978), paradigms.

This is not to ignore the applications which have been attempted. Lateralised visual functions have been studied in dyslexia (Chapter 6) and minimal brain damage (Beaumont, 1976); in pathological groups in conjunction with handedness (Chapter 9); and in psychiatric patients (Chapter 11). The applications of laterality research have also been discussed in an educational context, although in view of the wildness of some of the proposals (see Chapter 1), it is perhaps better that progress has not been made towards real applications. However, a more systematic approach to the relative performance of the two hemispheres seems worthy of exploration, and it might well be that relatively standardised forms of the DVF task would emerge which might find application in a number of applied environments.

## Neuropsychological Models

It is perhaps appropriate to conclude by raising yet again the question of what kind of an understanding of brain–behaviour relationships we hope to gain

---

[1] Users of microcomputers for DVF research should pay careful attention to the persistence of the phosphor in the VDU or television which they employ. A solution to long persistence is the use of reverse video.

from DVF research. It may be that if we are unclear about where we are going it is not surprising that we find it difficult to find the way.

By looking into mirrors we gain, from an early age, a good idea of our own appearance (although, curiously, a reversed view of that seen by everyone who confronts us). This is only accurate in so far as we meet simple mirrors with a plane surface in two dimensions. If all we ever met were more complicated mirrors, like the distorting mirrors in fairgrounds and amusement palaces, which deviate from a plane surface in one or two dimensions, then we should find it considerably more difficult to gain an accurate idea of how others see us.

Observing the function of the brain in terms of performance variables is rather like seeing oneself reflected in a mirror. However, given that neuro-psychologists are agreed that there are many dimensions which influence the observed performance, it is not surprising that we find difficulty in making sense of the "images" that we see. In so far as you may be able to conceive what you would look like in an $n$-dimensional reflecting surface with a complex topography, you will see how difficult it is to form a clear idea of how the brain works from performance data alone.

Perhaps the crucial difficulty is that we have not yet decided what kind of model we are hoping to establish. Consider a building and the variety of plans which may be drawn to represent aspects of that building. There is the physical plan, elevations and sections; there are drawings both isometric and perspective; there are the plumbing and heating systems represented as diagrams; there is the electrical and communications circuitry; there is the pattern of human movement within the building; functional allocation of space; the organisational structure of the group of people who inhabit the building; and so on. All these plans have different purposes, and may have little physical resemblance, as plans, one to the other. The problem with neuropsychology is that we are trying to develop functional plans, yet expecting the result to look like a physical plan of the building. We hope to understand the purposes of the organisation which uses the building, how it is organised, who works in which room and how all the rooms communicate with each other, all from a single line of research, and we hope to express it all in a single plan.

Perhaps it would be more productive to concentrate on one aspect, the functional structure of our object of study, and until that is clearly understood make no attempt to relate that to the physical structures in which the functions are carried out. If we took one thing at a time, worked out how the brain operates in cognitive terms, then we might make greater progress in eventually understanding how the physiological apparatus of the brain achieves the psychological operations of which it is capable. DVF studies are clearly going to have a place in that process of discovery and, whatever the outcome, it looks like being "fun finding out".

# REFERENCES

AARON, P. G. and HANDLEY, A. C. (1975). Directional scanning and cerebral asymmetries in processing visual stimuli. *Percept. mot. Skills* **40**, 719–725.

ACHILLES, E. M. (1920). Experimental studies in recall and recognition. *Arch. Psychol.* No. 44.

ADAMS, J. (1971). Visual perception of direction and number in right and left visual fields. *Cortex* **7**, 227–235.

AKELAITIS, A. J. (1941). Studies on the corpus callosum: II. The higher visual functions in each homonymous field following complete section of the corpus callosum. *Arch. Neurol. Psychiat. (Chicago)* **45**, 788–796.

AKELAITIS, A. J. (1943). Studies on the corpus callosum: VII. Study of language functions (tactile and visual lexia and graphia) unilaterally following section of the corpus callosum. *J. Neuropath. exp. Neurol.* **2**, 226–262.

AKELAITIS, A. J. (1944). A study of gnosis, praxis and language following section of the corpus callosum and anterior commissure. *J. Neurosurg.* **1**, 94–102.

ALBERT, M. L. and OBLER, L. K. (1978). *The Bilingual Brain.* Academic Press, New York and London.

ALBERT, M. L., RECHES, A. and SILVERBERG, R. (1975). Hemianopic colour blindness. *J. neurol. neurosurg. Psychiat.* **38**, 546–549.

ALIVISATOS, B. and WILDING, J. (1980). Hemispheric differences in matching Stroop-type letter stimuli. *Bull. Br. Psychol. Soc.* **33**, 17.

ALLARD, F. and BRYDEN, M. P. (1979). The effect of concurrent activity on hemispheric asymmetries. *Cortex* **15**, 5–17.

ALPERN, M. (1962a). Types of movement. In *The Eye, Vol.3: Muscular Mechanisms* (H. Davson, ed.), pp. 63–151. Academic Press, New York and London.

ALPERN, M. (1962b). Introduction to movements of the eyes. In *The Eye, Vol.3: Muscular Mechanisms* (H. Davson, ed.), pp. 3–5. Academic Press, New York and London.

ALPERN, M. (1971). Effector mechanisms in vision. In *Woodworth and Schlosberg's Experimental Psychology* (J. W. Kling and L. A. Riggs, eds), pp. 369–394. London.

AMADEO, M., ROEMER, R. A. and SHAGASS, C. (1977). Can callosal speed of transmission be inferred from verbal reaction time? *Biol. Psychiat.* **12**, 289–298.

ANASTASOPOULOS, G. K. (1959). Linksseitige Hemiplegie mit Alexie, Agraphie und Aphasie bei einem polyglotten Rechtshänder. *Dt. Z. NervHeilk* **179**, 120–144.

ANDERSON, I. and CROSLAND, H. R. (1933). A method of measuring the effect of primacy of report in the range of attention experiment. *Am. J. Psychol.* **45**, 701–713.

ANDREASSI, J. L., OKAMURA, H. and STERN, M. (1975). Hemispheric asymmetries in the visual cortical evoked potential as a function of stimulus location. *Psychophysiol.* **12**, 541–546.

ANDREWS, R. J. (1977). Aspects of language lateralisation correlated with family handedness. *Neuropsychologia* **15**, 769–778.

ANNETT, M. (1964). A model of the inheritance of handedness and cerebral dominance. *Nature, Lond.* **204**, 59–60.

ANNETT, M. (1970). A classification of hand preference by association analysis. *Br. J. Psychol.* **61**, 303–321.

ANNETT, M. (1972). The distribution of manual asymmetry. *Br. J. Psychol.* **63**, 343–358.

ANNETT, M. (1974). Handedness in the children of two left-handed parents. *Br. J. Psychol.* **65**, 129–131.

ANNETT, M. (1975). Hand preference and the laterality of cerebral speech. *Cortex* **11**, 305–328.

ANNETT, M. (1976). A coordination of hand preference and skill replicated. *Br. J. Psychol.* **67**, 587–592.

ANNETT, M. (1978). *A Single Gene Explanation of Right and Left Handedness and Brainedness.* Lanchester Polytechnic, Coventry.

ANNETT, M. (1979). Family handedness in three generations predicted by the right shift theory. *Ann. Hum. Genet., Lond.* **42**, 479–491.

ANNETT, M. and ANNETT, J. (1979). Individual differences in right and left reaction time. *Br. J. Psychol.* **70**, 393–404.

ANZOLA, G. P., BERTOLINI, G., BUCHTEL, H. A. and RIZZOLATTI, G. (1977). Spatial compatibility and anatomical factors in simple and choice reaction time. *Neuropsychologia* **15**, 295–302.

APRIL, R. S. and HAN, M. (1980). Crossed aphasia in a right-handed bilingual Chinese man. *Arch Neurol.* **37**, 342–436.

APRIL, R. S. and TSE, P. C. (1977). Crossed aphasia in a Chinese bilingual dextral. *Arch. Neurol.* **34**, 766–770.

ARRIGONI, G. and DE RENZI, E. (1964). Constructional apraxia and hemispheric locus of lesion. *Cortex* **1**, 170–197.

ASSAL, G., PERENTES, E. and DERVAZ, J.-P. (1981). Crossed aphasia in a right handed patient. Postmortem findings. *Arch. Neurol.* **38**, 455–458.

ATKINSON, J. and EGETH, H. (1973). Right hemisphere superiority in visual orientation matching. *Canad. J. Psychol.* **27**, 152–158.

AULHORN, E. and HARMS, H. (1972). Perimetry of various visual functions. In *Handbook of Sensory Physiology* (D. Jameson and L. M. Hurvich, eds), Vol. 7/4, pp. 102–144. Springer Verlag, Berlin.

AXELROD, S., HARYADI, T. and LEIBER, L. (1977). Oral report of words and word approximations presented to the left or right visual field. *Brain and Language* **4**, 550–557.

BAGNARA, S., SIMION, F., UMILTA, C. and RONCATO, S. (1980). Sex-related differences in hemispheric asymmetries in processing simple geometrical figures. *Percept. mot. Skills* **51**, 223–229.

BARRETT, G., BLUMHARDT, L., HALLIDAY, A. M., HALLIDAY, E. and KRISS, A. (1976). A paradox in the lateralisation of the visual evoked response. *Nature, Lond.* **261**, 253–255.

BARROSO, F. (1976). Hemispheric asymmetry of function in children. In *Neuropsychology of Language* (R. W. Rieber, ed.) pp. 157–180. Plenum Press, New York.

BARRY, C. (1981). Hemispheric asymmetry in lexical access and phonological encoding. *Neuropsychologia* **19**, 473–478.

BARTZ, A. E. (1962). Eye-movement latency, duration, and response time as a function of angular displacement. *J. exp. Psychol.* **64**, 318–324.

BASSO, A., BISIACH, E. and CAPITANI, E. (1977). Decision in ambiguity: Hemispheric dominance or interaction. *Cortex* **13**, 96–99.

BEATON, A. A. (1979). Duration of the motion after-effect as a function of retinal focus and visual field. *Percept. mot. Skills* **48**, 143–146.

BEAUMONT, J. G. (1974). Handedness and hemisphere function. In *Hemisphere Function in the Human Brain* (S. J. Dimond and J. G. Beaumont, eds), pp. 89–120. Elek Science, London.

BEAUMONT, J. G. (1976). The cerebral laterality of "minimal brain damage" children. *Cortex* **12**, 373–382.

BEAUMONT, J. G. (1981). Split-brain studies and the duality of consciousness. In *Aspects of Consciousness*, Vol. 2 (G. Underwood and R. G. Stevens, eds), pp. 189–213. Academic Press, London and New York.

BEAUMONT, J. G. and DIMOND, S. J. (1973a). Transfer between the cerebral hemispheres in human learning. *Acta Psychol.* **37**, 87–91.

BEAUMONT, J. G. and DIMOND, S. J. (1973b). Brain disconnection and schizophrenia. *Br. J. Psychiat.* **123**, 661–662.

BEAUMONT, J. G. and DIMOND, S. J. (1973c). The clinical assessment of interhemispheric psychological functioning. *J. neurol. neurosurg. Psychiat.* **36**, 445–447.

BEAUMONT, J. G. and DIMOND, S. J. (1975). Interhemispheric transfer of figural information in right- and non-right-handed subjects. *Acta Psychol.* **39**, 97–104.

BEAUMONT, J. G. and RUGG, M. D. (1978). Neuropsychological laterality of function and dyslexia: a new hypothesis. *Dyslexia Rev.* **1**, 18–22.

BEAUMONT, J. G., THOMSON, M. E. and RUGG, M. D. (1981). An intrahemispheric integration deficit in dyslexia. *Curr. psychol. Res.*, in press.

BEGLEITER, H. (1979). *Evoked Brain Potentials and Behaviour.* Plenum Press, New York.

BENSON, D. F. and BARTON, M. I. (1970). Disturbances in constructional ability. *Cortex* **6**, 19–46.

BENTON, A. L. (1978). The interplay of experimental and clinical approaches in brain lesion research. In *Recovery from Brain Damage* (S. Finger, ed.), pp. 49–68. Plenum Press, New York.

BENTON, A. L. (1980). The neuropsychology of facial recognition. *Am. Psychol.* **35**, 176–186.

BENTON, A. L. and PEARL, D. (eds) (1978). *Dyslexia: An Appraisal of Current Knowledge.* Oxford University Press, New York.

BENTON, A. L. and VAN ALLEN, M. W. (1968). Impairment in facial recognition in patients with cerebral disease. *Cortex* **4**, 344–358.

BERENBAUM, S. and HARSHMAN, R. (1980). On testing group differences in cognition resulting from differences in lateral specialisation: reply to Fennell *et al.* *Brain and Language* **11**, 209–220.

BERLIN, C. I. (1977). Hemispheric asymmetry in auditory tasks. In *Lateralization in the Nervous System* (S. Harnad, R. W. Doty, L. Goldstein, J. Jaynes and G. Krauthamer, eds), pp. 303–323. Academic Press, New York and London.

BERLUCCHI, G. (1972). Anatomical and physiological aspects of visual functions of corpus callosum. *Brain Research* **37**, 371–392.

BERLUCCHI, G., HERON, W., HYMAN, R., RIZZOLATTI, G. and UMILTA, C. (1971). Simple reaction times of ipsilateral and contralateral hand to lateralised visual stimuli. *Brain* **94**, 419–430.

BERLUCCHI, G., BRIZZOLARA, D., MARZI, C. A., RIZZOLATTI, G. and UMILTA, C.

(1974). Can lateral asymmetries in attention explain interfield differences in visual perception? *Cortex* **10**, 177–185.

BERLUCCHI, G., CREA, F., DI STEFANO, M. and TASSINARI, G. (1977). Influence of spatial stimulus-response compatability on reaction time of ipsilateral and contralateral hand to lateralised light stimuli. *J. exp. Psychol.: Human Percept. Perform.* **3**, 505–517.

BERLUCCHI, G., BRIZZOLARA, D., MARZI, C. A., RIZZOLATTI, G. and UMILTA, C. (1979). The role of stimulus discriminability and verbal codability in hemispheric specialization for visuospatial tasks. *Neuropsychologia* **17**, 195–202.

BERTELSON, P., VANHAELEN, H. and MORAIS, J. (1977). Left hemifield superiority and the extraction of physiognomic information. Paper presented at the EBBS workshop, Rotterdam, 31 March–2 April.

BERTOLINI, G., ANZOLA, G. P., BUCHTEL, H. A. and RIZZOLATTI, G. (1978). Hemispheric differences in the discrimination of the velocity and duration of a simple visual stimulus. *Neuropsychologia* **16**, 213–220.

BESNER, D., GRIMSELL, D. and DAVIS, R. (1979). The mind's eye and the comparative judgment of number. *Neuropsychologia* **17**, 373–380.

BEVER, T. G. and CHIARELLO, R. (1974). Cerebral dominance in musicians and nonmusicians. *Science, N.Y.* **185**, 537–539.

BEVER, T. G., HURTIG, R. R. and HANDEL, A. B. (1976). Analytic processing elicits right ear superiority in monaurally presented speech. *Neuropsychologia* **14**, 175–182.

BEVILACQUA, L., CAPITANI, E., LUZZATI, C. and SPINNLER, H. R. (1979). Does the hemisphere stimulated play a specific role in delayed recognition of complex abstract patterns? A tachistoscopic study. *Neuropsychologia* **17**, 93–97.

BIERSDORF, W. R. and NAKAMURA, Z. (1971). Electroencephalogram potentials evoked by hemi-retinal stimulation. *Experientia* **27**, 402–403.

BINGLEY, T. (1958). Mental symptoms in temporal lobe epilepsy and temporal lobe gliomas. *Acta. Psychiat. et Neurol. Suppl.* **120**, 33.

BIRKETT, P. (1977). Measures of laterality and theories of hemispheric process. *Neuropsychologia* **15**, 693–696.

BIRKETT, P. (1978). Hemisphere differences in the recognition of nonsense shapes: cerebral dominance or strategy effects. *Cortex* **14**, 245–249.

BIRKETT, P. (1980). Predicting spatial activity from hemispheric "non-verbal" lateralisation: sex, handedness and task differences implicate encoding strategy effects. *Acta Psychol.* **46**, 1–14.

BIRNBAUM, M. H. (1978). Holistic aspects of visual style: a hemispheric model with implications for vision therapy. *J. Am. Optom. Assoc.* **49**, 1133–1141.

BLUMHARDT, L. D., BARRETT, G. and HALLIDAY, A. M. (1977). The asymmetrical visual evoked potential to pattern reversal in one half field and its significance for the analysis of visual field defects. *Br. J. Opthalmol.* **61**, 454–461.

BOGEN, J. E. (1977). Some educational aspects of hemispheric specialisation. In *The Human Brain* (M. C. Wittrock, ed.), pp. 133–152. Prentice-Hall, Englewood Cliffs, New Jersey.

BOGEN, J. E. (1979). The callosal syndrome. In *Clinical Neuropsychology* (K. M. Heilman and E. Valenstein, eds), pp. 308–359. Oxford University Press, New York.

BOLES, D. B. (1979). Laterally biased attention with concurrent verbal load: multiple failures to replicate. *Neuropsychologia* **17**, 353–361.

BOWERS, D. and HEILMAN, K. M. (1976). Material specific hemispheral arousal. *Neuropsychologia* **14**, 123–127.

BOWERS, D., HEILMAN, K. M., SATZ, P. and ALTMAN, A. (1978). Simultaneous performance on verbal, nonverbal and motor tasks by righthanded adults. *Cortex* **14**, 540–556.

BOWMAN, A. M. (1920). Size v. intensity as a determinant of attention. *Am. J. Psychol.* **31**, 87–90.

BOWMAN, M. and LEWIS, M. S. (1980). Sites of subcortical damage in diseases which resemble schizophrenia. *Neuropsychologia* **18**, 597–601.

BOYLE, G. J. (1975). Report order in tachistoscopic recognition. *Aust. J. Psychol.* **27**, 269–272.

BRABYN, L. B. and MCGUINNESS, D. (1979). Gender differences in response to spatial frequency and stimulus orientation. *Percept. Psychophys.* **26**, 319–324.

BRACKEN, B. A., LEDFORD, T. L. and MCCALLUM, R. S. (1979). Effects of cerebral dominance on college-level achievement. *Percept. mot. Skills* **49**, 445–446.

BRADSHAW, G. J., HICKS, R. E. and ROSE, B. (1979). Lexical discrimination and letter-string identification in the two visual fields. *Brain and Language* **8**, 10–18.

BRADSHAW, J. L. (1974). Peripherally presented and unreported words may bias the perceived meaning of a centrally fixated homograph. *J. exp. Psychol.* **103**, 1200–1202.

BRADSHAW, J. L. (1980). Right hemisphere language: familial and nonfamilial sinistrals, cognitive deficits and writing hand position in sinistrals, and the concrete–abstract, imageable–nonimageable dimensions in word recognition. A review of interrelated issues. *Brain and Language* **10**, 172–188.

BRADSHAW, J. L. and GATES, E. A. (1978). Visual field differences in verbal tasks: effects of task familiarity and sex of subject. *Brain and Language* **5**, 166–187.

BRADSHAW, J. L. and NETTLETON, N. C. (1981). The nature of hemispheric specialization in man. *The Behavioral and Brain Sciences* **4**, 51–93.

BRADSHAW, J. L. and PERRIMENT, A. D. (1970). Laterality effect and choice reaction time in a unimanual 2-finger task. *Percept. Psychophys.* **7**, 185–188.

BRADSHAW, J. L. and TAYLOR, M. J. (1979). A word-naming deficit in nonfamilial sinistrals? Laterality effects of vocal responses to tachistoscopically presented letter strings. *Neuropsychologia* **17**, 21–32.

BRADSHAW, J. L., NETTLETON, N. C. and PATTERSON, K. (1973). Identification of mirror-reversed and non-reversed facial profiles in same and opposite fields. *J. exp. Psychol.* **99**, 42–48.

BRADSHAW, J. L., BRADLEY, D. and PATTERSON, K. (1976a). The perception and identification of mirror reversed patterns. *Q. J. exp. Psychol.* **28**, 221–246.

BRADSHAW, J. L., GATES, A. and PATTERSON, K. (1976b). Hemispheric differences in processing visual patterns. *Q. J. exp. Psychol.* **28**, 667–681.

BRADSHAW, J. L., BRADLEY, D., GATES, A. and PATTERSON, K. (1977a). Serial, parallel or holistic identification of single words in the two visual fields? *Percept. Psychophys.* **21**, 431–438.

BRADSHAW, J. L., GATES, A. and NETTLETON, N. C. (1977b). Bihemispheric involvement in lexical decisions: handedness and a possible sex difference. *Neuropsychologia* **15**, 277–286.

BRADSHAW, J. L., NETTLETON, N. C. and TAYLOR, M. (1981). Right hemisphere language and cognitive deficit in sinistrals. *Neuropsychologia* **19**, 113–132.

BRAINE, L. G. (1968). Asymmetries of pattern perception observed in Israelis. *Neuropsychologia* **6**, 73–88.

BRANCH, C., MILNER, B. and RASMUSSEN, T. (1964). Intracarotid sodium amytal for the lateralisation of cerebral dominance. *J. Neurosurg.* **21**, 399–405.

BREBNER, J. C. (1973). S-R compatability and changes in RT with practice. *Acta Psychol.* **37**, 93–106.

BRIDGMAN, C. S. and SMITH, K. U. (1945). Bilteral neural integration in visual perception after section of the corpus callosum. *J. comp. Neurol.* **83**, 57–68.

BRINKMAN, J. and KUYPERS, H. G. J. M. (1972). Splitbrain monkeys: cerebral control of ipsilateral and contralateral arm, hand and finger movements. *Science, N.Y.* **176**, 536–539.

BRINKMAN, J. and KUYPERS, H. G. J. M. (1973). Cerebral control of contralateral and ipsilateral arm, hand and finger movements in the splitbrain rhesus monkey. *Brain* **96**, 653–674.

BROCA, P. P. (1861). Perte de la parole. Ramollissement chronique et destruction partielle du lobe anterior gauche du cerveau. *Bull. Soc. Anthrop., Paris* **II**.

BROMAN, M. (1978). Reaction time difference between the left and right hemispheres for faces and letter discrimination in children and adults. *Cortex* **14**, 578–591.

BROOKS, R. M. and GOLDSTEIN, A. G. (1963). Recognition by children of inverted photographs of faces. *Child Dev.* **34**, 1033–1040.

BROWN, J. L. (1962). Differential hand usage in three-year-old children. *J. genet. Psychol.* **100**, 167–175.

BROWN, J. W. (1979). Language representation in the brain. In *Neurobiology of Social Communication in Primates: An Evolutionary Perspective* (H. D. Steklis and M. J. Raleigh, eds), pp. 113–195. Academic Press, New York and London.

BRUNORI, P., LADAVAS, E. and RICCI-BITTI, P. E. (1979). Differential aspects in the recognition of facial expression of emotions. *Ital. J. Psychol.* **6**, 265–272.

BRYDEN, M. P. (1960). Tachistoscopic recognition of non-alphabetic material. *Canad. J. Psychol.* **14**, 78–86.

BRYDEN, M. P. (1964). Tachistoscopic recognition and cerebral dominance. *Percept. mot. Skills* **19**, 686.

BRYDEN, M. P. (1965). Tachistoscopic recognition, handedness and cerebral dominance. *Neuropsychologia* **3**, 1–8.

BRYDEN, M. P. (1970). Left–right differences in tachistoscopic recognition as a function of familiarity and pattern orientation. *J. exp. Psychol.* **84**, 120–122.

BRYDEN, M. P. (1973). Perceptual asymmetry in vision: relation to handedness, eyedness and speech lateralisation. *Cortex* **9**, 418–435.

BRYDEN, M. P. (1976). Response bias and hemispheric differences in dot localization. *Percept. Psychophys.* **19**, 23–28.

BRYDEN, M. P. (1978). Strategy effects in the assessment of hemispheric asymmetry. In *Strategies of Information Processing* (G. Underwood, ed.), pp. 117–149. Academic Press, London and New York.

BRYDEN, M. P. and ALLARD, F. (1976). Visual hemifield differences depend on typeface. *Brain and Language* **3**, 191–200.

BRYDEN, M. P. and RAINEY, C. A. (1963). Left–right differences in tachistoscopic recognition. *J. exp. Psychol.* **66**, 568–571.

BUCHSBAUM, M. S. and DRAGO, D. (1977). Hemispheric asymmetry and the effects of attention on visual evoked potentials. In *Language and Hemispheric Specialisation in Man: Cerebral ERPs* (J. E. Desmedt, ed.), pp. 243–253. Karger, Basel.

BUCHSBAUM, M. S. and FEDIO, P. (1969). Visual information and evoked responses from the left and right hemispheres. *Electroenceph. Clin. Neurophysiology* **26**, 266–272.

BUCHSBAUM, M. S. and FEDIO, P. (1970). Hemispheric differences in evoked potentials to verbal and nonverbal stimuli in left and right visual fields. *Physiol. Behav.* **5**, 207–210.

BUCHTEL, H., CAMPARI, F., DE RISIO, C. and ROTA, R. (1980). Hemispheric differences in discriminative reaction time to facial expressions. *Ital. J. Psychol.*, in press.

BUFFERY, A. W. H. (1974). Asymmetrical lateralisation of cerebral functions and the effects of unilateral brain surgery in epileptic patients. In *Hemispheric Function in the Human Brain* (S. J. Dimond and J. G. Beaumont, eds), pp. 204–234. Elek Science, London.

BUFFERY, A. W. H. (1976). Sex differences in the neuropsychological development of verbal and spatial skills. In *The Neuropsychology of Learning Disorders: Theoretical Approaches* (R. M. Knights and D. J. Bakker, eds), pp. 187–205. University Park Press, Baltimore, Maryland.

BUFFERY, A. W. H. (1978). Neuropsychological aspects of language development: an essay on cerebral dominance. In *The Development of Communication* (N. Waterson and C. Snow, eds), pp. 25–46. Wiley, Chichester.

BUFFERY, A. W. H. and GRAY, J. A. (1972). Sex differences in the development of spatial and linguistic skills. In *Gender Differences: their Ontogeny and Significance* (C. Ounsted and D. C. Taylor, eds), pp. 123–157. Churchill-Livingstone, Edinburgh.

BUNGE, M. (1980). *The Mind–Body Problem.* Pergamon, Oxford.

BUNT, A. H., MINCKLER, D. S. and JOHANSON, G. W. (1977). Demonstration of bilateral projection of the central retina of the money with horseradish peroxidase neuronography. *J. comp. Neurol.* **171**, 619–630.

BURG, A. (1966). Visual acuity as measured by dynamic and static tests: a comparative evaluation. *J. appl. Psychol.* **50**, 460–466.

BURKE, R. S. and DALLENBACH, K. M. (1924). Minor studies from the Psychology Laboratory of Cornell. LXVII. Position v. intensity as a determinant of attention of left handed observers. *Am. J. Psychol.* **35**, 267–269.

BUTLER, D. C. and MILLER, L. K. (1979). Role of order of approximation to English and letter array length in the development of visual laterality. *Devel. Psychol.* **15**, 522–529.

BUTLER, S. (1979). Interhemispheric relations in schizophrenia. In *Hemisphere Asymmetries of Function in Psychopathology* (J. Gruzelier and P. Flor-Henry, eds), pp. 47–58. Elsevier/North-Holland Biomedical Press, Amsterdam.

BUTLER, S. R. and NORRSELL, U. (1968). Vocalisation possibly initiated by the minor hemisphere. *Nature, Lond.* **220**, 793.

CALLAWAY, E., TUETING, P. and KOSLOW, S. H. (1978). *Event-related Potentials in Man.* Academic Press, New York and London.

CAMPBELL, R. (1978). Asymmetries in interpretating and expressing a posed facial expression. *Cortex* **14**, 327–342.

CAPLAN, D., HOLMES, J. M. and MARSHALL, J. C. (1974). Word classes and hemispheric specialisation. *Neuropsychologia* **12**, 331–337.

CAREY, S., DIAMOND, R. and WOODS, B. (1980). Development of face recognition—a maturational component? *Devel. Psychol.* **16**, 257–269.

CARMON, A. and BECHTOLDT, H. P. (1969). Dominance of the right hemisphere for stereopsis. *Neuropsychologia* **7**, 29–39.

CARMON, A. and NACHSHON, I. (1971). Effects of unilateral brain damage on perception of temporal order. *Cortex* **7**, 410–418.

CARMON, A. and NACHSHON, I. (1973). Hemifield differences in binocular fusion. *Percept. mot. Skills* **36**, 175–184.

CARMON, A., NACHSHON, I., ISSEROFF, A. and KLEINER, M. (1972). Visual field differences in reaction time to Hebrew letters. *Psychon. Sci.* **28**, 222–224.

CARMON, A., KLEINER, M. and NACHSHON, I. (1975). Visual hemifield effects in dichoptic presentation of digits. *Neuropsychologia* **13**, 289–296.

CARMON, A., NACHSHON, I. and STARINSKY, R. (1976). Developmental aspects of visual hemifield differences in perception of verbal material. *Brain and Language* **3**, 463–469.

CARPENTER, R. H. S. (1977). *Movements of the Eyes*. Pion, London.

CARR, M. S., JACOBSON, T. and BOLLER, F. (1981). Crossed aphasia: analysis of four cases. *Brain and Language* **14**, 190–202.

CARR, S. (1980). Interhemispheric transfer of stereognostic information in chronic schizophrenics. *Br. J. Psychiat.* **136**, 53–58.

CARTER, D. B. (1953). A further demonstration of phi movement cerebral dominance. *J. Psychol.* **36**, 299–309.

CARTER, G. L. and KINSBOURNE, M. (1979). The ontogeny of right cerebral lateralisation of spatial mental set. *Devel. Psychol.* **15**, 241–245.

CHAPMAN, L. J. and CHAPMAN, J. P. (1973). Problems in the measurement of cognitive deficit. *Psychol. Bull.* **79**, 380–385.

CHARMAN, D. K. (1979). An examination of the relationship between subliminal perception, visual information processing, levels of processing and hemispheric asymmetries. *Percept. mot. Skills.* **49**, 451–455.

CHASTAIN, G. and LAWSON, L. (1979). Identification asymmetry of parafoveal stimulus pairs. *Percept. Psychophys.* **26**, 363–368.

CHESHER, E. C. (1936). Some observations concerning the relation of handedness to the language mechanism. *Bull. neurol. Inst. N.Y.* **4**, 556–562.

CIBA (1979). *Brain and Mind* Symposium 69 (new series). Excerpta Medica, Amsterdam.

CLARKE, E. and O'MALLEY, C. D. (1968). *The Human Brain and Spinal Cord*. University of California Press, Berkeley.

CLAUDE, H. and SCHAEFFER, H. (1921). Un nouveau cas d'hémiplégie gauche avec aphasie chez un droitier. *Revue neurol.* **37**, 170–175.

CLEM, R. K. and POLLACK, R. H. (1975). Illusion magnitude as a function of visual field exposure. *Percept. Psychophys.* **17**, 450–454.

CLOONEY, J. L. and MURRAY, D. J. (1977). Same–different judgments in paranoid and non-paranoid schizophrenic patients: a laterality study. *J. abnorm. Psychol.* **86**, 655–658.

COBB, W. A. and MORTON, H. B. (1970). Evoked potentials from the human scalp to visual half-field stimulation. *J. Physiol.* **208**, 39–40.

COHEN, A. S. (1977). Components of asymmetrical visual encoding of geometrically transformed scripts. *Percept. mot. Skills* **44**, 755–765.

COHEN, G. (1972). Hemisphere differences in a letter classification task. *Percept. Psychophys.* **11**, 139–142.

COHEN, G. (1973). Hemispheric differences in serial versus parallel processing. *J. exp. Psychol.* **97**, 349–356.

COHEN, G. (1975a). Hemispheric differences in the utilization of advance information. In *Attention and Performance V* (P. M. A. Rabbitt and S. Dornic, eds), pp. 20–32. Academic Press, London and New York.

COHEN, G. (1975b). Hemisphere differences in the effects of cuing in visual recognition tasks. *J. exp. Psychol: Human Percept. Perform.* **1**, 366–373.

COHEN, G. (1976). Components of the laterality effect in letter recognition: asymmetries in iconic storage. *Q. J. exp. Psychol.* **28**, 105–114.

COHEN, G. (1977). *The Psychology of Cognition*. Academic Press, London and New York.

COHEN, G. (1979). Comment on "Information processing in the cerebral hemispheres: selective activation and capacity limitations" by Hellige, Cox and Litvac. *J. exp. Psychol: General* **108**, 309–315.

COHEN, G. and FREEMAN, R. H. (1978). Individual differences in reading strategies in relation to handedness and cerebral asymmetry. In *Attention and Performance VII* (J. Requin, ed.), pp. 411–427. Lawrence Erlbaum Associates, Hillsdale, New Jersey.

COHEN, M. E. and ROSS, L. E. (1977). Saccade latency in children and adults: effects of warning interval and target eccentricity. *J. exp. child Psychol.* **23**, 539–549.

COLBOURN, C. J. (1978). Can laterality be measured? *Neuropsychologia* **16**, 283–289.

COLBOURN, C. J. (1979). Laterality measurement and theory. In *Hemisphere Asymmetries of Function in Psychopathology* (J. Gruzelier and P. Flor-Henry, eds), pp. 65–76. Elsevier/North-Holland Biomedical Press, Amsterdam.

COLBOURN, C. J. and LISHMAN, W. A. (1979). Lateralization of function and psychotic illness: a left hemisphere deficit? In *Hemisphere Asymmetries of Function in Psychopathology* (J. Gruzelier and P. Flor-Henry, eds), pp. 539–559. Elsevier/North-Holland Biomedical Press, Amsterdam.

COLONNO, A. and FAGLIONI, P. (1966). The performance of hemisphere-damaged patients on spatial intelligence tests. *Cortex* **2**, 293–307.

COLTHEART, M. (1980a). Iconic memory and visible persistence. *Percept. Psychophys* **27**, 183–228.

COLTHEART, M. (1980b). Deep dyslexia: a right hemisphere hypothesis. In *Deep Dyslexia* (M. Coltheart, K. E. Patterson and J. C. Marshall, eds), pp. 326–380. Routledge and Kegan Paul, London.

COLTHEART, M. and ARTHUR, B. (1971). Tachistoscopic hemifield effects with hemifield report. *Am. J. Psychol.* **84**, 355–364.

COLTHEART, M., PATTERSON, K. E. and MARSHALL, J. C. (eds) (1980) *Deep Dyslexia.* Routledge and Kegan Paul, London.

CONEY, J. and KIRSNER, K. (1976). Hemispheric processes in STM. *Univ. W. Austr. Res. Rep.* No.5, University Western Australia, Perth, Australia.

CONNOLLY, J. F. and GRUZELIER, J. H. (1980). Visual field advantages to hemisphere-specific tasks in schizophrenia patients. Personal communication, September 1980.

CONNOLLY, J. F., GRUZELIER, J. H., KLEINMAN, K. M. and HIRSCH, S. R. (1979). Lateralised abnormalities in hemisphere-specific tachistoscopic tasks in psychiatric patients and controls. In *Hemisphere Asymmetries of Function in Psychopathology* (J. Gruzelier and P. Flor-Henry, eds), pp. 491–509. Elsevier/North-Holland Biomedical Press, Amsterdam.

CONRAD, K. (1949). Cited by Zangwill (1960).

CORBALLIS, M. C. (1980). Laterality and myth. *Am. Psychol.* **35**, 284–295.

CORBALLIS, M. C. and MORGAN, M. J. (1978). On the biological basis of human laterality. *The Behavioral and Brain Sciences* **2**, 261–336.

COREN, S. and PORAC, C. (1979). Normative data on hand position during writing. *Cortex* **15**, 679–682.

CORWIN, T. R. and BOYNTON, R. M. (1968). Transitivity of visual judgments of simultaneity. *J. exp. Psychol.* **78**, 560–568.

COTTON, B., TZENG, O. J. L. and HARDYCK, C. (1980). Role of cerebral hemispheric processing in the visual half-field stimulus–response compatability effect. *J. exp. Psychol. Human Percept. Perform.* **6**, 13–23.

CRAFT, J. L. and SIMON, J. R. (1970). Processing symbolic information from a visual display: interference from an irrelevant directional cue. *J. exp. Psychol.* **83**, 415–420.

CRITCHLEY, M. (1964). The neurology of psychotic speech. *Br. J. Psychiat.* **110**, 353–364.

CROSLAND, H. R. (1931). Letter-position effects, in the range of attention experiment, as affected by the number of letters in each exposure. *J. exp. psychol.* **14**, 477–507.

CROSLAND, H. R. (1939). Superior elementary-school readers contrasted with inferior readers in letter position, "range of attention", scores. *J. educ. Res.* **32**, 410–427.

CROSS, J. F., CROSS, J. and DALY, J. (1971). Sex, race, age and beauty as factors in recognition of faces. *Percept. Psychophys.* **10**, 393–396.

CROVITZ, H. F. and LIPSCOMB, D. B. (1963). Dominance of temporal visual fields at a short duration of stimulation. *Am. J. Psychol.* **76**, 631–637.

CROVITZ, H. F. and ZENER, K. (1962). A group test for assessing hand and eye dominance. *Am. J. Psychol.* **75**, 271–276.

CULVER, C. M., TANLEY, J. C. and EASON, R. G. (1970). Evoked cortical potentials: relation to hand and eye dominance. *Percept. mot. Skills* **30**, 407–414.

CURCIO, F., MACKAVEY, W. and ROSEN, J. (1974). Role of visual acuity in tachistoscopic recognition of 3-letter words. *Percept. mot. Skills* **38**, 755–761.

CURTIS, J. N. and FOSTER, W. S. (1917). Minor studies from Cornell University XXXIV. Size vs. intensity as a determinant of attention. *Am. J. Psychol.* **28**, 293–296.

CURTISS, S. (1977). *Genie: A Psycholinguistic Study of a Modern-day "Wild Child".* Academic Press, New York and London.

DALLENBACH, K. M. (1923). Position vs. intensity as a determinant of clearness. *Am. J. Psychol.* **34**, 282–286.

DARWIN, C. J. and BADDELEY, A. D. (1974). Acoustic memory and the perception of speech. *Cog. Psychol.* **6**, 41–60.

DAVIDOFF, J. B. (1975a). Hemispheric differences in the perception of lightness. *Neuropsychologia* **13**, 121–124.

DAVIDOFF, J. B. (1975b). *Differences in Visual Perception.* Crosby Lockwood Staples, London.

DAVIDOFF, J. B. (1976). Hemispheric sensitivity differences in the perception of colour. *Q. J. exp. Psychol.* **28**, 387–394.

DAVIDOFF, J. B. (1977). Hemispheric differences in dot detection. *Cortex* **13**, 434–444.

DAVIS, R. and SCHMIT, V. (1973). Visual and verbal coding in the interhemispheric transfer of information. *Acta psychol.* **37**, 229–240.

DAVISON, K. and BAGLEY, C. R. (1969). Schizophrenia-like psychoses associated with organic disorders of the central nervous system. A review of the literature. In *Current Problems in Neuropsychiatry* (R. N. Herrington, ed.), pp. 113–184. Royal Medico-Psychological Association/Headley Bros., Ashford, Kent.

DAWSON, J. L. M. B. (1977). An anthropological perspective on the evolution and lateralisation of the brain. *Ann. N.Y. Acad. Sci.* **229**, 424–447.

DAX, M. (1865). Lésions de la moitié, gauche de l'encéphale coincident avec l'oubli des signes de la pensée. *Gaz. Hebdom.* **11**, 259–260.

DAY, J. (1977). Right hemisphere language processing in normal right handers. *J. exp. Psychol.: Human Percept. Perform.* **3**, 518–528.

DAY, J. (1979). Visual half field word recognition as a function of syntactic class and imageability. *Neuropsychologia* **17**, 515–519.

DEE, H. L. and FONTENOT, D. J. (1973). Cerebral dominance and lateral differences in perception and memory. *Neuropsychologia* **11**, 167–173.

DEE, H. L. and HANNAY, H. J. (1973). Asymmetry in perception: attention versus other determinants. *Acta psychol.* **37**, 241–247.

DENES, G. and CAVIEZEL, F. (1981). Dichotic listening in crossed aphasia. *Arch. Neurol.* **38**, 182–185.

DE RENZI, E. and FAGLIONI, P. (1965). The comparative efficiency of intelligence and vigilance tests in detecting hemispheric cerebral damage. *Cortex* **1**, 410–433.

DE RENZI, E. and SPINNLER, H. (1966a). Facial recognition in brain damaged patients. *Neurology* **16**, 145–152.

DE RENZI, E. and SPINNLER, H. (1966b). Visual recognition in patients with unilateral cerebral disease. *J. nerv. ment. Dis.* **142**, 515–525.

DE RENZI, E. and SPINNLER, H. (1967). Impaired performance on colour tasks in patients with hemispheric damage. *Cortex* **3**, 194–217.

DE RENZI, E., FAGLIONI, P. and FERRARI, P. (1980). The influence of sex and age on the incidence and type of aphasia. *Cortex* **16**, 627–630.

DEWEY, D. and DALLENBACH, K. M. (1924). Size vs. intensity as a determinant of attention. *Am. J. Psychol.* **35**, 121–125.

DICK, A. O. (1972). Visual hierarchical feature processing: the relation of size, spatial position and identity. *Neuropsychologia* **10**, 171–177.

DIMOND, S. J. (1970). Hemispheric refractoriness and control of reaction time. *Q. J. exp. Psychol.* **22**, 610–617.

DIMOND, S. J. (1971). Hemisphere function and word registration. *J. exp. Psychol.* **87**, 183–186.

DIMOND, S. J. (1972). *The Double Brain*. Churchill-Livingstone, Edinburgh.

DIMOND, S. J. (1976). Depletion of attentional capacity after total commissurotomy in man. *Brain* **99**, 347–356.

DIMOND, S. J. (1978a). Depletion of awareness and double-simultaneous stimulation in split-brain man. *Cortex* **14**, 604–607.

DIMOND, S. J. (1978b). *Introducing Neuropsychology. The Study of Brain and Mind*. C. C. Thomas, Springfield, Illinois.

DIMOND, S. J. (1979a). Performance by split-brain humans on lateralised vigilance tasks. *Cortex* **15**, 43–50.

DIMOND, S. J. (1979b). Symmetry and asymmetry in the vertebrate brain. In *Brain, Behaviour and Evolution* (D. A. Oakley and H. C. Plotkin, eds), pp. 189–218. Methuen, London.

DIMOND, S. J. (1979c). Disconnection and psychopathology. In *Hemisphere Asymmetries of Function in Psychopathology* (J. Gruzelier and P. Flor-Henry, eds), pp. 35–46. Elsevier/North-Holland Biomedical Press, Amsterdam.

DIMOND, S. J. and BEAUMONT, J. G. (1971a). The use of two cerebral hemispheres to increase brain capacity. *Nature, Lond.* **232**, 270–271.

DIMOND, S. J. and BEAUMONT, J. G. (1971b). Hemisphere function and vigilance, *Q. J. exp. Psychol.* **23**, 443–448.

DIMOND, S. J. and BEAUMONT, J. G. (1972a). Hemispheric control of hand function in the human brain. *Acta psychol.* **36**, 32–36.

DIMOND, S. J. and BEAUMONT, J. G. (1972b). On the nature of the interhemispheric effects of fatigue. *Acta psychol.* **36**, 443–449.

DIMOND, S. J. and BEAUMONT, J. G. (1972c). A right hemisphere basis for calculation in the human brain. *Psychon. Sci.* **26**, 137–138.

DIMOND, S. J. and BEAUMONT, J. G. (1972d). Hemisphere function and colour naming. *J. exp. Psychol.* **46**, 87–92.

DIMOND, S. J. and BEAUMONT, J. G. (1972e). Perceptual integration between and within the cerebral hemispheres. *Br. J. Psychol.* **63**, 509–514.

DIMOND, S. J. and BEAUMONT, J. G. (1973). Differences in the vigilance performance of the right and left hemispheres. *Cortex* **9**, 259–265.

DIMOND, S. J. and BEAUMONT, J. G. (eds) (1974a). *Hemisphere Function in the Human Brain*. Elek Science, London.

DIMOND, S. J. and BEAUMONT, J. G. (1974b). Experimental studies of hemisphere function in the human brain. In *Hemisphere Function in the Human Brain* (S. J. Dimond and J. G. Beaumont, eds), pp. 48–88. Elek Science, London.

DIMOND, S. J. and BEAUMONT, J. G. (1974c). Hemisphere function and paired-associate learning. *Br. J. Psychol.* **65**, 275–278.

DIMOND, S. J., GIBSON, A. R. and GAZZANIGA, M. S. (1972). Cross field and within field integration of visual information. *Neuropsychologia* **10**, 379–382.

DIMOND, S. J., BURES, J., FARRINGTON, L. J. and BROUWERS, E. Y. M. (1975). The use of contact lenses for the lateralisation of visual input in man. *Acta Psychol.* **39**, 341–349.

DIMOND, S. J., SCAMMELL, R. E., BROUWERS, E. Y. M. and WEEKS, R. (1977). Functions of the centre section (trunk) of the corpus callosum in man. *Brain* **100**, 543–562.

DIMOND, S. J., SCAMMELL, R., PRYCE, I. J., HUWS, D. and GRAY, C. (1980). Some failures of intermanual and cross-lateral transfer in chronic schizophrenia. *J. abnorm. Psychol.* **89**, 505–509.

DONCHIN, E. (1975). Brain electrical correlates of pattern recognition. In *Signal Analysis and Pattern Recognition in Biomedical Engineering* (G. F. Inbar, ed.), pp. 199–218. Wiley, Chichester.

DONCHIN, E., KUTAS, M. and McCARTHY, G. (1977a). Electrocortical indices of hemispheric utilisation. In *Lateralisation in the Nervous System* (S. Harnad, R. W. Doty, L. Goldstein, J. Jaynes and G. Krauthamer, eds), pp. 339–384. Academic Press, London and New York.

DONCHIN, E., McCARTHY, G. and KUTAS, M. (1977b). Electroencephalographic investigation of hemispheric specialisation. In *Language and Cerebral Specialisation in Man: Cerebral ERPs* (J. E. Desmedt, ed.), pp. 212–242. Karger, Basel.

DONCHIN, E., RITTER, W. and McCALLUM, W. C. (1978). Cognitive psychophysiology: the endogenous components of the ERP. In *Event-related Potentials in Man* (E. Callaway, P. Tueting and S. H. Koslow, eds), pp. 349–411. Academic Press, New York and London.

DUGGAN, L. (1950). An experiment on immediate recall in secondary school children. *Br. J. Psychol.* **40**, 149–154.

DURNFORD, M. and KIMURA, D. (1971). Right hemisphere specialisation for depth perception reflected in visual field differences. *Nature, Lond.* **231**, 394–395.

DYER, D. W. and HARCUM, E. R. (1961). Visual perception of binary patterns by preschool children and by school children. *J. educ. Psychol.* **52**, 161–165.

DYER, F. N. (1973). Interference and facilitation for colour naming with separate bilateral presentations of the word and color. *J. exp. Psychol.* **99**, 314–317.

EASON, R. G. and WHITE, C. T. (1967). Averaged occipital responses to stimulation of sites in the nasal and temporal halves of the retina. *Psychonom. Sci.* **7**, 309–310.

EASON, R. G., GROVES, P., WHITE, C. T. and ODEN, D. (1967a). Evoked cortical potentials: relation to visual field and handedness. *Science, N.Y.* **156**, 1643–1646.

EASON, R. G., GROVES, P. and BONNELLI, L. (1967b). Differences in occipital evoked potentials recorded simultaneously from both cerebral hemispheres in man. *Proc. 75th Ann. Conv. A.P.A.* **2**, 95–96.

EATON, E. M. (1979). Hemisphere-related visual information processing in acute schizophrenia before and after neuroleptic treatment. In *Hemisphere Asymmetries of Function in Psychopathology* (J. Gruzelier and P. Flor-Henry, eds), pp. 511–526. Elsevier/North-Holland Biomedical Press, Amsterdam.

EFRON, R. (1963a). The effect of handedness on the perception of simultaneity and temporal order. *Brain* **86**, 261–284.

EFRON, R. (1963b). The effect of stimulus intensity on the perception of simultaneity in right and left handed subjects. *Brain* 86, 285–294.

EGETH, H. (1971). Laterality effects in perceptual matching. *Percept. Psychophys.* 9, 375–376.

EGETH, H. and EPSTEIN, J. (1972). Differential specialisation of the cerebral hemispheres for the perception of sameness and difference. *Percept. Psychophys.* 12, 218–220.

EHRLICHMAN, H. and WEINBERGER, A. (1978). Lateral eye movements and hemispheric asymmetry: a critical review. *Psychol. Bull.* 85, 1080–1101.

EKMAN, P. and OSTER, H. (1979). Facial expressions of emotion. *A. Rev. Psychol.* 30, 527–554.

ELLENBERG, L. and SPERRY, R. W. (1979). Capacity for holding sustained attention following commissurotomy. *Cortex* 15, 421–438.

ELLIS, H. D. and SHEPHERD, J. W. (1974). Recognition of abstract and concrete words presented in left and right visual fields. *J. exp. Psychol.* 103, 1035–1036.

ELLIS, H. D. and SHEPHERD, J. W. (1975). Recognition of upright and inverted faces presented in the left and right visual fields. *Cortex* 11, 3–7.

ELLIS, H. D. and YOUNG, A. W. (1977). Age-of-acquisition and recognition of nouns presented in the left and right visual fields: a failed hypothesis. *Neuropsychologia* 15, 825–828.

ELLIS, H. D., SHEPHERD, J. W. and BRUCE, A. (1973). The effects of age and sex upon adolescents' recognition of faces. *J. genet. Psychol.* 123, 173–174.

ELLIS, H. D., SHEPHERD, J. W. and DAVIES, G. M. (1979). Identification of familiar and unfamiliar faces from internal and external features: some implications for theories of face recognition. *Perception* 8, 431–441.

ENDO, L. M., SHIMIZU, A. and HORI, T. (1978). Functional asymmetry of visual fields for Japanese words in Kana (syllable-based) writing and random-shape recognition in Japanese subjects. *Neuropsychologia* 16, 291–297.

ERWIN, B. J. and ROSENBAUM, G. (1979). Parietal lobe syndrome and schizophrenia: comparison of neuropsychological deficits. *J. abnorm. Psychol.* 88, 234–241.

ERWIN, D. E. and NEBES, R. D. (1976). Right hemisphere involvement in the functional properties of visual persistence. Annual meeting Eastern Psychological Association, New York City.

ETTLINGER, G., JACKSON, C. V. and ZANGWILL, O. L. (1955). Dysphasia following right temporal lobectomy in a right handed man. *J. neurol. neurosurg. Psychiat.* 18, 214–217.

FAGLIONI, P., SPINNLER, H. and VIGNOLO, L. A. (1969). Contrasting behavior of right and left hemisphere damaged patients on a discriminative and a semantic task of auditory recognition. *Cortex* 5, 366–389.

FAIRWEATHER, H. (1976). Sex differences in cognition. *Cognition* 4, 231–280.

FAIRWEATHER, H., BRIZZOLARA, D., TABOSSI, P. and UMILTA, C. (1981). Functional cerebral lateralisation: dichotomy or plurality? In preparation.

FEDIO, P. and BUCHSBAUM, M. (1971). Unilateral temporal lobectomy and changes in evoked responses during recognition of verbal and non-verbal material in the left and right visual fields. *Neuropsychologia* 9, 261–271.

FENNELL, E. B., BOWERS, D. and SATZ, P. (1977a). Within-modal and cross-modal reliabilities of two laterality tests. *Brain and Language* 4, 63–69.

FENNELL, E. B., BOWERS, D. and SATZ, P. (1977b). Within-modal and cross-modal reliabilities of two laterality tests among left handers. *Percept. mot. Skills.* 45, 451–456.

FERNÁNDEZ-MARTÍN, F., MARTÍNEZ-LAGE, J. M., MADOZ, P. and MARAVÍ, E. (1968). La afasia cruzada. Estudio clínico con comprobación anatómica de un Caso. *J. neurol. Sci.* **7**, 565–570.

FILBEY, R. A. and GAZZANIGA, M. S. (1969). Splitting the normal brain with RT. *Psychonom. Sci.* **17**, 335–336.

FINLAY, D. C. and FRENCH, J. (1978). Visual field difference in a facial recognition task using signal detection theory. *Neuropsychologia* **16**, 103–107.

FLEMINGER, J. J., DALTON, R. and STANDAGE, K. F. (1977). Handedness in psychiatric patients. *Br. J. Psychiat.* **131**, 448–452.

FLOR-HENRY, P. (1969). Psychosis and temporal lobe epilepsy: a controlled investigation. *Epilepsia* **10**, 363–395.

FLOR-HENRY, P. (1974). Psychosis, neurosis and epilepsy. *Br. J. Psychiat.* **124**, 144–150.

FLOR-HENRY, P. (1976). Lateralised temporal-limbic dysfunction and psychopathology. In *Origins and Evolution of Language and Speech* (S. R. Harnad, H. D. Steklis, and J. Lancaster, eds), *Ann. N.Y. Acad. Sci.* **280**, 777–795.

FLOR-HENRY, P. (1979). Laterality, shifts of cerebral dominance, sinistrality and psychosis. In *Hemisphere Asymmetries of Function in Psychopathology* (J. Gruzelier and P. Flor-Henry, eds), pp. 3–19. Elsevier/North-Holland Biomedical Press, Amsterdam.

FONTENOT, D. J. (1973). Visual field differences in the recognition of verbal and non-verbal stimuli in man. *J. comp. physiol. Psychol.* **85**, 564–569.

FONTENOT, D. J. and BENTON, A. L. (1972). Perception of direction in the right and left visual fields. *Neuropsychologia* **10**, 447–452.

FORGAYS, D. G. (1953). The development of differential word recognition. *J. exp. Psychol.* **45**, 165–168.

FRIEDLINE, C. L. and DALLENBACH, K. M. (1929). Distance from point of fixation vs. intensity as a determinant of attention. *Am. J. Psychol.* **41**, 464–468.

FRIEDMAN, D., SIMSON, R., RITTER, W. and RAPIN, I. (1977). CNV and P300 paradigms for the study of language. In *Language and Hemispheric Specialisation in Man: Cerebral ERPs* (J. E. Desmedt, ed.), pp. 205–210. Karger, Basel.

FRISEN, L. and GLANSHOLM, A. (1975). Optical and neural resolution in peripheral vision. *Investigative Ophthalmol.* **14**, 528–536.

FUDIN, R. (1976). Analysis of superiority of the right visual field in bilateral tachistoscopic word-recognition. *Percept. mot. Skills* **43**, 683–688.

FUDIN, R. and KENNY, J. T. (1972). Some factors in the recognition of tachistoscopically presented alphabetical arrays. *Percept. mot. Skills* **35**, 951–959.

FUDIN, R. and MASTERSON, C. C. (1975). Hemispheric factors and scanning dynamics in the processing of briefly exposed stimuli by human subjects: bibliography. *Percept. mot. Skills* **41**, 299–310.

FUDIN, R. and MASTERSON, C. C. (1976a). Note on duration of stimulus exposure in experiments on covert scanning of laterally shown targets. *Percept. mot. Skills* **42**, 223–226.

FUDIN, R. and MASTERSON, C. C. (1976b). Integration of post-exposural scanning and cerebral dominance explanations of lateral differences in tachistoscopic recognition. *Percept. mot. Skills* **42**, 355–359.

FURST, C. J. (1976). EEG asymmetry and visuospatial performance. *Nature, Lond.* **260**, 254–225.

GALIN, D. (1974). Implications for psychiatry of left and right cerebral specializations. A neuropsychological context for unconscious processes. *Arch. gen. Psychiat.* **31**, 572–583.

GALIN, D. (1976). Educating both halves of the brain. *Childhood Education* **53**, 17–20.

GALIN, D. (1977). Lateral specialisation and psychiatric issues: speculations on development and the evolution of consciousness. *Ann. N.Y. Acad. Sci.* **299**, 397–411.

GALIN, D. and ELLIS, R. R. (1975). Asymmetry in evoked potentials as an index of lateralised cognitive processes: relation to EEG alpha asymmetry. *Neuropsychologia* **13**, 45–50.

GALPER, R. E. and COSTA, L. (1980). Hemispheric superiority for recognising faces depends on how they are learned. *Cortex* **16**, 21–38.

GARDNER, E. and BRANSKI, D. (1976). Unilateral cerebral activation and perception of gaps: a signal detection analysis. *Neuropsychologia* **14**, 43–53.

GARDNER, E. B. and WARD, A. W. (1979). Spatial compatability in tactile–visual discrimination. *Neuropsychologia* **17**, 421–425.

GARDNER, H. (1975). *The Shattered Mind*. Knopf, New York.

GARDNER, H. (1978). What we know (and don't know) about the two halves of the brain. *J. aesth. Educ.* **12**, 113–119.

GARREN, R. B. (1980). Hemispheric laterality differences among four levels of reading attainment. *Percept. mot. Skills* **50**, 119–123.

GAZZANIGA, M. S. (1967). The split brain in man. *Scient. Am.* **217**, 24–29.

GAZZANIGA, M. S. (1968). Short-term memory and brain-bisected man. *Psychon. Sci.* **12**, 161–162.

GAZZANIGA, M. S. (1969). Eye position and visual motor coordination. *Neuropsychologia* **7**, 379–382.

GAZZANIGA, M. S. (1970). *The Bisected Brain*. Appleton-Century-Crofts, New York.

GAZZANIGA, M. S. (1972). One brain—two minds. *Am. Scient.* **60**, 311–317.

GAZZANIGA, M. S. (1975a). Partial commissurotomy and cerebral localization of function. In *Cerebral Localization* (K. J. Zülch, O. Creutzfeldt, and G. C. Galbraith, eds), pp. 133–143. Springer-Verlag, Berlin.

GAZZANIGA, M. S. (1975b). Beyond lateralisation. In *Les Syndromes de Disconnexion Calleuse chez l'Homme* (F. Michel and B. Schott, eds), pp. 173–178. Hôpital Neurologique, Lyons.

GAZZANIGA, M. S. and FREEDMAN, H. (1973). Observations on visual processes after posterior callosal section. *Neurology* **23**, 1126–1130.

GAZZANIGA, M. S. and HILLYARD, S. A. (1971). Language and speech capacity of the right hemisphere. *Neuropsychologia* **9**, 273–280.

GAZZANIGA, M. S. and HILLYARD, S. A. (1973). Attention mechanisms following brain bisection. In *Attention and Performance IV* (S. Kornblum, ed.), pp. 221–238. Academic Press, New York and London.

GAZZANIGA, M. S. and LEDOUX, J. E. (1978). *The Integrated Mind*. Plenum Press, New York.

GAZZANIGA, M. S. and SPERRY, R. W. (1967). Language after sectioning of the cerebral commissures. *Brain* **90**, 131–148.

GAZZANIGA, M. S., BOGEN, J. E. and SPERRY, R. W. (1962). Some functional effects of sectioning the cerebral commissures in man. *Proc. nat. Acad. Sci. USA* **48**, 1765–1769.

GAZZANIGA, M. S., BOGEN, J. E. and SPERRY, R. W. (1965). Observations on visual perception after disconnexion of the cerebral hemispheres in man. *Brain* **88**, 221–236.

GAZZANIGA, M. S., GLASS, A. V., SARNO, M. T. and POSNER, J. B. (1973). Pure word deafness and hemispheric dynamics: a case history. *Cortex* **9**, 136–143.

GAZZANIGA, M. S., RISSE, G. L., SPRINGER, S. P., CLARK, A. B. and WILSON, D. H.

(1975). Psychologic and neurologic consequences of partial and complete cerebral commissurotomy. *Neurology (Minneap.)* **25**, 10–15.

GAZZANIGA, M. S., LeDOUX, J. E. and WILSON, D. H. (1977). Language, praxis and the right hemisphere: clues to some mechanisms of consciousness. *Neurology (Minneap.)* **27**, 1144–1147.

GAZZANIGA, M. S., VOLPE, B. T., SMYLIE, C. S., WILSON, D. H. and LeDOUX, J. E. (1979). Plasticity in speech organisation following commissurotomy. *Brain* **102**, 805–815.

GEFFEN, G., BRADSHAW, J. L. and WALLACE, G. (1971). Interhemispheric effects on reaction time to verbal and nonverbal visual stimuli. *J. exp. Psychol.* **87**, 415–422.

GEFFEN, G., BRADSHAW, J. L. and NETTLETON, N. C. (1972). Hemispheric asymmetry: verbal and spatial encoding of visual stimuli. *J. exp. Psychol.* **95**, 25–31.

GEFFEN, G., BRADSHAW, J. L. and NETTLETON, N. C. (1973). Attention and hemispheric differences in reaction time during simultaneous audiovisual tasks. *Q. J. exp. Psychol.* **25**, 404–412.

GEFFEN, G., TRAUB, E. and STIERMAN, I. (1978). Language laterality assessed by unilateral ECT and dichotic monitoring. *J. neurol. neurosurg. Psychiat.* **41**, 354–360.

GESCHWIND, N. and LEVITSKY, W. (1968). Human brain: left–right asymmetries in temporal speech region. *Science, N.Y.* **161**, 186–187.

GIBSON, A. R., DIMOND, S. J. and GAZZANIGA, M. S. (1972). Left field superiority for word matching. *Neuropsychologia* **10**, 463–466.

GIBSON, W. C. (1962). Pioneers of localization of function in the brain. *J. Am. Med. Assoc.* **180**, 944–951.

GILBERT, C. (1977). Non verbal perceptual abilities in relation to left handedness and cerebral lateralisation. *Neuropsychologia* **15**, 779–791.

GILBERT, C. and BAKAN, P. (1973). Visual asymmetry in the perception of faces. *Neuropsychologia* **11**, 355–362.

GILL, K. M. and McKEEVER, W. F. (1974). Word length and exposure time effects on the recognition of bilaterally presented words. *Bull. Psychonom. Soc.* **4**, 173–175.

GILLILAND, K. and HAINES, R. F. (1975). Binocular summation and peripheral visual response time. *Am. J. Optom. Physiol. Optics.* **52**, 834–839.

GLANVILLE, A. D. and DALLENBACH, K. M. (1929). The range of attention. *Am. J. Psychol.* **41**, 207–236.

GOING, M. and READ, J. D. (1974). Effects of uniqueness, sex of subject and sex of photograph on facial recognition. *Percept. mot. Skills* **39**, 109–110.

GOLDBERG, E., VAUGHAN, H. G. and GERSTMAN, L. J. (1978). Nonverbal descriptive systems and hemispheric asymmetry: shape versus texture discrimination. *Brain and Language* **5**, 249–257.

GOLDMAN, P. S., LODGE, A., HAMMER, L. R., SEMMES, J. and MISHKIN, M. (1968). Critical flicker frequency after unilateral temporal lobectomy in man. *Neuropsychologia* **6**, 355–363.

GOLDSTEIN, A.G. and CHANCE, J. E. (1964). Recognition of children's faces. *Child Dev.* **35**, 129–136.

GOLDSTEIN, A. G. and CHANCE, J. E. (1971). Visual recognition memory for complex configurations. *Percept. Psychophys.* **9**, 237–241.

GOLDSTEIN, K. (1939). *The Organism*. American Book: New York.

GOLDSTEIN, M. N. and JOYNT, R. J. (1969). Long term follow-up of a callosal-sectioned patient. *Arch. Neurol.* **20**, 96–102.

GOLEMAN, D. (1977). Split brain psychology: fad of the year. *Psychology Today* **11**, 89–90, 149, 151.

GOODGLASS, H. and CALDERON, M. (1977). Parallel processing of verbal and musical stimuli in right and left hemispheres. *Neuropsychologia* **15**, 397–407.

GOODGLASS, H. and QUADFASEL, F. A. (1954). Language laterality in left handed aphasics. *Brain* **77**, 521–548.

GORDON, H. W. (1980). Cognitive asymmetry in dyslexic families. *Neuropsychologia* **18**, 645–656.

GORDON, H. W. and CARMON, A. (1976). Transfer of dominance in speed of verbal response to visually presented stimuli from right to left hemisphere. *Percept. mot. Skills* **42**, 1091–1100.

GORDON, H. W., BOGEN, J. E. and SPERRY, R. W. (1971). Absence of deconnexion syndrome in two patients with partial section of the neocommissures. *Brain* **94**, 327–336.

GOTT, P. S. (1973). Language after dominant hemispherectomy. *J. neurol. neurosurg. Psychiat.* **36**, 1082–1088.

GOTT, P. S. and BOYARSKY, C. L. (1972). The relation of cerebral dominance and handedness to visual evoked potentials. *J. Neurobiol.* **3**, 65–77.

GOTT, P. S., ROSSITER, V. S., GALBRAITH, G. C. and SAUL, R. E. (1975). Visual evoked responses in commissurotomy patients. In *Cerebral Localization* (K. J. Zülch, O. Creutzfeldt and G. C. Galbraith, eds), pp. 144–149. Springer-Verlag, Berlin.

GOTT, P. S., ROSSITER, V. S., GALBRAITH, G. C. and SAUL, R. E. (1977). Visual evoked response correlates of cerebral specialisation after human commissurotomy. *Biol. Psychol.* **5**, 245–255.

GRANT, D. W. (1980). Visual asymmetry on a color-naming task: a developmental perspective. *Percept. mot. Skills* **50**, 475–480.

GRANT, D. W. (1981). Visual asymmetry on a colour naming task: A longitudinal study with primary school children. *Child Dev.* **52**, 370–372.

GRAVES, R., LANDIS, T. and GOODGLASS, H. (1981). Laterality and sex differences for visual recognition of emotional and non-emotional words. *Neuropsychologia* **19**, 95–102.

GREENWOOD, P. M., ROTKIN, L. G., WILSON, D. H. and GAZZANIGA, M. S. (1980). Psychophysics with the split brain subject: on hemispheric differences and numerical mediation in perceptual matching tasks. *Neuropsychologia* **18**, 419–434.

GRIFFITHS, D. and SARAGA, E. (1979). Biological theories about women. *Science for People* (summer).

GROSS, K., ROTHENBERG, S., SCHOTTENFELD, S. and DRAKE, C. (1978). Duration thresholds for letter identification in left and right visual fields for normal and reading-disabled children. *Neuropsychologia* **16**, 709–715.

GROSS, M. M. (1972). Hemispheric specialisation for processing of visually presented verbal and spatial stimuli. *Percept. Psychophys.* **12**, 357–363.

GRUZELIER, J. (1979). Synthesis and critical review of the evidence for hemisphere asymmetries of function in psychopathology. In *Hemisphere Asymmetries of Function in Psychopathology* (J. Gruzelier and P. Flor-Henry, eds), pp. 647–672. Elsevier/North-Holland Biomedical Press, Amsterdam.

GRUZELIER, J. (1981). Cerebral laterality and psychopathology: fact and fiction. *Psychol. Med.*, in press.

GRUZELIER, J. and FLOR-HENRY, P. (eds) (1979). *Hemisphere Asymmetries of Function in Psychopathology*. Elsevier/North-Holland Biomedical Press, Amsterdam.

GRUZELIER, J. and HAMMOND, N. (1976). Schizophrenia: a dominant hemisphere temporal-limbic disorder? *Res. Commun. Psychol. Psychiat. Behav.* **1**, 33–72.

GRUZELIER, J. and HAMMOND, N. (1979). Lateralised auditory processing in medicated and unmedicated schizophrenic patients. In *Hemisphere Asymmetries of Function in*

*Psychopathology* (J. Gruzelier and P. Flor-Henry, eds), pp. 603–636. Elsevier/North-Holland Biomedical Press, Amsterdam.

GRUZELIER, J. H., EAVES, F. F. and CONNOLLY, J. F. (1980). Habituation and phasic reactivity in the electrodermal system: reciprocal hemispheric influences. Paper presented to the British Psychological Society conference on Lateral Asymmetries and Cerebral Function, University of Leicester, 3–5 September, 1980.

GUR, R. C. (1977). Motoric laterality imbalance in schizophrenia. A possible concomitant of left hemisphere dysfunction. *Arch. gen. Psychiat.* **34**, 33–37.

GUR, R. C. (1978). Left hemisphere dysfunction and left hemisphere overactivation in schizophrenia. *J. abnorm. Psychol.* **87**, 226–238.

GUR, R.E., LEVY, J. and GUR, R. C. (1977). Clinical studies of brain organization and behaviour. In *Biological Bases of Psychiatric Disorders* (A. Frazer and A. Winokur, eds), pp. 115–137. Spectrum, New York.

HACKMAN, R. B. (1940). An experimental study of variability in ocular latency. *J. exp. Psychol.* **27**, 546–558.

HAINES, R. F. and GILLILAND, K. (1973). Response time in the full visual field. *J. appl. Psychol.* **58**, 289–295.

HALL, J. A. (1978). Gender effects in decoding nonverbal cues. *Psychol. Bull* **85**, 845–857.

HALLIDAY, A. M., BARRETT, G., BLUMHARDT, L. D. and KRISS, A. (1979). The macular and paramacular subcomponents of the pattern evoked response. In *Human Evoked Potentials: Applications and Problems* (D. Lehmann and E. Callaway, eds), pp. 135–151. Plenum Press, New York.

HAMMOND, N. and GRUZELIER, J. H. (1978). Laterality, attention and rate effects in the auditory temporal discrimination of chronic schizophrenics: the effect of treatment with chlorpromazine. *Q. J. exp. Psychol.* **30**, 91–103.

HANNAY, H. J. (1976). Real or imagined incomplete lateralisation of function in females? *Percept. Psychophys.* **19**, 349–352.

HANNAY, H. J. (1979). Asymmetry in reception and retention of colors. *Brain and Language* **8**, 191–201.

HANNAY, H. J. and BOYER, C. L. (1978). Sex differences in hemispheric asymmetry revisited. *Percept. mot. Skills* **47**, 315–321.

HANNAY, H. J. and MALONE, D. R. (1976a). Visual field effects and short term memory for verbal material. *Neuropsychologia* **14**, 203–209.

HANNAY, H. J. and MALONE, D. R. (1976b). Visual field recognition memory for right-handed females as a function of familial handedness. *Cortex* **12**, 41–48.

HANNAY, H. J. and ROGERS, J. P. (1979). Individual differences and asymmetry effects in memory for unfamiliar faces. *Cortex* **15**, 257–267.

HANNAY, H. J., ROGERS, J. P. and DURANT, R. F. (1976a). Complexity as a determinant of visual field effects for random forms. *Acta Psychol.* **40**, 29–34.

HANNAY, H. J., VARNEY, N. R. and BENTON, A. L. (1976b). Visual localization in patients with unilateral brain disease. *J. neurol. neurosurg. Psychiat.* **39**, 307–313.

HANSCH, E. C. and PIROZZOLO, F. J. (1980). Task relevant effects on the assessment of cerebral specialization for facial emotion. *Brain and Language* **10**, 51–59.

HARCUM, E. R. (1978). Lateral dominance as a determinant of temporal order of responding. In *Asymmetrical Function of the Brain* (M. Kinsbourne, ed.), pp. 141–266. Cambridge University Press, Cambridge.

HARDYCK, C. (1977). A model of individual differences in hemispheric functioning. In *Studies in Neurolinguistics*, Vol. 3 (H. Avakaian-Whitaker and H. A. Whitaker, eds), pp. 223–256. Academic Press, New York and London.

HARDYCK, C. and PETRINOVICH, L. F. (1977). Left handedness. *Psychol. Bull.* **84**, 385–404.

HARDYCK, C., TZENG, O. J. L. and WANG, W. S.-Y. (1977). Cerebral laterality effects in visual half field experimentation. *Nature, Lond.* **269**, 705–707.

HARDYCK, C., TZENG, O. J. L. and WANG, W. S.-Y. (1978). Cerebral lateralisation of function and bilingual decision processes: is thinking lateralized? *Brain and Language* **5**, 56–71.

HARE, R. D. (1979). Psychopathy and laterality of cerebral function. *J. abnorm. Psychol.* **88**, 605–610.

HARVEY, L. O., Jr. (1978). Single representation of the visual midline in humans. *Neuropsychologia* **16**, 601–610.

HATTA, T. (1975). Hemisphere asymmetries in the perception and memory of random forms. *Psychologia* **19**, 157–162.

HATTA, T. (1976a). Functional hemispheric asymmetries in perception of digit and line orientation. *Jap. J. Psychol.* **47**, 268–276.

HATTA, T. (1976b). Asynchrony of lateral onset as a factor in differences in visual field. *Percept. mot. Skills* **42**, 163–166.

HATTA, T. (1977a). Recognition of Japanese Kanji in the left and right visual fields. *Neuropsychologia* **15**, 685–688.

HATTA, T. (1977b). Lateral recognition of abstract and concrete Kanji in Japanese. *Percept. mot. Skills* **45**, 731–734.

HATTA, T. (1978). Visual field differences in a mental transformation task. *Neuropsychologia* **16**, 637–641.

HATTA, T. and DIMOND, S. J. (1980). Comparison of lateral differences for digit and random form recognition in Japanese and Westerners. *J. exp. Psychol: Human Percept. Perform.* **6**, 368–374.

HAUN, F. (1978). Functional dissociation of the hemispheres using foveal visual input. *Neuropsychologia* **16**, 725–733.

HEATON, R. K., BAADE, L. E. and JOHNSON, K. L. (1978). Neuropsychological test results associated with psychiatric disorders in adults. *Psychol. Bull.* **85**, 141–162.

HÉCAEN, H. (1978). Right hemisphere contribution to language functions. In *Cerebral Correlates of Conscious Experience* (P. A. Buser and A. Rougeul-Buser, eds), pp. 199–214. North-Holland, Amsterdam.

HÉCAEN, H. and ALBERT, M. L. (1978). *Human Neuropsychology*, Wiley, New York.

HÉCAEN, H. and ANGELERGUES, R. (1962). Agnosia for faces (prosopagnosia). *A.M.A. Arch. Neurol.* **7**, 92–100.

HÉCAEN, H. and PIERCY, M. (1956). Paroxysmal dysphasia and the problem of cerebral dominance. *J. neurol. neurosurg. Psychiat.* **18**, 194–201.

HEILMAN, K. M. and ABELL, T. VAN DEN (1979). Right hemisphere dominance for mediating cerebral activation. *Neuropsychologia* **17**, 315–321.

HELLIGE, J. B. (1975). Hemispheric processing differences revealed by differential conditioning and reaction time performance. *J. exp. Psychol.: General* **104**, 309–326.

HELLIGE, J. B. (1976). Changes in same–different laterality patterns as a function of practice and stimulus quality. *Percept. Psychophys.* **20**, 267–273.

HELLIGE, J. B. (1978). Visual laterality patterns for pure- versus mixed-list presentation. *J. exp. Psychol: Human Percept. Perform.* **4**, 121–131.

HELLIGE, J. B. (1980a). Effects of perceptual quality and visual field of probe stimulus presentation on memory search for letters. *J. exp. Psychol.: Human Percept. Perform.* **6**, 639–651.

HELLIGE, J. B. (1980b). Cerebral hemisphere asymmetry: methods, issues and implications. *Educ. Commun. Technol.* **28**, 83–98.

HELLIGE, J. B. and COX, P. J. (1976). Effects of concurrent verbal memory on recognition of stimuli from the left and right visual fields. *J. exp. Psychol.: Human Percept. Perform.* **2**, 210–221.

HELLIGE, J. B. and WEBSTER, R. (1979). Right hemisphere superiority for initial stages of letter processing. *Neuropsychologia* **17**, 653–660.

HELLIGE, J. B., COX, P. J. and LITVAC, L. (1979). Information processing in the cerebral hemispheres: selective hemispheric activation and capacity limitations. *J. exp. Psychol.: General* **108**, 251–279.

HERMELIN, B. and O'CONNOR, N. (1971). Functional asymmetry in the reading of Braille. *Neuropsychologia* **9**, 431–435.

HERON, W. (1957). Perception as a function of retinal locus and attention. *Am. J. Psychol.* **70**, 38–48.

HERRON, J., GALIN, D., JOHNSTONE, J. and ORNSTEIN, R. E. (1979). Cerebral specialisation, writing posture and motor control of writing in left handers. *Science, N.Y.* **205**, 1285–1289.

HEYWOOD, S. and CHURCHER, J. (1980). Structure of the visual array and saccadic latency: implications for oculomotor control. *Q. J. exp. Psychol.* **32**, 335–341.

HICKS, R. (1975). Intrahemispheric response competition between vocal and unimanual performance in normal adult human males. *J. comp. physiol. Psychol.* **89**, 50–60.

HIGENBOTTAM, J. A. (1973). Relationship between sets of lateral and perceptual preference measures. *Cortex* **9**, 402–409.

HILLIARD, R. D. (1973). Hemispheric laterality effects on a facial recognition task in normal subjects. *Cortex* **9**, 246–258.

HILLSBERG, B. (1979). A comparison of visual discrimination performance of the dominant and nondominant hemispheres in schizophrenia. In *Hemisphere Asymmetries of Function in Psychopathology* (J. Gruzelier and P. Flor-Henry, eds), pp. 527–538. Elsevier/North-Holland Biomedical Press, Amsterdam.

HILLYARD, S. A. (1971). The psychological specificity of the contingent negative variation and late evoked potential. *Electroenceph. clin. Neurophysiol.* **31**, 302–330.

HILLYARD, S. A. and WOODS, D. L. (1979). Electrophysiological analysis of human brain function. In *Handbook of Behavioural Neurobiology, Vol. 2 Neuropsychology* (M. S. Gazzaniga, ed.), pp. 345–378. Plenum Press, New York.

HINES, D. (1972a). Bilateral tachistscopic recognition of verbal and nonverbal stimuli. *Cortex* **8**, 315–322.

HINES, D. (1972b). A brief reply to McKeever, Suberi and VanDeventer's comment on "Bilateral tachistoscopic recognitions of verbal and nonverbal stimuli". *Cortex* **8**, 480–482.

HINES, D. (1975). Independent functioning of the two cerebral hemispheres for recognising bilaterally presented visual half field stimuli. *Cortex* **11**, 132–143.

HINES, D. (1976). Recognition of verbs, abstract nouns and concrete nouns from the left and right visual half fields. *Neuropsychologia* **14**, 211–216.

HINES, D. (1977). Differences in tachistoscopic recognition between abstract and concrete words as a function of visual half field and frequency. *Cortex* **13**, 66–73.

HINES, D. (1978). Visual information processing in the left and right hemispheres. *Neuropsychologia* **16**, 593–600.

HINES, D. and SATZ, P. (1971). Superiority of right visual half-fields in right handers for recall of digits presented at varying rates. *Neuropsychologia* **9**, 21–26.

HINES, D. and SATZ, P. (1974). Cross-modal asymmetries in perception related to asymmetry in cerebral function. *Neuropsychologia* **12**, 239–247.

HINES, D., SATZ, P., SCHELL, B. and SCHMIDLIN, S. (1969). Differential recall of digits in the left and right visual half fields under free and fixed order of recall. *Neuropsychologia* **7**, 13–22.

HINES, D., SATZ, P. and CLEMENTINO, T. (1973). Perceptual and memory components of the superior recall of letters from the right visual half-fields. *Neuropsychologia* **11**, 175–180.

HINES, D., SUTKER, L. W., SATZ, P. and ALTMAN, A. (1976). Recall of letters from the left and right visual half-fields under unilateral and bilateral presentation. *Percept. mot. Skills* **42**, 531–539.

HIRATA, K. and BRYDEN, M. P. (1976). Right visual field superiority for letter recognition with partial report. *Canad. J. Psychol.* **30**, 134–139.

HIRATA, K. and OSAKA, R. (1967). Tachistoscopic recognition of Japanese letter materials on left and right visual fields. *Psychologia* **10**, 7–18.

HIRSCH, I. J. and SHERRICK, C. E. (1961). Perceived order in different sense modalities. *J. exp. Psychol.* **62**, 423–432.

HOCHBERG, F. H. and LEMAY, M. (1975). Arteriographic correlates of handedness. *Neurology* **25**, 218–222.

HOCK, H. S. (1973). The effects of stimulus structure and familiarity on same–different comparison. *Percept. Psychophys.* **14**, 413–420.

HOLMES, J. M. and MARSHALL, J. C. (1974a). Handedness and lateralised word perception: reading habits versus hemispheric specialisation. *IRCS (Eye; Neurobiol; Psychol.)* **2**, 1462.

HOLMES, J. M. and MARSHALL, J. C. (1974b). Word perception in the visual half fields: the effects of exposure duration on laterality measures and accuracy. *IRCS (Eye; Neurobiol. Psychol.)* **2**, 1609.

HONDA, H. (1977). Shift of perceptual laterality difference by loading of verbal and nonverbal discrimination tasks. *Jap. J. Psychol.* **48**, 70–79.

HONDA, H. (1978). Shift of visual laterality differences by loading of auditory discrimination tasks. *Jap. J. Psychol.* **49**, 8–14.

HOWELLS, T. H. (1938). A study of ability to recognise faces. *J. abnorm. soc. Psychol.* **33**, 124–127.

HUBEL, D. H. and WIESEL, T. N. (1959). The receptive fields of simple neurons in the cat's striate cortex. *J. Physiol.* **148**, 574–691.

HUBER, A. (1962). Homonymous hemianopia after occipital lobectomy. *Am. J. Ophthalmol.* **54**, 623–629.

ISSEROFF, A., CARMON, A. and NACHSON, I. (1974). Dissociation of hemifield reaction time differences from verbal stimulus directionality. *J. exp. Psychol.* **103**, 145–149.

ITO, H. (1980). Crossed aphasia in right handed man. *Adv. Neurol. Sci.* **24**, 547–555.

IZARD, C. E. (1971). *The Face of Emotion.* Appleton-Century-Crofts, New York.

JABLONOWSKA, K. and BUDOHOSKA, W. (1976). Hemispheric differences in the visual analysis of the verbal and nonverbal material in children. *Acta Neurobiologiae Experimentalis* **36**, 693–701.

JASPER, H. H. (1932). A laboratory study of diagnostic indices of bilateral neuromuscular organisation in stutterers and normal speakers. *Psychol. Monogr.* **43**, 72–174.

JASPER, H. H. and RANEY, E. T. (1937). The phi test of lateral dominance. *Am. J. Psychol.* **49**, 450–457.

JAYNES, J. (1976). *The Origin of Consciousness in the Breakdown of the Bicameral Mind.* Houghton Mifflin, New York.

JEEVES, M. A. (1972). Hemisphere differences in response rates to visual stimuli in children. *Psychonom. Sci.* **27**, 201–203.

JEEVES, M. A. (1979). Some limits to interhemispheric integration in cases of callosal agenesis and partial commissurotomy. In *Structure and Function of Cerebral Commissures* (I. Steele Russell, M. W. Van Hof and G. Berlucchi, eds), pp. 449–474. Macmillan, London.

JEEVES, M. A. and DIXON, N. F. (1970). Hemisphere differences in response rates to visual stimuli. *Psychonom. Sci.* 20, 249–251.

JEEVES, M. A., SIMPSON, D. A. and GEFFEN, G. (1979). Functional consequences of the transcallosal removal of intraventricular tumours. *J. neurol. neurosurg. Psychiat.* 42, 134–142.

JOHNSON, J. D. and GAZZANIGA, M. S. (1969). Cortical–cortical pathways involved in reinforcement. *Nature, Lond.* 223, 71.

JOHNSTONE, E. C., CROW, T. J., FRITH, C. D., HUSBAND, J. and KREEL, L. (1976). Cerebral ventricular size and cognitive impairment in chronic schizophrenia. *Lancet,* 30 October, 924–926.

JONES, B. (1979). Sex and visual field effects on accuracy and decision making when subjects classify male and female faces. *Cortex* 15, 551–560.

JONES, B. (1980). Sex and handedness as factors in visual field organization for a categorization task. *J. exp. Psychol.: Human Percept. Perform.* 6, 494–500.

JONIDES, J. (1979). Left and right visual field superiority for letter classification. *Q. J. exp. Psychol.* 31, 423–439.

JOYNT, R. J. (1974). The corpus callosum: history of thought regarding its function. In *Hemispheric Disconnection and Cerebral Function* (M. Kinsbourne and W. L. Smith, eds), pp. 117–125. Charles C. Thomas, Springfield, Illinois.

JOYNT, R. J. (1977). Inattention syndromes in split-brain man. In *Hemi-Inattention and Hemisphere Specialization*, Advances in Neurology, Vol. 18 (E. A. Weinstein and R. P. Friedland, eds), pp. 33–39. Raven Press, New York.

JULESZ, B., BREITMEYER, B. and KROPFL, W. (1976). Binocular-disparity-dependent upper–lower hemifield anisotropy as revealed by dynamic random dot stereograms. *Perception* 5, 129–141.

JUOLA, J. F. (1973). Repetition and laterality effects on recognition memory for words and pictures. *Memory and Cognition* 1, 183–192.

KAIL, R., CARTER, P. and PELLEGRINO, J. (1979). The locus of sex differences in spatial ability. *Percept. Psychophys.* 26, 182–186.

KAIL, R. V. and SIEGEL, A. W. (1978). Sex and hemispheric differences in the recall of verbal and spatial information. *Cortex* 14, 557–563.

KALLMAN, H. J. and CORBALLIS, M. C. (1975). Ear asymmetry in reaction to musical sounds, *Percept. Psychophys.* 17, 368–370.

KANISZA, G. (1979). *Organization in Vision.* Praeger, New York.

KAPLAN, C. D. and TENHOUTEN, W. D. (1975). Neurolinguistic sociology. *Sociolinguistics Newsletter* 6, 4–9.

KAPPAUF, W. E. and YEATMAN, F. R. (1970). Visual on- and off-latencies and handedness. *Percept. Psychophys.* 8, 46–50.

KAROL, E. A. and PANDYA, D. N. (1971). The distribution of the corpus callosum in the rhesus monkey. *Brain* 94, 471–486.

KAUFER, I., MORAIS, J. and BERTELSON, P. (1975). Lateral differences in tachistoscopic recognition of bilaterally presented verbal material. *Acta psychol.* 39, 369–376.

KEEFE, B. and SWINNEY, D. (1979). On the relationship of hemispheric specialisation and developmental dyslexia. *Cortex* 15, 471–481.

KELLY, R. (1978). Hemispheric specialization of deaf children: are there any implications for instruction? *Am. Ann. Deaf* 123, 637–645.

KELLY, R. R. and TOMLINSON-KEASEY, C. (1977). Hemispheric laterality of deaf children for processing words and pictures visually presented to the hemifields. *Am. Ann. Deaf* **122**, 525–533.

KELLY, R. R. and TOMLINSON-KEASEY, C. (1978). A comparison of deaf and hearing children's hemispheric laterality for processing visually presented words and pictures. Paper presented to Annual Meeting of the American Educational Research Association, Toronto, Canada.

KEMP, A. A. and HAUDE, R. H. (1979). Visual field–cerebral hemisphere differences in perception of visual nonverbal stimuli. *Percept. mot. Skills* **48**, 1127–1131.

KENNEDY, F. (1916). Stock-brainedness, the causative factor in the so-called "crossed aphasias". *Am. J. med. Sci.* **152**, 849–859.

KERSHNER, J. R. (1974). Ocular–manual laterality and dual hemisphere specialization. *Cortex* **10**, 293–301.

KERSHNER, J. R. (1977). Cerebral dominance in disabled readers, good readers and gifted children: search for a valid model. *Child Dev.* **48**, 61–67.

KERSHNER, J. R. and JENG, A. G-R. (1972). Dual functional asymmetry in visual perception: effects of ocular dominance and postexposural processes. *Neuropsychologia* **10**, 437–446.

KERSHNER, J., THOMAE, R. and CALLAWAY, R. (1977). Nonverbal fixation control in young children induces a left-field advantage in digit recall. *Neuropsychologia* **15**, 569–576.

KERTESZ, A. and SHEPPARD, A. (1981). The epidemiology of aphasia and cognitive impairment in stroke: age, sex, aphasia type and laterality differences. *Brain* **104**, 117–128.

KIM, Y., ROYER, F., BONSTELLE, C. and BOLLER, F. (1980). Temporal sequencing of verbal and nonverbal material: the effect of laterality of lesion. *Cortex* **16**, 135–143.

KIMURA, D. (1961). Cerebral dominance and the perception of verbal stimuli. *Canad. J. Psychol.* **15**, 166–171.

KIMURA, D. (1966). Dual functional asymmetry of the brain in visual perception. *Neuropsychologia* **4**, 275–285.

KIMURA, D. (1969). Spatial localisation in left and right visual fields. *Canad. J. Psychol.* **23**, 445–458.

KIMURA, D. and DAVIDSON, W. (1975). Right arm superiority for tapping with distal and proximal joints. *J. hum. mov. Stud.* **1**, 199–202.

KIMURA, D. and VANDERWOLF, C. H. (1970). The relation between hand preference and the performance of individual finger movements by left and right hands. *Brain* **93**, 769–774.

KINSBOURNE, M. (1970). The cerebral basis of lateral asymmetries in attention. *Acta Psychol.* **33**, 193–201.

KINSBOURNE, M. (1973). The control of attention by interaction between the cerebral hemispheres. In *Attention and Performance IV* (S. Kornblun, ed.), pp. 239–256. Academic Press, New York and London.

KINSBOURNE, M. (1974). Mechanisms of hemispheric interaction in man. In *Hemispheric Disconnection and Cerebral Function* (M. Kinsbourne and W. L. Smith, eds), pp. 260–285. Charles C. Thomas, Springfield, Illinois.

KINSBOURNE, M. (1975a). The mechanism of hemispheric control of the lateral gradient of attention. In *Attention and Performance V* (P. M. A. Rabbitt and S. Dornic, eds), pp. 81–97. Academic Press, London and New York.

KINSBOURNE, M. (1975b). Cerebral dominance, learning and cognition. In *Progress in Learning Disabilities*, Vol. III (H. R. Myklebust, ed.), pp. 201–218. Grune and Stratton, New York.

KINSBOURNE, M. (1976a). The neuropsychological analysis of cognitive deficit. In *Biological Foundations of Psychiatry*, Vol. 1 (R. G. Grenell and S. Gabay, eds), pp. 527–589. Raven Press, New York.

KINSBOURNE, M. (1976b). The ontogeny of cerebral dominance. In *Neuropsychology of Language* (R. W. Rieber, ed.), pp. 181–191. Plenum Press, New York.

KINSBOURNE, M. (1978). Biological determinance of functional bisymmetry and asymmetry. In *Asymmetrical Function of the Brain* (M. Kinsbourne, ed.), pp. 3–13. Cambridge University Press, Cambridge.

KINSBOURNE, M. and COOK, J. (1971). Generalized and lateralised effects of concurrent verbalization on a unimanual skill. *Q. J. exp. Psychol.* **23**, 341–345.

KINSBOURNE, M. and HICKS, R. E. (1978). Functional cerebral space: a model for overflow, transfer and interference effects in human performance: a tutorial review. In *Attention and Performance VII* (J. Requin, ed.), pp. 345–362. Lawrence Erlbaum Associates, Hillsdale, New Jersey.

KINSBOURNE, M. and SMITH, W. L. (eds) (1974). *Hemispheric Disconnection and Cerebral Function.* Charles C. Thomas, Springfield, Illinois.

KINSBOURNE, M. and WARRINGTON, E. K. (1964). Observations on colour agnosia. *J. neurol. neurosurg. Psychiat.* **27**, 296–299.

KIRSNER, K. (1979). Hemispheric differences in recognition memory for letters. *Bull. Psychonom. Soc.* **13**, 2–4.

KIRSNER, K. (1980). Hemisphere-specific processes in letter matching. *J. exp. Psychol.: Human Percept. Perform.* **6**, 167–179.

KLATZKY, R. (1972). Visual and verbal coding of laterally presented pictures. *J. exp. Psychol.* **96**, 439–448.

KLATZKY, R. L. and ATKINSON, R. C. (1971). Specialisation of the cerebral hemispheres in scanning for information in short-term memory. *Percept. Psychophys.* **10**, 335–338.

KLEIN, D., MOSCOVITCH, M. and VIGNA, C. (1976). Attentional mechanisms and perceptual asymmetries in tachistoscopic recognition of words and faces. *Neuropsychologia* **14**, 55–66.

KNEHR, C. A. (1941). The effects of monocular vision on measures of reading efficiency and perceptual span. *J. exp. Psychol.* **29**, 133–154.

KNIGHTS, R. M. and BAKKER, D. J. (eds) (1976). *The Neuropsychology of Learning Disorders: Theoretical Approaches.* University Park Press, Baltimore, Maryland.

KOBRICK, J. L. (1965). Effects of physical location of visual stimuli on intentional response time. *J. Engin. Psychol.* **4**, 1–8.

KOCH, S. A., POLZELLA, D. J. and DA POLITO, F. (1980). Cerebral asymmetry in the perceived duration of colour stimuli. *Percept. mot. Skills* **50**, 1230–1246.

KOERNER, F. and TEUBER, H-L. (1973). Visual field defects after missile injuries to the geniculo-striate pathway in man. *Exp. Brain Research* **18**, 88–113.

KOETTING, J. F. (1970). Word recognition as a function of locus in the four lateral visual fields: the iota phenomenon. *Am. J. Optom.* **7**, 56–66.

KRASHEN, S. D. (1976). Cerebral asymmetry. In *Studies in Neurolinguistics*, Vol. 2. (H. Whitaker and H. A. Whitaker, eds), pp. 157–192. Academic Press, New York and London.

KRÄUPL TAYLOR, F. (1966). *Psychopathology: Its Causes and Symptoms.* Butterworth, London.

KROLL, J. F. and HERSHENSON, M. (1980). Two stages in visual matching. *Canad. J. Psychol.* **34**, 49–61.

KROLL, N. E. A. and MADDEN, D. J. (1978). Verbal and pictorial processing by hemisphere as a function of the subject's Verbal Scholastic Aptitude Test score. In *Attention and Performance VII* (J. Requin, ed.), pp. 375–390. Lawrence Erlbaum Associates, Hillsdale, New Jersey.

KRONFOL, Z., HAMSHER, K. de S., DIGRÉ, K. and WAZIRI, R. (1978). Depression and hemispheric functions: changes associated with unilateral ECT. *Br. J. Psychiat.* **132**, 560–567.

KRYNICKI, V. E. and NAHAS, A. D. (1979). Differing lateralized perceptual-motor patterns in schizophrenic and non-psychotic children. *Percept. mot. Skills* **49**, 603–610.

KUHN, T. S. (1970). *The Structure of Scientific Revolutions.* 2nd edition. University of Chicago Press, Chicago.

LADAVAS, E., UMILTA, C. and RICCI-BITTI, P. E. (1980). Evidence for sex differences in right hemisphere dominance for emotions. *Neuropsychologia* **18**, 361–366.

LAGRONE, C. W., Jr. (1942). An experimental study of the relationship of peripheral perception to factors in reading. *J. exp. Educ.* **11**, 37–49.

LAKE, D. A. and BRYDEN, M. P. (1976). Handedness and sex differences in hemispheric asymmetry. *Brain and Language* **3**, 266–282.

LAMBERT, A. J. and BEAUMONT, J. G. (1981a). Imageability and report position in lateral word recognition. Submitted for publication.

LAMBERT, A. J. and BEAUMONT, J. G. (1981b). Comparative processing and report position in lateral word recognition. *Cortex*, in press.

LANDIS, T., ASSAL, G. and PERRET, E. (1979). Opposite cerebral hemispheric superiorities for visual associative processing of emotional facial expressions and objects. *Nature, Lond.* **278**, 739–740.

LASSEN, N. A., INGVAR, D. H. and SKINHOJ, E. (1978). Brain function and blood flow. *Scient. Am.*, October, 50–59.

LATOUR, P. L. (1962). Visual threshold during eye movements. *Vision Res.* **2**, 261–262.

LAUGHERY, K. R., ALEXANDER, J. F. and LANE, A. B. (1971). Recognition of human faces: effects of target exposure time, target position, pose position and type of photograph. *J. appl. Psychol.* **55**, 477–483.

LAWSON, N. C. (1978). Inverted writing in right and left handers in relation to lateralisation of face recognition. *Cortex* **14**, 207–211.

LEDLOW, A. (1976). A reaction time and evoked potential investigation of lateral asymmetries in a stimulus classification task. Unpublished doctoral dissertation, University of Texas, Austin.

LEDLOW, A., SWANSON, J. M. and KINSBOURNE, M. (1978a). Differences in reaction times and average evoked potentials as a function of direct and indirect neural pathways. *Ann. Neurol.* **3**, 525–530.

LEDLOW, A., SWANSON, J. M. and KINSBOURNE, M. (1978b). Reaction times and evoked potentials as indicators of hemispheric differences for laterally presented name and physical matches. *J. exp. Psychol.: Human Percept. Perform.* **4**, 440–454.

LEDOUX, J. E., WILSON, D. H. and GAZZANIGA, M. S. (1977). Manipulo-spatial aspects of cerebral lateralisation: clues to the origin of lateralisation. *Neuropsychologia* **15**, 743–750.

LEEHEY, S. C. (1976). Face recognition in children: evidence for the development of right hemisphere specialization. Unpublished Ph.D. thesis, Massachusetts Institute of Technology.

LEEHEY, S. C. and CAHN, A. (1979). Lateral asymmetries in the recognition of words, familiar faces and unfamiliar faces. *Neuropsychologia* **17**, 619–635.

LEEHEY, S. C., CAREY, S., DIAMOND, R. and CAHN, A. (1978). Upright and inverted faces: The right hemisphere knows the difference. *Cortex* **14**, 411–419.

LE FEBVRE, P. Y. and KUBOSE, S. K. (1975). Effects of visual field of presentation and stimulus characteristics on visual discrimination learning. *Bull. Psychonom. Soc.* **5**, 13–15.

LEFTON, L. A., FISHER, D. F. and KUHN, D. M. (1978). Left-to-right processing of alphabetic material is independent of retinal location. *Bull. Psychonom. Soc.* **12**, 171–174.

LEHMANN, D. and CALLAWAY, E. (1979). *Human Evoked Potentials: Applications and Problems.* Plenum Press, New York.

LEHMANN, D. and JULESZ, B. (1978). Lateralised cortical potentials evoked in humans by dynamic random-dot stereograms. *Vision. Res.* **18**, 1265–1271.

LEHTONEN, J. B. and KOIVIKKO, M. J. (1971). The use of a non-cephalic reference electrode in recording evoked potentials in man. *Electroenceph. clin. Neurophysiol.* **31**, 154–156.

LEIBER, L. (1976). Lexical decisions in the right and left cerebral hemispheres. *Brain and Language* **3**, 443–450.

LEMAY, M. (1976). Morphological cerebral asymmetries of modern man, fossil man and nonhuman primates. *Ann. N.Y. Acad. Sci.* **280**, 349–366.

LESSER, R. (1974). Verbal comprehension in aphasia: an English version of three Italian tests. *Cortex* **10**, 247–263.

LEVINE, D. N. (1978). Prosopagnosia and visual object agnosia: a behavioural study. *Brain and Language* **5**, 341–368.

LEVINE, D. N. and CALVANIO, R. (1980). Visual discrimination after lesion of the posterior corpus callosum. *Neurology* **30**, 21–30.

LEVY, J. (1970). Information processing and the higher psychological functions in the disconnected hemispheres of human commissurotomy patients. Unpublished Ph.D. thesis, California Institute of Technology, California.

LEVY, J. (1974a). Psychobiological implications of bilateral asymmetry. In *Hemisphere Function in the Human Brain* (S. J. Dimond and J. G. Beaumont, eds), pp. 121–183. Elek Science, London.

LEVY, J. (1974b). Cerebral asymmeries as manifested in split-brain man. In *Hemispheric Disconnection and Cerebral Function* (M. Kinsbourne and W. L. Smith, eds), pp. 165–183. Charles C. Thomas, Springfield, Illinois.

LEVY, J. (1978). Lateral differences in the human brain in cognition and behavioural control. In *Cerebral Correlates of Conscious Experience* (P. A. Buser and A. Rougeul-Buser, eds), pp. 285–298. North-Holland, Amsterdam.

LEVY, J. and GUR, R. C. (1980). Individual differences in psychoneurological organization. In *Neuropsychology of Left-handedness* (J. Herron, ed.), pp. 199–210. Academic Press, New York and London.

LEVY, J. and NAGYLAKI, T. (1972). A model for the genetics of handedness. *Genetics* **72**, 117–128.

LEVY, J. and REID, M. (1976). Variations in writing posture and cerebral organization. *Science, N.Y.* **194**, 337–339.

LEVY, J. and REID, M. (1978). Variations in cerebral organization as a function of handedness, hand posture in writing and sex. *J. exp. Psychol.: General* **107**, 119–144.

LEVY, J. and TREVARTHEN, C. (1976). Metacontrol of hemispheric function in human split-brain patients. *J. exp. Psychol.: Human Percept. Perform.* **2**, 299–312.

LEVY, J. and TREVARTHEN, C. (1977). Perceptual, semantic and phonetic aspects of elementary language processes in split-brain patients. *Brain* **100**, 105–118.

LEVY, J., TREVARTHEN, C. and SPERRY, R. W. (1972). Perception of bilateral chimeric figures following hemispheric disconnexion. *Brain* **95**, 61–78.

LEY, R. G. and BRYDEN, M. P. (1979). Hemispheric differences in processing emotions and faces. *Brain and Language* **7**, 127–138.

LIPTON, J. P. (1977). On the psychology of eyewitness testimony. *J. appl. Psychol.* **62**, 90–95.

LISHMAN, W. A. (1968). Brain damage in relation to psychiatric disability after hand injury. *Br. J. Psychiat.* **114**, 373–410.

LISHMAN, W. A. (1973). The psychiatric sequelae of head injury: a review. *Psychol. Med.* **3**, 304–318.

LISHMAN, W. A. and McMEEKAN, E. R. L. (1976). Hand preference patterns in psychiatric patients. *Br. J. Psychiat.* **129**, 158–166.

LISSAUER, H. (1889). Ein Fall von Seelenblindheit nebst Beitrage zur Theorie derselben. *Archiv. für Psychiatrie und Nervenkrankheiten* **21**, 222–270.

LOMAS, J. and KIMURA, D. (1976). Intrahemispheric interaction between speaking and sequential manual activity. *Neuropsychologia* **14**, 23–33.

LONGDEN, K., ELLIS, C. and IVERSEN, S. D. (1976). Hemispheric differences in the discrimination of curvature. *Neuropsychologia* **14**, 195–201.

LORDAHL, D. S., KLEINMAN, K. M., LEVY, B., MASSOTH, N. A., PESSIN, M. S., STORANDT, M., TACKER, R. and VANDERPLAS, J. M. (1965). Deficits in recognition of random shapes with changed visual fields. *Psychonom. Sci.* **3**, 245–246.

LOVELL, H.W., WAGGONER, R. W. and KAHN, E. A. (1932). Critical study of a case of aphasia. *Arch. Neurol. Psychiat.* **28**, 1179–1181.

LUCHINS, D. J., WEINBERGER, D. R. and WYATT, R. J. (1979). Schizophrenia: evidence of a subgroup with reversed cerebral asymmetry. *Arch. gen. Psychiat.* **36**, 1309–1311.

LURIA, A. R. (1966). *Higher Cortical Functions in Man.* Tavistock Publications, London.

LURIA, A. R. and MAJOVSKI, L. V. (1977). Basic approaches used in American and Soviet clinical neuropsychology. *Am. Psychol.* **32**, 959–968.

LURIA, S. M. (1974). Visual masking, handedness and laterality. *Percept. mot. Skills* **38**, 803–811.

MACKAVEY, W., CURCIO, F. and ROSEN, J. (1975). Tachistoscopic word recognition performance under conditions of simultaneous bilateral presentation. *Neuropsychologia* **13**, 27–33.

MADDESS, R. J. (1975). Reaction time to hemiretinal stimulation. *Neuropsychologia* **13**, 213–218.

MADDESS, R. J., ROSENBLOOD, L. K. and GOLDWATER, B. C. (1973). An improved technique for monitoring fixation in tachistoscopic tasks. *Q. J. exp. Psychol.* **25**, 398–403.

MALATESHA, R. (1976). Differences in hemispheric functions between dyslexics and normal readers. Unpublished Ph.D. thesis, University of South Carolina.

MALONE, D. R. and HANNAY, H. J. (1978). Hemispheric dominance and normal color memory. *Neuropsychologia* **16**, 51–59.

MANDELBAUM, J. and SLOAN, L. L. (1947). Peripheral visual acuity with special reference to scotopic illumination. *Am. J. Ophthalmol.*, Series 3, **30**, 581–588.

MANDES, E. (1980). Visual field accuracy and eye movement direction: a child's eye view. *Percept. mot. Skills* **50**, 631–636.

MANNING, A. A., GOBLE, W., MARKMAN, R. and LaBRECHE, T. (1977). Lateral cerebral differences in the deaf in response to linguistic and nonlinguistic stimuli. *Brain and Language* **4**, 309–321.

MARCEL, T. and PATTERSON, K. E. (1978). Word recognition and production: reciprocity in clinical and normal studies. In *Attention and Performance VII* (J. Requin, ed.), pp. 209–226. Lawrence Erlbaum Associates, Hillsdale, New Jersey.

MARCEL, T. and RAJAN, P. (1975). Lateral specialisation for recognition of words and faces in good and poor readers. *Neuropsychologia* 13, 489–497.

MARCEL, T., KATZ, L. and SMITH, M. (1974). Laterality and reading proficiency. *Neuropsychologia* 12, 131–140.

MARKOVITZ, H. and WEITZMAN, D. O. (1969). Monocular recognition of letters and Landolt C's in left and right visual hemifields. *J. exp. Psychol.* 79, 187–189.

MARSDEN, C. D. (1976). (Letter on Johnstone *et al.*'s "Cerebral atrophy and cognitive impairment in chronic schizophrenia".) *Lancet*, 13 November, p. 1079.

MARSH, G. R. (1978). Asymmetry of electrophysiological phenomena and its relation to behaviour in humans. In *Asymmetrical Function of the Brain* (M. Kinsbourne, ed.), pp. 292–317. Cambridge University Press, Cambridge.

MARSHALL, J. C. (1973). Some problems and paradoxes associated with recent accounts of hemispheric specialisation. *Neuropsychologia* 11, 463–470.

MARSHALL, J. C. and HOLMES, J. M. (1974). Sex, handedness and differential hemispheric specialisation for components of word perception. *IRCS (Eye, Neurobiol., Psychol.)* 2, 1344.

MARSHALL, J. C., CAPLAN, D. and HOLMES, J. M. (1975). The measure of laterality. *Neuropsychologia* 13, 315–321.

MARTIN, C. M. (1978). Verbal and spatial encoding of visual stimuli: the effects of sex, hemisphere and yes-no judgments. *Cortex* 14, 227–233.

MARTIN, M. (1978). Hemispheric asymmetries for physical and semantic selection of visually presented words. *Neuropsychologia* 16, 717–724.

MARTIN, M. (1979). Hemispheric specialisation for local and global processing. *Neuropsychologia* 17, 33–40.

MARZI, C. A. (1980). Hemiretinal differences in detection. Paper given at the course on Neuropsychology and Behaviour. Erice, Sicily.

MARZI, C. A. and BERLUCCHI, G. (1977). Right field superiority for recognition of famous faces in normals. *Neuropsychologia* 15, 751–756.

MARZI, C. A., DI STEFANO, M., TASSINARI, G. and CREA, F. (1979). Iconic storage in the two hemispheres. *J. exp. Psychol.: Human Percept. Perform.* 5, 31–41.

MATTE-BLANCO, I. (1965). A study of schizophrenic thinking: its expression in terms of symbolic logic and its representation in terms of multi-dimensional space. *Int. J. Psychiat.* 1, 91–96.

MAZZUCCHI, A., FERRARI, A. and MORETTI, G. (1977). Prevalente frequenza della prosopagnosia nel sesso maschile. *Riv. Neurol.* 47, 454–464.

McCARTHY, R. A. (1980). Visual field differences in sequential letter classification tasks. Unpublished Ph.D. thesis, University of Leicester.

McCONKIE, G. W. and RAYNER, K. (1976). Asymmetry of the perceptual span in reading. *Bull. Psychonom. Soc.* 8, 365–368.

McFIE, J. (1969). The diagnostic significance of disorders of higher nervous activity: syndromes related to frontal, temporal, parietal and occipital lesions. In *Handbook of Clinical Neurology, Volume 4: Disorders of Speech, Perception, and Symbolic Behaviour* (P. J. Vinken and G. W. Bruyn, eds), pp. 1–12. North-Holland, Amsterdam.

McGLONE, J. (1977). Sex differences in the cerebral organization of verbal functions in patients with unilateral brain lesions. *Brain* 100, 775–793.

McGLONE, J. (1978). Sex differences in functional brain asymmetry. *Cortex* 14, 122–128.

McGLONE, J. (1980). Sex differences in human brain asymmetry: a critical survey. *The Behavioral and Brain Sciences* 3, 215–263.

McGLONE, J. and DAVIDSON, W. (1973). The relation between cerebral speech laterality and spatial ability with special reference to sex and hand preference. *Neuropsychologia* **11**, 105–113.

McGRANE, D. (1977). Bilateral asymmetry and behaviour: three papers, three preferences in recognition of conflicting verbal stimuli presented tachistoscopically. *Irish J. Psychol.* **3**, 215–222.

McKEEVER, W. F. (1971). Lateral word recognition: effects of unilateral and bilateral presentation, asynchrony of bilateral presentation and forced order of report. *Q. J. exp. Psychol.* **23**, 410–416.

McKEEVER, W. F. (1974). Does post-exposural directional scanning offer a sufficient explanation for lateral differences in tachistoscopic recognition? *Percept. mot. Skills* **38**, 43–50.

McKEEVER, W. F. (1976). On Orenstein's and Meighan's finding of left visual field superiority for bilaterally presented words. *Bull. Psychonom. Soc.* **8**, 85–86.

McKEEVER, W. F. (1977). Lateral tachistoscopic recognition, cerebral dominance and dyslexia. *Bull. Orton Soc.* **27**, 26–36.

McKEEVER, W. F. (1979). Handwriting posture in left handers: sex, familial sinistrality and language laterality correlates. *Neuropsychologia* **17**, 429–444.

McKEEVER, W. F. and GILL, K. M. (1972a). Visual half field differences in the recognition of bilaterally presented single letters and vertically spelled words. *Percept. mot. Skills* **34**, 815–818.

McKEEVER, W. F. and GILL, K. M. (1972b). Interhemispheric transfer time for visual stimulus information varies as a function of the retinal locus of stimulation. *Psychonom. Sci.* **26**, 308–310.

McKEEVER, W. F. and GILL, K. M. (1972c). Visual half field differences in masking effects for sequential letter stimuli in the right and left handed. *Neuropsychologia* **10**, 111–117.

McKEEVER, W. F. and HOFF, A. L. (1979). Evidence of a possible isolation of left hemisphere visual and motor areas in sinistrals employing an inverted handwriting posture. *Neuropsychologia* **17**, 445–455.

McKEEVER, W. F. and HULING, M. D. (1970a). Right hemispheric superiority in graphic reproduction of briefly viewed dot figures. *Percept. mot. Skills* **31**, 201–202.

McKEEVER, W. F. and HULING, M. D. (1970b). Lateral dominance in tachistoscopic word recognition of children at two levels of ability. *Q. J. exp. Psychol.* **22**, 600–604.

McKEEVER, W. F. and HULING, M. D. (1971a). Bilateral tachistoscopic word recognition as a function of hemisphere stimulated and interhemispheric transfer time. *Neuropsychologia* **9**, 281–288.

McKEEVER, W. F. and HULING, M. D. (1971b). Lateral dominance in tachistoscopic word recognition performances obtained with simultaneous bilateral input. *Neuropsychologia* **9**, 15–20.

McKEEVER, W. F. and JACKSON, T. L. (1979). Cerebral dominance assessed by object- and colour-naming latencies: sex and familial sinistrality. *Brain and Language* **7**, 175–190.

McKEEVER, W. F. and SUBERI, M. (1974). Parallel but temporally displaced visual half field metacontrast functions. *Q. J. exp. Psychol.* **26**, 258–265.

McKEEVER, W. F. and VAN DEVENTER, A. D. (1975). Dyslexic adolescents: evidence of impaired visual and auditory language processing associated with normal lateralization and visual responsivity. *Cortex* **11**, 361–378.

McKEEVER, W. F. and VAN DEVENTER, A. D. (1977). Visual and auditory language processing asymmetries: influences of handedness, familial sinistrality and sex. *Cortex* **13**, 225–241.

McKEEVER, W. F. and VAN DEVENTER, A. D. (1980). Inverted handwriting position, language laterality, and the Levy-Nagylaki genetic model of handedness and cerebral organization. *Neuropsychologia* **18**, 99–102.

McKEEVER, W. F., SUBERI, M. and VAN DEVENTER, A. D. (1972). Fixation control in tachistoscopic studies of laterality effects: comment and data relevant to Hines' experiment. *Cortex* **8**, 473–479.

McKEEVER, W. F., VAN DEVENTER, A. D. and SUBERI, M. (1973). Avowed, assessed and familial handedness and differential hemispheric processing of brief sequential and non-sequential visual stimuli. *Neuropsychologia* **11**, 235–238.

McKEEVER, W. F., GILL, K. M. and VAN DEVENTER, A. D. (1975). Letter versus dot stimuli as tools for "splitting the normal brain with reaction time". *Q. J. exp. Psychol.* **27**, 363–373.

McKEEVER, W. F., HOEMANN, H. W., FLORIAN, V. A. and VAN DEVENTER, A. D. (1976). Evidence of minimal cerebral asymmetries for the processing of English words and American sign language in the congenitally deaf. *Neuropsychologia* **14**, 413–423.

McKELVIE, S. J. (1976). The effects of verbal labelling on recognition memory for schematic faces. *Q. J. exp. Psychol.* **28**, 459–474.

McKINNEY, J. P. (1966). Lateral asymmetry in the stability of the visual field. *Psychonom. Sci.* **5**, 175–176.

McKINNEY, J. P. (1967). Handedness, eyedness and perceptual stability of the left and right visual fields. *Neuropsychologia* **5**, 339–344.

MEADOWS, J. C. (1974a). Disturbed perception of colours associated with localised cerebral lesions. *Brain* **97**, 615–632.

MEADOWS, J. C. (1974b). The anatomical basis for prosopagnosia. *J. neurol. neurosurg. Psychiat.* **37**, 489–501.

MENDEL, K. (1914). Über Rechtshirnigkeit bei Rechtshändern. *Neurol. Zentbl* **33**, 291–293.

METZGER, R. L. and ANTES, J. R. (1976). Sex and coding strategy effects on reaction time to hemisphere probes. *Memory and Cognition* **4**, 157–171.

MEYER, A. (1971). *Historical Aspects of Cerebral Anatomy.* Oxford University Press, London.

MEYER, G. E. (1976). Right hemispheric sensitivity for the McCollough effect. *Nature, Lond.* **204**, 751–753.

MICELLI, G., CALTAGIRONE, C., GAINOTTI, G., MASULLO, C., SILVERI, M. C. and VILLA, G. (1981). Influence of sex, age, literacy and pathological lesion on incidence, severity and type of aphasia. In preparation.

MICHAELS, C. F. (1973). An examination of hemispheric asymmetry in the visual processing of linguistic items. *Haskins Labs Status Report on Speech Research* 35–36, 121.

MILES, W. R. (1936). The reaction time of the eye. *Psychol. Monogr.* **47**, 268–293.

MILLER, L. (1975). Contralateral masking in word recognition. 16th Annual Meeting of Psychonomic Society, Denver, Colorado.

MILLER, L. K. and BUTLER, D. (1980). The effect of set size on hemifield asymmetries in letter recognition. *Brain and Language* **9**, 307–314.

MILLER, L. K. and TURNER, S. (1973). Development of hemifield differences in word recognition. *J. educ. Psychol.* **65**, 172–176.

MILNER, A. D. and DUNNE, J. J. (1977). Lateralised perception of bilateral chimaeric faces by normal subjects. *Nature, Lond.* **268**, 175–176.

MILNER, A. D. and JEEVES, M. A. (1979). A review of behavioural studies of agenesis of the corpus callosum. In *Structure and Function of Cerebral Commissures* (J. Steele

Russell, M. W. Van Hof and G. Berlucchi, eds), pp. 428–448. Macmillan, London.

MILNER, A. D. and LINES, C. (1982). Interhemispheric pathways in simple reaction-time to lateralised light flash. *Neuropsychologia*, in press.

MILNER, B. (1971). Interhemispheric differences in the localization of psychological processes in man. *Brit. Med. Bull.* **27**, 272–277.

MILNER, B., BRANCH, C. and RASMUSSEN, T. (1964). Observations on cerebral dominance. In *Disorders of Language* (A. V. S. De Reuck and M. O'Connor, eds), pp. 200–222. Churchill, London.

MILNER, B., TAYLOR, L. B. and SPERRY, R. W. (1968). Lateralized suppression and dichotically presented digits after commissural section in man. *Science, N.Y.* **161**, 184–185.

MILSTEIN, V., SMALL, I. F., MALLOY, F. W. and SMALL, J. G. (1979). Influence of sex and handedness on hemispheric functioning. *Cortex* **15**, 439–449.

MIRSKY, A. F. (1969). Neuropsychological bases of schizophrenia. *Ann. Rev. Psychol.* **20**, 321–348.

MISHKIN, M. and FORGAYS, D. G. (1952). Word recognition as a function of retinal locus. *J. exp. Psychol.* **43**, 43–48.

MORGAN, A. H., MACDONALD, H. and HILGARD, E. R. (1974). EEG alpha: lateral asymmetry related to task and hypnotizability. *Psychophysiology* **11**, 275–282.

MOSCOVITCH, M. (1973). Language and the cerebral hemispheres: reaction time studies and their implications for models of cerebral dominance. In *Communication and Affect: Language and Thought* (P. Pliner, L. Krames and T. Alloway, eds), pp. 89–126. Academic Press, New York and London.

MOSCOVITCH, M. (1976). On the representation of language in the right hemisphere of right-handed people. *Brain and Language* **3**, 47–71.

MOSCOVITCH, M. (1977). The development of lateralisation of language functions and its relation to cognitive and linguistic development: A review and some theoretical speculations. In *Language Development and Neurological Theory* (S. J. Segalowitz and F. A. Gruber, eds), pp. 194–211. Academic Press, New York and London.

MOSCOVITCH, M. (1979). Information processing and the cerebral hemispheres. In *Handbook of Behavioral Neurobiology, Vol. 2: Neuropsychology* (M. S. Gazzaniga, ed.), pp. 379–446. Plenum Press, New York.

MOSCOVITCH, M. and KLEIN, D. (1980). Material-specific perceptual interference for visual words and faces: Implications for models of capacity limitations, attention and laterality. *J. exp. Psychol.: Human Percept. Perform.* **6**, 590–604.

MOSCOVITCH, M. and SMITH, L. C. (1979). Differences in neural organization between individuals with inverted and noninverted handwriting postures. *Science, N.Y.* **205**, 710–713.

MOSCOVITCH, M., SCULLION, D. and CHRISTIE, D. (1976). Early versus late stages of processing and their relation to functional hemispheric asymmetries in face recognition. *J. exp. Psychol.: Human Percept. Perform.* **2**, 401–416.

MOWERY, G. L. and BENNETT, A. E. (1957). Some technical notes on monopolar and bipolar recordings. *Electroenceph. clin. Neurophysiol.* **9**, 377.

MYKLEBUST, H. R. (ed.) (1978). *Progress in Learning Disabilities*, Vol. IV. Grune and Stratton, New York.

NATALE, M. and GUR, R. (1980). Differential hemispheric lateralization of positive and negative emotions in normals. Paper given at the Third INS European Conference. Chianciano-Terme, Italy.

NAYLOR, H. (1980). Reading disability and lateral asymmetry: an information-processing analysis. *Psychol. Bull.* **87**, 531–545.

NEBES, R. D. (1971). Superiority of the minor hemisphere in commissurotomized man for the perception of part–whole relations. *Cortex* **7**, 333–349.

NEBES, R. D. (1973). Perception of spatial relationships by the right and left hemispheres in commissurotomised man. *Neuropsychologia* **11**, 285–289.

NEBES, R. D. (1974a). Hemispheric specialisation in commissurotomised man. *Psychol. Bull.* **81**, 1–14.

NEBES, R. D. (1974b). Dominance of the minor hemisphere in commissurotomised man for the perception of part–whole relationships. In *Hemispheric Disconnection and Cerebral Function* (M. Kinsbourne and W. L. Smith, eds), pp. 155–164. Charles C. Thomas, Springfield, Illinois.

NEIL, D. O., SIMPSON, H. and GRIBBEN, J. A. (1971). Hemiretinal effects in tachistoscopic letter recognition. *J. exp. Psychol.* **91**, 129–135.

NEVILLE, H. G. and BELLUGI, U. (1978). Patterns of cerebral specialization in congenitally deaf adults: a preliminary report. In *Understanding Language through Sign Language Research* (P. Siple, ed.), pp. 239–257. Academic Press, New York and London.

NEVILLE, H. J. (1975). The development of cerebral specialization in normal and congenitally deaf children: an evoked potential and behavioral study. Paper presented to Third Annual Meeting of the International Neuropsychology Society, Tampa, Florida.

NEVILLE, H. J. (1976). The functional significance of cerebral specialization. In *Neuropsychology of Language* (R. W. Rieber, ed.), pp. 193–227. Plenum Press, New York.

NEVILLE, H. J. (1978). Electroencephalographic testing of cerebral specialisation in normal and congenitally deaf children: a preliminary report. In *Language Development and Neurological Theory* (S. J. Segalowitz and F. A. Gruber, eds), pp. 121–131. Academic Press, New York and London.

NEWCOMBE, F. and RATCLIFF, G. (1973). Handedness, speech lateralization and abilities. *Neuropsychologia* **11**, 399–407.

NEWMAN, S. and ALBINO, R. C. (1979). Hemisphere differences and judgments of simultaneity of brief light flashes. *Percept. mot. Skills* **49**, 943–956.

NICE, D. S. and HARCUM, E. R. (1976). Evidence from mutual masking for serial processing of tachistoscopic letter patterns. *Percept. mot. Skills* **42**, 991–1003.

NICOLETTI, R. and FAIRWEATHER, H. (1979). La specializzazione emisferica negli effetti di ripetizione e compatibilità. *Giornal. Ital. Psicol.* **6**, 541–559.

NIEDERBUHL, J. and SPRINGER, S. P. (1979). Task requirements and hemisphere asymmetry for the processing of single letters. *Neuropsychologia* **17**, 689–692.

OLDFIELD, R. C. (1971). The assessment and analysis of handedness: the Edinburgh inventory. *Neuropsychologia* **9**, 97–113.

OLSON, M. E. (1973). Laterality differences in tachistoscopic word recognition in normal and delayed readers in elementary school. *Neuropsychologia* **11**, 343–350.

OOSTENBRUG, M. W. M., HORST, J. W. and KUIMPER, J. W. (1978). Discrimination of visually perceived intervals of time. *Percept. Psychophys.* **24**, 21–34.

ORBACH, J. (1952). Retinal locus as a factor in the recognition of visually perceived words. *Am. J. Psychol.* **65**, 555–562.

ORENSTEIN, H. B. (1976). A reply to McKeever's "On Orenstein's and Meighan's finding of left visual field recognition superiority for bilaterally presented words". *Bull. Psychonom. Soc.* **8**, 87.

ORENSTEIN, H. B. and MEIGHAN, W. B. (1976). Recognition of bilaterally presented words varying in concreteness and frequency: lateral dominance or sequential processing? *Bull. Psychonom. Soc.* **7**, 179–180.

ORNSTEIN, R. E. (1977). *The Psychology of Consciousness*. 2nd edition. Harcourt, Brace, Jovanovich, New York.

OSAKA, N. (1978). Naso-temporal differences in human reaction time in the peripheral visual field. *Neuropsychologia* **16**, 299–303.

OSCAR-BERMAN, M., GOODGLASS, H. and CHERLOW, D. G. (1973). Perceptual laterality and iconic recognition of visual materal by Korsakoff patients and normal adults. *J. comp. Physiol. Psychol.* **82**, 316–321.

OXBURY, J. M. (1975). The right hemisphere and hemispheric disconnection. In *Recent Advances in Clinical Neurology No. 1* (W. B. Matthews, ed.), pp. 1–22. Churchill-Livingstone, Edinburgh.

PAIVIO, A. and ERNEST, C. H. (1971). Imagery ability and visual perception of verbal and nonverbal stimuli. *Percept. Psychophys.* **10**, 429–432.

PAPANICOLAOU, A. C. (1980). Cerebral excitation profiles in language processing: the photic probe paradigm. *Brain and Language* **9**, 269–280.

PARKER, R., SATZ, P. and HORNE, E. F. (1976). Visual pathways, acuity dominance and visual half field asymmetry. *J. gen. Psychol.* **95**, 233–240.

PATERSON, A. and ZANGWILL, O. L. (1944). Disorders of visual space perception associated with lesions of the right cerebral hemisphere. *Brain* **67**, 331–358.

PATTERSON, K. and BADDELEY, A. D. (1977). When face recognition fails. *J. exp. Psychol.: Human Learning and Memory* **3**, 406–417.

PATTERSON, K. and BRADSHAW, J. L. (1975). Differential hemispheric mediation of nonverbal stimuli. *J. exp. Psychol.: Human Percept. Perform.* **1**, 246–252.

PAVY, D. (1968). Verbal behaviour in schizophrenia. A review of recent studies. *Psychol. Bull.* **70**, 164–178.

PENNAL, B. E. (1977). Human cerebral asymmetry in color discrimination. *Neuropsychologia* **15**, 563–568.

PERENIN, M. T. and JEANNEROD, M. (1978). Visual function within the hemianopic field following early cerebral hemidecortication in man: spatial localization. *Neuropsychologia* **16**, 1–13.

PERL, N. and HAGGARD, M. (1975). Practice and strategy in a measure of cerebral dominance. *Neuropsychologia* **13**, 347–354.

PETERS, M. (1980). Why the preferred hand taps more quickly than the non-preferred hand: three experiments on handedness. *Canad. J. Psychol.* **34**, 62–71.

PETERS, M. and DURDING, B. (1979). Left-handers and right-handers compared on a motor task. *J. mot. Behav.* **11**, 103–111.

PETERS, M. and PEDERSON, K. (1978). Incidence of left handers with inverted writing position in a population of 5910 elementary school children. *Neuropsychologia* **16**, 743–746.

PETRUSIC, W. M., VARRO, L. and JAMIESON, D. G. (1978). Mental rotation validation of two spatial ability tests. *Psychol. Res.* **40**, 139–148.

PHIPPARD, D. (1977). Hemifield differences in visual perception in deaf and hearing subjects. *Neuropsychologia* **15**, 555–561.

PIAZZA, D. M. (1980). The influence of sex and handedness in the hemispheric specialization of verbal and nonverbal tasks. *Neuropsychologia* **18**, 163–176.

PIC'L, A. K., MAGARO, P. A. and WADE, E. A. (1979). Hemispheric functioning in paranoid and nonparanoid schizophrenia. *Biol. Psychiat.* **14**, 891–903.

PILLON, B., DESI, M. and LHERMITTE, F. (1979). Deux cas d'aphasie croisée avec jargonographie chez des droitiers. *Rev. Neurol.* **135**, 15–30.

PIROT, M., PULTON, T. W. and SUTKER, L. W. (1977). Hemispheric asymmetry in reaction time to color stimuli. *Percept. mot. Skills* **45**, 1151–1155.

PIROZZOLO, F. J. (1977). Lateral asymmetries in visual perception: a review of tachistoscopic visual half field studies. *Percept. mot. Skills* **45**, 695–701.

PIROZZOLO, F. J. (1978). Cerebral asymmetries and reading acquisition. *Academic Therapy* **13**, 261–266.

PIROZZOLO, F. J. (1979). *The Neuropsychology of Developmental Reading Disorders.* Praeger, New York.

PIROZZOLO, F. J. and RAYNER, K. (1977). Hemispheric specialization in reading and word recognition. *Brain and Language* **4**, 248–261.

PIROZZOLO, F. J. and RAYNER, K. (1979). Cerebral organization and reading disability. *Neuropsychologia* **17**, 485–491.

PIROZZOLO, F. J. and RAYNER, K. (1980). Handedness, hemispheric specialization and saccadic eye movement latencies. *Neuropsychologia* **18**, 225–229.

PITBLADO, C. (1979a). Cerebral asymmetries in random-dot stereopsis: reversal of direction with changes in dot size. *Perception* **6**, 683–690.

PITBLADO, C. (1979b). Visual field differences in perception of the vertical with and without a visible frame of reference. *Neuropsychologia* **17**, 381–392.

PITBLADO, C., PETRIDES, M. and RICCIO, G. (1979). Visual field asymmetries in letter recognition: evidence for asymmetry in early visual registration. *Percept. mot. Skills* **49**, 183–191.

PIZZAMIGLIO, L. and ZOCCOLOTTI, P. (1981). Sex and cognitive influence on visual hemifield superiority for face and letter recognition. *Cortex* **17**, 215–226.

POFFENBERGER, A. T. (1912). Reaction time to retinal stimulation with special reference to the time lost in conduction through nerve centers. *Arch. Psychol.* **23**, 1–73.

POHL, W., BUTTERS, N. and GOODGLASS, H. (1972). Spatial discrimination systems and cerebral lateralization. *Cortex* **8**, 305–314.

POIZNER, H. and LANE, H. (1979). Cerebral asymmetry in the perception of American sign language. *Brain and Language* **7**, 210–226.

POIZNER, H., BATTISON, R. and LANE, H. (1979). Cerebral asymmetry for American sign language: the effects of moving stimuli. *Brain and Language* **7**, 351–362.

POLICH, J. M. (1978). Hemispheric differences in stimulus identification. *Percept. Psychophys.* **24**, 49–57.

POLZELLA, D. J., DA POLITO, F. and HINSMAN, M. C. (1977). Cerebral asymmetry in time perception. *Percept. Psychophys.* **21**, 187–192.

PÖPPEL, E. (1977). The structure of the visual field. In *Neuronal Mechanisms in Visual Perception* (E. Pöppel, R. Held and J. E. Dowling, eds), NRP-Bulletin Vol. 15/3, pp. 369–375. Boston, MIT Press.

PORAC, C. and COREN, S. (1976). The dominant eye. *Psychol. Bull.* **83**, 880–897.

POSNER, M. I. (1980). Orienting of attention. *Q. J. exp. Psychol.* **32**, 3–25.

POWERS, P., ANDRIKS, J. and LOFTUS, E. (1979). Eyewitness accounts of females and males. *J. appl. Psychol.* **64**, 339–347.

PREILOWSKI, B. (1979). Consciousness after complete surgical section of the forebrain commissures in man. In *Structure and Function of Cerebral Commissures* (I. Steele Russell, M. W. Van Hof and G. Berlucchi, eds), pp. 441–420. Macmillan, London.

PRING, T. (1981a). The effects of stimulus-size and exposure duration on visual field asymmetry. *Cortex* **17**, 227–239.

PRING, T. R. (1981b). The effects of concreteness/imageability, sex and hand of responding on visual field asymmetries in a lexical decision task. *Cortex*, in press.

RAINS, J. D. (1963). Signal luminance and position effects in human reaction time. *Vision Res.* **3**, 239–251.

RAPACZYNSKI, W. and EHRLICHMAN, H. (1979). Opposite visual field hemifield superiorities in face recognition as a function of cognitive style. *Neuropsychologia* **17**, 645–652.

RASMUSSEN, C. T., ALLEN, R. and TATE, R. D. (1977). Hemispheric asymmetries in the cortical evoked potential as a function of arithmetical computations. *Bull. Psychonom. Soc.* **10**, 419–421.

RASMUSSEN, T. and MILNER, B. (1975). Clinical and surgical studies of the cerebral speech areas in man. In *Cerebral Localization* (K. J. Zülch, O. Creutzfeldt and G. C. Galbraith, eds), pp. 238–257. Springer-Verlag, Berlin.

RASMUSSEN, T. and MILNER, B. (1977). The role of early left brain injury in determining lateralisation of cerebral speech function. In *Evolution and Lateralization of the Brain* (S. J. Dimond and D. A. Blizard, eds), pp. 355–369. *Ann. N. Y. Acad. Sci.* **299**.

RATCLIFF, G. and DAVIES-JONES, G. A. B. (1972). Defective visual localization in focal brain wounds. *Brain* **95**, 49–60.

RATCLIFF, G., DILA, C., TAYLOR, L. B. and MILNER, B. (1978). Arteriographic correlates of cerebral dominance for speech. Paper presented at the International Neuropsychology Symposium, Oxford, England.

RAUSCH, M. A., PRESCOTT, T. E. and DEWOLFE, A. S. (1980). Schizophrenic and aphasic language: discriminable or not? *J. consult. clin. Psychol.* **48**, 63–70.

RAYNER, K. (1978a). Foveal and parafoveal cues in reading. In *Attention and Performance VII* (J. Requin, ed.), pp. 149–162. Lawrence Erlbaum Associates, Hillsdale, New Jersey.

RAYNER, K. (1978b). Eye movement latencies for parafoveally presented words. *Bull. Psychonom. Soc.* **11**, 13–16.

REGAN, D. (1972). *Evoked Potentials in Psychology, Sensory Physiology and Medicine*. Chapman and Hall, London.

REITAN, R. M. (1976). Neurological and physiological bases of psychopathology. *A. Rev. Psychol.* **27**, 189–216.

REITSMA, P. (1975). Visual asymmetry in children. In *Lateralization of Brain Functions* (Boorhaave Committee for Postgraduate Education), pp. 85–98. University of Leiden Press, Leiden.

REYNOLDS, C. R. and TORRANCE, E. P. (1972). Perceived changes in styles of learning and thinking (hemisphericity) through direct and indirect training. *J. creative Behav.* **12**, 247–252.

REYNOLDS, D. McQ. and JEEVES, M. A. (1978a). A developmental study of hemisphere specialisation for alphabetical stimuli. *Cortex* **14**, 259–267.

REYNOLDS, D.McQ. and JEEVES, M. A. (1978b). A developmental study of hemisphere specialisation for recognition of faces in normal subjects. *Cortex* **14**, 511–520.

RICHARDS, W. (1970). Stereopsis and stereoblindness. *Exp. Brain Res.* **10**, 380–388.

RICHARDSON, J. T. E. (1976). How to measure laterality. *Neuropsychologia* **14**, 135–136.

RICHARDSON, J. T. E. (1978). A factor analysis of self-reported handedness. *Neuropsychologia* **16**, 747–748.

RICHARDSON, J. T. E. and FIRLEJ, M. D. E. (1979). Laterality and reading attainment. *Cortex* **15**, 581–595.

RISBERG, J. (1980). Regional cerebral blood flow measurements by [133]Xe-inhalation methodology and applications in neuropsychology and psychiatry. *Brain and Language* **9**, 9–34.

RISSE, G. L., LEDOUX, J. E., SPRINGER, S. P., WILSON, D. H. and GAZZANIGA, M. S. (1978). The anterior commissure in man: functional variation in a multisensory system. *Neuropsychologia* **16**, 23–31.

RIZZOLATTI, G. (1979). Interfield differences in reaction times to lateralised visual stimuli in normal subjects. In *Structure and Function of Cerebral Commissures* (I. Steele-Russell, M. W. Van Hof and G. Berlucchi, eds), pp. 390–399. Macmillan Press, London.

RIZZOLATTI, G. and BUCHTEL, H. A. (1977). Hemispheric superiority in reaction time to faces: a sex difference. *Cortex* 13, 300–305.

RIZZOLATTI, G., UMILTA, C. and BERLUCCHI, G. (1971). Opposite superiorities of the right and left cerebral hemispheres on discriminative reaction time to physiognomical and alphabetical material. *Brain* 94, 431–442.

RIZZOLATTI, G., BERTOLINI, G. and BUCHTEL, H. A. (1979). Interference of concommitant motor and verbal tasks on simple reaction time: a hemispheric difference. *Neuropsychologia* 17, 323–329.

ROBERTSHAW, S. and SHELDON, M. (1976). Laterality effects in judgment of the identity and position of letters: a signal detection analysis. *Q. J. exp. Psychol.* 28, 115–121.

ROSEN, J. J., CURCIO, F., MACKAVEY, W. and HEBERT, J. (1975). Superior recall of letters in the right visual field with bilateral presentation and partial report. *Cortex* 11, 144–154.

ROSENTHAL, R. and BIGELOW, L. B. (1972). Quantitative brain measurements in chronic schizophrenia. *Br. J. Psychiat.* 121, 259–264.

ROSS, P. and TURKEWITZ, G. (1981). Individual differences in cerebral asymmetries for facial recognition. *Cortex* 17, 199–214.

ROSS, P., PERGAMENT, L., and ANISFELD, M. (1979). Cerebral lateralisation of deaf and hearing individuals for linguistic comparison judgments. *Brain and Language* 8, 69–80.

ROTHSCHILD, K. (1931). The relation of Broca's center to lefthandedness. *Am. J. med. Sci.* 182, 116–118.

RUGG, M. D. and BEAUMONT, J. G. (1978). Interhemispheric asymmetries in the visual evoked response: effects of stimulus lateralisation and task. *Biol. Psychol.* 6, 283–292.

RUGG, M. D. and BEAUMONT, J. G. (1979). Late positive component correlates of verbal and visuo-spatial processing. *Biol. Psychol.* 9, 1–11.

RUSSO, M. and VIGNOLO, L. A. (1967). Visual figure ground discrimination in patients with unilateral cerebral disease. *Cortex* 3, 113–127.

SACKEIM, H., GUR, R. and SAUCY, M. (1978). Emotions are expressed more intensely on the left side of the face. *Science, N.Y.* 202, 434–436.

SAFER, M. A. (1981). Sex and hemisphere differences in access to codes for processing emotional expressions and faces. *J. exp. Psychol: General*, 110, 86–100.

SAFFRAN, E. M., BOGYO, L. C., SCHWARTZ, M. F. and MARIN, O. S. M. (1980). Does deep dyslexia reflect right hemisphere reading? In *Deep Dyslexia* (M. Coltheart, K. E. Patterson and J. C. Marshall, eds), pp. 381–406. Routledge and Kegan Paul, London.

SALIS, D. L. (1980). Laterality effects with visual perception of musical chords and dot patterns. *Percept. Psychophys.* 28, 284–292.

SALMASO, D. (1979). Hemispheric differences in a novelty task. Experimental Psychology Society, York Meeting.

SASANUMA, S. and KOBAYASHI, Y. (1978). Tachistoscopic recognition of line orientation. *Neuropsychologia* 16, 239–242.

SASANUMA, S., ITOH, M., MORI, K. and KOBAYASHI, Y. (1977). Tachistoscopic recognition of kana and kanji words. *Neuropsychologia* 15, 547–553.

SATZ, P. (1976). Cerebral dominance and reading disability: an old problem revisited.

In *The Neuropsychology of Learning Disorders: Theoretical Approaches* (R. M. Knights and D. J. Bakker, eds), pp. 273–294. University Park Press, Baltimore, Maryland.

SATZ, P. (1977). Laterality tests: an inferential problem. *Cortex* **13**, 208–212.

SATZ, P. (1979). A test of some models of hemispheric speech organization in the left- and right-handed. *Science, N.Y.* **203**, 1131–1133.

SCHALLER, M. J. and DZIADOSZ, G. M. (1975). Individual differences in adult foveal asymmetries. *J. exp. Psychol.: Human Percept. Perform.* **1**, 353–365.

SCHALLER, M. J. and DZIADOSZ, G. M. (1976). Developmental changes in foveal tachistoscopic recognition between prereading and reading children. *Devel. Psychol.* **12**, 321–327.

SCHEERER, E. (1974). Task requirement and hemifield asymmetry in tachistoscopic partial report performance. *Acta psychol.* **38**, 131–147.

SCHMIT, V. and DAVIS, R. (1974). The role of hemispheric specialisation in the analysis of Stroop stimuli. *Acta psychol.* **38**, 149–158.

SCHMULLER, J. (1979). Hemispheric asymmetry for alphabetic identification: scaling analyses. *Brain and Language* **8**, 263–274.

SCHMULLER, J. (1980). Stimulus repetition in studies of laterality. *Brain and Language* **10**, 205–207.

SCHMULLER, J. and GOODMAN, R. (1979). Bilateral tachistoscopic perception, handedness and laterality. *Brain and Language* **8**, 81–91.

SCHMULLER, J. and GOODMAN, R. (1980). Bilateral tachistoscopic perception, handedness and laterality. II. Nonverbal stimuli. *Brain and Language* **11**, 12–18.

SCHMULLER, J. and PLATT, S. (unpublished). Hemispheric asymmetry and individual differences in word decoding strategy. Unpublished manuscript, Clark University, Worcester, Massachusetts.

SCHNEIDER, G. E. (1969). Two visual systems. *Science, N.Y.* **163**, 895–902.

SCHOLES, R. J. and FISCHLER, I. (1979). Hemispheric function and linguistic skill in the deaf. *Brain and Language* **7**, 336–350.

SCHWANTES, F. M. (1978). Stimulus position functions in tachistoscopic identification tasks: scanning, rehearsal and order of report. *Percept. Psychophys.* **23**, 219–226.

SCHWARTZ, M. and SMITH, M. L. (1980). Visual asymmetries with chimeric faces. *Neuropsychologia* **18**, 103–106.

SCULLY, J. P. (1978). Hemisphere differences in memory. In *Practical Aspects of Memory* (M. M. Gruneberg, P. E. Morris and R. N. Sykes, eds), pp. 451–458. Academic Press, London and New York.

SEAMON, J. G. (1974). Coding and retrieval processes and the hemispheres of the brain. In *Hemisphere Function in the Human Brain* (S. J. Dimond and J. G. Beaumont, eds), pp. 184–203. Elek Science, London.

SEAMON, J. G. and GAZZANIGA, M. S. (1973). Coding strategies and cerebral laterality effects. *Cog. Psychol.* **5**, 249–256.

SEARLEMAN, A. (1977). A review of right hemisphere linguistic capabilities. *Psychol. Bull.* **84**, 503–528.

SEGALOWITZ, S. J. and STEWART, C. (1979). Left and right lateralisation for letter matching: strategy and sex differences. *Neuropsychologia* **17**, 521–525.

SEGALOWITZ, S. J., BEBOUT, L. J. and LEDERMAN, S. J. (1979). Lateralisation for reading musical chords: disentangling symbolic, analytic and phonological aspects of reading. *Brain and Language* **8**, 315–323.

SEKULER, R., TYNAN, P. and LEVINSON, E. (1973). Visual temporal order: a new illusion. *Science, N.Y.* **180**, 210–212.

SELNES, O. A. (1974). The corpus collosum: some anatomical and functional considerations with special reference to language. *Brain and Language* **1**, 111–139.

SEMMES, J. (1968). Hemispheric specialisation: a possible clue to mechanism. *Neuropsychologia* **6**, 11–26.

SENATOR, ?. (1904). Reported in Kennedy (1916).

SHANON, B. (1979). Lateralisation effects in lexical decision tasks. *Brain and Language* **8**, 380–387.

SHEPHERD, J. W. and ELLIS, H. D. (1973). The effect of attractiveness on recognition memory for faces. *Am. J. Psychol.* **86**, 627–633.

SHEPHERD, J. W., DEREGOWSKI, J. B. and ELLIS, H. D. (1974). A cross-cultural study of recognition memory for faces. *Int. J. Psychol.* **9**, 205–211.

SHIMKUNAS, A. (1978). Hemispheric asymmetry and schizophrenic thought disorder. In *Language and Cognition in Schizophrenia* (S. Schwartz, ed.), pp. 193–235. Lawrence Erlbaum Associates, Hillsdale, New Jersey.

SHINE, L. C., II, WIANT, J. and DA POLITO, F. (1972a). Effect of learning on hemisphere dominance and free recall in a single subject. *Psychol. Rep.* **31**, 227–230.

SHINE, L. C., II, WIANT, J. and DA POLITO, F. (1972b). Effect of learning on hemisphere dominance and free recall. *Percept. mot. Skills* **35**, 596–598.

SHUKLA, G. D. and KATIYAR, B. C. (1980). Psychiatric disorders in temporal lobe epilepsy: the laterality effect. *Br. J. Psychiat.* **137**, 181–182.

SHUMAN, R. B. (1978). Inquiry and discovery as teaching strategies in English. *Illinois Schools J.* **58**, 18–27.

SIDTIS, J. J. and BRYDEN, M. P. (1978). Asymmetric perception of language and music: evidence for independent processing strategies. *Neuropsychologia* **16**, 627–632.

SILVERBERG, R., BENTIN, S., GAZIEL, T., OBLER, L. K. and ALBERT, M. L. (1979). Shift of visual field preference for English words in native Hebrew speakers. *Brain and Language* **8**, 184–190.

SIMION, F., BAGNARA, S., BISACCHI, P., RONCATO, S. and UMILTA, C. (1980). Laterality effects, levels of processing and stimulus properties. *J. exp. Psychol.: Human Percept. Perform.* **6**, 184–195.

SIMON, J. R. (1968). Effect of ear stimulated on reaction time and movement time. *J. exp. Psychol.* **78**, 344–346.

SLONIM, P. S., WEISSMAN, S., GLAZER, E. and NETTLER, P. A. (1975). Effects of training on dynamic stereo acuity performance in males and females. *Percept. mot. Skills* **40**, 359–362.

SMITH, K. U. (1947). Bilateral integrative action of the cerebral cortex in man in verbal association and sensorimotor coordination. *J. exp. Psychol.* **37**, 367–376.

SMITH, L. C. and MOSCOVITCH, M. (1979). Writing posture, hemispheric control of movement and cerebral dominance in individuals with inverted and noninverted postures during writing. *Neuropsychologia* **17**, 637–644.

SMITH, N. C. and RAMUNAS, S. (1971). Estimation of visual field effects by use of a single report technique: evidence for order of report artifact. *J. exp. Psychol.* **87**, 23–28.

SOUQUES, M. A. (1910). Aphasie avec hémiplegie gauche chez un droiter. *Revue neurol.* **20**, 547–549.

SPELLACY, F. and BLUMSTEIN, S. (1970). The influence of language set on ear preference in phoneme recognition. *Cortex* **6**, 430–439.

SPERLING, G. (1960). The information available in brief visual presentations. *Psychol. Monogr.* **74**, Whole No. 498.

SPERRY, R. W. (1961). Cerebral organization and behaviour. *Science, N.Y.* **133**, 1749–1757.

SPERRY, R. W. (1964a). *Problems Outstanding in the Evolution of Brain Function.* American Museum of Natural History, New York.

SPERRY, R. W. (1964b). The great cerebral commissure. *Scient. Am.* **210**, 45–52.

SPERRY, R. W. (1966). Brain bisection and mechanisms of consciousness. In *Brain and Conscious Experience* (J. C. Eccles, ed.), pp. 298–313. Springer-Verlag, Berlin.

SPERRY, R. W. (1968a). Hemisphere deconnection and unity in conscious awareness. *Am. Psychol.* **23**, 723–733.

SPERRY, R. W. (1968b). Mental unity following surgical disconnection of the cerebral hemispheres. *The Harvey Lectures* **62**, 293–323.

SPERRY, R. W., GAZZANIGA, M. S. and BOGEN, J. E. (1969). Interhemispheric relationship: the neocortical commissures: syndromes of hemisphere disconnection. In *Handbook of Clinical Neurology*, Vol. IV (P. K. Vinkin and G. W. Bruyn, eds), pp. 273–290. North Holland, Amsterdam.

SPERRY, R. W., ZAIDEL, E. and ZAIDEL, D. (1979). Self-recognition and social awareness in the deconnected minor hemisphere. *Neuropsychologia* **17**, 153–166.

SPRINGER, S. P. (1977). Tachistoscopic and dichotic listening investigations of laterality in normal human subjects. In *Lateralization in the Nervous System* (S. Harnad, R. W. Doty, L. Goldstein, J. Jaynes and G. Krauthamer, eds), pp. 325–336. Academic Press, New York and London.

STEPHENSON, W. A. and GIBBS, F. A. (1951). A balanced non-cephalic reference electrode. *Electroenceph. Clin. Neurophysiol.* **3**, 237–240.

STEVENS, S. S. (1975). *Psychophysics.* Wiley: New York.

STONE, J., LEICESTER, J. and SHERMAN, S. M. (1973). The naso-temporal division of the monkey's retina. *J. comp. Neurol.* **150**, 333–348.

STONE, M. A. (1980). Measures of laterality and spurious correlation. *Neuropsychologia* **18**, 339–345.

STRAUSS, E. and MOSCOVITCH, M. (1981). Perception of facial expression. *Brain and Language* **13**, 308–332.

SUBERI, M. and MCKEEVER, W. F. (1977). Differential right hemispheric memory storage of emotional and non-emotional faces. *Neuropsychologia* **15**, 757–768.

SUBIRANA, A. (1952). La droiterie. *Schweizer Arch. Neurol. Psychiat.* **69**, 321–359.

SUGISHITA, M., IWATA, M., TOYOKURA, Y., YOSHIOKA, M. and YAMADA, R. (1978). Reading of ideograms and phonograms in Japanese patients after partial commissurotomy. *Neuropsychologia* **16**, 417–426.

SUGISHITA, M., TOYOKURA, Y., YOSHIOKA, M. and YAMADA, R. (1980). Unilateral agraphia after section of the posterior half of the truncus of the corpus callosum. *Brain and Language* **9**, 215–225.

SWANSON, J., LEDLOW, A. and KINSBOURNE, M. (1978). Lateral asymmetries revealed by simple reaction time. In *Asymmetrical Function of the Brain* (M. Kinsbourne, ed.), pp. 274–291. Cambridge University Press, Cambridge.

TAPLEY, S. M. and BRYDEN, M. P. (1977). An investigation of sex differences in spatial ability: mental rotation of three-dimensional objects. *Canad. J. Psychol.* **31**, 122–130.

TAYLOR, M. A., GREENSPAN, B. and ABRAMS, R. (1979). Lateralized neuropsychological dysfunction in affective disorder and schizophrenia. *Am. J. Psychiat.* **136**, 1031–1034.

TAYLOR, P. J., DALTON, R. and FLEMINGER, J. J. (1980). Handedness in schizophrenia. *Br. J. Psychiat.* **136**, 375–383.

TENG, E. L. and SPERRY, R. W. (1973). Interhemispheric interaction during simultaneous bilateral presentation of letters as digits in commissurotomised patients. *Neuropsychologia* **11**, 131–140.

TENG, E. L. and SPERRY, R. W. (1974). Interhemispheric rivalry during simultaneous bilateral task presentation in commissurotomised patients. *Cortex* **10**, 111–120.

TENHOUTEN, W. D., THOMPSON, A. L. and WALTER, D. O. (1976). Discriminating social groups by performance on two lateralised tests. *Bull. L.A. Neur. Socs.* **41**, 99–108.

TERRACE, H. S. (1959). The effects of retinal locus and attention on the perception of words. *J. exp. Psychol.* **58**, 382–385.

TEUBER, H-L. (1962). Effects of brain wounds implicating right or left hemisphere in man. In *Interhemispheric Relations and Cerebral Dominance* (V. B. Mountcastle, ed.), pp. 131–157. The Johns Hopkins Press, Baltimore, Maryland.

THOMAS, E. A. C. and WEAVER, W. B. (1975). Cognitive processing and time perception. *Percept. Psychophys.* **17**, 363–367.

THOMPSON, P. (1980). Margaret Thatcher: a new illusion. *Perception* **9**, 483–484.

THOMPSON, R. F. and PATTERSON, M. M. (1974). *Biolectric Recording Techniques*, Part B. Academic Press, New York and London.

TOMLINSON-KEASEY, C. and KELLY, R. R. (1979a). Is hemispheric specialisation important to school achievement? *Cortex* **15**, 97–107.

TOMLINSON-KEASEY, C. and KELLY, R. R. (1979b). A task analysis of hemispheric function. *Neuropsychologia* **17**, 345–351.

TOMLINSON-KEASEY, C., KELLY, R. R. and BURTON, J. K. (1978). Hemispheric changes in information processing during development. *Devel. Psychol.* **14**, 214–223.

TORRANCE, E. P. and REYNOLDS, C. (1980). *Preliminary Norms—Technical Manual for Your Style of Learning and Thinking Form C*. Department of Educational Psychology, University of Georgia, Athens, Georgia.

TRAVIS, L. E. and MARTIN, R. (1934). A study of retinal summation. *J. exp. Psychol.* **17**, 773–786.

TRESHER, H. H. and FORD, F. R. (1937). Colloid cyst of the third ventride: report of a case; operative removal with section of the posterior half of the corpus callosum. *Arch. Neurol. Psychiat. (Chicago)* **37**, 959–973.

TREVARTHEN, C. (1974a). Analysis of cerebral activities that generate and regulate consciousness in commissurotomy patients. In *Hemisphere Function in the Human Brain* (S. J. Dimond and J. G. Beaumont, eds), pp. 235–263. Elek Science, London.

TREVARTHEN, C. (1974b). Functional relations of disconnected hemispheres with the brain stem and with each other: monkey and man. In *Hemispheric Disconnection and Cerebral Function* (M. Kinsbourne and W. L. Smith, eds), p. 187–207. Charles C. Thomas, Springfield, Illinois.

TREVARTHEN, C. (1975). Psychological activities after forebrain commissurotomy in man: concepts, and methodological hurdles in testing. In *Les syndromes de disconnexion calleuse chez l'homme* (F. Michel and B. Schott, eds), pp. 181–210. Hôpital Neurologique, Lyons.

TREVARTHEN, C. and SPERRY, R. W. (1973). Perceptual unity of the ambient visual field in human commissurotomy patients. *Brain* **96**, 547–570.

TSAO, Y-C., FEUSTEL, T. and SOSEOS, C. (1979). Stroop interference in the left and right visual fields. *Brain and Language* **8**, 367–371.

TUCKER, D. M., ANTES, J. R., STENSLIE, C. E. and BARNHARDT, T. M. (1978). Anxiety and lateral cerebral function. *J. abnorm. Psychol.* **87**, 380–383.

TURNER, S. and MILLER, L. K. (1975). Some boundary conditions for laterality effects in children. *Devel. Psychol.* **11**, 342–352.

TZENG, O. J. L., HUNG, D. L., COTTON, B. and WANG, W. S-Y. (1979). Visual lateralisation effect in reading Chinese characters. *Nature, Lond.* **282**, 499–501.

UMILTA, C., FROST, N. and HYMAN, R. (1972). Interhemispheric effects on choice reaction time in one-, two- and three-letter displays. *J. exp. Psychol.* **93**, 198–204.

UMILTA, C., RIZZOLATTI, G., MARZI, C. A., ZAMBONI, G., FRANZINI, C., CAMARDA, R. and BERLUCCHI, G. (1974). Hemispheric differences in the discrimination of line orientation. *Neuropsychologia* 12, 165–174.

UMILTA, C., SIMION, F. and HYMAN, R. (1976). The repetition effect for verbal and non-verbal stimuli in the two visual fields. *Ital. J. Psychol.* 111, 305–316.

UMILTA, C., BAGNARA, S. and SIMION, F. (1978a). Laterality effects for simple and complex geometrical figures, and nonsense patterns. *Neuropsychologia* 16, 43–49.

UMILTA, C., BRIZZOLARA, D., TABOSSI, P. and FAIRWEATHER, H. (1978b). Factors affecting face recognition in the cerebral hemispheres: familiarity and naming. In *Attention and Performance VII* (J. Requin, ed.), pp. 363–374. Lawrence Erlbaum Associates, New Jersey.

UMILTA, C., SALMASO, D., BAGNARA, S. and SIMION, F. (1979). Evidence for a right hemisphere superiority and for a serial search in a dot detection task. *Cortex* 15, 597–608.

UMILTA, C., SAVA, D. and SALMASO, D. (1980). Hemispheric asymmetries in a letter classification task with different typefaces. *Brain and Language* 9, 171–181.

UNDERWOOD, G. (1977). Attention, awareness and hemispheric differences in word recognition. *Neuropsychologia* 15, 61–67.

VANDERPLAS, J. M. and GARVIN, E. A. (1959). The association value of random shapes. *J. exp. Psychol.* 57, 147–154.

VELLA, E. J., BUTLER, S. R. and GLASS, A. (1972). Electrical correlate of right hemisphere function. *Nature: New Biol.* 136, 125–126.

VELLUTINO, F. R., BENTLEY, W. L. and PHILLIPS, F. (1978). Inter- versus intra-hemispheric learning in dyslexic and normal readers. *Devel. med. Child Neurol.* 20, 71–80.

VENABLES, P. H. (1978). Cognitive disorder. In *Schizophrenia: Towards a New Synthesis* (J. K. Wing, ed.), pp. 117–137. Academic Press, London; Grune and Stratton, New York.

VIROSTEK, S. and CUTTING, J. E. (1979). Asymmetries for Ameslan handshapes and other forms in signers and non-signers. *Percept. Psychophys.* 26, 505–508.

VOLKMANN, F. C. (1962). Vision during voluntary saccadic eye movements. *J. Optic. Soc. Am.* 52, 571–578.

VOLKMANN, F. C., SCHICK, A. M. L. and RIGGS, L. A. (1968). Time Course of visual inhibition during voluntary saccades. *J. Optic. Soc. Am.* 58, 362–369.

VROON, P. A., TIMMERS, H. and TEMPELAARS, S. (1977). On the hemispheric representation of time. In *Attention and Performance VI* (S. Dornic, ed.), pp. 231–245. Lawrence Erlbaum Associates, Hillsdale, New Jersey.

WADA, J. A., CLARKE, R. and HAMM, A. (1975). Cerebral hemispheric asymmetry in humans. *Arch. Neurol.* 32, 239–246.

WAGNER, J. (1918). Experimentelle Beitrage zür Psychologie des Lasens. *Z. Psychol.* 80, 1–75.

WALLACE, R. J. (1971). S-R compatability and the idea of a response code. *J. exp. Psychol.* 88, 354–360.

WALSH, K. W. (1978). *Neuropsychology. A Clinical Approach.* Churchill Livingstone, Edinburgh.

WALTERS, J. and ZATORRE, R. J. (1978). Laterality differences for word identification in bilinguals. *Brain and Language* 6, 158–167.

WARD, T. B. and ROSS, L. E. (1977). Laterality differences and practice effects under central backward masking conditions. *Memory and Cognition* 5, 221–226.

WARREN, L. R. and MARSH, G. R. (1978). Hemispheric asymmetry in the processing of Stroop stimuli. *Bull. Psychonom. Soc.* 12, 214–216.

WARRINGTON, E. K. and JAMES, M. (1967a). Tachistoscopic number estimation in patients with unilateral cerebral lesions. *J. neurol. neurosurg. Psychiat.* **30**, 468–474.

WARRINGTON, E. K. and JAMES, M. (1967b). An experimental investigation of facial recognition in patients with unilateral cerebral lesions. *Cortex* **3**, 317–326.

WARRINGTON, E. K. and RABIN, P. (1970). Perceptual matching in patients with cerebral lesions. *Neuropsychologia* **8**, 475–487.

WASTELL, D. G. (1977). Statistical detection of individual evoked responses: an evaluation of Woody's adaptive filter. *Electroenceph. Clin. Neurophysiol.* **42**, 835–839.

WEISENBURG, S. and McBRIDE, K. (1935). *Aphasia: A Clinical and Psychological Study.* The Commonwealth Fund, New York.

WEXLER, B. E. (1980). Cerebral laterality and psychiatry: a review of the literature. *Am. J. Psychiat.* **137**, 279–291.

WEXLER, B. E. and HENINGER, G. R. (1979). Alterations in cerebral laterality during acute psychotic illness. *Arch. gen. Psychiat.* **36**, 278–284.

WHITAKER, H. A. and OJEMANN, G. A. (1977). Lateralisation of higher cortical functions: a critique. *Ann. N. Y. Acad. Sci.* **299**, 459–473.

WHITE, A. M. and DALLENBACH, K. M. (1932). Position vs. intensity as a determinant of the attention of left handed observers. *Am. J. Psychol.* **44**, 175–179.

WHITE, K. G. and SILVER, A. B. (1975). Cerebral hemispheres serve as two channels for visual information processing. *Bull. Psychonom. Soc.* **6**, 51–52.

WHITE, M. J. (1969a). Laterality differences in perception: a review. *Psychol. Bull.* **72**, 387–405.

WHITE, M. J. (1969b). Identification and localisation within digit and letter spans. *Psychonom. Sci.* **17**, 279–280.

WHITE, M. J. (1970). Signal detection analysis of laterality differences: some preliminary data, free of recall and report-sequence characteristics. *J. exp. Psychol.* **83**, 174–176.

WHITE, M. J. (1971a). Brain function and the enumeration of visual stimuli. *Aust. J. Psychol.* **23**, 73–76.

WHITE, M. J. (1971b). Visual hemifield differences in the perception of letters and contour orientation. *Canad. J. Psychol.* **25**, 207–212.

WHITE, M. J. (1972). Hemispheric asymmetries in tachistoscopic information-processing. *Br. J. Psychol.* **63**, 497–508.

WHITE, M. J. (1973a). Vocal and manual response latencies to bilateral and unilateral tachistoscopic letter displays. *Q. J. exp. Psychol.* **25**, 41–47.

WHITE, M. J. (1973b). Does cerebral dominance offer a sufficient explanation for laterality differences in tachistoscopic recognition? *Percept. mot. Skills* **36**, 479–485.

WHITE, M. J. and BARR-BROWN, M. (1972). Role of the right hemisphere in tachistoscopic recognition. *J. gen. Psychol.* **87**, 143–144.

WHITE, M. J. and WHITE, K. G. (1975). Parallel-serial processing and hemispheric functions. *Neuropsychologia* **13**, 377–382.

WHITELEY, A. M. and WARRINGTON, E. K. (1977). Prosopagnosia: a clinical, psychological and anatomical study of three patients. *J. Neurol. Neurosurg. Psychiat.* **40**, 395–403.

WICKELGREN, W. A. (1967). Strength theories of disjunctive visual detection. *Percept. Psychophys.* **2**, 331–337.

WIGAN, A. L. (1844). *The Duality of the Mind: A New View of Insanity.* Longman, London.

WILKINS, A. and STEWART, A. (1974). The time course of lateral asymmetries in visual perception of letters. *J. exp. Psychol.* **102**, 905–908.

WILLIAMS, D. and GASSEL, M. M. (1962). Visual function in patients with homonyous hemianopia. Part 1: The visual fields. *Brain* 85, 175–250.

WILLIS, T. (1664). *Cerebri Anatome.* London.

WILSON, D. H., CULVER, C., WADDINGTON, M. and GAZZANIGA, M. (1975). Disconnection of the cerebral hemispheres. *Neurology (Minneap.)* 25, 1149–1153.

WILSON, D. H., REEVES, A. and GAZZANIGA, M. S. (1978). Division of the corpus callosum for uncontrollable epilepsy. *Neurology* 28, 649–653.

WING, J. K. (ed.) (1978a). *Schizophrenia: Towards a New Synthesis.* Academic Press, London; Grune and Stratton, New York.

WING, J. K. (1978b). Clinical concepts of schizophrenia. In *Schizophrenia: Towards a New Synthesis* (J. K. Wing, ed.), pp. 1–30. Academic Press, London; Grune and Stratton, New York.

WITELSON, S. F. (1977a). Developmental dyslexia: two right hemispheres and none left. *Science, N.Y.* 195, 309–311.

WITELSON, S. F. (1977b). Neural and cognitive correlates of developmental dyslexia: age and sex differences. In *Psychopathology and Brain Dysfunction* (C. Shagass, S. Gershon and A. J. Friedhoff, eds), pp. 15–49. Raven Press, New York.

WITELSON, S. F. (1977c). Early hemisphere specialization and interhemispheric plasticity: an empirical and theoretical review. In *Language Development and Neurological Theory* (S. J. Segalowitz and F. A. Gruber, eds), pp. 213–287. Academic Press, New York and London.

WITELSON, S. F. (1977d). Anatomical asymmetry in the temporal lobes: its documentation phylogenesis and relationship to functional asymmetry. *Ann N.Y. Acad. Sci.* 299, 328–356.

WITRYOL, S. L. and KAESS, W. A. (1957). Sex differences in social memory tasks. *J. abnorm. soc. Psychol.* 54, 343–346.

WODEHOUSE, P. G. (1969). *A Pelican at Blandings.* Herbert Jenkins, London.

WOLFF, P. H., HURWITZ, I. and MOSS, H. (1977). Serial organization of motor skills in left- and right-handed adults. *Neuropsychologia* 15, 539–546.

WOLFORD, G. and HOLLINGSWORTH, S. (1974). Retinal location and string position as important variables in visual information processing. *Percept. Psychophys.* 16, 437–442.

WOOD, C. C., GOFF, W. R. and DAY, R. S. (1971). Auditory evoked potentials during speech perception. *Science, N.Y.* 173, 1248–1251.

WORRALL, N. and COLES, P. (1976). Visual field differences in recognising letters. *Percept. Psychophys.* 20, 21–24.

WYKE, M. and CHOROVER, S. L. (1965). Comparison of spatial discrimination in the temporal and nasal sectors of the monocular visual field. *Percept. mot. Skills* 20, 1037–1045.

WYKE, M. and ETTLINGER, G. (1961). Efficiency of recognition in left and right visual fields. *Arch. Neurol.* 5, 659–665.

WYMAN, D. and STEINMAN, R. M. (1973). Latency characteristics of small saccades. *Vision Res.* 13, 2173–2175.

YARMEY, A. D. (1974). Proactive interference in short-term retention of human faces. *Canad. J. Psychol.* 28, 333–338.

YARMEY, A. D. (1979a). The effects of attractiveness, feature saliency and liking on memory for faces. In *Love and Attraction* (M. Cook and G. Wilson, eds), pp. 51–53. Pergamon Press, Oxford and New York.

YARMEY, A. D. (1979b). Through the looking glass: sex differences in memory for self-facial poses. *J. Res. Personality* 13, 450–459.

YENI-KOMSHIAN, G. H., ISENBERG, D. and GOLDBERG, H. (1975). Cerebral dominance and reading disability: left visual field deficit in poor readers. *Neuropsychologia* 13, 83–94.

YEUDALL, L. T. and FROMM-AUCH, D. (1979). Neuropsychological impairments in various psychopathological populations. In *Hemisphere Asymmetries of Function in Psychopathology* (J. Gruzelier and P. Flor-Henry, eds), pp. 401–428. Elsevier/North-Holland Biomedical Press, Amsterdam.

YIN, R. K. (1969). Looking at upside-down faces. *J. exp. Psychol.* 81, 141–145.

YIN, R. K. (1970). Face recognition by brain injured patients: a dissociable ability. *Neuropsychologia* 8, 395–402.

YOUNG, A. W. (1981). Asymmetry of cerebral hemispheric function during development. To appear in *Brain and Behaviour: A Developmental Perspective* (J. Dickerson and H. McGurk, eds). Blackie, Glasgow.

YOUNG, A. W. and BION, P. J. (1979). Hemispheric laterality effects in the enumeration of visually presented collections of dots by children. *Neuropsychologia* 17, 99–102.

YOUNG, A. W. and BION, P. J. (1980a). Absence of any developmental trend in right hemisphere superiority for face recognition. *Cortex* 16, 213–221.

YOUNG, A. W. and BION, P. J. (1980b). Hemifield differences of naming bilaterally presented nouns varying on age of acquisiton. *Percept. mot. Skills* 50, 366.

YOUNG, A. W. and BION, P. J. (1981a). Accuracy of naming laterally presented known faces by children and adults. *Cortex* 17, 97–106.

YOUNG, A. W. and BION, P. J. (1981b). Identification and storage of line drawings presented to the left and right cerebral hemispheres of adults and children. *Cortex*, in press.

YOUNG, A. W. and ELLIS, A. W. (1981). Asymmetry of cerebral hemispheric function in normal and poor readers. *Psychol. Bull.* 89, 183–190.

YOUNG, A. W. and ELLIS, H. D. (1976). An experimental investigation of developmental differences in ability to recognise faces presented to the left and right cerebral hemispheres. *Neuropsychologia* 14, 495–498.

YOUNG, A. W., BION, P. J. and ELLIS, A. W. (1979). A comparison of visual hemifield asymmetries for naming bilaterally presented picture and print stimuli. International Neuropsychology Society, Second European Conference, Holland.

YOUNG, A. W., BION, P. J. and ELLIS, A. W. (1980). Studies toward a model of laterality effects for picture and word naming. *Brain and Language* 11, 54–65.

YOUNG, G. (1977). Manual specialization in infancy: implications for lateralization of brain function. In *Language Development and Neurological Theory* (S. J. Segalowitz and F. A. Gruber, eds), pp. 289–311. Academic Press, New York and London.

YOUNG, L. R. and SHEENA, D. (1975). Survey of eye movement recording methods. *Behav. Res. Meth. Instr.* 7, 397–429.

ZAIDEL, E. (1973). Linguistic competence and related functions in the right hemisphere of man following cerebral commissurotomy and hemispherectomy. Unpublished doctoral dissertation, California Institute of Technology.

ZAIDEL, E. (1975). A technique for presenting lateralized input with prolonged exposure. *Vision Res.* 15, 283–289.

ZAIDEL, E. (1976). Auditory vocabulary of the right hemisphere following brain bisection or hemidecortication. *Cortex* 12, 191–211.

ZAIDEL, E. (1977). Unilateral auditory language comprehension in the Token Test following cerebral commissurotomy and hemispherectomy. *Neuropsychologia* 15, 1–18.

ZAIDEL, E. (1978a). Auditory language comprehension in the right hemisphere following cerebral commissurotomy and hemispherectomy: a comparison with child language and aphasia. In *Language Acquisition and Language Breakdown* (A. Caramazza and E. B. Zurif, eds), pp. 229–276. The Johns Hopkins University Press, Baltimore.

ZAIDEL, E. (1978b). Lexical organisation in the right hemisphere. In *Cerebral Correlates of Conscious Experience* (P. A. Buser and A. Rougeul-Buser, eds), pp. 177–198. North-Holland, Amsterdam.

ZAIDEL, E. (1978c). Concepts of cerebral dominance in the split brain. In *Cerebral Correlates of Conscious Experience* (P. A. Buser and A. Rougeul-Buser, eds), pp. 263–284. North-Holland, Amsterdam.

ZAIDEL, E. (1979). Performance on the ITPA following cerebral commissurotomy and hemispherectomy. *Neuropsychologia* 17, 259–280.

ZANGWILL, O. L. (1960). *Cerebral Dominance and its Relation to Psychological Function.* Oliver and Boyd, Edinburgh.

ZANGWILL, O. L. (1976). Thought and the brain. *Brit. J. Psychol.* 67, 301–314.

ZANGWILL, O. L. (1979). Two cases of crossed aphasia in dextrals. *Neuropsychologia* 17, 167–172.

ZENHAUSERN, R. (1978). Imagery, cerebral dominance and style of thinking: a unified field model. *Bull. Psychonom. Soc.* 12, 381–384.

ZOCCOLOTTI, P. and OLTMAN, P. K. (1978). Field dependence and lateralisation of verbal and configurational processing. *Cortex* 14, 155–163.

ZUCKERMAN, M., LIPETS, M. S., KOIVUMAKI, J. H. and ROSENTHAL, R. (1975). Encoding and decoding nonverbal cues of emotion. *J. Personality Soc. Psychol.* 32, 1068–1076.

ZURIF, E. B. and BRYDEN, M. P. (1969). Familial handedness and left–right differences in auditory and visual perception. *Neuropsychologia* 7, 179–187.

# SUBJECT INDEX